Berliners

Berliners: Both Sides of the Wall

Anne Armstrong

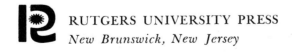 RUTGERS UNIVERSITY PRESS
New Brunswick, New Jersey

Library of Congress Cataloging in Publication Data

Armstrong, Anne.
    Berliners: both sides of the wall.

    1. Berlin—Politics and government—1945–
2. Berlin—Social life and customs. 3. Youth—
Berlin. I. Title.
DD881.A8   914.3′155′0387   73–7591
ISBN   0–8135–0713–8

In memory of A. K.
because Berlin was his second home, too.

Contents

Illustrations

List of Abbreviations

C.D.U.: Christian-Democratic Union (in West Germany and West Berlin)

D.K.P.: New Communist Party (in West Germany and West Berlin)

E.K.D.: Evangelical Church of Germany (Lutheran)

F.D.J.: Free German Youth (East German youth organization)

F.D.P.: Free Democratic Party (in West Germany and West Berlin)

G.D.R.: German Democratic Republic (East Germany)

K.P.D.: Communist Party of Germany (former name for the communist party)

L.D.P.: Liberal Democratic Party (in East Germany)

N.P.D.: National Democratic Party (nationalist party in West Germany)

S.D.S.: Socialist German Students (in West Germany and West Berlin)

S.E.D.: Socialist Unity Party (the socialist-communist party in East Germany)

S.P.D.: Social Democratic Party (the socialist part of West Germany and West Berlin)

VOPO—*Volkspolizei:* People's Police (in East Germany)

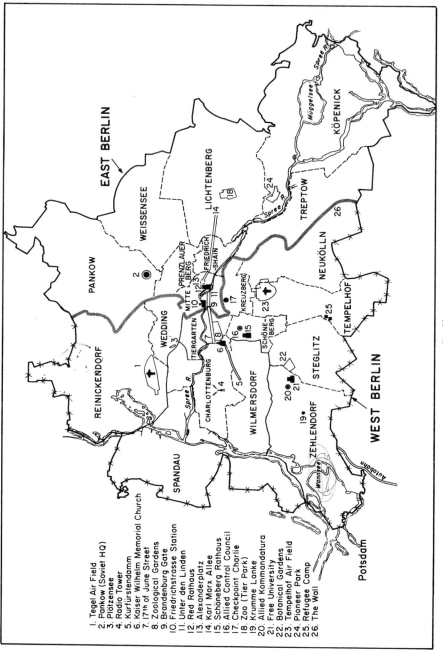

1. Tegel Air Field
2. Pankow (Soviet HQ)
3. Plötzensee
4. Radio Tower
5. Kurfürstendamm
6. 17th of June Street
7. Kaiser Wilhelm Memorial Church
8. Zoological Gardens
9. Brandenburg Gate
10. Friedrichstrasse Station
11. Unter den Linden
12. Red Rathaus
13. Alexanderplatz
14. Karl Marx Allee
15. Schöneberg Rathaus
16. Allied Control Council
17. Checkpoint Charlie
18. Zoo (Tier Park)
19. Krumme Lanke
20. Allied Kommandatura
21. Free University
22. Botanical Gardens
23. Tempelhof Air Field
24. Pioneer Camp
25. Refugee Camp
26. The Wall

Berlin

Preface

Berlin Ist Einmalig:
Berlin Is Unique!

"If you dropped me from a helicopter blindfolded into one of Berlin's forests I should know instantly that I was in Berlin," one of my Berliners insisted. The Berlin air is famous in Germany, and Berlin atmosphere is famous throughout the world. As a symbol of imperial Germany, of nazi terror, of the Cold War, Berlin has been admired and feared, hated and loved. Behind the symbol stand the Berliners, native-born and adopted, a special breed not quite like other Germans, as unique as their city is unique.

Berlin air genuinely has a distinctive savor. It is effervescent and pungent, invigorating in a brisk, northern style as Attic air is invigorating in the south. Cold dry winds sweep across the unbroken Eurasian plain to swirl and settle over the cluster of lakes and forests of the Old Mark Brandenburg, borrow the scent of pines and firs and sandy soil, mixing these with the city smells of aged wood and freshly poured concrete, of sooty coke fires burning in colorful, tiled stoves, of spicy *Wurst* hanging in rows in immaculate delicatessens, of freshly ground, freshly brewed coffee poured steaming into sparkling porcelain cups, of fragrant wines and yeasty beers and rich, zesty foods.

Berlin is a kaleidoscope of images, of scents and sounds. Berlin is the opulent matron gossiping with her friends as they consume strawberry *Torte* piled high with sweet, whipped cream. It is the tired workman who stops to swallow a pungent frankfurter and a half liter of beer on his way to the subway and the gang of construction workers sprawled on a half-built wall, laughing and flirting with a passing girl during their mid-morning coffee break. It is giggling school girls exchanging confidences over Cokes and sundaes in the American-type drugstore and intense students expostulating, arguing as they devour piping hot goulash soup and drink raw, red wine in a dimly lit co-op; it is two distinguished-looking white-haired men reminiscing over a bottle of sound Burgundy, and a young couple two tables away recklessly ordering champagne to celebrate their engagement. Berlin is a prostitute self-consciously slipping into a pew at a midnight church service; it is an old woman alone on a park bench.

Berlin is night clubs, sex shops and grimy back courtyards. It is chic boutiques, fashionable shoppers, scrubbed children, businesslike men. It is a middle-aged woman west of the Wall waving across to her mother and sisters; it is an old woman dragging a too-heavy suitcase through customs, pausing to call good-bye to her daughter and grandchildren before she crosses over into the West. It is the guards in the watchtowers with powerful field glasses and precision rifles.

It is angry students demonstrating on the streets and on campus; it is patient, courteous students debating with honest citizens or handing out mimeographed position papers along the Kurfürstendamm. It is harassed, irate, or tolerantly amused professors hectically trying to cope with the fringe of revolution. It is scrupulously correct civil servants, canny trade unionists, earnest politicians. It is communist officials, new and old leftists, socialists and conservatives; it is former nazis, and antinazis and now and then an occasional present-day nazi.

Berlin is unique. No visitor strolling down West Berlin's Kurfürstendamm would mistake it for the fashionable shopping street of any other city. The mixture of orderliness and surging vitality is uniquely Berlin's. Berliners bustle and bounce along the Kurfürstendamm, affluent, tidy, usually conventional. Brisk, purposeful, individual, the Berliner also appears relaxed, always ready for a chat or a joke. Nothing is more typical of Berlin than the pedestrian lawfully waiting at an intersection for the traffic light to change even though there is not a car in sight. When I, an anarchistic New Yorker, look both ways and dash despite the red light, Berliners look at me, in a kindly way of course, but puzzled as though I had possibly escaped from the zoo.

In Berlin the walls of subway stations are lined with sparkling yellow or aqua tiles. Neat underground shops offer flowers for the visitor or penitent husband, books, baby clothes and even antiques, and the trains, clean, quiet and distinctly announced, run swiftly and on time. Berlin's streets are broad, clean and well lit, engineered from their inception for the orderly flow of modern traffic or of troop transports.

The city boasts abundant parks, forests and lakes. It is entirely sur-

Fig. 1. Sidewalk café on the Kurfürstendamm (photo by Landesbildstelle, West Berlin)

rounded by a network of lakes and canals; much of the traffic of the city
moves on its waterways. Hardest hit by wartime bombing were the
central areas of the city, including most of the old slum districts. Because
of this and because of intelligent, imaginative reconstruction much of
Berlin's housing is modern, fresh, cheerful, pleasantly set in green areas
of grass, trees and shrubs. Almost every Berlin neighborhood is safe for
citizens to wander in day and night, and shady park lanes and benches
are the haven of the elderly, especially of lonely old women. They sit
and read or knit or watch children playing, hugging their loneliness but
quite free of fear.

Berlin, East and West, is a modern, progressive, prosperous city. It is
also an impressively large city, with a total area of 341 square miles, a
total population (1970) of more than three million people.* The Wall
which divides the city stretches twenty-eight miles. The border between
West Berlin and the German Democratic Republic is eighty miles long.
The three German cities of Dresden, Frankfort on Main and Leipzig
would all fit into the area of West Berlin alone.

Berlin is one of Europe's leading industrial and commercial centers.
West Berlin is Germany's largest industrial city, employing 285,000 industrial workers. Its per capita G.N.P. is greater than that of France
or Great Britain. The products of West Berlin's electronics and electrical
industry, of Telefunken and Siemens, are symbols of quality and precision throughout the world. In an average year West Berlin's exports
total more than Portugal's. West Berlin employs more electrical workers
than Austria and Switzerland combined. High productivity, highly specialized, highly skilled technicians make Berlin a desirable prize, far
more than merely a psychological symbol in the Cold War.

But Berlin is also a great deal more than physical size and industrial
productivity. Beyond these, Berlin is the humor and courage of Berliners,
of Berliners who crowded good-naturedly into shelters and cracked ironic
jokes about themselves and their leaders while their city fell into ruins
about them, and then trudged doggedly off to work the next morning.
Berlin is the Berliners, especially the Berlin women, who, because there
were virtually no men, swept up the rubble, stacked the bricks and then
slowly, painfully and with little real hope but with stubborn determination, began to rebuild their cities and their lives. Berlin is the women

* The area of East Berlin is 156 square miles, of West Berlin 185 square miles. In
1970 the population of East Berlin was approximately 1.1 million, of West Berlin 2.15
million, for a total of 3.35 for Greater Berlin. The five boroughs of New York City,
including inland water, cover 365.4 square miles, with a population of 7,895,563 million
people in 1970.

who cleared away the rubble of the past, dealt with the black market, coped with the occupation, many in the direct way that conquered women have always coped, fed their families, brought new babies into the world, and slowly got themselves and their civilization back onto its feet. Gradually, they even learned to hope a little. Berlin is their courage, their effort and that fragile hope.

Berlin is also the West Berliners who stood fast during the blockade, grateful to the Allies, supporting, encouraging them on the outside chance that they just might succeed. It is the determined workers, ingenious businessmen and creative city planners who extracted the last pfennig of productivity from the Marshall Plan and Bonn aid to revive the city's economy, restore industry and transform the rubble heap into a vital, modern city.

Berlin is the ugly Wall that rips through the city from north to south. It is the Berliners on both sides of the Wall who live with the reality of division and isolation, with the awareness that their city is the bone of contention which at any moment could loose the dogs of war. It is tension, strain and pressure.

There is a Berlin song which says that God created Berlin in the center of the world. Certainly to a Berliner living in a city torn between East and West it must seem so. In June, 1963, United States President John Kennedy stood in the square in front of West Berlin's city hall to announce. *"Ich bin ein Berliner!"* The massed thousands of West Berliners cheered wildly, wanting to believe him. Saddened and shocked by the Wall Ulbricht had built two years before, in August, 1961, puzzled and disappointed by the equanimity with which the Western allies had reacted, West Berliners nevertheless seemed to accept the American president's assurances of continued support of the freedom of their island half-city. In 1963, despite the Wall, the majority of Berliners had not begun to despair.

Ten, eleven years is a long time to live in a threatened, divided city. It is a long time to cling to verbal assurances. Hope for the reunification of Berlin and of Germany has ebbed each year. Continuing hope for the survival of West Berlin's independence demands the exertion of faith and courage. The gay and gallant Berliners who laughed their way through bombing and blockade, through decades of crises and ultimata today seem less gay and only by a formidable act of will gallant.

On the surface West Berlin presents a prosperous and busy façade. East Berlin has stirred from its long lethargy to construct its own small miracle of recovery, its own bustle and prosperity. Both West and East Berliners rejoice in the opportunities afforded by the Four Power agreement for Western visits to the East, and many Berliners hope that the agreement will lead to a general easing of tension, but no one is quite sure. Beneath the surface vitality and hope there is a pervasive uneasiness, in some circles alarm.

Nevertheless most Berliners stay in Berlin. Almost every Berliner I have interviewed has assured me that he intends to stay. Why? No one offers a clear-cut or entirely rational reason. Most of my Berliners simply smile, shrug and say, *"Berlin ist einmalig."* Apparently it is. To a great extent it is unique because of Berliners.

Who are the Berliners? Why do they love their city and want to remain there in spite of endemic crisis and an uncertain future? No single book could hope to answer those questions, but in my interviews I have at least posed the questions.

For more than ten years I have interviewed Berliners in both parts of the divided city, tried to discover who they are, how they live, how they feel about their city, and why they stay. My own experience with Berlin dates back to 1947, when I served for a year in the military government. Some of the Berliners I interviewed are friends and acquaintances I have known since 1947. I have visited Berlin often since then, accumulating impressions, acquaintances, and data. In 1963 I began conducting interviews with the intention of writing a book on Berlin. Some of the interviews, then, have been conducted over a period of years. Others are the result of a single conversation. Some of the Berliners around whom chapters are built are individuals, others are composites constructed from multiple interviews. Pastor Carl, for instance, is based on the personality of one real clergyman, but I have incorporated the views of two or three other pastors into his chapters. Walter and Gerd, the worker and the apprentice, are based on dozens of interviews with scores of workers and incorporate statistics and data.

Obviously, the interviews in West Berlin bear a different character from those in East Berlin. Many of the West Berliners are close personal friends. Even those whom I met only once or twice could talk with me at leisure and were free to express their views frankly. Most of my interviews in the East were arranged for me or resulted from accidental meetings, and they were necessarily hurried, limited in depth, and discreet. In both East and West Berlin I took no shorthand notes nor did I ever use a tape recorder. Instead I listened, took occasional notes, and then when I got back to my room transcribed or recorded my recollection and impressions of the person, of the setting, and of the interview. Naturally, I have tried to be as accurate as possible, but my report does not pretend to literal accuracy. I have tried to capture the atmosphere, the viewpoint, and, where possible, the actual words of each Berliner interviewed. I have tried to present their opinions and not mine, to let Berliners speak for themselves.

Naturally, I have chosen as broad a spectrum of opinion and background as I could: men and women, young, middle-aged, and elderly, workers, businessmen, and professional people, but I have not aimed at a statistically perfect cross-section. This study is not in any sense a quantitative analysis. If you belong to the school of thought which holds that, if you can't count it, it doesn't count, I fear you will shudder at my nonmethod.

However, I hope that my survey is scientific in the older sense of that word, that it contributes to depth of understanding and to insight. I hope that it presents a dimension of social and political history, something more than just journalism, which can be lost in traditional, scholarly analysis. I love Berlin and Berliners. I have deep personal ties with the city. I also speak German fluently and with the smallest hint of a Prussian intonation. Perhaps my personal commitment and my empathy help transmute data into insight.

I have tried to portray Berlin and Berliners both objectively and impressionistically to create a composite portrait of a specific place and time in history. I believe that it is a vitally, perhaps crucially important place and time, that in a sense Berlin since 1945 has been the center of the world. It has certainly been the center of my world and of the world of my Berliners.

Berliners, East and West, are caught up in the drama of their city, but they are not passive pawns on a great-power chessboard. They are real and vital individuals involved deeply and personally in an immediate and continuing tragedy. They play their roles with gallantry. They go on living in divided, threatened Berlin day by day, dealing with each crisis as it comes, working, producing, laughing, wondering and often worrying, joking about themselves, sometimes on the edge of despair.

These are my Berliners, the Berliners I should like you to meet.

Berliners

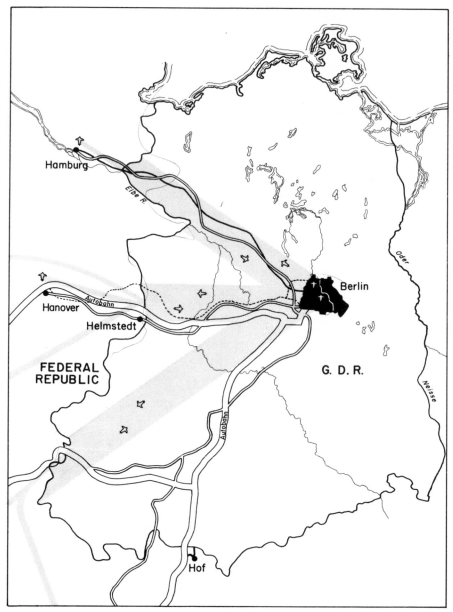

Traffic Routes between West Berlin and West Germany

1

Historical Background

Berlin is unique. Few cities in recent history have presided over such drama, such disaster as Berlin. The ugly wall that for a decade has severed the city and the death strip running around the periphery of West Berlin cutting it off from its natural hinterland are only recent symbols of an old tragedy.

Perhaps Berlin's chief tragedy is that it surged so rapidly, so blatantly, to its status as a world city. Berlin is young for a European city, brashly new. No ancient ruins, no walled old town with picturesque, winding medieval streets, no famous Romanesque or Gothic churches lure the tourist to Berlin. During the thirteenth century the twin trading towns of Berlin and Cölln on the River Spree, outposts on the northern and eastern flank of the Holy Roman Empire, prospered modestly. Only with the succession of the Hohenzollerns to the electorate of Brandenburg in 1415 was a certain amount of European attention attracted to little Berlin. In 1440 the Hohenzollerns established their residence in Berlin.

The rise of Brandenburg-Prussia signaled the rise of Berlin, its growth in size, in prosperity, and in prestige. Progressive, paternalistic princes, the Hohenzollerns encouraged trade, patronized learning and the arts, and fostered intellectual freedom and religious toleration. Hopeful and hard-working young people from all over Germany streamed to the new capital to seek opportunity and to help it grow and prosper. Spanish Jews and French Huguenots sought refuge and brought their diligence and skills to add to the sophistication of the city. Throughout the seventeenth and eighteenth centuries, the Hohenzollern princes imported architects and artists to build and decorate palaces, public buildings, parks, and squares. They sponsored poets, professors, and scientists. In 1680 Berlin had only about ten thousand inhabitants. By the mid-

3

eighteenth century it was an impressive city with over a hundred thousand people, and it had grown to a center of learning and progress.

During the struggle against Napoleon, Berlin came into its own. Crushed by the defeat at Jena in 1806, Prussia nevertheless became the storm center of national and progressive feeling, attracting rebels and reformers, poets, military officers, and musicians who looked to the Prussian Queen Luise rather than to the rather weak king to spearhead the struggle for national freedom and unity. The constitutional reforms of Freiherr vom Stein, the military reforms of Gerhard Johann David von Scharnhorst and August Gneisenau made Prussia the most modern state in Europe. The victories of Wellington and Nelson, supported by their Prussian allies, destroyed French hegemony and stimulated hope for the unification of Germany.

Dynamic, modern Prussia became the nucleus around which German national unity was constructed. In 1871, when Bismarck succeeded in creating a German national state, Berlin, by then with a population of almost a million, emerged as the new imperial capital. Between 1871 and 1914 Berlin's population almost quadrupled. Industrial production soared, commerce thrived. The university, founded in 1809, and the many scientific and scholarly institutes made Berlin a world-famous center, especially in the fields of mathematics and history. Opera houses, concert halls, and theaters attracted the world's leading conductors, singers, and composers. By 1914 Berlin had grown from an insignificant provincial town to a full-fledged imperial city, one of the great cities of the world.

Berlin shared Germany's destiny, plunging from world power to disaster in 1918. Defeat, inflation, unemployment, and social unrest plagued the almost four million Berliners in the period following the Versailles settlement. The undercurrent of despair ran through the cultural revival of the 1920s. Weimar Berlin remained a world-famous center of music, learning, and the arts, and excelled in the new art of the film, but the city was also a center of decadence.

From 1933 until 1945, Berlin became the symbol of nazi Germany. Never a nazi stronghold, center of both the leftwing and rightwing opposition to National Socialism, Berlin nevertheless was the site of the burning of the Reichstag, of the Chancellery from which Hitler ruled and in which he later died. It was the Berlin Olympic stadium which witnessed many of the largest, most flamboyant nazi rallies, which rang to the demagogic speeches of Goebbels and Hitler and resounded with the blare of brass bands and the shouts of *Sieg Heil.* The nazis took control of the provincial Prussian government by force; they never won a free election in Berlin, but to the world, especially to nazi Germany's enemies, Berlin symbolized nazi tryranny.

When the war began in 1939, obviously, Berlin became general headquarters. The War Office, the General Staff, and Hitler's personal headquarters were all in Berlin. In addition, the city was a major production center for strategically vital supplies. Inevitably it became a major target of Allied strategy. Early Allied bombing raids focused primarily on industrial targets in the Ruhr and Rhineland, but after January 1943, the around-the-clock saturation bombing of Berlin began. During the last half of 1943 and throughout all of 1944, the raids continued with increasing ferocity, increasing devastation. Whole sections of the city were obliterated by block busters and firebombs; whole neighborhoods were reduced to rubble.

On Hitler's birthday, 20 April 1945, the Red Army reached the outskirts of Greater Berlin. For twelve days the murderous battle for Berlin pressed to its ruthless, inexorable end. House by house, street by street, Red Army units forced back the German and Ukrainian defenders. Ukrainian and S.S. units fought with literal desperation, knowing that for them surrender was unthinkable. Whole blocks not yet entirely destroyed by bombing were demolished by artillery.

On 30 April Hitler abandoned his capital and the German people to their fate, committing suicide in the bunker in the Chancellery. On the second of May the last German defenders of Berlin surrendered. The remnants of the High Command had already evacuated the city, flying to a temporary headquarters in Flensburg. On 8 May the war officially ended with the signing of Germany's unconditional surrender. Berlin, capital of the nazi German Reich, became the symbol of Germany's total defeat. For an entire week, the Red Army tore through the city, raping and pillaging. By July Berlin was under the rule of the four-power Allied military Kommandatura.

In 1945 Berlin was little more than a heap of rubble. During the bombings, women and especially children had been evacuated; military units recruited from the Berlin area had suffered especially high losses. In consequence the population, which had reached almost five million in 1939, had dropped to less than three million by May 1945. Seventy-five per cent of the city's housing was uninhabitable; twelve per cent was totally destroyed. Public utilities such as gas, electricity, subways, and streetcars had ceased functioning; garbage was not collected; sewage disposal was interrupted; there was insufficient food and less fuel.

On 17 May local government was revived and by mid-July had begun to restore city services. The reconstruction of the thoroughly deva-

Fig. 2. Downtown Berlin, May, 1946 (photo by Landesbildstelle, West Berlin)

stated city was a slow, painful process hampered by the growing division among the Allies as well as by the policy of taking reparations out of current production and by the dismantling of industrial plants. Almost a quarter of Berlin's industrial capacity had been destroyed by war losses. Another forty-three per cent was lost through dismantling, leaving the city crippled economically and burdened with massive unemployment. All commodities were scarce but especially fuel, food, tools, and consumer goods. Inevitably a black market sprang up, and soon all goods and services were valued not in the worthless reichsmark but in cigarettes, the coin of the occupation.

By 1946 it was clear that the Soviets intended to make all Berlin communist. It was also clear that Berlin Social Democrats and trade union leaders were determined to resist with or without the support of the Western occupying powers. In October 1946 the first Berlin city elections shattered Soviet optimism. The Communist Party polled less than twenty per cent of the vote in all Berlin, most of their support coming from the Soviet-occupied sector.

Tension mounted, and pressure on German socialists and trade unionists was increased. The Soviets tried to force the merger of the West Berlin Social Democratic Party (S.P.D.) with the communists in the newly formed Socialist Unity Party (S.E.D.), and to foster communist domination of West Berlin trade unions, but the West Berliners resisted.

In West Germany the three Allied occupation authorities decided to introduce new currency to help end the black market and curb inflation. The United States, Great Britain, and France had tried to arrive at an agreement with the Soviet Union to introduce new currency into all Germany in accordance with the stipulation of the Potsdam Agreement that Germany was to be administered as a single economic entity, but after repeated failures to win any co-operation from their Eastern ally, they decided to introduce the new deutsche mark (D-mark) into their three Western zones. The Soviets threatened that they would consider this a violation of the Potsdam Agreement and warned of reprisals.

By the beginning of 1948 the Berlin atmosphere had chilled to the degree that the Soviets began to tighten controls on access to West Berlin. In March the Soviet commander walked out of the Allied Control Council; the Soviets increased their pressure on traffic to Berlin. By April Berlin was effectively blockaded, and in June the Soviets withdrew from the four-power Kommandatura which governed Berlin's four sectors. The Cold War was on, and Berlin was its focal point.

The British and American Allies responded to the Soviet move with a swiftly improvised airlift to supply necessary food, fuel and supplies to West Berlin. West Berliners, as astonished as the Soviets and perhaps as doubtful of the outcome, welcomed the Allied decision and remained cheerfully intransigent, stubbornly refusing to submit to Soviet threats.

Throughout the fall of 1948 procommunist demonstrators picketed the Berlin Town Hall in East Berlin, harassing government officials and interfering with the deliberations of the Assembly. By the beginning of December the government found it impossible to function in East Berlin and so anticommunist officials marched out of the old city hall and fled to West Berlin, where they established headquarters in the borough hall in Schöneberg. On 5 December, free elections were held in West Berlin. On 21 December the Allied Kommandatura resumed meetings as a three-power body representing only the West. By the end of 1948, Berlin had become virtually two separate cities.

In May 1949 the Soviets abandoned their blockade of Berlin and acknowledged the right of the Western Allies to have access to the city. In the same month, the Western Allies accorded to West Berlin local autonomy under an occupation statute, and West Germany adopted a new constitution under which West Berlin was declared to be a land in the new Federal Republic. In October the Russians proclaimed that their zone of occupation was the German Democratic Republic. There were now two German governments as well as two Berlin governments.

The introduction of the D-mark into West Berlin, the beginning of Marshall Plan aid and assistance from the new Federal Republic stimulated the reconstruction and the economic revival of West Berlin. Rubble was cleared, housing began to spring up, factories started to turn out goods and shops displayed consumer goods. By the early 1950s, West Berlin had already begun to look like a thriving Western city. The contrast between the dynamic growth of the economy in West Berlin, between its well-lit streets and well-fed citizens, and the drab, dingy streets and empty shops of East Berlin was already striking.

Between 1945 and August 1961, a total of more than two and a half million people fled from the Soviet zone of Germany, seeking asylum in the West. Of these, the great majority fled by way of West Berlin. By 1961 the tide of refugees reached flood level. In June and July about a thousand people a day streamed from East to West Berlin, many of them skilled, highly educated and young.

Early on the morning of 13 August 1961, the East Berlin authorities began to construct a wall along the line separating East from West Berlin. Since August 1961 the Wall has become the symbol of the divided and isolated city. Despite it and despite guards with dogs and high-

powered rifles, refugees still try to escape into West Berlin; many ha
been killed or wounded in the attempt.

In the ten years since the building of the Wall, the temperature of the
Cold War has fluctuated and tension in Berlin has increased and dimin-
ished. Periods of harassment and pinpricks, of threats and ultimata
have been succeeded by periods of thaw and *détente*. As recently as the
summer of 1968, the Soviets launched a series of diplomatic attacks on
Bonn, attempting to cut off the political ties between West Berlin and
the Federal Republic. The atmosphere grew very chilly. However, as
soon as former West Berlin mayor Willy Brandt took office as Chancellor of the Federal Republic, he introduced his *Ost Politik,* his policy
of attempting to normalize relations between West Germany and the
U.S.S.R. On 12 August 1970 he signed a treaty in Moscow with the
Soviet Union which seemed to indicate that it was interested in estab-
lishing friendlier relations with Bonn. The West Germans stipulated
that a four-power agreement on Berlin was a prior condition to ratification of the Bonn-Moscow treaty by the Bonn parliament.

In March 1970, for the first time in eleven years, representatives of
France, Great Britain, the Soviet Union and the United States met in
Berlin to attempt to negotiate an agreement concerning access to the
city and its future status. Once again Berlin had become the focal point
of the intersection of East and West.

Berliners watched the progress of the negotiations with the cool
detachment of experienced players in the game of international diplomacy, but not without an undercurrent of tension, certainly not without deep concern for their future as individuals and as a city. Berliners
are accustomed to living at the storm center of crisis. They have experienced little but crisis since 1945, perhaps since 1933.

They accepted the Berlin agreement of 3 September 1971 with grati-
fication and gratitude, sincerely thankful that West Berliners would be
permitted to visit relatives in the East, but the underlying tension and
doubt persist. Old Berlin hands sense a growing scepticism, in some
quarters a growing fear. Many Berliners confidently trust that the
agreement will lead to genuine *détente,* to a new era of decreased tension. Others shake their heads, wondering whether *détente* means de-
nouement.

Berliners react to their new situation as they always have reacted, as
individuals. Let us examine the lives and views of some Berlin individuals
over the past decade.

2

Sigrid

It was a mild evening in June 1967. Sigrid and I had finished an early dinner celebrating my arrival in West Berlin, and we were enjoying a leisurely stroll down the Kurfürstendamm. I was experiencing that mood of unreality and light-headedness that comes from the sudden translation of jet flight. It was delightful to be in Berlin again, carried along on the tide of vitality that is the Kurfürstendamm on a warm spring evening, but it was not yet entirely real.

Sigrid smiled patiently while I examined every shop window, carefully inspecting the Rosenthal china, striking sportswear in a chic boutique, cameras and books and jewelry. Each time I return to Berlin I am enchanted by the air of opulent cleanliness and bustling vigor. I drank in all the impressions, joyfully observed young couples arm in arm, teen-aged boys decked out in the Berlin version of the latest "mod" costume, camera-laden tourists searching for a good restaurant, spritely young girls and dowdy, substantial matrons windowshopping or sipping coffee in the sidewalk cafés. The restaurants and cafés were crowded, the shops glittered with the abundance of their offerings, and Berliners chatted and laughed and bounced along in all their customary gaiety. It was good to be back in Berlin and very good to be enjoying an evening with an old friend.

Sigrid and I had much to catch up on, but she realized that I was tired from my flight and so we postponed serious conversation until the next day. That evening we were both content with light gossip and a leisurely stroll. Neither of us had planned an encounter with tragedy.

As we walked, we noticed that there were an unusual number of policemen and police cars on the street. We stopped an American Army MP at the next crossing, and I asked him why there were so many policemen in evidence.

10

Fig. 3. Strollers on the Kurfürstendamm in front of an American-type drugstore (photo by Landesbildstelle, West Berlin)

"Students, ma'am," he said, and he explained that the Shah of Iran was visiting West Berlin and the police were expecting a student demonstration to protest oppression in Iran. "There'll be trouble," he predicted, "but the Berlin police are ready for it." He glanced at his watch and said, "Just about now. The Shah and his party went to the opera and they should be getting out and heading this way any minute."

His watch and his information were accurate. We continued our walk, and in a very few minutes we saw the first knot of demonstrators. A small band of dark-skinned young men marched down the center of the street carrying a large placard. Just as they reached our corner, they set fire to the placard and shouted some sort of slogan.

"They're Iranian students, I think," Sigrid said.

A white-helmeted policeman hurried the demonstrators on briskly but politely, and they disappeared around the corner.

By then a small crowd of curious onlookers had gathered, and Sigrid and I moved around the fringe. Even before we saw the surging crowd of demonstrators marching from the direction of the opera toward the Kurfürstendamm, a large fleet of police trucks drew up and parked in a row along the curb near us. Swiftly and with frightening precision one policeman after another leaped from the trucks to the sidewalk and charged toward the approaching demonstrators, clubs swinging. Sigrid and I backed against the nearest shop window and watched. Many other spectators also backed away; still others fled without ceremony. Loudspeakers ordered the marchers to disperse, but they came on, many of them arm-in-arm, chanting.

The police charged into the massed students; clubs flailed; the crowd surged. Sigrid and I had difficulty seeing over the heads of the people closer to the curb so we could not tell exactly what happened. We heard the sharp strident squawk of the ambulance siren over the shouts and the scuffling. Craning our necks we saw that several young men fell before the police onslaught; a few were carried off on stretchers to the waiting ambulances.

"There isn't anything we can do, and we can't get closer. Should we leave?" I asked.

Sigrid had just agreed when a young woman in a fawn-colored suede jacket pushed through the crowd, rushed toward us, and amazingly threw herself into my arms weeping. Blood streamed down her cheek from a shallow cut on her forehead.

"My friend," she sobbed, "he's hurt! They've taken him away. They wouldn't let me go with him; they just pushed me away. I don't know where they've taken him. I don't know how badly he was hurt!"

We soothed her and assured her that he would be all right and firmly shepherded her away from the congestion and the danger.

"Would you like a drink?" I asked. "Some coffee?"

She shook her head, still dazed. She thanked me but said, "No. If he's conscious, he will have them call me, and I can go to him. I'd better go home and wait."

We both agreed and walked slowly with her to the next subway station. Sigrid and I were both too badly shocked to be able to say much.

"I'll go home with her, shall I?" Sigrid suggested.

I agreed, and we decided to meet at my pension the following morning.

"I'll come at ten," Sigrid said.

I kissed her and waved good-bye to her and to our sudden acquaintance. "I hope your friend is all right," I said, and she managed a smile and thanked me. Slowly, still stunned, I turned and walked to my pension. That was not the welcome I had expected on my return to Berlin.

I was deeply disturbed by the violence, and so, despite my travel fatigue, I slept badly. The following morning I read in the paper that one young man had died from his injuries, and several more were in the hospital. When Sigrid arrived to join me over late coffee, she assured me that it was not the friend of our young woman who had been killed.

"The student who was killed was married,'" she explained. "His wife is expecting a baby in November. My friends have been telephoning since seven this morning, and, of course, they are all terribly upset about it."

I said that the police claimed the students had used knives and thrown stones. They said they had acted in self-defense.

"Perhaps they did, or thought they did, but this is going to cause trouble," she predicted.

We drank our coffee rather soberly. Sigrid was right. The demonstration against the Shah on 2 June 1967 and the shooting of Benno Ohnesorge marked the beginning of the violent phase of student rebellion in West Berlin. Although Sigrid has never considered herself a radical, even she was active in the events which followed. When Ohnesorge's body left Berlin on its way to his home in Hanover, West Germany, for burial, thousands of Berlin students, many in rattle-trap cars, black banners streaming from their radio antennae, began the drive along the *Autobahn* across the German Democratic Republic (G.D.R.) to West Germany. When they reached the border of the communist area, they discovered thousands of East German young people in the uniform of the Communist Free German Youth organization massed to welcome them and proclaim their sympathy. The East German authorities refused to charge the students the usual fee for using the *Autobahn,* and they waived the normal requirement of visas. Many of the students, even new leftist radicals, were embarrassed by this uninvited alliance with the old left; however they had no choice but to accept the offer.

Sigrid went along. Although she never became a member of any political group, radical or otherwise, she did have friends among the activists, and she certainly sympathized with the general student reaction to the death of their fellow-student, to what they considered the brutality of the police. In the weeks following that June incident, she not only went to Hanover for the funeral, she also attended rallies and meetings and signed protest petitions.

"The head of the police must go!" she told me over coffee the following week. "We are supposed to be living in a democratic city with a government responsible to the will of the people!"

She was very emphatic, and apparently her feelings were typical even of moderate students and of a good many average Berlin citizens. The pressure on the governing mayor and the police head mounted. Eventually both Erich Duensing, the police chief, and the mayor were forced from office.

Despite this, student unrest increased. A little over a year later, Erich Duensing's successor, Georg Moch, was pressured into retiring prematurely. Demonstration followed demonstration, meetings multiplied. Throughout the summer, the politically active students, primarily new leftists, issued pamphlets and mimeographed bulletins. Every evening groups of three or four students stood at intervals along the Kurfürstendamm distributing the latest literature, debating with passing citizens.

That summer Sigrid and I often stopped to listen to the exchange of opinion between students representing the Socialist German Students' Organization (S.D.S.) and Berliners of all classes. Sometimes the retort of the citizen was acrimonious or impatient, more often it was tolerant and humorous, but I noticed that moderate Sigrid was growing impatient with her fellow citizens.

"They don't understand!" she exploded as we walked briskly away from one sidewalk debate. "They are *Spiesser*—Philistines! They are narrow-minded, provincial, and moral cowards! Oh, not that I agree with this garbage," she waved the mimeograph pages we had just accepted from a bearded but extremely tidy apostle of the left. "These far leftists are silly to be so ideological, so doctrinaire. They have a good issue, a genuine grievance, but, as always, they insist on weakening their case by wrapping the real problem in ritualistic cant about monopoly capitalism or exploitation of the masses! They only alienate people."

She took a breath and then went on. "Just because they are silly doesn't mean that everything they say is worthless or that older people shouldn't listen to them. There are real problems, and the average Berliner just doesn't want to know about them. All they can worry about is the Wall and their fixed idea of communism. They are frozen into the attitudes of the Cold War; they can't see that we have moved into a different era with new and different problems."

"Have some coffee," I suggested, "or a Coke," pressing her into the next sidewalk café.

She grinned apologetically. "Sorry, I was sounding off, wasn't I? But they do make me mad, and the Springer Press makes me even madder."

Apparently Sigrid's anger was not peculiar to her. Hostility between the students and the citizens grew, and the Springer Publishing House became the symbol and the focal point of student hostility toward the establishment. The organs of the Springer Press, especially the newspaper *Bild,* with its mass circulation of four million readers, consistently exposed the radicalism of the extremists and steadily criticized the excesses of the protesters. The students considered this a concerted campaign against them, and in their turn they picketed the publishing house, issued pamphlets, and made speeches denouncing Axel Springer and all his works.

During the fall and winter of 1967–68, the students turned their wrath against the American war in Vietnam, and this sharply increased the hostility, fear, and suspicion of the average Berliner, grateful to the United States and staunchly anticommunist. Just after Klaus Schütz took over his new duties as governing mayor, about thirty thousand students, supported by the West Berlin S.E.D., massed to voice their opposition to the Vietnam conflict. Later that fall, the leftist students urged West German recognition of the German Democratic Republic, and the debates along the Kurfürstendamm grew more heated, less tolerant. Still, except for the incident of the Shah's visit, until early 1968 the protests remained peaceful. The leaders of the S.D.S. kept strict control over their rank and file. They policed all demonstrations and kept them from getting out of hand.

In February, 1968, Mayor Schütz took the occasion of a speech in the City Hall Square to reaffirm West Berlin's loyalty to the principles of freedom and peace. This sparked a violent reaction by student protesters. Stones flew, police retaliated, and scores of injured policemen and students were carried off in ambulances. Just before Easter, the attempted assassination of new leftist leader Rudi Dutschke precipitated further riots and increased violence. The Easter troubles exploded into the confrontation of thousands of angry students with masses of increasingly angry police. Students stormed City Hall, marched down the Kurfürstendamm, and attacked the Springer building. They damaged property, destroyed police cars, and two people died.

In May, trade unionists for the first time made common cause with the students to protest the plans of the National Democratic Party (N.P.D.), a small rightist party described as neonazi, to hold its party congress in West Berlin. Fifty thousand workers and students marched through working-class neighborhoods to protest any encroachment of the neonazis on democratic Berlin. The N.P.D. canceled its meeting.

During the summer the debate in the Bonn parliament on the proposed emergency legislation, a law to grant special powers to the federal government in the event of a national emergency, gave rise to student protest throughout Germany. Delegations from many universities, including sizable ones from West Berlin's Free University and Technical University, converged on Bonn, picketing and chanting in front of the parliament building.

By the fall of 1968 hostility had reached the point of outright warfare. A small but highly organized group of students (about five hundred, according to press reports), led by the most extreme radicals, attacked the courthouse on Tegeler Weg in Charlottenburg, where Horst Mahler, the lawyer who had defended many of the demonstrators arrested after the spring riots, was on trial. The students carried pikes and sticks and wore protective helmets. The police countercharged, wearing new helmets with plastic plates to protect the face and neck. They used water cannons, tear gas, and truncheons and used them most effectively. About one hundred and fifty people were injured, mostly police. The students barricaded one of the bridges over the Spree and held it for half an hour. Later, at a mass meeting at the Technical University, students cheered wildly when police casualties were announced.

This was perhaps the high point of the tension and violence. After that the leftist movement began to split, and the more moderate students, previously sympathetic because there were underlying and just grievances, pulled back from identification with such brutality. The leaders on the far left had become professional revolutionaries, opposed to order of any kind, unwilling to compromise.

Sigrid remained both sympathetic and critical. In June, 1968, when we were again celebrating my arrival in Berlin with a festive dinner on the Kurfürstendamm, she told me about her experiences as a patient in a large Berlin hospital.

"It was awful!" she said. She had suffered a burst appendix and at first had been too weak to notice the attitude of her fellow patients in the women's surgery ward, and while she was dangerously ill they showed a normal human sympathy and concern. However as soon as she was out of danger, out of severe pain, and began to convalesce, the underlying hostility of the Berlin citizen to the genus student began to emerge.

"Of course, they always knew I was a student, but while I was very sick they felt sorry for me. Gradually, though, as I became stronger, they showed their resentment and began to look at me as though I were a zoo specimen, 'One of those!' Truly, they hate students, and especially women students."

I asked why women especially, and she explained that they regarded the males merely as troublemakers, "as they call them, *Radicalinskys*, but female students are immoral and underminers of society."

"Excuse me," I interrupted, "but how do they imagine that you are immoral all by yourselves? Do they think you are all lesbians?"

She laughed and said, "No, just some of us! But you are being too rational and too liberated. These Berlin women are very old-fashioned and very conventional. Girls who live in communes or live with their young men are anathema to them."

"Well, surely they didn't think of you as a scarlet woman?" I asked.

"Not after a while. When they got used to me they gradually decided I was fairly decent, anyway normal."

"No bombs in your nightie or bearded boys under the bed?"

She giggled. "Exactly, and even the students who came to see me were all clean-shaven and rather neat and inoffensive, so they slowly pulled in their horns, or their claws. Still, I resented their attitude. It is so unjust to condemn all twenty-something thousand students in Berlin because a few hundred are violent or revolutionary; and that is what they do."

I sympathized, but I said I also understood the average middle-aged Berliner's reaction. I still remember the blockade and so do they. For two decades West Berlin has been the exposed salient, the outer glacis surrounded by Soviet power. Naturally average Berliners hate and fear communism, and so they must almost automatically hate and fear anything they associate with communism.

"Student rebellion at Columbia University is just one incident in New York's complex urban crisis," I told her, "but student revolt in West Berlin is a crisis in itself. Last time I was in East Berlin, Sigrid, I spoke with one of the official journalists there, and he smiled like a cream-fed tomcat when he spoke of the student violence in West Berlin. He said that if things continue that way, the communists won't have to lift a finger, West Berlin will drop into the communist sphere like a ripe plum. Your average Berliner may not be sophisticated, but he knows that much. He knows it from experience, and naturally he is afraid."

Sigrid said she understood but was still resentful and hurt. After all, she is a child of her generation, and in Germany what we call the generation gap is real and often tragic. Like many advanced German students, she is over thirty. She has already completed her final examination and won her diploma in architecture. She is now working on a dissertation and hopes to have her doctorate in sociology within a year.

It is not unusual for a student at a German university to be thirty or thirty-five before completing his degree or degrees. The course of study is inordinately long, but for Sigrid the road has been longer than for most students because she did not enter the university directly from the Gymnasium.

Sigrid's family did not belong to the traditional European academic class. Her father began life as a mechanic. As a young man he worked days and went to trade school at night to qualify as a master mechanic. To this day he is proud that he was able to qualify as a master in two trades. Ultimately he established his own machine shop and entered the ranks of small businessmen.

During the war he served as a noncommissioned officer in the Luftwaffe and eventually became chief mechanic at an airfield near Königsberg in East Prussia, very near the family home. Towards the end of the war, when the Red Army began to penetrate German territory, he was able to arrange to have his wife and two children flown out of East Prussia with a friendly air-force pilot. Although they could bring only what belongings they could carry, they were lucky to escape, transferred as they were from plane to plane, from pilot to pilot until they reached the relative safety of West Germany. There, in the small, provincial town of Rinteln on the Weser in Lower Saxony, the family settled and Sigrid grew up.

As soon as her father was demobilized, he joined his family in the West, and he immediately set to work to re-establish his lost business. By dint of long hours of very hard work, of stinting and saving, he finally was able to establish his family as part of Rinteln's respectable middle class.

As a symbol of their new affluence and status, both Sigrid and her younger brother Otto were encouraged to attend the Gymnasium, the traditional academic secondary school which prepares young people to enter the university. Their father believed that the *Abitur*, the certificate of completion of the Gymnasium which entitles the graduate to enter any German university, conferred a certain social cachet upon his children, even upon a girl, but he firmly opposed allowing Sigrid to go on to attend the university.

"Do I want an intellectual daughter?" he asked. "You are no beauty. It will be hard enough for you to get a husband without making a bluestocking of yourself." Intellectual women, he still believes, are too independent, inclined to be bossy and unfeminine, and perhaps he feared he would feel insecure if his daughter were better educated than he. He was able to insist, indeed to order, and so after finishing the Gymnasium, Sigrid reluctantly entered a secretarial school and completed the course.

A year later she began work in the office of a small business firm not far from her home, but she had quietly decided that she would not allow her father to curtail her opportunity, to limit her life. She saved just as stringently as he had done, and, after little more than a year, she boldly announced that she would move to West Berlin. Her parents were hurt and indignant, but by then she was of age, and she had saved enough to establish herself.

She arrived in Berlin in 1958 when she was exactly twenty-one. She quickly found a rented room and an office job; then she investigated the possibility of entering the faculty of architecture at Berlin's Technical University. She discovered that she lacked some prerequisites, so she spent almost a year filling in the gaps in her background and in 1959 enrolled as a candidate for a degree in architecture.

Throughout her student years she has had to work to support herself. She works full time between semesters, part time during the semester. She has lived very simply and frugally, and she has worked very hard. By 1970 she was ready to take her final examination in architecture, and she had completed all the credits and examinations for a doctorate in sociology.

"My father still disapproves of scientific females," she told me, "but he is also a little proud of me. When he can speak of his daughter the doctor, he will be overjoyed, but he will still not like it!"

She told me a little about the requirements for the degree in architecture. "The examination wasn't hard so much as exhausting," she explained. "After all those semesters, one knows one's stuff, but it was a lot of writing! There were four written examinations, each in a different phase of the work, each six hours long. There was a single oral examination covering six or seven disciplines.

"After I passed both the written and oral exams, I had to do a practicum, that is an original architectural plan. I worked on that for three months and then presented it to a faculty committee. The whole committee had to approve it, but my grade was assigned by my sponsoring professor. They accepted it, and I was qualified to become a diplomate engineer. I am an architect, you know, but the degree is in engineering."

I asked her what happens to a candidate who fails either his written or oral examination, and she explained that he may automatically take either or both again after six months. If he fails the second time, he must have a very good excuse, such as sickness, to be allowed to take it a third time; however she assured me that most students who get as far as the final examination usually pass at least at the second trial.

That evening we sipped our wine slowly and talked a good deal about her parents. Sigrid resents them and unequivocally rejects their values.

"My parents are loveless and shallow. They have spent all their adult lives struggling for material success, for security, for status. They sacrificed every comfort, every joy, year after year, and expected their children to sacrifice them too. There were no little treats for us, no outings. We never went to the circus or to the ballet or took interesting vacations. I almost never had a pretty dress and my brother Otto had to work to buy his own bicycle even though by then my father could well have afforded it. My mother wore old, dowdy dresses and never went to the hairdresser, and both she and my father were always tired, always irritable and impatient. Otto and I had a gloomy household, a gloomy childhood."

I reminded her that her parents had lost everything they had when they fled from East Prussia in 1945. "They had to feed and clothe you and put a roof over your head. They had to work hard, rebuild and save."

"Of course they did," she admitted, "but they didn't have to renounce every pleasure, every joy, or go on living frugally, meanly, after they began to have enough to eat and a place to live. I know people who lost vast estates or large businesses, the parents of some of my fellow students, and they are gay and relaxed and happy."

I asked her whether she didn't think it might be harder for a self-made small businessman to lose the little security he had built up than for the heir to ten or twelve generations of nobility to lose his estates.

"I'm not sure," I ventured, "that you see the shock, the emotional dislocation that the war and the flight inflicted, especially on people who were not very sophisticated, basically not very secure. I have laughed with any number of Silesian countesses or Pomeranian barons about the ludicrous adventures of the trek, but they can laugh because who and what they are doesn't depend on what they own; their identity wasn't shattered because they were uprooted."

Sigrid nodded in half-agreement, but I could see that nothing would nullify her basic resentment, not at least for many years. I wondered whether her parents reacted with equal resentment, baffled at their children's lack of gratitude for all their hard work and sacrifice, never understanding that the children had longed for tenderness and love. The generation gap in many such German middle-class families can be very real, very tragic.

We talked a little about this generation gap, and Sigrid said, "Well at least my father was never a nazi. I think he was too selfish to be anything besides frugal! In some families the children blame their parents for the nazi crimes, for the war and for losing it. The parents try to explain the conditions in Germany in the 1930s, but, of course, they rarely succeed. The young people ask how their parents could have let it happen, and they despise them. The parents resent the failure of their children even to try to understand. I know many cases like that."

I said there must also be many students of about her age who had never known a father. Germany lost between three and four million people in the Second World War, at least three million males. That represented about ten per cent of the total male population, but, of course, a much higher percentage of the young men of an age to become fathers. Sigrid agreed that many of her fellow students were fatherless.

"You're a Christian, aren't you?" she asked, abruptly changing the subject. I admitted that I was. "Well, I suppose I am too. I mean, I believe in God. I even believe in Christ and in the creed, although some of my friends think I am a little silly to admit it. I read a lot of books on theology, Barth and Tillich, Niebuhr and Bonhoeffer. I love Martin Buber. I am very much interested in religion, but not in church. I think that is because of my parents."

"My parents are Lutheran, of course," she said. "Most East Prussians are. They are very pious, very churchy, and that has rather put me off church. They are the grim, sober kind of Christians. You know, the kind that keep fast days strictly. I rather think it's because they like to punish themselves instead of because they love God! They do without things they need, things we needed as children, to contribute to the church, and that could be good, only they never did it cheerfully, with love. They suffered grimly. When they take a trip, they always attend church along the way, and they are brutally critical of neighbors and friends who skip church. My papa is a member of the church council; he doesn't drink or smoke, and yet, you know, I believe he is less a believer than I am. He and his friends don't really believe in the whole Bible, but they pretend that they do, and they refuse to discuss it!

"No," she said firmly, shaking her head, "if they are Christians, then I do not want to go to church. I do, of course, once in a while, and I should like to be married in church, but I cannot like my parents' kind of religion. I think a good many students feel as I do, but I also think many of us are more truly religious than our parents."

I agreed with her emphatically.

3

Rainer

"Thank the Lord this is my last semester here!" The dark-haired young man swept off his horn-rimmed glasses and slammed them dangerously onto the desk. He grinned at me, a little embarrassed by his own vehemence. "No, maybe it's not so bad as all that. Some of it has been fun and, of course, I love Berlin, but it has honestly become impossible for someone like me to teach at the Free University, even in the law faculty. I am grateful that I received a call to one of the new West German universities. If I hadn't, I swear I would have left the academic world and taken a job in the federal government, even if it meant spending the rest of my life in Bonn!"

I smiled, remembering the dismal year I had spent in provincial Bonn. "Things must be bad here," I said, and I asked whether it was his personal political views that had caused trouble with his students.

Rainer has a mobile, expressive face. He raised his eyebrows, registering self-irony. "I don't need any views, Frau Doctor. They know my name."

His is a well-known military family. He has an older brother who is prominent in the Church, a younger one who had just entered the Bonn Foreign Service.

"Definitely Establishmentarian," he said, "although between us, you know perfectly well what I think of that Bonn crowd. Still, to our dear radical students, anyone who isn't an incendiary is a conservative, anyone whose father was a general, a nazi general as they would say in their ignorance, is *ipso facto* reactionary. Unless I wear African robes or Chinese pajamas with a 'Heil Mao' arm band, they are bound to label me as the Enemy."

I said things hadn't reached that stage in the City University in New York. "In fact, I find that radical students, especially the blacks, prefer an honest-to-God conservative any day to a liberal or even to an old

22

leftist. They know where they are with a conservative, and they hate being patronized."

He nodded. "Even here there is an element of grudging respect in their hostility. Liberals they simply can't take seriously; us they seem to fear, although quite foolishly, if you ask me. Again, between us, I think we are quite as inept politically as the liberals, even if our basic principles are more realistic."

Rainer is tall and athletic-looking for an academic man. In addition to teaching legal history in the law faculty of West Berlin's Free University, he is an ardent yachtsman and an accomplished equestrian. The impressively thick-rimmed glasses are for reading, or perhaps, I suspected, for effect, to make an elegant and perhaps too good-natured young man appear serious and academic.

He looks younger than his thirty-five years, especially without his glasses, and he can never resist a grin or a quip. He impressed me as precisely the sort of young professor who would normally be popular with students, and so I was sad but not surprised to learn that in the tumultuous situation at the Free University in October of 1970, in spite of having a loyal following of moderate and nonpolitical students, he has been harassed and tormented by his faculty's Red cell to the extent that he seriously considered abandoning his profession.

"Our Red cell is not very large," he said. He explained that almost every faculty in both the Free University and the Technical University has an organized cadre of radical students who form what they call a Red cell and who use this organization to attempt to dominate the political activities of their faculty. "Most Red cells have fifteen to twenty members, but politically related disciplines like economics, sociology, and political science have much larger ones. Economics, for instance, has about two hundred members in its Red cell. Medicine and the natural sciences, on the other hand, have been relatively free of the plague. They have only a handful of radicals, who haven't much influence.

"At the law faculty we were also lucky until recently. During the first year or two of the disturbances, we were almost untouched. We took it for granted that law students tended to be serious and professional-minded and also, by and large, conservative. In any case, most of them wanted to get their degrees as quickly as possible and get on with their profession, but in the past year or two, there has been a change, perhaps because radicalism has become chic. Perhaps it is a fashion which even law students cannot resist? Anyway, some of them can't."

He offered me a cigarette from a silver box and came around from behind his desk to light it for me. "I was only a kid back in 1948 when

the Free University was founded, and in those days my family was living in West Germany, so I don't remember much about it, but my
professor, the head of my institute, was one of the original founders of
the Free University. In 1948, he must have been about as old as I am
now. He was an assistant at the old Humboldt University in East Berlin.
Well, you remember what happened."

I said that I did indeed. "I was living in Berlin at the time. In fact,
my office was in Dahlem, almost on the campus of the new university.
I have particularly close associations with the Free University because
my own professor at Columbia was active in getting American funds to
help establish it. I was more or less in at the birth."

"I hope you won't be in at the death," he commented. "Well, you
can imagine how my professor feels about what has been going on here
during the past few years. He and his fellow assistants, professors, and
students left the Humboldt University because they could no longer
stomach the curtailment of academic freedom. They couldn't teach
what they believed, and students couldn't discuss ideas and problems
freely; they couldn't get objective books or attend scholarly meetings,
and both students and professors were subjected to increasing harassment from the political hacks. They left. They simply picked up their
books and notebooks and walked out, crossed over to the Western half
of the city, and settled in Dahlem. They held classes in private houses,
in some of the scientific institutes over here, or in the professors' living
rooms. At first they lived and worked like Gypsies, but they achieved
what they had come for, freedom."

He shrugged sadly, "And now, just a little over twenty years later,
some of their own students are trying to destroy academic freedom by
their violence and intolerance. It is hard on old socialists like my professor. He is a Jew, so for two reasons, both race and politics, he had
to leave Germany in the 1930s. He had just got his doctorate when Hitler
came to power, and he was working toward his habilitation here in
Berlin. Luckily he got a fellowship to Cambridge to specialize in Anglo-
Saxon law. He went to England, supposedly just for a year, but they
let him stay. He taught there until the war began, then he worked in the
British War Office.

"It took a lot of guts and dedication for a man like that to come back
to Berlin after the war, but Humboldt asked him, and he accepted. Of
course, he'd been used to England. He couldn't swallow East Berlin.
Poor guy, he fled from the nazi dictatorship in 1933, then from the communists in 1948, and now he is going to have to run away from our

anarchists. He hasn't yet reached retirement age, but he is retiring this year on a reduced pension and is going to Ireland to write. He and I don't always see eye to eye, and I can't say we are close friends, but I have always respected his integrity, and I can't help feeling sorry for him."

"Will he be homesick?" I asked, thinking of the many German refugees I have known in New York.

"Probably. It's funny, isn't it, but these old socialists who pride themselves on not being nationalistic are often the most sentimental, or at least, I find them so. But most of his old friends have left or are leaving the Free University, either retiring or transferring to other universities in Germany or abroad. In Ireland he'll be close enough to fly over to have a look at Berlin or to see a German play or hear some music now and then. He won't feel quite so bad as if he were part of the dissolution here."

"Depressing," I said, and stubbed out my cigarette. He agreed, glanced at his watch, and suggested that we move on to some place more comfortable to continue our talk.

"I have a meeting later in the neighborhood of your hotel. You're at the Hilton, aren't you? Why don't we drive down to the Kudamm, have a drink there somewhere, and then I'll drop you off on my way to my meeting?"

I said good, and he stuffed his decorative glasses into his breast pocket. While he searched impatiently for prodigal car keys, I noticed how well cut, how English his tweeds were. He examined his pockets one after another, shuffled the papers on the desk, and dug into the pocket of a raincoat draped over an adjacent chair, but no car keys. I did not giggle, but he reminded me so much of myself that I was at pains not to. He looked in the wastebasket and under books. Finally he looked inside the silver cigarette box and said, "Aha! I put them here so that I would be sure to find them!"

He held the door for me, and we passed through into the antiseptic hall, down a stone staircase to the glass-walled entrance hall. It was warm outside for a fall day in Berlin. I was grateful for my light dress and pitied Rainer in thick tweeds. He waved an arm at the building across the street, an immaculate white, modern stone-and-glass building emblazoned with one of the ubiquitous, smeary blood-red slogans, "For a Socialist Program of Study" and below that, "Get rid of the State Commissar!"

"A friend of mine at the Technical University tells me that a whole crew of workmen do nothing but wash away or paint over those slogans every morning, and then, during the day, the students paint them on again," I said.

"I wouldn't doubt it. Do you know about the State Commissar?" he asked, and then told me: "In the spring of 1970 the entire graduating class in the faculty of architecture over at the Technical University simply refused to take the final examination. They insisted that individual examinations were competitive and therefore capitalistic, and they announced that they would take the exam collectively."

"You mean they cheated?" I asked, and he waved a monitory finger at me.

"You, my dear Frau Doctor, are a reactionary! But so were the professors of the architecture faculty. They ignored the results of the co-operative exam and refused to award any degrees that spring. Naturally, the whole class rebelled and a good many of their fellow students joined them in a lusty strike."

"Was it a destructive strike?" I asked, as we walked briskly toward the parking lot.

"Bad enough," he said. "They pulled out all the conventional stops like boycotting classes, painting slogans on the walls, harassing students who insisted on taking exams. They even incarcerated a dean in his office and threatened him and his family with violence unless he agreed to their demands. I have a few friends over at the Technical University, and they said it was pretty wild. The radicals certainly destroyed a lot of equipment and broke some windows, and they made it impossible for the architecture faculty to function."

"What was their objective?" I asked. "To get the faculty to award degrees without a valid final examination?"

"Exactly," he said. "Well, the faculty met and went over the records of the graduating class and decided they could award degrees to about forty per cent of the class without a valid final exam on the basis of their accumulated record, but the students weren't satisfied, and they intensified their strike. Things got pretty well out of hand; damage and violence increased; and so the city government stepped in. The Senate appointed a commissar, I guess you would say commissioner, to take charge of the faculty of architecture during the emergency and to sort out the whole question of exams and degrees."

"Oh, that's the commissar they want to get rid of," I said.

"Yes. That's what the slogans are about. No sooner had he been appointed than students from the Free University joined with the Technical University students to protest police-state methods, tyranny, terror and all the rest, but the strike petered out when the semester ended. The commissar is still there, and all we have left is slogans on walls."

I asked whether the architecture students had gone back to their classes this fall, and he said that by and large they had, but he had no idea what would happen when the time came for final examinations in the spring.

"Explosive situation," he said.

By then we had reached the parking lot and were climbing into his red Volkswagen. "You see those cars with a round seal like a big dot on their side windows?" He pointed to two or three of the parked cars, and I looked and nodded.

"Those dots mean that the car's driver is prepared to give first aid in an emergency. We are in a revolutionary situation, or anyway an untidy one. You can see why people like us shy away from lamp posts."

"Or from Berlin," I suggested, snapping down the button to lock my door.

As he headed the car out of the parking lot and turned into the avenue leading toward downtown Berlin, he continued:

"I have a friend who writes for the newspaper *Die Welt*. He fumes every time he visits the Free University and sees all the student cars in the parking lot. He is only in his early thirties, but he says that when he was a student, he rode to class on a bicycle. He insists that today's students are too affluent, too spoiled and too soft, and that is why some of them are rebellious and juvenile, and the others lack the moral fiber to resist the extremists and fight back."

"It sounds a bit too simple," I suggested.

Rainer nodded. "Well, Kurt is a bit simple, but I think there may be just a grain of truth in it. There is certainly some reason why the bulk of our students who are certainly not revolutionaries or anarchists allow themselves to be bulldozed by a handful of radicals. For whatever reason it seems the majority do lack moral courage or anyway leadership."

"Perhaps because leadership has been a naughty word for so long?" I said.

"Political leadership is certainly out of style," he replied.

We talked a little about the beginning of the student unrest, and I told him about my many talks with Sigrid and her friends.

"You must also know some of the people at the Otto Suhr Institute," he suggested, and I admitted that I did. "As you might expect of the faculty of political science, it has been one of the hotbeds of the revolt from the beginning," he said. "The original faculty was made up largely

Fig. 4. Otto Suhr Institute—Department of Political Science, Free University (photo by Ullstein Bilderstein, West Berlin)

of leftists from the emigration, socialists and old-line German communists or former communists who spent the Hitler years in England or the States or even in the U.S.S.R. Of course, they were old leftists, but they attracted a left-leaning student population, and suddenly, some of the old leftists bloomed into new leftists, second childhood, possibly. Not surprisingly, many of the student leaders of the movement come from the Suhr Institute. Your colleagues, Madame!"

I said it didn't surprise me. "You know I deplore violence and harassment as much as you do," I said, "but surely there must be some legitimate grounds for grievance among the students or else the moderates, however spoiled or lacking in leadership, wouldn't tolerate the violence and disruption. The extremists must have been able to clothe their violence in garments of idealism and reform at least at first."

"Oh, of course," he admitted. "At the beginning I was a strong advocate of reform. Most of us assistants were."

By then we were moving into a more crowded section of town, and he had to slow down and give more attention to his driving. When he had successfully maneuvered around a bus and skimmed through a changing traffic light, he continued.

"Well, you know enough about German universities to know what the condition of assistants has been. We were serfs!"

I told him that I did know a little about it. "Several years back I had a tentative offer from a very prominent professor to work as his assistant. It was in my second favorite German city, but much as I should have loved living there and been flattered to teach at that university, I refused even to apply for the job. I liked the man's politics too."

"I can understand your refusal," Rainer said. "I spent a year as an exchange instructor at a mid-Western American law school, and I can imagine that anyone who was used to the free and easy atmosphere of an American faculty just couldn't take the formality, the stiffness, the lack of freedom that is part of the life of a junior faculty member here. My particular professor is very decent, so I have been lucky, but some professors are little dictators, and they can make the lives of their assistants pure hell, or they could until the recent reforms."

I said that I understood that under the old German system each professor was virtually autonomous, that he ran his own little research and teaching center and his assistants worked directly under him, responsible to no one else.

"Exactly. We didn't have departments as you do, with an assortment of full professors, associates, assistants, and instructors, each with at least some voice in running the department. As you say, here each full professor was more or less his own department. Under the German tradition of academic freedom, a German professor was guaranted the freedom to teach in his own field no matter how narrow that might be. He could teach what he liked, and he alone decided when he would give his lectures, when he would offer examinations. He decided which students to accept as doctoral candidates and what subjects they might choose for their dissertations. He chose his own assistants and decided how much to pay them. They weren't hired by the department or by the administration as in the States, and although the funds for their salaries came from the university, the professor decided on the amount and doled it out, and he had virtual life-and-death power over his assistant's habilitation."

He paused, threading his way through traffic, to make sure I knew what habilitation is.

"Well," I said, "I know an assistant has to write a book or complete a research project to qualify as a professor, and he has to complete it within a certain time, doesn't he?"

"Six years, and that is, or was, the rub. You see unless he completed the habilitation research and received a call from a university within six years, he would have to leave the academic profession. If I hadn't finished my work and got my call by next year, I should have had to go into the civil service or private practice. Many assistants do because obviously there are many more assistants than there are professorial chairs available."

"It sounds harshly competitive," I said, and he agreed that it was.

"If the system operates fairly, it is supposed to insure the survival of only the best scholars, but under the old system a professor could choose to be unfair. He could specify the research topic, possibly in some field in which he but not the assistant was interested, and only he had the final approval of the work. If the assistant irritated or angered him during his six years, the professor could retaliate when it came time to approve the habilitation, and there was no appeal."

"Good Lord, that did make him a dictator. Virtual life or death power indeed," I said.

"Academic life or death anyway. Meanwhile, during the years the assistant was working on his project, he also taught classes, advised students, graded exams, and did research for his professor. Two thirds or more of the actual teaching at our universities is done by assistants and most of the grading and advising. Students complain that they seldom see their professors, who are very remote and tend to be interested not in students but in their own research. Assistants complain that they haven't time for their own work."

"No wonder," I said.

We had reached the Berlin Hilton, and Rainer turned his Volkswagen into the parking lot.

"I decided to come right here because there is always room here to park," he explained. "Do you know what I should like right now?" he asked as he helped me out of the car. "A bottle of champagne to celebrate your book, my call, and my liberation from the Unfree U.!"

"At four in the afternoon?" I asked, pretending to be conventional. "But you have to go to a meeting."

He waved meetings aside and promised that we should nibble some cheese with our champagne.

"It is a very special occasion!" he insisted.

Not until after the careful selection of the vintage, the ceremonial delivery of the chilled bottle, and the skillfully quiet extraction of the cork, after the toasts to liberation, did we return to our discussion of the misery of assistants under the old dispensation.

"Some fellows never get a chance to work on their own research until evenings and weekends because their professors keep them doing chores for them. I've known assistants who virtually wrote a famous professor's latest scholarly work and were never mentioned in the acknowledgements, not even a footnote."

"That's unethical!" I protested.

"It's also bad for the young man's career. He spends months or years working on a project and receives no academic credit for it. Did you know that in the traditional German university the names of assistants don't even appear in the catalogue? They may teach two thirds of the courses, but they are academic nonpersons."

He raised his glass again: "Well, here's to the new order for assistants!" I toasted and sipped wholeheartedly.

He went on, "Did you know there are some professors who expect their assistants to be body slaves? They walk their dogs, wash their cars, and even buy birthday presents for their wives."

"Isn't there some committee, some board to which assistants could complain if they are exploited or treated unjustly?" I asked.

"Not under the old system. If an assistant absolutely could not get along with his professor or found he couldn't make progress toward his habilitation, he could try to get another professor to take him on. If he was lucky, he might find a better situation, but as long as he worked under a professor, he was dependent on him. When the habilitation work

was finished, it was submitted to a committee, but only the professor decided when it was good enough to submit, and even though the entire
committee voted on the acceptance of the habilitation, the sponsoring
professor's vote was decisive. He had to approve it before it could be
accepted."

"But isn't the assistant under civil service and doesn't that give him
some rights?"

"Yes and no," Rainer answered. "An assistant does fill a civil service
line, but it is a temporary six-year line, and it gives him no tenure or
other civil service rights. As I said, even his salary was paid by the professor out of a general fund, and the professor could fire him whenever
he wanted."

I asked whether the assistants were organized in any way, and he said
that in 1968, they had formed a Federal Conference of Assistants which
was now working to improve the lot of their members throughout West
Germany. "The West German ministers of education and the Conference
of University Rectors or Deans have also endorsed plans to improve the
status of assistants, so it is moving."

"In Berlin you have the new university law. That surely has helped
the assistants, hasn't it?" I asked.

"A great deal," he agreed. "The law went on the books in August 1969
and so the reforms began to be implemented in the fall semester. In
the first place, our salaries are now paid directly by the university instead of by our professors, and in addition, the law specifies that at
least two thirds of our duty time is to be reserved for our own individual
research. That is, only one third of our working hours can be devoted
to teaching, counseling or working for the professor."

"That sounds like a great improvement. Is the professor any less
dictatorial?" I asked.

"We are in the process of setting up something like a departmental
system now throughout the university. The philosophy faculty, which is
the largest at the Free University with something like seventy-three
chairs, started dividing into departments as far back as the fall of 1968.
They appointed a committee to work out the new organization and by
now they have separate departments of psychology, history, art history,
and so on, each of which supervises appointments of assistants, habili-
tations and so on."

"That sounds better," I said. He promised to get me a copy of the
university reform law so that I could study it in detail at my leisure.

"I'll have our youngest assistant drop it off at your hotel," he offered.

I said that I understood that the new law had also given assistants and students a greater voice in determining departmental and university policy. He shook his head dubiously.

"I certainly favored giving students and assistants greater voice than they had under the old system, but I think the new law goes too far in the other direction. It just about insures that the radicals can dominate all levels of decision making."

I asked how, and he explained that in voting for the senate and for most of the subsidiary committees which run the university, the full professors, assistants, and students each elect one third of the representatives.

"The Red cells in each faculty or department dominate all elections. They bulldoze and steamroller their candidates into office. Many of the assistants are also radical, and many of the older, more moderate professors have already resigned or transferred out of Berlin, leaving their chairs to be filled by younger, usually more radical men.

"No, I believe in reform, but I think this plan is a sellout. Worse, I think that in turning over the universities to the extremists, we are making them ungovernable. These radicals are not communists but anarchists and theoreticians. They haven't the first notion of how to run anything. They don't want to govern, they want to destroy. Honestly, Frau Doctor, I am really very glad I am leaving! *Prost!*"

We drank a little more of our champagne, and the waiter brought us some cheese to nibble. Rainer admitted that the new university law was still too new for one to be sure how things would work out, but he was pessimistic.

"There are still problems in the German universities, aren't there?" I asked. "The students complain of overcrowding, of lack of attention, of the growing impersonality of the atmosphere. Does the Berlin reform tackle these questions?"

He shook his head. "Both the Berlin Senate and the universities themselves have committees working on these problems, but I think the root lies in the basic nature of the German university concept. You see, I am a real radical, not an official one."

I said that most genuine conservatives were.

"Most conservatives believe in tradition, but in the case of the medieval university, much as I love the tradition, I think it has to go by the board. The two basic principles of the old German university, academic freedom and the unity of study and research, seem to me to be incompatible with the modern idea of mass education. Today the university simply is not a community of scholars. It is basically a training school to turn out doctors and lawyers, engineers and technicians on a

Fig. 5. Slogan announcing "People's Commune of Dahlem" on Free University building (photo by Ullstein Bilderstein, West Berlin)

mass scale for a sophisticated, technological society. You and I may
mourn the passing of the community of dedicated scholars and feel
the kind of nostalgia we feel for cavalry regiments or hoop skirts, but
I think we admit that the reality of modern demands must be faced."

I nodded, silently picturing a company of a guards regiment in full
panoply trotting down the broad sweep of Unter den Linden.

"The students are right when they complain of overcrowded classes,"
he continued. "Some of them are like mass meetings. I taught a seminar
with more than eighty law students, which you will admit is absurd.
They are also right when they say they seldom see their professors and
that even the assistants have little time for them. I think this all boils
down to about three separate factors. The course of study is too long;
incompetent or lazy students are not weeded out; and hiring and promotion of professors and assistants still depends more on research than
on teaching.

"We've made a beginning. In the past year or two, we have been
appointing teaching assistants and professors. These are supposed to be
competent in their fields and good teachers, but they won't be expected to produce research, just to teach. For example, a young man
or woman no longer needs a doctorate to be appointed as a teaching
assistant. He just needs a diploma in his field. The teaching professor
doesn't require habilitation."

"That sounds excellent," I said. "Do the students approve the change?"

"I think most of them do, but they want even more teaching assistants.
One of the demands of the radicals, and in this they have the support
of many moderates, is for more tutorials and for seminars with no more
than twenty students. I admit that this would be ideal, but I don't
think they realize how expensive it would be under present conditions.

"You know that under German law anyone who completes his *Abitur*
has the legal right to enter any German university. The university may
restrict the number of students it will admit to a given faculty such as
medicine, but by law it must admit every applicant with the *Abitur*.
There are no entrance exams or complicated admissions procedures as
there are in the States."

He continued, "The worst thing is that once a student is admitted to
most of our universities, he may take as long as he likes or needs to complete his degree. In Germany academic freedom included freedom of
study, and that has always meant that the student may take whatever
courses he wishes, attend lectures or not as he sees fit, decide for himself when he is ready to take examinations, and more or less study as
long as he wishes. It is not uncommon for a student to take five or six

Fig. 6. Overcrowding in lecture halls at the Free University. These students are watching a television lecture (photo by Ullstein Bilderstein, West Berlin)

semesters to complete a three- or four-semester course, so it is no wonder
our classrooms are overcrowded."

"Is there any solution to this?" I asked.

"Some of us have been advocating greater regulation of the course of
study. One method might be to require all students to take a matricu-
lation exam after three or four semesters. Those who pass will go on
to advanced courses. Those who fail may retake the examination at the
end of the following semester; any who fail then leave the university."

"I can see that that would weed out some deadwood, and it would
also spur some of the lazy students on to work a little faster, but I suppose the students don't like the plan."

"The radicals don't," he said. "They complain that it infringes on
their freedom of study, but the Technical University has always used
this system. They have to. Obviously, a student cannot go on to advanced science or technical courses unless he has mastered the basic
stuff. Anyway, whether or not the radical students object, the Free
University has begun to introduce these qualifying exams in more and
more disciplines, and in the long run, I believe the majority of students will benefit from it."

I asked whether there was any plan to shorten the course of study,
especially in fields like medicine and chemistry.

"I've read," I said, "that your chemistry students often study for as
long as ten or twelve years."

He nodded. "The average German student spends about five or six
years at the university. Since our university begins with the equivalent of
your third year of college, that would be the same as an average of
three to four graduate years. This is about normal for a lawyer or an
M.D., but it is a lot for an engineer or businessman. It means that
our average student is twenty-five or twenty-six before he is ready to
enter his profession, and the specialist, let's say the surgeon or research
chemist, is likely to be over thirty."

"It can't be healthy, can it," I asked, "for young people to prolong
their adolescence into their thirties, and that is what they're doing if
they are students that long."

"Exactly. A young man is an adolescent until he is able to make himself independent, establish himself professionally, marry, and support a
family. Our students are living on part-time jobs and government stipends. In other words, they are only half-adult, and I agree with your
implication that this makes them both restless and irresponsible and
perhaps contributes to their malaise and their radicalism."

"But is there a solution?" I asked. "With the proliferation of knowledge, especially in medicine and the natural sciences, is there any realistic way of shortening the course of study? Wouldn't it be dangerous to turn out instant doctors or quickie engineers?"

He grinned and suggested a second bottle. I started to say, "Oh, no!" but he forestalled me with, "It's a celebration." I am easily persuaded when the conversation is interesting and the vintage good. He signaled the waiter, and again we watched reverently as he performed the traditional rite. "This is to your book," he proposed. I thanked him and drank to my Berliners.

"What we've been doing," he said, returning to the question of proliferation of knowledge, "is to add more semesters. New knowledge in a field? Tack on another semester! But that is useless as well as silly because technical knowledge goes out of date so quickly. A young doctor or chemist or biologist who has been at the university for ten years finds that much that he learned in his early semesters is obsolete by the time he finishes; what he learns in the tacked-on semesters is at least obsolescent by the time he begins to work. There simply is no way to keep up with the explosion of knowledge except by continuing education, by reading, experience, and independent research."

He suggested that the function of the modern university should be to teach the basic data and concepts and equip the student to keep learning. For medical students, he advocated a curtailed university course covering fundamentals and methods, supplemented by seminars, films and lectures in the hospital where the young doctor interns, by evening and summer university courses and by reading in medical journals.

"As for the research chemist or biologist, he must really learn his speciality by working in it, but in these fields, too, the university could offer summer or evening updating seminars."

I said that I thought the students should support changes which would shorten their required course of study, and he said that many did, but there was also some opposition.

"Not only among the radicals," he said. "It goes back to our traditional principle of freedom of study. Even some moderates object to any infringement of that right, no matter how necessary under existing conditions. You know that German university students have always enjoyed much more freedom than your American college students."

"They are older," I suggested.

"Yes, our first-year students are about as old as your juniors, but I think ours have even more freedom than your graduate students. American students have to be admitted to the college or law school or graduate school; they have to be accepted by a department; they have to follow a curriculum, meet requirements for a degree, take exams at prescribed times. A German student simply registers with a faculty, signs up for the courses he wants to take, attends lectures or doesn't, takes whatever examinations he wishes and whenever he thinks he is ready, and until now, may take as many years as he needs to accumulate credits."

"I've heard that," I said, "but how does the university know when he has completed his course?"

"When he signs up for courses, a record is made in his faculty's office. At the end of each semester, he collects certificates of attendance from the assistant in charge of each course and certificates of having passed exams that he took. When he has accumulated enough certificates, he presents them to the faculty office and can file for his final examination."

"That sounds very free, but doesn't the student get a little lost? Doesn't he need just a little more direction than that, and perhaps some advice once in a while?"

"Yes, I think that in our modern, mass universities he probably does. In the first place, the sheer number of students tends to make the entering student feel isolated and disoriented. In the second place, we can no longer take it for granted that the university student is either mature or a dedicated scholar; we no longer have an elitist university."

"So you think they need more guidance, firmer lines?"

"A little more guidance, a bit firmer direction, but I don't want to see us go to the other extreme and begin to treat our students the way some of your giant American universities treat theirs, half like children, half like robots. I enjoyed my year in America, but, frankly, I was appalled at the lack of freedom the students enjoyed, at the indignity of all the petty, bureaucratic regulations. My image of an American university student is of a dazed adolescent wandering down some endless corridor with an I.B.M. card in his hand looking for a line to stand in."

I laughed and said, "We also have some small colleges. But I sympathize with your revulsion against bureaucracy. I share it. Perhaps there is a middle way?"

"I hope so," he said, "But you do see that the whole concept of higher education is in question, that our universities not only have basic problems, they are in themselves a problem."

"Yes, and I can see why many perceptive students are disgruntled and dissatisfied. What I do not see is why people like you and me, as well as people older and more powerful than we could not have grappled with the problems and tried to solve them before the student unrest reached the violent stage."

He shrugged. "Democracy, I suppose. No politician is ever going to vote to spend money to solve a problem which is not apparent to his constituents as a problem and preferably a threat. Now it may be too late to work out rational solutions. We have let the extremists seize the initiative, build up their influence and power by exploiting the genuine grievances. Now, as I said, they have achieved virtual control of both Berlin universities."

"But the radicals are still only a small minority, aren't they?"

"Oh, the really dedicated radicals are only a small cadre, perhaps a hundred, at most two hundred, at each of the universities, but as I said, they terrorize the moderates and the nonpolitical students, and so can control many of the student elections."

"We are back to the student radicals," I said with a sigh.

"Here in Berlin whenever we talk about the universities or about politics, we somehow always get back to them." He sighed too and poured champagne.

"I shall get quite high," I said, "and you will never get to your meeting." He said it was just a meeting, and this was a celebration.

"Strange, isn't it," I said, "that Berlin, which has been a symbol of the counterrevolution since 1945, or at least since 1948, should have become the storm center of revolution?"

"Strange," he agreed, "but on the other hand, Berlin has always been a more progressive, more innovating city than any other in Germany. Our universities were always more flexible, more modern. I suppose we naturally attracted a more progressive, radical type of student."

"Of course, once you gained the reputation for being a center of radicalism, even more radical students would come to Berlin to study, and the more serious, more moderate or less political sort would choose a quieter school."

"Exactly," he said. "By now Berlin is known as the hotbed of revolution. Our figures show that about forty percent of all the students elected throughout the Free University, that is to the university senate and to the various subsidiary committees, are not only radical but are so far left that they are considered enemies of the constitution, meaning that they advocate the violent overthrow of the government."

"Surely," I said, "nowhere near forty percent of the student body are revolutionaries. Haven't the nonrevolutionary or counterrevolutionary students or professors done anything to fight back? Isn't there any opposition organization to the Red cells?"

"Nothing really effective, I'm afraid. I belong to a group of professors called the Emergency Committee [literally, Emergency Community], which includes a few prominent professors such as Professor Löwenthal of political science, Professor von Simson of history, and Professor Sandmann of economic history. On the one hand, this group is working for some of the needed university reforms I spoke about, and on the other, it will try to oppose the terrorist and criminal activities of the extremists. The press has been kind, and there seems to be a good deal of public sympathy, but so far I have not seen any concrete results."

"What about the students?" I asked.

"There is a new group of reform socialists who also want to bring about reforms without violence, but they are too new for me to have any opinion of their effectiveness. The average moderate student seems to be basically nonpolitical and not organization-minded. I find him cowed and intimidated and simply too passive, too much involved with his personal, professional goals to be any match for a cadre of tough-minded, dedicated, ruthless radicals. Some students just avoid coming to class. They sit in the library or at home and study, but they refuse to buck the picket lines or contend with the revolutionaries."

"I find that sad," I said.

"I find it tragic. They and we have just about turned over two great universities to a small bunch of anarchists. They have forced some of our best scholars into retirement or retreat to other schools. As I said, I love Berlin, and I have enjoyed being at the Free University, but I am very grateful to be leaving.

"Well," he said, rousing himself, "I suppose I should make some effort to attend that meeting. Would you like some coffee?"

4

Wolfgang

Wolfgang carried the coffee tray in from the kitchen and set it on the cluttered desk. He poured steaming coffee carefully into the cups, offered cream and sugar, and then held out a plate of cookies.

"My mother sent them to me. She thinks that because I live alone I must be starving."

We laughed, and he offered me a cigarette and lit it for me. The cigarettes were Russian and came out of a crumpled pack. He struggled with two or three matches before one stayed lit. I thought of Rainer's silver box and matching butane lighter.

"These blasted matches!" he complained. "You would think that now that the German Democratic Republic has achieved such a high G.N.P. we would be able to manufacture matches that actually light and don't break."

I suggested that perhaps in a socialist society matches have a low priority. He nodded.

"But that's one of our little psychological errors. The average man in the street uses matches all day long, and small but constant irritations are apparent, and they build up. How often does he use a jet plane or a precision lens?"

I glanced around at Wolfgang's room. It was a large room, comfortably shabby. I was sitting on a faded chintz-covered couch, probably his bed. Behind me the wall was lined with books. An old-fashioned and very heavy oak desk covered with papers and books stood at one end of the room and opposite my couch were two chairs and a low round table.

"I'm very comfortable here," he said, following my glance. "I was lucky to find a room this size all to myself. There isn't a bath—I share the landlady's—but I have a good-sized balcony overlooking the garden, and that's a quiet, cool place to work when the weather is good."

42

He pointed to the cubbyhole from which he had emerged with the tray: "As you see, I've made a kitchen out of that storeroom. It's not elaborate, but I can cook the few things I need. Most students just have rented rooms without a kitchen."

I asked him to tell me about his landlady.

"She's nice. I'm lucky there too because not all of them are, but Frau D. is the mother of three grown boys, all married and scattered, and so she is happy to have a young man to look after. She cooks for me once in a while, does my laundry, darns my socks and does most of the cleaning. I'm supposed to do my own day-to-day cleaning, but you know how it is with a student. Sometimes I just get busy and forget. She doesn't mind. She comes in and picks up after me."

I was beginning to get used to asking people what they paid for rent and how much their stipends were, so I didn't hesitate.

"Well," he said, "I pay a little more than most students. I think the average student pays about fifty marks a month for rent. I pay eighty, but that includes a meal now and then, laundry and heat. I looked around until I found a room in an old building. I like the high ceilings and large rooms, but they cost a little more."

Wolfgang told me that he was just beginning his sixth year at East Berlin's Humboldt University and that he had started work on his dissertation in the faculty of philosophy.

"I'm writing on the influence of philosophy on nineteenth century colonialism. I don't suppose I'll finish it this year, but I certainly hope to finish sometime next year."

I offered him one of my cigarettes. He examined the box and asked, "English?" I said I'd bought them on the plane.

"I don't see these very often. We get American ones now and then." He lit mine and then his and said he liked it.

"I am a little more anxious than the average student to finish my degree quickly because I started late. I'm already thirty-two. I taught in an elementary school before I decided to get a university education. I did not begin until I was twenty-seven, and that is very late."

He then told me a little about his background. He was born in Pomerania in the area beyond the Oder-Neisse line which fell under Polish administration in 1945. Before the war his father had been a forester, and his family had lived in a charming house at the edge of a huge wood.

"I was the youngest. My oldest brother was drafted when he was eighteen and killed in Russia before he was nineteen. Then there were two sisters. They are both married and one is in West Germany. I was the baby. I guess I was about nine or ten when the war ended.

"During the last months of the war millions of German families fled from the Eastern provinces, but my mother refused to go with her brother's family when they left. My father was missing in the East. She was afraid that if he returned and found that we had fled, he might never find us again, so we stayed on in Pomerania and waited for the Poles. I don't remember much of those years except that the schools were closed for a while, and I liked that, and we were always cold and there wasn't much to eat, and I liked that less. I remember that my mother had to go out to work and that my father finally got home near the end of 1946 or early in 1947. He was thin and sick and he couldn't work at all for a long time. Later, when he was able, he did casual odd jobs because in the Polish territory Germans weren't allowed to work as foresters.

"In 1949 the Polish authorities gave permission for Germans to emigrate to the Soviet Zone of Germany, and we moved to a village near Rostock. Fortunately, my father was able to find a job as forester again, and my mother was able to stop working. When I was sixteen I left school and worked with my father in the forest for a year. I had always liked school, but I guess I was restless.

"You see," he said apologetically, "I am not proletarian."

"No," I said, carefully suppressing the natural "of course not."

"Being a professional forester my father counted as a bourgeois, and during those first years after the war, only the children of workers and peasants or of victims of fascism could hope to enter a university. Even teacher's college was beyond my reach, so I didn't know quite what to do with my life. I liked the forest work, but I longed to continue my studies. I couldn't even become a qualified forester without more education.

"Apparently there was too great a shortage of teachers and technicians to keep that restriction. By the time I was eighteen, I thought I might be admitted to teacher's college, so I went back to school, finished, applied to the training school at Rostock and was accepted. After three years I passed my examination and began to teach the third grade."

I asked whether he had liked teaching small children, and he said he had enjoyed it tremendously.

"It was not what I really wanted to do, but I found that I liked the kids. They were fun, and I had a marvellous time trying to be a jack of all trades—teaching drawing when I can't draw a cat and music when I can't read notes, as well as teaching German, arithmetic and geography. What I liked best was taking the children on nature walks because I knew the forest intimately, and they were always fascinated by stories about trees and animals."

"But you didn't stay on."

"No, I always hoped that I would some day be permitted to go on to a university, and when I was twenty-seven, the opportunity came. I applied for admission to Humboldt and was accepted. I had a stipend from the first year, and this year I was awarded the Karl Marx Fellowship."

I realized that the Karl Marx Fellowship was both a very great honor and the highest stipend awarded university students, so I congratulated him. I also asked just how much money it amounted to and how well he could live on it.

"I get 450 marks a month for the Karl Marx. The average student gets 190 marks or up to 300 if his parents are in a low-income group or have four or more children. It's graduated, you know, according to need."

"So that means most students get between 190 and 300, and you get 450. Yes," I said, "that's a considerable difference. Can the student with about 200 marks a month live on that during the semester or does he have to work or get help from his parents?"

"Well," said Wolfgang, "in the first place, he can add to his stipend by getting good grades. If he achieves what you would call a *B* average, he gets an additional 40 marks a month, if he has something like a *B+* or *A−*, he gets 80 marks additional. That doesn't sound like much, but it does help, and it's an incentive. I think the average student who gets, say 200, 250 a month can just live on it. It will pay rent and food during the semester. If he wants extras, he will have to work part time or get help from parents, and he will probably work between semesters to buy his clothes and save a little for spending money during the semesters. He can't afford luxuries on the basic stipend, but he can get by. With my 450 marks I can afford to live alone, for example, and I can buy meat once in a while or a bottle of decent wine and real coffee, or I can take a girl out now and then."

I said that I thought 300 or even 450 marks a month seemed very little to live on even without luxuries.

"Prices are low here for basics, especially for students," he explained. "Those who live in government-run student homes pay only nominal rent. Students who board with families or rent rooms also pay very little, as I've said, and food prices here, at least for staples like rice and potatoes and bread, are very low. I get my lunch at the university dining hall for about ten cents a day."

"Ten cents U.S.?" I asked, astounded. "What do you get for that?"

"Nothing fancy," he said, "but enough to eat and not bad, either. There's soup, a main course and dessert. If I want a salad or a glass of beer, those are extra, but all the prices are low. Altogether I guess I spend about a hundred marks a month on food and perhaps another hundred on clothing, books, and odds and ends.

"Books are very cheap here," he said. "The average technical or text-book costs about ten to twenty marks. Besides, as a doctoral candidate I get an extra allowance of 600 marks for books and research materials, and the University provides me with stationery for my dissertation and with a typist."

"You are indeed fortunate," I said. "Are there any teaching duties connected with your award?"

"No. Some candidates are fellows, and they teach as assistants or do research work for professors part time. They get a small salary in addition to the basic student allowance, and they have four years in which to complete their dissertations."

"Do they get typing services and stationery?" I asked.

"All our doctoral candidates do, even those who are not resident students. I should say that most doctoral candidates work only part time on their dissertations. They get jobs in industry or business or government, but they are allowed one day free from their jobs to work on their dissertations. In the summer they get four weeks free in addition to their normal vacations. This is the best method for married students because they can earn almost a full salary while they are working toward their degrees. They get special tax benefits too."

I said that it sounded like a good program. "But what about you? What category are you in?"

"I am what we call an aspirant. That means that I work full time on my research without a job, without teaching, and so I am supposed to finish in three years. The average aspirant gets a stipend of 300 marks a month for the first year, 350 the second, and 400 the third, and so he can live fairly comfortably on that. Because of my Karl Marx, of course, I'm even better off."

He told me that students receive their stipends for twelve months a year and not just during the semesters.

"So, you see, if I get a job between semesters, I can save all I earn."

I asked whether jobs were available, and he said, "Easily. Most students work in factories or on farms near their homes, but quite a few work in youth camps for the summer. That is fun because they can swim and more or less get a free vacation, but the pay isn't much. Still, we don't need very much. That's what I usually do, I guess, because I used to be a teacher, and I like kids."

He told me that students who choose not to work can go to camps and summer homes run for students at the sea or in the mountains or they can arrange exchange visits to student homes in other East European countries.

"It's very cheap because we just exchange rooms and eat at the dining hall. Last summer I went with a group to Hungary. We worked on a farm there for half the summer and then traveled around the other half. The Hungarian students took us around, arranged dances, and even taught us a little Magyar. It was fun and good experience.

"Students from the Soviet Union or from Poland visit us here in the summer and we show them around."

"Do you get many Czech visitors?" I asked innocently.

He grinned and said, "Not as many as we used to."

By then the coffee pot was empty. He looked at it ruefully.

"I know it's pretty early in the day, but would you like a schnapps? I have some Yugoslav *slivovitz*."

I noticed how frequently he smiled and what a relaxed, boyish face he had. Wolfgang is fairly tall, perhaps just six feet, square-shouldered, slightly stocky. He has dark blond, very thick hair, clear grey eyes, good hands. His clothes are the sort you do not notice or remember, obviously not expensive but in discreet good taste, as though he had done the best possible with limited resources. I realized by his occasional grin and slight cocking of the head that he did not always tell me all that he would like to tell, but I thought that what he said, as much as he said, was probably true. We both clearly understood that he did not say everything.

I smiled at him and let myself be persuaded. "A very small one," I said, and he got up and hunted for glasses.

"No, on the whole, we students are fortunate. If there is a ruling class in socialist countries, and, of course, we both know there is not, then it is the technicians, the intellectuals, and they treat students, especially advanced students, as apprentice intellectuals. We live comparatively well, not in luxury, but without insecurity."

"Is there a price?" I asked frankly. He did not pretend to misunderstand.

"Frau Doctor, as you know, there is always a price. In the first place, even though I'm over twenty-five, which is the usual age to quit the Free German Youth, I keep up my membership. I'm not as active as I used to be. I haven't time now that I'm trying to finish my dissertation on schedule, but I have to be reasonably active or they'd drop me. They weed out deadwood, you know, and it is a good thing for a student to keep up his membership."

"You mean you wouldn't have your Karl Marx if you weren't an F.D.J. [Free German Youth] member?"

"Probably not, although in some fields, such as physics or chemistry, it wouldn't matter as much. In any field touching on politics it matters a great deal, especially when you come from a bourgeois background."

"I hadn't forgotten," I said. "Is the F.D.J. very active at the university?"

"Yes," he said. "Even though most students do drop out at twenty-five, the group still organizes all of the sports and club activities for students."

I asked whether there were many extracurricular activities.

"That's one of the things the socialists are good at. They have organized all kinds of sports and clubs, not just soccer and the usual field sports, but skiing, boating, and even flying. Then there are chess clubs, a drama group that I belong to, a newspaper, a debating society, and so on.

"I'm active in the drama group. We put on two or three plays a year and have our own little theater. We do experimental plays as well as classics, and we have a lot of fun. I am also in the sailing and skiing clubs. Our sailing club has a boathouse and several boats on one of the Berlin lakes, and we also take trips up to the Baltic during warm weather and sail there. All the expenses are paid for by the government. That's true of our ski club's outings to the Harz Mountains too."

"Do most students belong to clubs?" I asked.

"You mean do they have to belong? No, there's no pressure, but I'd say that most students do join one or two clubs. There is such a variety that almost everyone can find something he enjoys, and as I said, the facilities are excellent, and it's all free."

He explained that there was a general student organization to which all students automatically belonged. "No one is forced to be active in it, but it arranges free films, concerts, lectures, and dances. Most people go once in a while to one or the other activity. Personally I think the dances are dull, but now and again I drop by on a Saturday evening."

"Is there much politics in your courses?" I asked.

"What is not political, Frau Doctor?" he asked. "Every student has to take a course in Marxism-Leninism during his introductory studies, and regardless of whether he's studying medicine or engineering or agriculture, he must pass that before he can go on to advanced work in his field. The engineers and scientists sometimes have a terrible time getting through it, I suppose because they are not used to the vocabulary, but get through it they must. A few years back I coached a friend who is now finishing his medical studies. I just poured it into him, like a tonic."

"Otherwise?" I asked.

"Otherwise, of course, it depends upon your field. There is always a little politics but much less in the technical, considerably more in the social fields. As for placement later, no one has to be a star member of the F.D.J. or a candidate for membership in the S.E.D. to get a good job, especially not in science or industry, but it always helps."

I hesitated before I asked whether there had been much repercussion among Humboldt students after the Czech crisis, but I found that he was willing to comment almost frankly.

"A considerable number of students here sympathized with the Czech move toward greater decentralization, greater independence. There were, of course, others who adhered strictly to the official Ulbricht view. A large group which hadn't commented publicly on the developments in the Czechoslovakian Socialist Republic before the Soviet intervention nevertheless expressed opposition to the use of force by the Soviets. Some students circulated petitions, held a meeting, and several were arrested.

"Since then, students are quiet, and they are discreet, but I think there is more off-the-record discussion, more speculation. I may be wrong, but I think there is more criticism now than before, more independence of viewpoint. I shouldn't like to be more explicit than that."

I did not ask him to be. Instead I asked him about unrest or dissension among nonstudents. I said that I had read some West German articles which indicated that delinquency and opposition were increasing among East German young people and asked whether he thought there was any truth in it.

"We have a little trouble," he said, "as who hasn't? There have been a few teen-age gangs who beat up old people, rape girls, rob shops, that sort of thing, but it's nothing like as bad as in West Berlin, I believe. Greater Berlin was a big city, and most of the slum sections were in East Berlin. It is inevitable that we have some urban problems, but we're doing our best to deal with them.

"There has even been a little trouble in our official youth clubs. You know how kids are—they like to be in style. Some of ours have begun to grow beards, affect freakish clothes, dig rock music, and groan when they are expected to listen to an uplifting lecture or watch a propaganda film. There have been a couple of incidents when kids broke up a meeting and even broke up furniture. We had to close one club for several weeks because there was so much violence, and some of the kids landed in jail.

"But our police have an excellent way of dealing with bearded, long-haired boys. Naturally, there is no law against beards or far-out outfits, but when a cop runs into a bunch of hippie types, he stops them and asks for their ID cards, which all citizens here are required to carry. Well, the cop looks at the cards, looks at the boys, and then runs them in because they do not look like their photographs. At the station the sergeant stares at the kids and says that they have false ID cards. When the boys protest, he calls in a barber and has them clipped and shaved and then says, 'Oh, well, now I see the cards are yours,' and lets them go, beardless and crewcut."

I laughed and said I supposed that also encouraged the others. "Yes," he said, "our party functionaries take rather a dim view of noncon-formism, especially when it is imitative of Western styles, but, relatively speaking, we have very little of it. There are, of course, occasional inci-dents which are amusing. Did you hear about the women students who were recruited to help out with the harvest and who went tramping down the streets of the village naked to the waist and singing nazi songs?"

"Nazi songs?" I asked, surprised and just a little shocked. "I mean, nakedness is within the mainstream of the *Zeitgeist,* but nazi songs?"

He laughed and said that there had been rather a lot of that. "You see, young people learn the old marching songs from their fathers or grand-fathers and they think it's fun to sing them, not so much because they sympathize with the nazis as because the songs are *verboten.* It's rather like your Western kids shouting, 'Mao, Mao' or 'Ho-Ho-Ho, Ho Chi Minh.' It is an act of defiance."

"We're having rather a problem with sex," he said. "Who doesn't? But I mean that our official attitude is rather pure. Even before the Czech crisis the F.D.J. launched a campaign to attack nudity and moral laxness. Not only Western but also Polish and Czech plays and films which violate our rather strict moral code have been banned, but still I think there has been a general moral weakening, perhaps because we are grow-ing too affluent, or else because we are too close to West Berlin."

I asked him whether on the whole he was satisfied with the condition of university education in the G.D.R. and with his life as a student in East Berlin.

He nodded. "On the whole I am more than satisfied. We have prob-lems, and, of course, off the record, I would have some criticisms, but I must honestly say that whatever criticism one may have of our govern-ment, we do put education first. We give our schools and universities the highest priority in budgeting and planning. I think the organization of our educational system is not only good but superb.

"As for me personally, I am very grateful. For a while I thought I should have to be content to be a laborer, and later an elementary school teacher. Now I am living comfortably in Berlin, working on my doctorate. In a few years I shall probably be teaching at a university. I have been very lucky. No, I haven't got everything I might want, but then who does? And by and large, I am satisfied, at least for now."

I gathered up my notebook and handbag, and he offered to walk with me to the subway. "I like Berlin," he said as he led me out of his room and down the stairs to the street. "Here we are in a quiet, tree-lined street that might be in a suburb, and yet we are only two block from the subway. In ten minutes you will be downtown. It's a convenient city. Most of all I like the people. They are so broad-minded and kind.

"When I finish my degree I shall probably go back to Rostock or somewhere out there because that is my home, but I shall always come back to visit Berlin. I'm sorry it's divided. I'd like to see West Berlin, too, but even if I can only see East Berlin, I love it. I guess it is because of the Berliners," he said. "No wonder you're writing a book about them."

"You're one of them," I said.

"For a while, and I'm glad."

We shook hands, and I waved as I started down the subway steps. I had liked Wolfgang and admired his openness. I never saw him again. It is often that way with East Berliners.

5

Irmingard

The street in East Berlin might have been in any of the older residential districts of West Berlin. The stately trees lining the street proclaimed that the neighborhood had been spared war damage. The brown, stucco, semidetached houses, solid and comfortable rather than pretty, probably dated from the 1920s. Flowers and flowering shrubs brightened the small squares in front of each house.

Eric, my East Berlin acquaintance, who had arranged the appointment with Irmingard had written her address and the time "4 P.M." in his precise, schoolboy's hand on the back of one of my cards. I examined it and saw that the number I sought was that of the corner house, its entrance almost blocked by an unruly but fragrant lilac bush. I pushed open the outer door and found myself in a musty entrance hall. In front of me, dark, uncarpeted wooden stairs led up to a second-floor apartment. On my right, a heavy door bore a printed card with Irmingard's name and academic title.

I knocked and almost immediately the door swung open. My first reaction to Irmingard was that she was exactly like my image of a female university professor. I guessed her to be in her early sixties. She had grey, rather shapeless hair, grey eyes half hidden by businesslike, rimless glasses, and she wore a grey, rather shapeless suit. She was tall for a woman, square rather than plump, and she walked and moved briskly, but she welcomed me with candor and friendliness.

We shook hands, and she led me into her living room, a large, square room which made no pretension of elegance but was shabby, comfortable and cheerful. Books and papers overflowed the desk and bookcases. Piles of books and papers teetered precariously on the couch and chairs and table. She removed a stack from an armchair so that I could sit down.

52

"Wine or tea?" she asked, her voice brisk but kind. "I have a rather nice Austrian wine that you might like."

"Much as I should like to try the wine," I said, "I think I should prefer tea. It looked warmer today than it is, and I came over without a coat."

"Tea, then, and we can have the wine later if you like." She handed me a brochure. "I got this for you. It explains our recent university reforms. Perhaps you could browse while I make the tea," she suggested and disappeared.

I studied the booklet and absorbed the atmosphere of the room, so like any apartment in an older West Berlin building inhabited by a professional woman.

Irmingard was an efficient woman. She returned in a very few minutes with the tea tray, and she was soon handing me my cup and a slice of excellent plum cake. I asked whether she had always been in the academic world.

"Goodness, no!" she said. "My father would be amazed to know that I ended up as anything half so respectable as a university professor. I am sure he expected the worst of me. I was a rebel when I was young. Do you know I actually quit school when I was seventeen to take a job in a factory? I'm sure the poor man thought I would never amount to anything."

"Political idealism," I asked, "or just adolescent rebellion?"

She hesitated. "A little of both, to be perfectly honest. You see, my parents were respectable, fairly prosperous middle-class Berliners. My father was a self-made man. As a boy he had wanted to be a high-school teacher, but in his family there had been too many children to educate and so he never had the opportunity. He worked in an office as a clerk. He saved his money, though, and worked hard, and after a few years, he was able to open a small business and become an entrepreneur. Later he bought a small factory and became a small-scale capitalist. He did fairly well.

"There were five of us children, and father was determined that each of us should have a professional education, I suppose, because he had been denied it. My oldest sister studied medicine and is a well-known internist in West Berlin. My second sister became a librarian. She and a younger brother who is a businessman both live in West Germany. My youngest brother studied law, but he was killed in the war. I guess I was father's only failure, at least at first."

"You were the black sheep?" I asked.

"I was the red ewe lamb," she said, and laughed. "My poor father! He always considered himself a very progressive man, but he was humiliated to have a daughter who was an out-and-out communist. My brothers and sisters were all docile and respectable. They followed precisely in the educational paths he set out for them, and they have remained conventional and bourgeois in their lives and in their politics. Well you can see! They have all gone to the West and are doing very well there."

"But you," I asked, "were you always a communist?"

"Always," she announced, "from the time I became interested in politics, and that was when I was in my early teens. We lived in Berlin, you know, and in those days, Berlin was a progressive city. I had a communist teacher at school who encouraged me to read Marx and Lenin. By the time I was fourteen or fifteen, I was buying the communist newspaper and hiding it from my parents, and when I was seventeen I joined the official communist youth organization. My parents were horrified, so I quit school, took a job in the Osram factory making light bulbs and moved away from home."

"You were brave," I said. "Did you lose contact with your parents?"

She shook her head. "No, they didn't cast me off into outer darkness, although I think they despaired that I would ever make anything worthwhile of my life, and my mother was terrified that I would get into serious trouble with the police. But they were progressive, my parents. They were not communists, and they certainly were appalled that their daughter was a communist, but they were basically broad-minded, and after all they loved me."

"You kept in touch then," I said.

"Oh yes, and I visited them most Sundays, but, of course, the atmosphere was strained. My mother worried more and more about my health. I guess I got thin and looked pretty ghastly."

"Didn't you eat properly?" I asked, knowing adolescents.

"Of course not!" she answered and laughed. "Besides, we young communists were very busy. No eight-hour day for us! Every evening after work a group of us would meet and go out to stick up posters or hand out literature all around Berlin, or we worked as ushers at party meetings and rallies. Late evenings we'd meet in our cellar office or in someone's room and drink beer or *ersatz* coffee and smoke too many cheap cigarettes and talk. Lord how we talked! Well, you know kids. Bull sessions from midnight until dawn, and then each morning, even Saturdays, I had to work in the factory."

"No wonder you got thin," I said.

"I almost had a breakdown," she said. "I lost something like fifteen pounds, and I got anemic and rundown. Besides, the glass dust from the light bulbs in the factory began to affect my lungs, so I finally had to quit my job."

"Did you return home?" I asked.

She shook her head. "No, I was stubborn, and, don't forget, I was still a communist. But I was lucky. I found a job in a children's home where I could live in and work evenings as a kind of aide, and so I was able to go back to school during the day."

"You finished your *Abitur?*" I asked.

"Within a year," she said. "Then my father insisted that I let him help me with my university education. Since I planned to go to Frankfort on Main to study, there wasn't any question of my living at home, and so we worked out a compromise. I remained a young communist, but I pulled in my horns a little until after I had completed my studies."

"Did you get your doctorate?" I asked.

"Not then. I didn't intend to teach. I rather thought I would go into the civil service, and I didn't need more than a diploma for that. I had just been hired by the Ministry of Labor when the nazis came to power. I think I had my job for about six weeks."

"Were you fired because you were a communist?" I asked.

"I was fired and arrested," she said. "You know we Germans keep excellent records."

"Everything in triplicate," I said.

"At least! The nazis had no trouble finding out exactly who were members of the German Communist Party and of all its affiliated organizations, and so as soon as Hitler was in power, all communists were interned."

"Were you in a concentration camp?" I asked.

"No. In fact, there weren't any K.Z.s [concentration camps] yet. During the first months, the nazis followed the traditional German practice of confining political prisoners in fortresses rather than in ordinary prisons with convicted criminals. I was in a fortress just outside Berlin. It was grim and rather damp, but it was palatial compared to a penitentiary.

"It was almost fun as first. I guess I was young enough to feel that I was a martyr, and at the beginning it was an adventure. During the early months, we political prisoners were allowed to circulate freely in the fortress, play cards, gossip, take exercise. We were allowed visitors, and we could have food and wine and even books sent in."

"Communists?" I asked, incredulous.

She laughed. "Those were the early days of the nazis. After a few months of comparative ease, I was transferred to a regular prison and that was less pleasant. I confess I felt less adventurous."

I asked how long she had been in prison, and she said she had been released after about two years.

"I was only a member of the youth group, after all, not a full-fledged party member, and I suppose they thought I was young and healthy and ought to be working. Naturally they kept a dossier on me, and I was labeled 'P.U.,' politically unreliable, so I was not permitted to work in the government or to teach, but I could work in private industry."

"Could you work in your field?" I asked.

"Hardly. A sociologist with a communist background wasn't very much in demand, so I took up shorthand and typing and got a job as a stenographer in private industry. I surprised myself by getting interested in the business. I suppose I take after my father and am a capitalist at heart, because I became assistant manager of the firm and was soon earning a very respectable salary."

I wondered whether it would be tactless to congratulate her, and so I just smiled and nodded.

"That was when I found this apartment," she said, "and gradually I was able to furnish it, not lavishly but comfortably. I was very lucky during the war. My office was bombed, and we had to relocate twice, but this entire neighborhood escaped."

This time I did congratulate her, and I asked whether she had had any further trouble with the nazis during the war.

"I was under surveillance, of course. Everyone who was 'P.U.' was, but even so I managed to keep in touch with former comrades. Communists had to be very careful, but the party did maintain an underground organization all through the war, and even we younger members were able to carry out occasional assignments."

"It was dangerous." I commented.

"Of course, but just being in Berlin during those years was dangerous. One tended to grow reckless. I realized that I might be rearrested any moment just for having been a communist. Many of our comrades were, and so I thought I might as well hang for a sheep as for a lamb."

"It was a desperate time," I said, remembering the courage of some of my conservative friends. "But after 1945 you must have found yourself a heroine."

"I found myself in demand," she said, "and that was a change. For years I had been a pariah, and suddenly I found that I could choose from among a dozen different jobs because there just were not enough bona fide antifascists to fill all the vacancies. Instead of having most doors closed to me, overnight a dozen different avenues had opened up."

"Did you begin teaching right away?" I asked.

"No. I got into teaching through the back door. I began by running for election to my local borough council. The next thing I knew, I had been elected, and I was appointed in charge of the borough schools. I didn't know a thing about running schools, but in those chaotic days, almost no one knew anything about the department he was running. The people who knew had run away or they were interned or at least disqualified."

"The schools had been closed, hadn't they? And weren't many of the children evacuated out of Berlin?" I asked.

"Yes. It was a total mess, but in a sense, that was fortunate because I wasn't required to know anything about educational theory or the technical side of school administration. All I needed was common sense and some organizing ability, and my business experience had given me that.

"First, we had to locate our schoolchildren. Tens of thousands had become lost, you know. They had been evacuated, and then after the war their parents couldn't find them. The Red Cross, the churches, and the city administration worked for months to locate and identify children, return them to parents or relatives, and assign them to schools. In many cases we found children but no parents, either because they had been killed or they too had been evacuated and couldn't be located. In the worst months of the bombing, many Berlin families had to move two or three or more times, and it often took months or even years to track them down at their ultimate addresses.

"Then we had to find buildings. Where whole neighborhoods were blotted out, of course the schools were demolished too. We took over private houses, rooms in factories or shops, parts of public buildings for temporary classrooms."

"Did you have teachers?" I asked.

"Goodness, no! You probably know that no profession was more nazi-dominated than elementary education. By the time we had screened the elementary schoolteachers and weeded out the nazi party members and the open sympathizers, there were very few left. The war had devoured many of the young men who might have become teachers, and many young women had gone into war industries. There simply were no qualified, antinazi teachers! We were forced to hunt for elderly, retired teachers to fill the gap, and we hired housewives, mothers and grandmothers, anyone who had a modicum of education and was politically clean, as temporary, emergency teachers.

"Of course, there were no textbooks. You can imagine what the nazi texts were like. Even introductory arithmetic texts had racist and militaristic problems and examples."

"Two Jews plus three Jews equal five Jews?" I asked, and she grinned.

"Something like that. Truly, the illustrations were always soldiers and tanks and heroes. We had no money to buy or manufacture textbooks or to order blackboards, erasers, paper and chalk, no budget for fuel to heat the buildings or lunches for the children."

"It sounds impossible," I said. "How did you manage?"

"My capitalistic background stood me in good stead. I scrounged. We organized neighborhood committees and teams. We collected scrap and sold it; we asked for donations and got them; we asked parents to volunteer to clean the classrooms, make the lunches, repair the roof or the furnace. We searched storerooms and attics and found some pre-Hitler texts. We got donations from abroad. I still don't know how we managed, but we got the schools open, and it was tremendous fun."

"I think you thrive on battles," I said.

"I do, I guess," she said. "After years of being discreet, of pussyfooting, of being hypocritical and cautious, it was a great relief to be able to throw myself into a project that used up all my energy and time. It helped work off the tensions of all those years of repression, and obviously it gave us all a great feeling of accomplishment.

"Our first schoolrooms were pretty shabby and education those first years was sketchy, but by 1948, the schools were open and they were beginning to function almost normally. I decided that the school system was beginning to need experts, so I gave up my job."

"Is that when you decided on an academic career?" I asked.

"Well, I decided that I should go back to the university and finish my doctorate," she said. "I applied to the Humboldt University and they gave me credit for most of the work I had done before 1933. I decided to take my degree in education instead of in sociology, but I specialized in the teaching of social science, so much of my earlier work was useful."

She told me that she was teaching courses in both method and content to students preparing to teach in secondary schools. I asked her whether she had any particular personal philosophy of education, whether there was any single goal she thought most important.

She considered for a moment. "Yes, I think one of the most serious challenges of our educational system is to learn to teach our children and young people to think for themselves, to question, to develop their critical faculties and their creative intellect. So much traditional, European education has always been just memorization, stuffing children

and even university students with facts, with knowledge. I believe the
time has come when we must change our goals and teach young people
on all levels of society, not just scientists and research scholars, to think
independently."

I said I agreed emphatically, and I longed to ask her whether this
kind of thinking was prevalent among her East Berlin colleagues. It certainly did not seem typical of what I had learned to think of as communist, but my experience in interviewing East Berliners had taught
me that this was the sort of question to avoid. A question which suggests
hostility, however unintentionally, immediately puts the Westerner on
the opposite side of the Wall, and this seems to cut off the flow of person-
to-person communication. I swallowed my natural curiosity, as I did many
times during my East Berlin visits.

"You see, in our socialist society we expect workers in industrial
plants to participate in management and also to take part in local government. If they are to do this effectively, obviously, they must be able
to think critically and independently."

I kept my reservations to myself and asked her about East Germany's
University Reform Law of 1968.

"You seem to have had much the same sort of problems in your
universities as the West Germans had in theirs, overcrowding, the pro-
longation of study, the proliferation of knowledge," I suggested.

"The problems were much the same in all technologically advanced
societies. Both the need for scientists and technologists and the scientific and technical knowledge exploded too suddenly for our antiquated
university system to be able to cope with the needs. It was a quantum
leap, if you will, both in the number of students to be educated and in
the amount of knowledge to be taught. In both Western and Eastern
universities we have had to struggle to find new methods of dealing with
the leap."

She smiled. "Naturally I think our socialist way is better. I have read
the West Berlin University Reform Law, and I find it only a stopgap,
only patching up the medieval system. We have tried a radical reform,
and I think our solution is more realistic."

I asked what she thought the basic difference in philosophy was between the Western and Eastern university reforms, and she answered:

"I think we have accepted the interrelationship between industry and
the academic community. I think the Western universities are trying to
deny this."

She explained: "We have accepted the fact that in the modern, technological world the university can no longer be an ivory tower, divorced

from social and industrial life, can no longer be a medieval community of scholars devoted to knowledge in the abstract, but must be both a part of the social community and part of the industrial world. Therefore, we have tried to bring industry into university education and the universities into industry."

"How?" I asked.

"For example, the university at Jena now works in full co-operation with the Zeiss works. There is a research committee on which directors and scientists from the Zeiss optical plant work together with state officials and professors and students from the University at Jena to decide what research will be done by university students and professors. We bring the industrial representatives into all phases of the university administration and planning, and members of the Jena academic community into the industrial research of the plant."

"Do you mean that the university conducts research projects for Zeiss?" I asked.

"I mean that the whole scope of study and research is planned jointly by the university, by the people from Zeiss, and by government representatives: the course of study, the texts and outside reading assigned as well as the research projects. The whole work of the university is integrated with the needs and goals of Zeiss."

"Does this have any bearing on recruitment of students to work in the Zeiss plant?" I asked.

"Yes, in many cases. Most of our students already have jobs assigned to them before they complete their exams, many of them with Zeiss, others with other firms, but all of our students will find it easier to fit into industrial management or research because of their experience in working with the Zeiss representatives."

We talked a little of other reforms such as shortening the course of study and increasing student participation in university administration.

"Of course, our students have always had a greater voice in university decisions than West German students had," she said. "We have always had more student representatives on various committees, but, under the reform law, students have an equal voice with professors in the new research collectives. We are trying to make the students feel that they are truly comrades and partners of their professors, and that their university education is not just a continuation of schooling but that it represents the beginning of their own independent research. We try to get students started on serious research projects, not just training projects or busy work, as early in their academic experience as possible. This way not only do they learn by valuable, practical experience but they feel that their years at the university are useful, that they are not just years of preparation but are already productive."

I asked whether this has improved the morale of students, and she replied that it was still too early to be sure but that she believed that it would do so.

"Shortening the course of study will also help." She explained that the entire course of study had been revised. "Under the new system, the average student spends five to five and a half years at the university, the average technical student only four years and that, I think, is a great improvement.

"We've done this by dividing the curriculum into phases. The beginning student spends one to two years, depending on his field, mastering basic principles in his discipline and also studying Marxism-Leninism, languages, and sports. You know we now require two foreign languages, of which one must be Russian, for every student regardless of his discipline."

I said that I had heard this.

"Every field is international these days," she said, "whether medicine or agriculture or physics, so I approve this change. Well, at the end of the introductory phase, the student must pass an examination to qualify to go on to the second phase. Next comes a year or two of special study in his field with emphasis on research. Each student must spend some portion of each week on his personal research project, and he devotes up to six months doing practical work in an industrial plant or a research institute. At the end of the practicum, most students will take their final examinations, written and oral, submit the results of their research projects, and receive their diplomas. Those who want to be specialists, university teachers or research scientists will return for additional research for their doctorates or advanced diplomas."

I asked her about provisions for continuing education and updating. She said that in the case of medical students, for instance, there would be Saturday seminars at the university after the internship. For qualified doctors there will be summer sessions, evening classes, and the meetings of the professional societies.

"In my own field of education we are doing quite a lot to keep our teachers and school administrators up to date," she said. "We are introducing a program under which every teacher in the country will be able to take a four-weeks' refresher course each year, two weeks in the winter and two in the summer. School principals have a program under which they get one day free from their school duties each week to attend classes and discussions, and they get four weeks free in addition to their normal vacations to attend intensive seminars.

"None of this is perfect," she said, "and no system can possibly keep the entire professional and technical population up to date at the rate that knowledge is exploding, but at least we are trying to cope."

I said that I saw that they were. "It seems as though the G.D.R. has made great strides in expanding its university system."

"When I think back to the state of our education in 1945, the bombed-out buildings, the destroyed libraries and laboratories, the shortage of teachers and of money, I think we have done splendidly. Humboldt University was fifty-four per cent destroyed and Dresden eighty per cent. Before the war, there were only seven universities in East Germany as compared to thirty-one in West Germany. Now we have forty-four institutions of university rank with 12,000 instructors and something over 120,000 students."

She opened a booklet and read me a statistic: "There were 31,512 students in the G.D.R. in 1951, 74,742 in 1955, and 113,400 in 1968. The percentage of children of workers and peasants has also increased: in 1946 they accounted for only four per cent of all university students, in 1950 for twenty-eight per cent, and in 1968 for forty-five per cent, so we have made strides toward democratization. Our constitution of 1968 guarantees every East German citizen the right of education, and this includes university education for everyone who is qualified."

"You are enthusiastic about your university system," I said, and she smiled.

"You will think I am an old party hack and am just grinding out propaganda, but in the case of our universities, I am perfectly sincere. I don't mean to try to convince you that I am entirely satisfied with the state of our socialist society or with our universities. Of course I am not. As an old communist I find that I am often disappointed by the reality as compared to the theory that I believed in and still believe in. After all, we are only human, and we have been struggling against very great odds."

I agreed that they had.

"We have made mistakes, and we have been imperfect. Even my beloved Humboldt University isn't perfect, despite the reforms. For instance, my classes are still far too large, and I scarcely ever know my students personally as people, and I regret that. Worse, I see no solution. Classes will get larger, not smaller.

"But then, nothing is perfect, and as I said, we have made great strides.

We still have problems in our universities and in our society, but we are making progress, and, don't forget, in the history of a nation, a quarter of a century is a very short time. We are only at the beginning."

"In general," I said, "you are pleased with your life, I think."

"I am very grateful. I still remember the nazi time and the postwar years, the terror, the bombing, the hunger, the disorder. I am grateful. I love my work, I have enjoyed my life, I appreciate the adventure."

I said it was getting late, and I was afraid I would freeze if I did not get back to West Berlin before the temperature dropped too far. "I came over without a coat because it looked so sunny this morning, but it is cool for spring."

"I wish I could lend you a coat or a jacket," she said, but we both knew that I could not return it. I assured her that I would hurry to the subway and be warm enough. I thanked her for our talk and for the tea and wine.

"It was fun for me," she said. "I wish we could talk again and you could tell me about your universities, about your students."

"I wish so too," I said. She walked with me to the door and waved from the stoop. "Thank you!" I said, and she smiled and waved, still very much the rebellious young woman who had kicked over the traces of a conventional, bourgeois upbringing to leave home at seventeen, take a factory job and plunge into the dangerous adventure of life in the communist party of pre-Hitler Berlin. I had liked Irmingard and thought that she had liked me. She was a colleague, and I regretted that we could not have been more open, more candid, and that we should probably never meet again. I walked briskly through the spring evening, hurrying to the warmth of the subway station, to the comfort of a relaxed and delicious dinner in West Berlin.

6

The Borough Mayor

Berlin, like London and New York, is a federation of boroughs. New York City has five boroughs, each headed by a borough president. Greater Berlin has twenty boroughs or districts (*Bezirke*), twelve of which are in West Berlin. Each borough has its own mayor, assembly, and civil service housed in its borough city hall or *Rathaus*. Herr M. was one of the borough mayors in West Berlin.

"It's an ugly building, actually," he told me as he showed me around the main floor of his borough *Rathaus,* "but we Berliners are proud of any building that survived the war!" The red brick structure *was* ugly, but the ceilings were high, the rooms spacious, the windows generous in admitting sunlight. Herr M. showed me into his private office and motioned me to a chair facing his massive, nineteenth-century desk. The chairs upholstered in stiff brown leather were firm but comfortable. Everything in the room was dark, the paneling, the desk, chairs, bookshelves and the somber carpet, but it was also solid, sober and restrained.

"Not my taste," Mayor M. said and smiled, "but elected officials are ephemeral tenants, and, as I said, we Berliners are grateful for anything that survived."

Herr M. is a short man, inches shorter than I. He has a round, balding head, a round cheerful face, and his movements are quick but economical. He wore dark, conventional, well-cut clothes without appearing either stuffy or fashionable.

"I am a socialist, Frau Doctor," he explained, "but I did not begin life as a carpenter or a dock worker. Like many socialist politicians of my generation, I come from the civil service. My people were working-class people. My father was a teamster and later a trucker. My mother's father kept a working-man's pub, and mother helped out there even

64

after we children were born. I grew up in a working-class neighborhood."

I asked him whether he had attended local schools.

"Yes," he said, "I began in the neighborhood elementary school, but I did very well and I had good teachers. When I was ten my teacher sent a note home to my parents asking them to come to see her. My mother went, and luckily my mother believed in education. My teacher was able to persuade her to send me to a Gymnasium the next year."

"Did you have to pay? Could your parents afford that?" I asked.

"My grandfather, the pub keeper, paid the fees and my mother went on working to buy me decent clothes and books. In those days a working-class boy was apt to feel out of place in a Gymnasium."

"Were the boys snobbish?" I asked.

He nodded. "It's a long time ago. I am over fifty, but I remember that some of the middle-class boys were very critical and unfriendly, but on the other hand, some of them were very kind. My mother spent most of her earnings to make me look respectable, and I never felt ashamed of my background, certainly not of my parents. I made a few good friends, some of them from middle-class homes."

He laughed. "I remember the first time I went home with one of my schoolmates to his home in Grunewald. He lived in one of those big old mansions set in its own park, and when we walked up the steps, a butler in livery opened the door. I guess my mouth fell open. I was afraid to walk on the carpets. We didn't even see his mother. He took me up to the top floor, and his old nanny gave us tea with lots of milk. He was a nice fellow. He used to lend me books. Later we were at the university together."

"Are you and he still friends?" I asked.

He shook his head sadly. "Alfred was killed on the Eastern Front in 1943. So many of the boys I went to school with didn't survive the war."

Just then the door swung open, and his neatly dressed, grey-haired secretary carried in a tray with coffee. Herr M. jumped to his feet and helped her settle the tray on his desk.

"Thank you, thank you, Frau D.," he said, and he introduced her to me. We shook hands and exchanged smiles, and Frau D. disappeared into the outer office.

"May I pour for you?" he asked, already suiting his action to the words. He offered me sugar and cream, and I accepted a sweet biscuit. "The coffee service survived the war too," he said.

"It looks as though it had survived several wars," I suggested, noting that it was Imperial Berlin porcelain, plain unembellished white but of very good quality.

"I'm sure Frau D. knows all about it, and she takes good care of it. She is motherly about me, about the young clerks, and about the whole mayor's office. She is a widow. Both her father and her husband died in nazi concentration camps. They were from old socialist families, prominent in the Berlin trade-union movement before 1933."

I could think of nothing to say, and he understood. "My father was a local trade-union leader," he went on, "and he was arrested soon after 1933, but I guess the nazis decided he was pretty small beer. They let him out after about six months, and he was able to go back to his regular job."

"Did you have any trouble with the nazis?" I asked.

"Well, in 1933 I was just finishing the Gymnasium. I used to play soccer with the young socialists, and I went along with my parents to S.P.D. and trade-union outings, but I had never been politically active. After 1933 my father advised me to be discreet, to keep my mouth shut and get on with my education."

"Did you have trouble getting into a university because of your father's arrest?" I asked.

He shook his head. "No, I don't doubt that they kept an eye on me, but those were the early days. The nazis didn't seize control of all aspects of society all at once; totalitarianism was a slow growth. I was able to study law, but after the first semester in Berlin, I thought it wise to transfer to a Catholic university in south Germany. The nazis had less influence in Catholic schools."

I asked whether his family was Catholic, and he said no.

"We were one of those old-fashioned socialist families which thought of religion as the opiate of the people. I was brought up an agnostic. When I was a little boy, I went to socialist Sunday school, not to church, and Sunday afternoons we went to socialist picnics or ball games."

"You say that as though you had changed your viewpoint," I said. "It's a personal question, but may I ask it?"

"Oh, yes, of course. I'm a Christian now. One of my sons was just ordained as a Lutheran minister. I guess it was the war, or the experience of the nazi time. I joined the Evangelical Church right after the war, perhaps partly as a gesture of opposition to the communists."

"Are you active in the Church?" I asked, and he said that he was. He was serving on several lay committees dealing with youth and welfare.

We talked a little about Berlin city politics, and I asked the inevitable questions: "What is Berlin's most urgent domestic political problem?"

His answer was also inevitable: "The political attitude of our young people.

"Do you remember when we used to complain that our German young people were too complacent, too indifferent, too apathetic to be interested in politics? I remember. I served on a committee which regularly drew up resolutions and drafted programs to try to interest young Berliners in politics. In those days young people, whether apprentices or secondary-school pupils or university students, seemed to regard all party politics as dirty or crooked, and they were afraid to make a commitment to any one party or even to any ideology or form of government."

I told him that I remembered that time. "We had an apathetic, conformist generation in the U.S. too," I told him.

"In Germany that kind of reaction was understandable. From about the turn of the century until 1945 our German youth had been too political, or at least too enthusiastic, too naïvely idealistic. Take for instance the *Wandervogel* movement of the early years of the century. They were young idealists who rebelled against the hypocrisy and artificiality of the bourgeois Wilhelmine era and who were searching for a freer, more natural, and more democratic life style."

"It sounds a little like the hippies, doesn't it?" I asked, and he nodded.

"Yes, in a way," he said, "except that the *Wandervögel* believed in political freedom and some of our modern rebels seem to willing to compromise with communism. I know their leaders say that they are opposed to the Soviet and East German forms of socialism, but they admire Che and Mao.

"Our German young people were too idealistic, they believed too easily; that is why some, a great many, were taken in by the nazis, at least at first. The nazis knew how to exploit that youthful enthusiasm and take advantage of that naïveté. No wonder, really, that modern young people are afraid to believe anything.

"I still think as I did several years back that our young people need more political education in the schools and on the job. Our Berlin schools are doing a much better job in the last several years, I believe. They teach civics, and they take the pupils on field trips to town halls, to Senate meetings, even to prisons and hospitals. When school classes come here to our borough hall, I usually try to arrange to be here, along with several department heads, to meet them. The youngsters ask some pretty frank questions, and I find them very well informed. I think that many are interested in politics and in public questions, but their interest needs to be stimulated and cultivated."

"And they're not all radicals?" I asked.

"Oh, no, certainly not. Mind you, the percentage of radicals is higher among secondary school pupils than it was, say three, four years ago. Many sixteen- and seventeen-year-olds now are reading radical literature, and even more of them are mouthing new left slogans, but these are still a small minority, especially among working-class youngsters. We Berliners live too close to the Wall and too close to our own past for the majority of young people to forget."

Our conversation turned to the position and duties of the district mayors, and I asked him whether he was elected directly by the voters. He explained:

"No. The mayors are elected indirectly by the borough assemblies.* Whenever there is a municipal or *Land* (state) election in West Berlin, the voter votes for delegates to his local borough assembly as well as for members of the Berlin House of Representatives. Each borough has forty-five assemblymen or women elected for a four-year term."

"And the assembly chooses the borough mayor?" I asked.

"Yes. The assembly meets and votes for the borough mayor and for members of the borough council, who are all elected for a six-year term. In my borough there are six members of the council. According to the constitution there may be as many as necessary up to seven."

I asked whether the local boroughs have much autonomy.

"When the new Berlin constitution was drawn up in 1950, there were people who favored a large measure of local self-government, and there were others who wanted a strong central government. What we have, I think, represents a compromise between the two extremes. While our borough assemblies do not actually legislate, they do exercise a substantial influence on the drafting of the local budget, and they supervise the administration in their districts. Schools, for instance, are largely administered on a local basis and so is housing, whereas the overall planning is city-wide."

I asked how often the assemblies meet, and he explained that they are required to meet at least once every two months, but they may meet as often as necessary.

"Certain times of the year, for instance, when they are drawing up budget requirements, they may be in almost continuous session."

"How large is your borough, Mayor M.?"

"Well, we are not the largest, but we are one of the larger boroughs. The largest, Neukölln, has a population of 278,000, which is as much as the city of Kiel. Even the smallest, Zehlendorf, has almost 100,000 people, enough for a good-sized European city."

* *Bezirksverordnetenversammlung,* translated by some scholars as borough council.

"So West Berlin is as large as twelve rather large cities?"

He nodded. "And all Berlin as large as twenty! You know that Greater Berlin with its present borders was only created in 1920 under the Weimar Republic. Before that the old city of Berlin had only 24 square miles of territory. Since 1920 Greater Berlin has had an area of 344 square miles. Paris has only 185 square miles and New York City 365.4, so you see Berlin ranks as a very large city in area. The periphery of all Berlin is 144 miles and the total area is as large as the whole Ruhr district. In 1920 Berlin had a population of more than four million and ranked as the third largest city in the world, the second in Europe. By 1943 we reached our peak of four and a half million, but by 1945 the population had declined by more than a third.

"We're still a pretty big city, though, with more than three million people, East and West, and over two million just in West Berlin."

"You are important economically, I know," I said.

"Oh, yes; but again, not as important as we once were. We used to be the financial capital of Germany. The Berlin stock exchange was Germany's Wall Street. All the leading banks, brokers, insurance companies, and many big businesses had their main offices here. I was just looking at some figures which showed that in 1924, 41 per cent of the German electrical industry, 25 per cent of the joint stock companies, and 11 per cent of all business firms in Germany were centered in Berlin."

"No longer?" I asked.

"Oh, we are still important in the electrical industry, in fashions, and in a few other light industries, but a great many businesses and banks have moved their front offices out to West Germany, leaving just a token office here.

"Don't misunderstand me," he went on, "we are holding our own. We still have more workers engaged in industry than any other German city. Don't forget that West Berlin industry lost about three-quarters of its prewar capacity through the bombings and the postwar dismantling. Machines and tools were removed from about four hundred and sixty firms. The most important factories were entirely dismantled and transported to the Soviet Union.

"Still, we had a lot of help in rebuilding both from the U.S.A. and from the Federal Republic. Between 1949 and 1962 West Berlin received about five billion D-marks from the Marshall Plan. Our industrial turnover rose from about 1,660 million marks in 1950 to 15,421 million in 1968, about half of that total in production goods, especially electronics and machine tools. Economically, industrially, West Berlin is still a force to be reckoned with."

"And a prize to be won," I said, and he nodded seriously.

"We are still working very hard, the city government, private enterprise, and the federal government in Bonn, to keep Berlin thriving economically and to attract both new business and young workers to the city, and we are doing very well."

"There is a special problem in Berlin, isn't there, because the average age of the population is older than in West Germany, older than normal? I suppose that means the birth rate is relatively low," I said.

"Exactly," he answered and took up a folder from his desk. "I had my assistant get some statistics together for you about population, employment and production." He leafed through the papers in the file and held out a chart to me.

"This graph shows the age of our population in relation to that in the Federal Republic. In West Berlin about twenty-five per cent of the population is over sixty-five, whereas in the Federal Republic, the figure is only eleven per cent. Then, not only have we proportionately too few young parents and workers and too many people on pensions, in hospitals, and otherwise, draining the city's economy, but we also lack the natural hinterland, the farms and villages and small towns surrounding the city from which new settlers would normally come. We are cut off from our surrounding provinces."

"So you import young people from the Federal Republic and from abroad?" I asked.

"We do, and we have done rather well. One of our projects was an advertising campaign to recruit young workers. In 1969 the Berlin Senate, in co-operation with the Labor Office and private industry fitted out two big buses and sent them around to more than a hundred cities and towns in the Federal Republic. The buses carried posters and brochures and applications for jobs."

"I suppose the brochures explained all the advantages of living and working in Berlin, all the inducements?"

"Everything," he said. "We told about the kinds of jobs available, wages and salaries, living conditions, cultural advantages."

"Surely for a young person from a provincial town, Berlin must seem very exciting culturally," I said.

"Three opera houses, two first-class symphony orchestras, lots of legitimate theaters, first-run films, museums, evening classes and, of course, all the more frivolous advantages of life in the big city. We also offer tax advantages for the newly arrived young worker; we help him find an apartment, lend him 3,000 marks if he marries, plus 10,000 marks at only two per cent interest for ten years to furnish his apartment. The Senate even pays for a visit home at the end of the first year."

"I've seen very attractive posters in several West German cities urging young people, especially young couples, to come to Berlin. Has the campaign been successful?"

He took out several sheets covered with statistics and showed them to me.

"You can search through these data for yourself, so I won't go into too much detail, but you can see that in 1967 and 1968, more people moved out of West Berlin than moved into it, but in 1969, that trend was reversed. In 1969, 13,741 more people moved into the city than left it. The figures for the first part of 1970 show a positive balance."

"So the young workers do come?"

"Yes. A high proportion of those who come are both young and workers, whereas many of those who leave are elderly, retired people going to join children or other relatives in West Germany. In 1969, the net gain of employed persons was almost nineteen thousand."

"That sounds encouraging, but do the young people stay in Berlin once they are here, or is it too early to know that?" I asked.

"It is too early to be sure how long they will stay, but so far we estimate that about fifty per cent stay. If that many stay and start families here, then it will have been worthwhile."

"Does the net gain through recruits outweigh the loss caused by the surplus of deaths over births?" I asked.

"Not until very recently. The statistics show that the surplus of deaths over births rose almost steadily from 1964 to 1969. In 1968, the total loss of population was almost twenty-two thousand. The population of West Berlin fell from 2,163,306 in 1967 to 2,141,441 at the end of 1968."

I studied the columns of figures and observed, "Yes, I see. The total West Berlin population dropped steadily from 2,200,228 at the end of 1964 to 2,134,020 by 1969. That is quite serious."

"Yes, but look at these new figures." He pulled out a mimeographed sheet with recent data. "At the beginning of 1970, the population deficit began to decrease, and in April and May, there was a net increase in population."

"So things are looking up?"

He nodded and smiled. "At least, we hope so, and we are certainly trying. I think we have a lot to offer. We still have a lot of job opportunities. Our G.N.P. is still rising and has risen consistently. Industrial production rose by three and five-tenths per cent in 1970. Our total an-

nual production of goods and serivces in West Berlin is almost as high as
the total in Czechoslovakia. There has been a rise in the cost of living,
something like four to five per cent in 1970, but the average income kept
well ahead of the rise in prices."

He showed me pages of statistics with cost of living and income for the
period from 1964 to 1970.

"We anticipate a slight slowing down in the rate of increase because
there has been a mild cooling of the economy in the Federal Republic,
and Berlin always reacts to that, but the economy was a bit overheated.
An adjustment is healthy, and we still have a surplus of jobs to fill * and
a healthy amount of purchasing power. I think our Berlin economy is
basically healthy."

"How are you doing with housing? Are there apartments available for
young workers who come here?" I asked.

"I thought you might like to see some of our housing, Frau Doctor."

"I would, very much," I said.

"I asked one of the experts from the Senate Housing Office to come by
with a car and take us on a tour of some of the newer housing developments."

He got up and went to the door and called quietly to Frau D. to ask
whether Matthaeus had arrived. Apparently he had. Mayor M. walked
out into the anteroom, and seconds later he reappeared with a middle-
sized, thick-set young man carrying a briefcase. He introduced us and we
shook hands. Matthaeus had a friendly grin which showed irregular
teeth. He cocked his head to one side and blushed a little when he smiled.

"Matt brought us an official Senate Mercedes and a driver, so we can
tour in style!" the mayor said.

We said goodbye to Frau D., and as we walked down the broad steps of
the *Rathaus,* Mayor M. told me that his father and Matt's grandfather
were close friends. "Old comrades, eh, Matt?"

"Birds of a feather," Matt said. "Jailbirds!" and he laughed without
bitterness. "Opa was a union organizer, and so, of course, the nazis didn't
like him much."

"He was in jail longer than my father," the mayor said, and Matt
nodded.

"Ah, here's our fat Mercedes! Hello Fritz, here are our guests."

The chauffeur smiled, saluted happily, and held open the car door for
us all. Matt climbed into the front seat and twisted around to face us.

"Yes," Matt continued, "I guess he was in for about two years, but they

* There were 21,131 job vacancies at the end of 1970 and only 6,597 unemployed.

let him out. Lucky, too, because my father was killed in the war and left my mother with four kids. Grandpa looked after us all."

I asked whether he was still alive, and Matt grinned.

"Sure. He's retired now, but he's still the party district leader. He has lots of time to collect dues and arrange meetings and chat with all the comrades."

The mayor laughed and said Opa and his father still got together on Saturday nights to drink beer and talk about old times at the corner pub and shake their heads over what the S.P.D. is coming to.

"They don't like the young Falcons. That's our party's youth group, and they've got pretty far out in the past few years. I confess I get impatient with them myself," Matt said, looking impatient.

Herr M. laughed. "Matt is one of our hard hats."

Matt grinned and shook his head. "No, no. I don't want to break kids' heads, but I do wish they'd get a little sense into them! I was only nine or ten when the war ended, so I don't remember very much about the nazi period, but I do remember the feeling of fear, and I know how my relatives and their friends suffered. We Berlin socialists have always fought against dictatorships. I hate to see Berlin young people who call themselves socialists making fools of themselves, flirting with any form of totalitarianism."

Herr M. nodded. "Matt is right about dictatorships. Berlin has always been progressive, socially and politically. I don't know whether you know that it was largely because of the general strike of Berlin trade unionists that the Kapp Putsch failed in 1920."

I said that I had not heard that, but that I knew the city was called "Red Berlin" in the days before World War I and during the 1920s.

"Red, meaning socialist, Frau Doctor," Matt interposed, "not communist. We were progressive in things like housing, public health, city planning, welfare, and public transportation. Our schools were always models for the rest of Germany, and our voters were the best informed, the most democratic in Germany, or at least I think so."

Herr M. laughed. "Matt is another *waschecht* Berliner!" *Waschecht* means washing true. "Color-fast," Matt explained.

"Dyed-in-the-wool?" I suggested.

"It means a real Berliner, usually one whose parents were born in Berlin," said Matt.

"Most Berliners, like most people from big cities, came from the provinces or else their parents did," Herr M. said.

"I know," I said, "the typical Berliner comes from Breslau."

"Came, Frau Doctor," the mayor said. "No more."

"The mayor means I make propaganda for our city, but it's not just because I work for the city government," Matt said.

"No," Mayor M. said, "he does it in his free time too. He's a regular Prussian."

"Never off duty?" I asked. "But you're not alone. Most of the Berliners I meet are propagandists for the city."

Matt nodded. "I think we should be proud of our political record. Berlin was never a nazi city, you know."

"I know the nazis never won a majority or a plurality here in a free election," I said.

"Not even nearly!" the mayor said. "In the Berlin city election of, what was it, March? anyway spring 1933, the Nazi Party made a very poor showing for a party already in power nationally. They got about a third of the seats."

"Were they furious?" I asked.

"Very," the mayor said. "They appointed a special commissioner for Berlin and took away most of the local autonomy of the city government. What it meant was that the *Gauleiter,* Goebbels, became virtual dictator of the city."

"The nazis hadn't much use for Berliners," Matt continued, "especially not for us socialists and trade unionists. It was Goebbels who said they'd had to take over Berlin by force. They could never have got it by free elections. Berliners don't fall for totalitarianism."

The car slowed down, and the chauffeur patted Matt on the arm. Matt turned quickly and looked out his window.

"Oh, here's our first project! I was so soothed by the sound of my own voice that we got here without my noticing it. This is one of our borough's older projects, Frau Doctor."

It was a large project, several blocks square. The trees and gardens and lawns were already well established. Many of the apartments had window boxes with plants in bloom.

"I think this is one of our best planned projects," Matt was saying. "You see, this is conceived of as a whole neighborhood, almost like an independent village. You'll notice as we drive around the outskirts that most of the buildings have parking lots in the back, facing this street. That's because the settlement itself is designed as a plaza. The houses face inward away from the street, and there is no car traffic inside the plaza."

"There are bicycle paths," the mayor said, "and there is also underground parking. A bus line runs along this street, and there are bus stops at each end of the project and in the middle and a subway entrance on the opposite side, so the people who live here have excellent public transportation to all parts of the city."

"That," Matt said, pointing to a modest steeple, "is the Protestant church. The Catholic church is just across a small V-shaped park. Between them is a parish house for both churches, which also serves as a community center for meetings of boy scouts, youth clubs, and so on."

Fritz pulled into one of the parking areas. We got out and began to stroll along a wide path into the interior of the project.

"Here are the two churches," Matt said, "and up ahead is the Sports Hall. Beyond that is a small swimming pool and a soccer field."

"You have everything!" I said, impressed with the convenience, the spic-and-span neatness and general cheerfulness of the area. I liked the asymmetrical, curving paths, the houses set at angles rather than all in a row close to the sidewalk. "What a lot of lawn and trees!" I said.

"Green spots!" Matt said. "That is an essential part of all our planning, the inclusion of as much green as possible, and we set the houses along curves, asymmetrically, so that each apartment gets the maximum amount of sun. We are a northern city: our Berliners like sunny apartments."

He pointed to a large building, perhaps fifteen stories high, set at right angles to the path and surrounded by a large green area.

"That is a bachelors' building," he explained. "It is for men and women bachelors, young people mostly, who live alone and need only one or two rooms plus a kitchen and bath and balcony. We put them all together in one corner of the project, both to save space by building a tall building and to give them privacy. Bachelors might be annoyed by crying or shouting children in the apartment next door, and families might be disturbed by the bachelors' late parties."

"Good idea," I said, "but suppose they don't stay bachelors?"

"Lots of them don't, of course, but then they move to a larger apartment or to one of the small houses on the other side. We have garden apartments for families and also small houses with up to four bedrooms."

We stood just under the bachelors' building, and the mayor pointed up to the balconies.

"The building is constructed in such a way that each balcony is set at a slightly different angle, so that each gets its share of sun and so that no one can see onto his neighbor's balcony. We understand that bachelors like privacy, especially at breakfast, and many take their breakfasts on the balconies."

I saw that most balconies had tables and chairs as well as window boxes.

"A couple of years back," Matt said, "during the C.D.U.-S.P.D. coalition, an important visitor from Bonn came to Berlin to inspect our housing projects. He was from the Christian Democratic Union and a very prim, pious Rhineland Catholic. When I told him about the bachelor apartments and especially about the privacy of the balconies, he was scandalized and indignant. We happened to be driving past on a Sunday morning, after early Mass I hardly need add, and we saw couple after couple sitting on the balconies enjoying late breakfast. My Catholic dignitary spluttered, 'but-but-breakfast! Couples! They are supposed to be bachelors!' 'Well, they are,' I told him, and he said we Berliners were pandering to immorality. He was horrified. I knew it wouldn't make him feel any better if I said that young people would sleep together anyway and they might as well be comfortable as have to go hiding in the bushes.''

"No, heavens, you couldn't say that to someone from Bonn!" I said.

"Especially not a V.I.P. from Bonn who was concerned with the proper use of federal funds," the mayor said.

"No," Matt agreed, "so I told him that this was really a very clever plot on our part because most of the couples ended up getting married. We know, because they apply for larger apartments. He seemed placated by that."

"Bonn," the mayor said darkly.

Past the bachelors' building farther along the curving path, we found a cluster of shops: a pub, a tailor's, a drugstore, and a good-sized modern market. Down the street were a bakery, a florist, and a stationery shop.

"That building over there," Matt said, "is for our elderly people. Each individual or couple has a one- or two-room apartment with a balcony. The apartments have small kitchens, but there is also a restaurant on the first floor and a big sitting room and recreation area. We show films and arrange lectures, and there are bridge and ping pong tournaments as well as theater parties and excursions. Inside there are ramps and elevators so that the old people don't have to climb stairs, and there's always a nurse on duty and a doctor on call."

"Marvellous," I said. "How good that you don't isolate them, stick them away in a settlement by themselves."

"They're too useful!" the mayor said. "We put them quite close to the family apartments and small houses so that the young parents can get to know them and employ them as baby sitters. They're within easy walking distance of the churches and community center too."

Matt nodded, "The old men like to sit around the soccer field and watch the boys and young men play or stroll to the pub and have a few beers and talk about sports or politics or old times with the younger men. The old ladies just about run the churches. It keeps them part of the community."

"Now here," Matt said, "is our school. This building in front, all glass and gardens, is the elementary school. Behind it, over there to the left, is the kindergarten. There's a secondary school a few blocks away. Youngsters who go to the Gymnasium or to special trade schools have to take buses or the *U-Bahn,* but the connections are good. They don't have to cross a street to catch a bus or get into the subway."

We walked a little farther beyond the school playground and came to a park green with lawn and trees. The terrain sloped down gradually until about a block ahead it was perhaps eight or ten feet below street level. A sturdy fence separated the deep ditch from the peripheral sidewalk.

"It looks like a zoo!" I said, meaning the kind of free zoo where lions enjoy maximum liberty to roam and are separated from the public by a ditch and fence.

"Exactly," Matt said. "It's a playground. Balls can't escape into the street or hit passers-by, and smaller children can't escape, nor can outsiders get in to sell them pot or pornography."

"Better and better," I said admiringly. "You really have thought of everything."

The mayor smiled politely. "Well, this is one of our showcase projects, of course. We are proud of all our housing, but some projects have only apartments or houses and perhaps a church or community center. We try to plan all of them with or near schools and shops, though."

"Yes," Matt said, "and we always plan for adequate parking space, road connections, and bus or subway services. Sometimes the subway or bus line has to be extended to serve a new project. We have built something over twenty-one kilometers of subway since the war, and more is in progress, and we've built or rebuilt 187 bridges."

The mayor nodded. "It has been a big job. A third of all Berlin apartments were entirely destroyed during the war. We had to begin by clearing away eighty million cubic meters of rubble before we could think about rebuilding."

"Eighty million cubic meters? I can't even conceive of how much that is, but I remember Berlin in 1947, mile after mile of rubble and not much left standing, not in downtown Berlin."

"Not much standing and little running," Herr M. said. "We had to get the electricity, the water, the garbage disposal, the sewer system, all the public utilities running. We had to find buses and gasoline and spare parts and drivers, and there were none. Then we had to start clearing away the rubble."

"We built about 338,000 new apartments in West Berlin between

Fig. 7. Kreuzberg, one of West Berlin's housing developments (photo by Landesbild-stelle, West Berlin)

1948 and 1968," Matt said. "About three-fourths of all the new apartments are what we call 'social' apartments, built at least in part with
public money."

"Are the social apartments for low-income people?" I asked.

"Low and middle," he answered, "and for people with special problems
such as handicaps or very large families."

The mayor said that by 1968 there was no longer an actual shortage of
apartments in West Berlin.

"Naturally we still have some old housing that needs to be replaced.
We are going on building apartments and projects and will gradually
replace all the old and inadequate housing."

I told them that I was very much impressed with the project and with
the overall planning. Herr M. promised to send some statistics around to
my hotel.

"Put lots of statistics in your book, Frau Doctor," he suggested. "It
impresses people."

We strolled back to the car and spent another hour driving around,
looking at several projects in the mayor's district and in neighboring districts.

"Matt just returned from New York," the mayor told me. "He was
invited by some committee to tour around the United States and compare
urban housing there with our Berlin experience."

"What did you think of New York's housing and city planning?" I
asked. Matt did not answer. He just grinned and covered his eyes with his
hands. I asked what he would recommend to New York as a first step in
coping with its housing problem.

"Follow our example, *gnädige* Frau," he said. "It's the only way. Bomb
it!" We laughed, and he went on: "I realize that New York has a problem
because Manhattan is an island, a rather small island. In Berlin we are
an island too, but we have a large territory. Before the war a large proportion of the population was crowded into the two or three boroughs of
mid-town Berlin which were almost obliterated. When we began to plan
the rebuilding of the city, we decided to move the population out, to
spread it thinner. With modern buses and subways and roads there's no
reason to have the population concentrated in the center of the city. We
have spread our projects out over as wide a territory as possible, keeping
the population per square mile much lower than before the war."

"That's how we get the green spaces," the mayor explained. "We limit
the number of people housed per square kilometer and insist on a fixed
ratio of green space to construction. Each small house has a small garden.

Each tall apartment building is set in a small park with the same proportion of green space per cubic meter of construction. This provides not only a pleasanter appearance and more quiet and breathing space, but it helps keep our famous Berlin air pure."

"And we've been doing this long before ecology became the in-thing," Matt said.

The mayor looked at his watch and suggested lunch.

"Since we are having a political morning, Frau Doctor, why don't we have lunch at the City Hall?"

"The rathskeller?" I asked.

"At Schöneberg," he said. "We'll meet all the city politicians. I suppose you have met a great many of them?"

I admitted that I had met a few and that I found many of them very like city politicians I knew in the States. "Only, perhaps, prouder of their city than most New York politicians," I said. "You have children, Mayor M.; are any of them on their way to becoming politicians?"

Fritz had driven into the large square in front of the Schöneberg *Rathaus* now called Kennedy Platz. He came around, opened our door and helped me out. We said good-bye and walked to the entrance to the rathskeller left of the main stairway to the *Rathaus*.

"I have three children, Frau Doctor," the Mayor said, "two boys and a girl. They are all interested in politics and in public, social questions. My oldest is a businessman in West Germany. He married a Munich girl he met while he was a student down there. My second oldest is the new pastor. The baby, Katie, is still a student. I sent her out of Berlin to avoid all the current turmoil. She is studying law, and I think she will go into politics. There are never enough young people interested in choosing politics as a career, especially not local politics. It's not glamorous enough for them."

"You don't regret your career, Mayor M.?" I asked.

"No, no. I've been very lucky, and I like my work. We've been through a lot in Berlin: my father's generation in the First World War, then the nazi period and the Second World War, terror, bombing, hunger, shortages, the Soviet menace at arm's length; but we have come through this far, and we have accomplished a lot."

"You have," I said, as we walked slowly into the rather somber but comfortable dining room.

"I can't say I have enjoyed all of it, but whatever happens in Berlin I am glad to have been part of it, and I hope my daughter will go into politics, preferably Berlin politics."

Matt, who had stopped to talk with an acquaintance in the hall, came
bounding up to the table we had chosen and pulled out a chair for me.

"I just saw the mayor in the hall. He's coming in with a couple of
cronies. I saw the headwaiter too, and there's venison today."

"But first we'll have an apéritif and drink to this lady's book," said
Mayor M.

"No, indeed," I said. "We must drink to Berlin and to your daughter
and to all young political recruits!"

7

The County Leader

"Sitting here on a mild summer evening, safe in a comfortable room, sipping Grand Marnier and talking with a gracious lady, those dramatic days seem very far away, as though they were in another life."

The county * leader raised his glass and we sipped. He was a distinguished-looking man with silver hair and finely chiselled features. The hand holding the fragile liqueur glass was graceful and well made.

"But then, that was all a very long time ago," he said, "a quarter of a century. Strange that those days seem more real to me than recent years, I suppose because in the middle of a struggle one is very much alive."

"In the midst of the struggle, Doctor, did you really believe that you could win?" I asked.

"We simply didn't know, but we knew that we had to try, that we had to fight. If we hadn't tried, if we hadn't fought during those first postwar months, you and I would not be sitting here in comfort and freedom. In fact, people like you and me would not be in Berlin, not in a communist Berlin." He paused and shook his head, perhaps imagining where he might be.

"West Berlin's present freedom was forged in those early months, I believe, and by a pathetic handful of Berliners still dazed and disoriented by the collapse of nazi Germany, by the chaos and confusion of the early occupation days."

"Most of your friends had returned to Berlin after May, 1945, hadn't they?" I asked, thinking of some of the old socialists who had spent years in concentration camps or abroad.

He nodded. "We drifted back gradually, from Dachau or Buchenwald, from America or England, a few from the U.S.S.R. Some of the younger

* I have used the word "county" organization and "county" leader because Dr. X used it.

men had managed to survive by escaping into the Wehrmacht. They came back more slowly, some of them not for years."

"Did you begin reorganizing your party right away?" I asked.

"The survivors of all the democratic parties and trade unions gathered immediately after the surrender and began to reform their party structures and unions. We had no idea what would happen to Berlin, whether the occupation of three sectors by the Western powers would be temporary or long-term, whether the Soviets would swallow up all Berlin, but we intended to stay free as long as possible."

"Did the democratic parties organize in the Soviet sector too?" I asked.

"Strangely enough, they did, and for the first months the Russians simply ignored us, I suppose because they thought us impotent. We socialists reformed our local clubs and county organizations and got ready to choose candidates for the first local elections."

"Why did the Soviets consider you so negligible? After all, prenazi Berlin had traditionally been an S.P.D. stronghold."

"Well," he considered, "as they read history, the democratic parties, socialists included, had failed in 1933. Weimar had failed, and we had allowed Hitler to come to power. Therefore they thought we had been rejected by history. With the nazis discredited and disfranchised, with the immense prestige of the victorious Red Army, the Russians honestly believed that the German communists would sweep the elections. In addition, they probably calculated that Berliners would be tacitly pressured into voting for the K.P.D. because of the overwhelming Soviet military presence. In Eastern Europe they counted on landslide victories simply because they expected the voters to be grateful for their liberation from nazi occupation by the Red Army."

"Naive, weren't they?" I said. "Almost as though they believed their own propaganda."

"People often do, Frau Doctor. That is one of the dangers of propaganda. I believe you wrote a book to that effect."

"In this case," I suggested, "it was to your advantage."

"It was. It gave us a breathing spell, a chance to organize. However on 11 November 1945 the Russians got their first shock when the first postwar elections in Eastern Europe devastated the communists."

"Hungary?" I asked, and he nodded.

"The Small Holder's Party, a sort of bourgeois-peasant party, polled 60 per cent, the socialists 20 per cent, and the Hungarian communists only 18 per cent in spite of Red Army presence."

"Did that have repercussions in Berlin?" I asked.

"Immediate," he said. "Just before the results of the Hungarian elections were known, Otto Grotewohl made a speech at an S.P.D. meeting in the Friedrichstadt Palace commemorating the 1917 Bolshevik revolution. He called for the unity of the entire working class, but he insisted that this unity must be voluntary co-operation, not compulsory merger brought about through external coercion. He said that the unification of the K.P.D. and the S.P.D. in the Soviet Zone and in East Berin would not make eventual reunification easier but would hamper it and perhaps make it impossible. This, you see, is a line which was acceptable to the Russians before the Hungarian results were known. The following day, after the disastrous returns were in, the Soviet government suppressed all reference to the Grotewohl speech. Not a line of it appeared in the Soviet-licensed S.P.D. press; in fact, there was no indication that a meeting had been held."

"The party line had changed?" I asked.

"Literally over night," he said. "Then on 25 November the Soviet Union got another shock when the free elections in Austria gave the communists there a scant 5 per cent. The Austrian socialists polled almost 50 per cent and so of course the Russians in Berlin began looking at the S.P.D. with different eyes."

"Did they start putting pressure on you?"

"Both the Soviets and the local K.P.D. began demanding the merger of the S.P.D. with the K.P.D., as well they might."

"How did the S.P.D. react to the demand? Were you unified in opposing it?" I asked.

"Oh, yes, even Grotewohl opposed it at first, but the Russians called him again and again to their headquarters at Karlshorst. God knows what they threatened or promised, but he finally capitulated and endorsed the merger in the name of the entire S.P.D."

"How did you and your friends react?" I asked.

"Oh, the county leaders in West Berlin refused to accept the decision. We simply said no, but in East Berlin and throughout the Soviet Zone, any socialist who refused to go along was branded as subversive and was subjected to investigation by the N.K.V.D. Many prominent socialists were arrested, and some simply disappeared; others were harassed and pressured into accepting the merger."

"What about the West German socialists? How did they react?"

"Early in February 1946 Grotewohl traveled to Braunschweig in West Germany to meet with Kurt Schumacher, the S.P.D. leader in the Western zones. Schumacher was a fiery and uncompromising champion of freedom."

"He had had some pretty fierce encounters with dictatorship," I said.

"Yes," the leader said and nodded gravely. "He was almost one of our martyrs."

"I remember seeing him at a meeting in about 1947. He still looked almost emaciated. You could still see traces of what he had been through in the K.Z."

"He was one of our greats," the leader said, "intense, intolerant, and not an easy man to work with, but brilliant and incorruptible. Naturally he vigorously opposed any merger with the communists, especially under pressure. He argued and persuaded, but Grotewohl, although he listened respectfully, could not agree. On the eleventh of February, just after this meeting, the Soviet Zone S.P.D. announced that it would merge with the K.P.D. to form the S.E.D., the Socialist Unity Party, by 1 May."

"That meant the split of the S.P.D. in Germany, but did the Berlin party split too?" I asked.

"Not right away and not without a fight," he said. "We were organized according to boroughs so that there were twelve western and eight eastern suborganizations, county organizations if you like, but the overall Berlin S.P.D. still functioned as a single party under a unified central committee. Despite Grotewohl's decision for the Zone, we Berlin socialists, East as well as West Berliners, decided to make a fight of it."

"Could you?" I asked. "Could they?"

"We tried, but even organizing a political fight wasn't a simple matter in the Berlin of 1946. Imagine the conditions. It was winter, one of the coldest winters northern Europe had ever experienced. There were almost no private automobiles left in the city. A few of us had cars that were still functioning, but it was often impossible to get gasoline. If a car broke down, and it often did in that cold weather, it was difficult to get spare parts. Public transportation was still erratic. Miles of tram lines had been torn up by the bombing; there was a shortage of cars, of spare parts, of drivers. The subway was as bad. I often had to wait half an hour or more for a tram or train, and once I was on board, service was likely to be interrupted by a power failure or because we had come to an unrepaired section of track. Just getting from one borough to another was a major undertaking, and getting from one end of Berlin to the other was a pilgrimage, especially in the ice and snow."

"And no telephones, I suppose?" I asked.

"Very few," he said. "Telephone service hadn't been fully restored. I was one of the few county leaders who still had a functioning telephone, probably because I live out here in a suburb where the bombing had been comparatively light. I often spent whole nights until dawn just trying to reach people by telephone."

"How did you reach other leaders or clubs without telephones?"

"We worked out a system. A shop or restaurant or pub would take messages. That is, they would if their telephones happened to be working," he explained.

"Frustrating?" I asked.

"Sometimes downright impossible. It often boiled down to walking, to tramping on foot in the snow from one house to another organizing opinion and votes."

"Had you got back your club houses and meeting halls after the nazi collapse or had they all been bombed out?" I asked.

"Most of them," he said, "especially those in midtown, but we met in offices or lofts or in each other's houses. You should have seen some of those meetings—four, five, or ten of us huddled together in thick coats or crowded around a coke stove drinking schnapps or *ersatz* coffee to try to keep warm. We were all cold and hungry most of the time."

I said, "Nine hundred calories a day, I remember."

"We had disagreements among ourselves, too," he said.

"Not about whether to join the S.E.D.?" I asked.

"No, but about the methods to use to keep from being absorbed. Do you remember Franz Neumann? He was the leader of a powerful and well-knit borough organization, and he was a clever politician, but he believed that we could resist the Russians by using conventional political methods."

"How?" I asked.

"By normal electioneering and by a plebiscite of the S.P.D. membership. He didn't realize the extent to which the Russians were able to put pressure on our S.P.D. Central Committee or the implication of the fact that it would be the Central Committee which would supervise and tally the poll. At that time no official county meeting could be held unless a representative of the Central Committee was present, and it was usually a Soviet-controlled committeeman who turned up. Under conditions like that, you can guess what the results of any election would be."

"How could you fight against those conditions?" I asked.

"Early in March 1946 five of us formed an action committee. We decided that since we were in a revolutionary situation we would need to use extraordinary methods. We knew that as Germans we had very little chance of resisting the Russians, but we hoped that we might enlist the support of the Western occupation authorities, especially the British. If you remember, at that time the British had a labor government. We hoped that they might look on us social democrats as comrades and support us against the communists."

"Were you able to convince them?" I asked. I remembered clearly that at that time official Allied policy still forbade military government officials to support any action which implied criticism of our Soviet ally.

"Well, we knew that to many Anglo-Saxons all Germans, even socialists, were suspect. We were still the defeated enemy, the Russians were still the glorious ally. Gradually, though, some of us had become acquainted with individual American and English officials who were more sympathetic, some because they were aware of the Soviet threat, others because they were partisans of freedom, and some who just liked us as individuals."

"The rule was still nonfraternization, wasn't it?" I asked.

"Yes," he said, "and the British were especially scrupulous, but nevertheless we began approaching individual officers. We realized that top-echelon people would not be able to help us, certainly not openly, so we concentrated on the middle level, and we were fortunate in finding several very staunch, if discreet, champions. These men risked their careers in violating their countries' official policy, but they were convinced that they were acting in their own national interest."

"How did they help?" I asked.

"Well, one British officer supplied us with equipment that we Germans simply couldn't get in those days, especially paper and cardboard for leaflets, letters, and posters. Another helped us arrange for a free vote of our membership without the supervision of our Soviet-controlled Central Committee."

"Did any Americans help?" I asked.

"It was a little harder to enlist the Americans at first. They were still influenced by their unconditional surrender theory and by the illusion of a four-power alliance, but gradually many individual Americans came to see that the Berlin socialists were fighting for their freedom and for the city's freedom, and many of them began to sympathize and eventually to support us. I believe that it was because many of these British and American military government officials had learned to admire our determination to resist Soviet pressure that they later decided to resist the Soviet blockade and to influence their governments to resist. If they had not by then been convinced of our dedication and stubbornness they might very well have allowed the Russians to take all of Berlin by default."

"You haven't mentioned the French," I said. "Were they involved in your struggle?"

"Not at first," he said. "I think they were the most sceptical in the early phase, but as the aims of Soviet policy became clearer, French policy toughened. M. Schumann began to exert greater influence in Paris, and he worked together with Konrad Adenauer to build a Franco-German entente. Naturally, this changed the atmosphere in Berlin. French military government officials became more friendly and more co-operative."

"How did the Russians react to all this? Were they aware of your activities?" I asked.

"Oh, yes," he said. "The city wasn't divided as it is now. Not only could we Berliners travel back and forth from one sector to another, but the occupation forces could too. Soviet jeeps and command cars drove through Western sector streets, Soviet officers attended receptions and had lunch in Western officers' clubs. They were well informed, and, of course, they harassed us. One of our five action-committee members was kidnapped. Those were the days when people simply disappeared. He never reappeared."

"You never found out what happened to him?" I asked.

He shook his head. "Not to this day. Naturally, they hoped to intimidate the remaining four, but we kept on fighting."

"When did you hold the election?"

"In March, and you can imagine that we had been campaigning day and night for weeks before. We voted by borough. The membership of the twelve Western boroughs voted 19,529 against, 2,937 for merger with the K.P.D. The East Berlin S.P.D. merged."

"Were you overjoyed?" I asked.

"We were jubilant, and we were greatly encouraged. We had learned that the Russians could be resisted, that we did not have to be swallowed up by communism, that if we dug in and resisted, we could find support among the Allies, and that there was hope for our city."

"There was still a long struggle ahead," I said. "That was only March 1946."

"Yes, indeed," he said. "By the way, would you like some coffee? I really must apologize for forgetting it. If my wife were here, she would have seen to it, but as you know, she is travelling with our daughter in the Alps. I'm afraid I get so absorbed in discussion that I forget my duties as a host, but my housekeeper will be glad to bring some coffee."

I thanked him and said I would welcome coffee and he got up and called to the plump Frau G. who had admitted me.

"The next battle was in October of that year when city-wide elections for municipal government were held. To no one's surprise by then, the communists were badly mauled. The total vote in all four sectors gave us socialists 48.7 per cent, the C.D.U. 22.2 per cent, the new S.E.D. only 19.9

per cent, and the L.P.D. 9.3 per cent. That represented an 80 per cent anti-Soviet, anticommunist vote, quite a slap in the face."

"How did the Russians react to the defeat?" I asked.

"The Cold War began to chill," he said. "The Soviet line was that former nazis were stirring up anticommunist and anti-Soviet opinion in West Berlin, leading West Berliners astray. The Soviet Zone Commander issued an order forbidding Soviet citizens, especially the wives of officials and of army personnel, from visiting West Berlin except in the line of duty."

"They were afraid they would be led astray too?" I asked.

"Corrupted," he said. "Of course, the world press was beginning by then to talk about a Berlin problem, and very slowly Berlin and Berliners were beginning to receive the first good press any Germans had enjoyed in the free world since the war, perhaps since 1933. English and American newspapers began to refer to Berliners with sympathy, even with admiration."

"And you think this led to increased co-operation between the Western Allies and West Berliners?" I asked.

"I am convinced of it. The entire situation was leading up to the blockade. Berlin became more and more a thorn in the Soviet flesh, and I think the Russians believed that they could take over the city without any serious resistance from the Western Allies. They may even have thought that the West would be grateful for an opportunity to withdraw from an untenable position. After all, when the blockade began there were only 1,500 French, 2,000 British, and 3,000 American troops in Berlin, a pitiful handful compared to the 300,000 Red Army troops stationed in and around the city. I am sure the Russians expected the West to withdraw gracefully and that they were both startled and chagrined when they were confronted with the airlift."

"Quite possibly," I said. "And you think that knowing they could count on the moral stamina of Berliners was at least one factor in the Western decision to resist, to defend the city?"

"Don't you, Frau Doctor? You were here with Military Government when the blockade began."

"I was a very young, inexperienced analyst," I said, "but I do think so, and I think General Clay and General Howley have both indicated as much."

The door leading to the corridor swung open, and Frau G. came in bearing the tray with coffee and demitasses.

"Thank you, Gerda," the leader said. She smiled and left us while he poured the strong coffee.

"More Grand Marnier?" he asked, brandishing the bottle. "You are not driving," he added.

"No," I said, "but I am dieting."

He laughed and said, "You Americans! Even your men are always dieting, but, of course, nowadays German women diet too, especially the younger ones."

"American influence," I said.

He nodded. "Yes, probably, but you are not going to persuade me to complain about American influence in Berlin! I am grateful to the Americans. Most Berliners are, but especially those of us who dug in our toes and fought and refused to give in to the Russians during those early years. Obviously we could not have succeeded for long without American support."

"British too," I said.

"Of course. We are still deeply aware of the Allied sacrifices in the airlift. Forty Royal Air Force and thirty-one United States Air Force men lost their lives in that operation. We haven't forgotten."

"You older Berliners who remember the postwar struggle and the blockade feel that way, but how about younger Berliners? Isn't there growing anti-American sentiment?"

"You mean because of the Vietnam War and the student anti-American protests? No. I think that America still has her staunchest friends in Europe in Berlin. The great majority of West Berliners have faith in America and above all remain grateful. They may be uncertain about the wisdom of the American involvement in Southeast Asia, but they are in no doubt about the commitment of the United States to freedom.

"You know that in Germany it is the custom that streets are named only after people who have died, never after living persons, but we renamed the Crown Prince Allee 'Clay Allee' in gratitude and affection. When General Clay visited Berlin in 1959 the Berliners greeted him tumultuously; they love the man. Quite a tribute for a former occupation commander, don't you think?"

"General Clay also has a great affection for Berlin and for Berliners," I said. "He himself said that he came here as an enemy, but he left as a friend."

"A very good friend," the leader said. "I think that it is very natural that Americans and Berliners should have become friends. We have a lot in common. We are both relaxed and informal and hate stuffiness. We both have a sense of humor. Most of the Americans I know love Berlin, do you agree?"

"I've never known an American who has lived here who doesn't love Berlin. We all come back whenever we can," I said.

"Yes," he said. "Berlin has something special, something unique. West Berlin is still not safe. We still have to go on fighting for our independence, for our freedom, but so far we have held on. With your help and with luck, I have confidence that we shall keep holding on."

8

Waltraud

Whenever I am in Berlin I find that I spend a lot of time at the Schöneberg *Rathaus,* now the central city hall of West Berlin. I feel quite at home climbing the broad steps to the entrance, greeting my old friend, the information clerk, in his little booth, clattering along the stone, high-ceilinged corridor, and bravely leaping on board the rickety *Paternoster.* On one of my recent visits, I held my breath and jumped carefully, easing myself out at the second floor, and I almost collided with a small, neat man in brown carrying an immense briefcase. He smiled and bowed, probably used to the minor social contretemps inherent in the use of a *Paternoster.* I smiled and apologized as he was swallowed by the clanking monster.

I looked up at the room numbers posted in the corridor and found that the room I sought was two corridors away. As I hurried down the dingy hall, I looked at my watch. My appointment with Waltraud was for two, and I would be exactly on time. I came to the room and noticed that the sign on the door read, "Frau Waltraud X, Member for Schöneberg, House of Representatives (S.P.D.)" and under that, "Fräulein W., Secretary." I knocked and was admitted by a small, smiling blond girl of about twenty.

"Frau Doctor?" she asked, and I nodded. "Frau X will be here any minute. Would you like to go into her office and wait?"

She led me through a small anteroom in which the desk and shelves were piled high with folders and papers into an inner room only slightly larger, just a little more comfortably furnished. She indicated a straight-backed wooden chair facing the plain wooden desk. She offered me a cigarette.

"I can bring you a magazine," she suggested, but I said that I had brought along a book. "She will be here any minute," she assured me.

I lit the cigarette I had accepted and settled down to read a paperback,

92

Fig. 8. The *Rathaus* at Schöneberg, showing the market in the square (photo by Landes-bildstelle, West Berlin)

but within a few minutes I heard the outer door open and close. A few
sentences were exchanged by feminine voices, and then Waltraud burst
into her office. She was carrying a net bag bulging with oranges and
tomatoes, an unwrapped loaf of bread, and assorted jars and bottles. She
tossed the bag onto a rather shabby leather couch and held out her
hand to me.

"Do please forgive me for being late!" she said. "Today one of my
committee meetings ran late, so I didn't get away in time, and I have to
do all my shopping during lunch hour. Wouldn't you know there'd be a
long line at the check-out counter? And then the rathskeller was crowded,
and I had to wait to be served, and, on the way back here, I met at
least three people who simply had to ask me questions. Some days are
like that! I'm really sorry to keep you waiting."

I told her that it had been a very few minutes and I had been glad
of a little rest between appointments. One of the oranges rolled out of
the net and onto the floor. She stooped to retrieve it.

"Not very dignified for a legislator," she said with a grin pointing
to the bag, "but very Prussian and typical for Berlin politicians. We
pride ourselves on our simplicity, on living just like ordinary citizens.
I have exactly one hour for lunch just like any other working woman,
and, of course, I do my own shopping and cooking and cleaning."

Waltraud is a slight, small-boned woman. She wears her dark hair
short, with crisp curls falling casually around her face. She has deep-set
dark eyes with prominent brows and lashes and an air of concentration
and purpose.

"Well, now, what do you want to know about me? My work in the
House of Representatives, in the socialist party, or my job in the civil
service?" she asked.

"I want to know a little about everything," I said, "about you as a
person, too, but first, perhaps we could talk about the legislature. What
would we call it in English, a house of representatives?"

"It's *Abgeordnetenhaus* in German. I guess you would translate that
as House of Representatives or House of Delegates. It is also a *Landtag*,
a state legislature, because Berlin is a *Land* or state in the Federal Republic, as you know."

"Yes," I said. "I know that the city government is also a *Land* government. How many representatives are there, and how long is your term?"

"There are 137 representatives," she said, "and we are elected for a
four-year term. Before 1958, representatives were elected on the basis of
proportional representation, but now each of us is elected by simple majority to represent geographical districts. You know that there are twelve

boroughs in West Berlin. Well, each borough is divided into districts according to its population. Schöneberg, for example, has seven districts, one of which I represent."

I asked about her work in the House of Representatives. "Does it take most of your time?"

"A lot of it," she replied. "The full House meets only twice a month unless we're especially busy, but each member usually serves on three committees, and these meet more frequently. One of my committees meets three times a week, one once a week, and the other only once a month. We have homework to do too, of course."

"Reading bills?" I asked.

"Yes, and studying testimony from the hearings or reading background reports on proposed legislation. I also have to keep up with newspaper editorials and letters from constituents on the bills under consideration."

"Do you have to serve your constituents directly, too?"

She nodded. "That is one of the advantages to the voter of the single-member district. Each citizen has an individual who represents him specifically, someone he has elected, someone responsible for and to him. When he has problems or complaints, he expects to see his representative, and rightly so. I spend several hours a week talking with constituents and many more answering their letters."

"You hold an office in the House, don't you?" I asked.

She nodded. "Yes, right after an election, the new House elects a presidium, which includes a president from the majority party, two vice presidents, one from each minority party, and four secretaries apportioned according to the strength of each party in the house. I am one of the S.P.D. secretaries."

"That means extra work, I suppose."

"Some," she said. "The presidium of ten meets between House sessions. It represents the House at official functions, such as receiving foreign dignitaries. Occasionally we travel abroad or to the Federal Republic as representatives of the Berlin government, and as individuals most of us are invited to lecture about Berlin politics both here in the city and in West Germany. It keeps us pretty busy."

"How is the Senate chosen?" I asked.

Waltraud explained: "Our Senate isn't a legislature. It is an administrative or executive body rather like a cabinet. It is composed of the mayors of each of the twelve boroughs plus a number of senators who are elected by the House of Representatives. The constitution allows up to sixteen elected senators. At present [1969], there are nine."

"Nine elected by the House, plus twelve mayors?" I asked.

"Yes. You see, each of the nine heads a department, such as justice, education, housing, and so on. The police president, for instance, comes under the jurisdiction of the senator for the interior."

"I see," I said. "Since these senators are elected indirectly, how does the public express approval or disapproval of their administration?"

"Oh, our Berliners make themselves heard!" she said. "They write letters both to the press and to the Senate, and, of course, they put pressure on us, the House of Representatives, since we are directly elected and are ultimately responsible for the actions and the acceptability of the Senate."

"Of course," I said. "What about your elections? Are your campaigns as exciting and as exhausting as ours?"

"Our elections get more American every time around. Unlike you, we limit the length of a campaign to about six weeks, and we strictly limit the amount of money spent, but we are gradually adopting most of the American advertising techniques. Our candidates stand on street corners and shake hands with men and women on their way to work. Workers hand out buttons and party literature. They ring doorbells and telephone registered voters. The party organizes rallies, hires sound trucks, and sticks up posters all over the district. The climax of the campaign is a city-wide rally where all the party's candidates appear and the candidate for Governing Mayor makes his final speech."

"Do Berlin citizens have as much fun with their political campaigns as Americans do?" I asked.

"Well," she said, considering my question, "perhaps there's not quite as much show business about our campaigns. I think in general we Berliners have more sense of humor than West Germans, but even we still like our politicans to be serious and dignified, so our campaigns can't be quite as light-hearted as yours, but we have definitely adopted the American view that candidates must create an image."

"Sad," I said, and she agreed. "Do average Berliners volunteer for campaign work and do they come out to the rallies?"

"We don't have anything like the number of woman workers you do," she said. "I wish we did, both because we need more volunteers and because I should like our German women to take more interest in politics, play a more active role."

"They think politics is undignified?" I asked.

"Some of them think it's dirty; others are just lazy, or perhaps I should say passive. We have a harder time than you getting citizens to help out during the campaign. Our campaign workers are usually the party regulars. On the other hand, a very high percentage of citizens come out to vote. Usually about eighty-six per cent of the eligible voters actually vote, and I think that is much higher than your average." *

I admitted that it was. "As a party leader you must be busy with party politics between campaigns as well," I suggested. "Do you hold a party office? Are you a member of a local club?"

She nodded. "In the S.P.D. one gets into politics through the local clubs. In Schöneberg, for instance, there are twelve socialist clubs, one in each electoral district."

"Exactly like New York." I said. "There they have assembly district clubs."

She said, "I suppose that is logical. Our club in Schöneberg meets once a month. We have about three hundred members who pay dues, but on the average, only about thirty or forty members turn up for regular meetings. When we have a famous speaker or some kind of a celebration, we may get up to eighty to attend, and, of course, just before election, more will come."

I said that was exactly like the American political clubs I was familiar with. I asked whether she was an officer of her local club and she shook her head.

"Not now, I haven't the time. I used to be the secretary and then vice president until I ran for the House of Representatives, but now I just serve on a few commitees. I'm still very active, but I find that I must squeeze in club work between other duties, so I'm careful not to take on too much."

I asked whether she always attended meetings.

"Oh yes. The local club is my grass-roots support." She added, "Not that just being a delegate to the *Land* House of Representatives isn't grass roots in itself. But I mean I have to keep close to my local organization. I get speakers for them, help plan their rallies, sometimes meet with the youth group or take groups on tours of the *Rathaus,* that sort of thing. My main job, though, is to help the treasurer in collecting the dues."

"Strategic," I said, and she grinned.

"It has always been a tradition in the German socialist party that

* In the election of 12 March 1967, of 1,718,400 registered voters, 1,481,700 voted with the following results:
S.P.D.—57% (81 seats); C.D.U.—33% (47 seats); F.D.P. (Free Democratic Party)—7% (9 seats)

In the election of 14 March 1971, which occurred after the interview, of 1,654,658 registered voters, 1,470,281 voted with the following results:
S.P.D.—50.4% (73 seats) ; C.D.U.—38.2% (54 seats) ; F.D.P.—8.5% (11 seats)

each member pays dues each month according to his income. Each member has a dues book and, when he pays, he gets a stamp. People with low incomes, some retired people, for instance, pay as little as one mark a month, and people who earn more pay up to thirty marks a month. Each member decides for himself how much he will pay per month."

"Like a church," I suggested.

She nodded, interested. "Yes, I suppose that comes from the days when socialism and trade unionism were rather like the working man's religion, perhaps like a secret lodge or fraternity. The S.P.D. has always been more than just a political party."

I asked whether she had grown up in socialist politics, whether her father had been a trade unionist.

"No. Quite the opposite," she said. "My parents were the sort of Germans who think of politics as indecent. My father is a Catholic, and I was brought up a Catholic. You probably know that there was always hostility between the Catholic Church and the S.P.D. To this day my father cannot reconcile himself to having a socialist daughter. Before the First World War no devout Catholic would join the S.P.D., and even in Weimar days being a socialist was almost as bad for a Catholic as being a communist. On their part most dedicated socialists regarded the Church of Rome as a bastion of reaction and as their political enemy."

"Did you remain a Catholic after you joined the party?" I asked.

"Yes. You see I joined after 1945, and by then the atmosphere had changed. I think it is still true that a 'good Catholic' does not join the S.P.D., still less become a socialist candidate, and so I guess I am not a good Catholic, but I am a Catholic. There is still some tension between our party leadership and the Roman hierarchy. After all, in the Catholic *Länder* the C.D.U. is their party and we are the opposition. We are political rivals."

"But there is no longer the anti-Christian sentiment of more doctrinaire times, is there?" I asked.

"No, Willy Brandt and his family are good Lutherans, and I should say that many, even most of our younger party members, now consider themselves Christians, but they are Protestants. Many prominent socialists are active in the Protestant Church. They serve on committees, participate in Church conventions, and so on. Certainly the S.P.D. is no longer antireligious, but my poor father cannot be reconciled. He has learned to accept the fact of my independence, to accept my decision, but he cannot like it."

"But surely your parents must be proud of you too?" I asked.

She shrugged. "A little perhaps, but, as I said, they don't have a high regard for politics or politicians, and as for female politicians! Well, in a way, I suppose they are a little proud of me. After all, we come from a very simple background, and I never had any formal education. I suppose they must think I have accomplished a little something."

"Are your parents Berliners?" I asked.

"No, both of them came from small villages, my mother from Silesia, my father from East Prussia. Neither had more than a sketchy education. My father never learned a craft. They were married just after the First World War and, like most Germans, they lost their small savings during the inflation of the 1920s. When I was a child, I remember that my father was out of work more often than not. All the years I was at school my mother worked as a concierge in a shabby old apartment house. I guess you'd call it a slum tenement. It was one of those grim, dingy buildings with the single toilet in the courtyard and only cold water and, of course, no central heating. As part of my mother's wages we were allowed a small flat in the basement, just one room and a small kitchen. No bath, of course."

"Were you the only child?" I asked.

She nodded. "Strange, too in those days. Most of my schoolmates had brothers and sisters. I never knew why there weren't more children. My mother isn't the kind of woman to talk about anything like that even now, not to anyone, last of all to me."

"Did you mind?" I asked, knowing the question was perhaps too personal.

"A little. I was lonely as a child. I am often lonely still, but one gets used to loneliness. That may be one reason why I never married."

"Very possibly. One learns to enjoy being alone."

"There are many women alone in Berlin, especially those of us over forty," she said. "I suppose because I was alone a lot, I became quieter and more serious than most children. I read a lot, and I hoped to be able to go on to the university, but, of course, we couldn't afford that even though, when the war began in 1939 and most of the younger men were drafted, my father found it easier to get work. The post office needed clerks so badly that they had to lower their educational qualifications. My father took the examination, was accepted, and began a whole new career at forty-five. He never made much money, but with the post office he had a secure income and a little status, and now he has his pension."

"But there still wasn't enough money for you to get a formal education?" I asked.

"No. He had to start at the bottom rung, of course. I couldn't even finish my *Abitur*. I took the examination for an intermediate diploma in 1942 and immediately got a job as a clerk with the *Autobahn* administration. I worked in one or another *Autobahn* office all over Germany until the end of the war. When the war ended I happened to be in Frankfort on the Oder, in what became part of the Soviet Zone."

"Did you have any trouble getting back to Berlin?" I asked.

"Not really. I was young and a woman, and my parents lived in Berlin, so I was allowed to return to them. The Soviets were interested in male labor, not so much in fragile female clerks."

"Had your parents been bombed out or evacuated during the war?" I asked.

"Luckily, no. There had been some bombing in the neighborhood, but our street got only a few bombs. Our house was just slightly damaged. It was a cramped and dismal flat to return to, but in 1945 I was grateful even for that. I found my mother living alone. My father, although he was overage for regular army service, had been in the Home Army and was called up during the last months of the war. It was just his luck to be taken prisoner. He was in a Red Army P.O.W. camp for several months, but the Soviets decided he was too old or too frail for labor camp in the U.S.S.R., and so they released him and let him come home to Berlin. He got back in October 1945. He looked pretty awful, thin and ragged, but he was able to go right back to work at the post office. They needed people desperately because there simply were no men in Berlin in 1945."

"Were you able to go back to work?" I asked.

"I worked as one of the *Trümmer Frauen,* the rubble women, for three months when I first got back. That was hard, dirty work, and depressing too, because we seemed to make no headway among all the miles and miles of rubble! And you should have seen my hands and my nails and my hair after a day's work! We had almost no soap and certainly no hot water. Each night I used to scrub and scrub with an old, worn-out brush trying to get my hands clean. I think 1 looked ten years older than my age after those few months. Some women kept on for years."

I told her that I remember the *Trümmer Frauen* from my first glimpse of Berlin in 1947. "There were still miles and tons of rubble then," I said.

"I was one of the lucky ones. In August 1945, I was able to get a job here in the Schöneberg City Hall, and I have been here ever since."

Looking at the trim, immaculately groomed professional woman sitting rather primly behind her desk, it was impossible to imagine the shabby, underfed, grubby *Trümmer Frau,* probably in shapeless black with a grimy black kerchief protecting her hair.

"Was your new job part of the city's civil service?" I asked.

"Yes," she said. "They transferred my rating from the national to the city civil service. I am not what we call a *Beamter,* an official. I don't have the education to qualify for that. With just a middle-level secondary education I could enter only the lowest ranks of the service as a clerk, but here in Berlin the city offers late afternoon classes twice a week which employees can attend to qualify for advancement. I registered right away, took the courses for three years, and then was accepted into the middle ranks—I suppose you would say the managerial level. I work in the personnel office."

"But you are still not an official?" I asked.

"No," she said. "Most officials have a university education. What I have earned by my afternoon classes and working experience puts me about on the level of people with an *Abitur.* I am grateful for that much!"

"Did your promotion make a difference in your life? Could you move from the basement flat?"

"Not right away. In the first place, there wasn't any place to move to! There just weren't enough apartments in Berlin, and there were so many people whose need was much greater than ours, people whose apartments were badly damaged or who had to live with relatives. We at least had a flat. In the second place, my salary as a city employee was very modest so we couldn't afford anything lavish, but as soon as I began work here, we did put our name on the list. Finally in 1950 we found an apartment, and I was so grateful because at last my poor mother could give up her job as concierge."

"Was the apartment in a new building?"

"Not new but newer. It was a prewar building that had been slightly damaged and restored. It was still far from luxurious, but it was more cheerful and at least had a bathroom and hot water and central heating. It has a nice big balcony, too. My parents still live there. They have modernized the kitchen and bath and made it very comfortable."

"You don't live with them?"

"No, when I became active in politics I decided to get a place of my own, and by then it was possible to find a small apartment in a new building."

"I suppose you wanted to be closer to the *Rathaus?*"

"That too," she said. "I can walk on good days or take the bus right in front of my door. My apartment is small, and the rooms are much smaller than in older houses, but everything is modern and efficient. I have a lot of books and records and my all-important telephone.

"It's one of the reasons I live alone. The telephone is likely to ring any time of the day or night, and in an emergency, I may have to start calling people even very late at night."

"Of course," I said. "You said before that you do your own cooking and cleaning. Do you like to cook?"

"I know one is supposed to say yes, but, honestly, I am usually too tired to enjoy it! By the time I get home I am too tired to be interested in eating, and so I make myself something very light and very simple like a salad and a can of soup or some scrambled eggs, and then I take a book and some fruit and stretch out in bed."

"Do you go out often in the evenings?" I asked.

"Not often," she said. "Sometimes I have to go to meetings or conferences, of course, and once in a while I go to the theater or to a film or concert with a woman friend, but usually I am too tired, and, frankly, I guess I am rather aloof."

"You are probably absorbed in your work," I ventured.

"I am that, but a single woman living in a city tends to become isolated, I think. Like many city people I don't even know who my neighbors are. If we meet in the elevator or the hall, we say hello and that's that. I go home to eat, read and sleep and then leave early the next morning. Weekends I usually visit my parents, so naturally I never get acquainted with any neighbors."

"Do you have close friends at work?" I asked.

"Not really," she said. "Again, maybe it is because I have too many different jobs. I divide my time between my civil service job, my work as a representative, and my party functions. Don't misunderstand me. My colleagues are all friendly enough, but we all tend to be rather formal and reserved. I keep my distance because I am afraid they might misunderstand any attempt at intimacy."

"You mean male colleagues?"

"Chiefly male colleagues. Most of them are married, of course. You know that there are very few men in Berlin in my age group, and those who exist are nearly certain to be married. I have grown used to that. I suppose I regret that I never married, but, on the other hand, I have an interesting life. I think my work is useful, and my life isn't all work either."

"Do you have hobbies?" I asked.

"When I have time for them," she said. "I belong to a tennis club, but I rarely get a chance to play. I like music and the theater, but again I almost never get to a play or concert. But I do read, and I like to travel. I am entitled to four weeks' vacation a year, and even though I cannot spare the time all at once, I do manage to take two, sometimes three, weeks, and I see to it that I get out of the country at least once a year, sometimes professionally. I've visited London and Paris and Vienna quite often, and I've been to Switzerland for skiing several winters. Once in a while I go to Italy just to get some sun and to relax. My life is lonely and a bit strenuous, but it is not dull."

"Do you find the time to go shopping or get your hair done?" I asked, noting that her hair was smartly cut, her beige and white knit dress attractive if a little severe.

She sighed. "A public official should look at least neat and respectable," she said, "but I am lucky if I find time to go to the hairdresser once a month. Normally I wash my hair myself, just as I do my own laundry and take my clothes to be cleaned in one of those automatic places. Shopping I have to do lunch hours or Saturday, and I am always in a rush, but I have one or two favorite shops where the saleswomen know my taste. They put aside dresses they think will suit me, and that saves a lot of time."

I told her that I liked her dress and she said, "I prefer tailored, simple clothes and plain colors. I have small bones and fortunately have stayed slim—I suppose because I am always rushing around, so I am easy to fit. I like clothes, you know. I wish I had more time to think about them!

"You know I live in a country in which formal education is very important. I am deeply conscious of my lack of education. There are very few of my colleagues who do not at least have the *Abitur,* and a great many have doctorates. I hate feeling inadequate, perhaps especially because I am a woman, and so I read all the time. I always have a book with me. Just now I am plowing through Suetonius. Don't laugh! He is interesting."

"No," I said, "I admire you, but Suetonius after a hard day rushing from meeting to meeting? Don't you find that kind of reading strenuous? When I'm exhausted I read mysteries."

"I do too, sometimes," she confessed. "I also admit that I often fall asleep after the first few pages, but I am determined to keep growing, to keep learning. Besides, I enjoy the challenge."

I asked how she happened to become interested in politics, coming from a nonpolitical family.

"I'm not really sure," she said, "except that there were one or two

people in my office at the *Rathaus* who were active in the S.P.D. I used
to have lunch with them from time to time, and they convinced me that
if everyone thought as my parents did, that is that politics is dirty and
honest people should avoid it, then we could never have a successful
democracy in Germany. It's true. If decent, average citizens won't take
up the burden of self-government, we would be asking for another
Hitler. Don't you agree?"

"Oh, entirely," I said, "but then I grew up in politics, so it is natural
for me to feel that way."

"You're right," she said, puzzling. "It was not natural for me. I suppose
in 1945 the consequences of the flight from political responsibility of
people like my parents were too obvious, too tragic. Besides, I liked some
of the young politicians I met, and I soon became absorbed in party
activities. In a political club, there is always work for willing hands."

"That's true. No one stays lonely who is a good worker."

"I soon found that out. My local club supplied plenty of work to fill up
empty evenings and weekends. I soon found myself promoted from
envelope-stuffing to serving on committees and collecting dues. I discovered that I was honestly fascinated by political issues, especially by
questions like public health, taxation and budgeting. I began to read
everything I could get my hands on, and gradually my friends in the
party began to take me and my views seriously, not only because I was a
worker but because I read."

"They would," I said. "How soon did they ask you to run for office?"

"Well, let's see. They made me a candidate for the House of Representatives in 1958. By then I had been a party member for twelve years.
I was lucky enough to be elected the first time around. I guess I come
from a safe district!"

"Twelve years of hard work! You deserved it," I said. "Do you have
trouble recruiting young people in the socialist party nowadays?"

"A lot of young men and women join when they are students," she
said, "but we find that when they begin to be active in their professions,
especially if they are successful, they have less and less time for politics
and gradually drop out. That means we are often left with the less
ambitious, the less able."

"The hacks," I said, and I said that in the States we very often experience the same thing.

"Also when they marry and acquire family responsibilities they can
no longer afford to give time to the party. Naturally this is especially
true of women, whom we often lose entirely after the first or second
baby."

"Don't they return when their children reach school age?" I asked. "Ours often do."

She shook her head. "Not many, not yet. German women are still too much bound by the image of the *Hausfrau*. It is hard to get wives and mothers to devote time to interests outside their homes. Only the really dedicated will do it, and there are very few of those, so the party usually must make do with old maids like me."

I said something polite and deprecatory. I asked what professions most of the political leaders followed, and she said that in the S.P.D. most were civil servants, lawyers or trade unionists.

"In the C.D.U. you find engineers and businessmen and an occasional clergyman. But I should say that lawyers predominate in both parties."

"In ours too," I said. I asked whether she had been tempted to give up her civil-service status and become a full-time, professional political functionary.

"I have been asked several times whether I would like to do that, but I enjoy my job, and besides I like to keep my independence. In the civil service, if I ever found I could not get along with some individual department head, I could ask to be transferred to another department. In the party it would be more difficult. I also like to keep my intellectual independence as a legislator. Having a job to fall back on gives me a great deal more freedom to have and to voice my own opinions."

I said that I could see that. "Do the borough governments have much autonomy?" I asked.

"Quite a bit," she said. "Each borough has its own department of youth, health, education, social welfare and so on and is relatively autonomous in these fields. We like to keep public services close to the people, and we also try to get private citizens to participate in their local governments."

In answer to my "How?" she explained that much of the planning and supervision of the borough departments is accomplished through committees, which include six members of the district assembly and seven private citizens on each committee.

"The citizens must be of voting age and should have special experience in the area in which the committee works. For example, on the education committee we have teachers, professors of education, and parents, and on the health committee, doctors, hospital administrators or nurses."

"What do these committees do?" I asked.

"They supervise the administration of the related department, help plan the budget for the coming year and look into complaints and inquiries by citizens about the operation of their departments. For example, if a patient is dissatisfied with treatment in a hospital or at a public health clinic, he would complain to the health committee."

"It keeps the civil servants on their toes," I suggested.

"It does. It is also another of the checks and balances which keep our civil service from becoming corrupt. Complete public scrutiny of most administrative decisions allows no room for bribes or favoritism."

"You are still very correct and very Prussian about the purity of the civil service, aren't you?" I asked.

"Very strict," she agreed, "and we should be. You probably know that in Berlin it is strictly forbidden for civil servants to accept any kind of gift from an individual or business firm. There is only one exception. At Christmas business firms are allowed to give inexpensive gifts like pencils or calendars, but they must give them to the departments not to individuals. If any one office gets too many calendars or appointment books, they contribute the surplus to a collection, which is then given to old people's homes or orphanages."

"Prussian indeed!" I said.

"It's wrong," she insisted, "to think that Prussian strictness or correctness is authoritarian or undemocratic. I think it is the opposite. Only when the individual members of government practice restraint and self-discipline and when the private citizen demands that they do so can free government operate."

I said that I agreed with her, that I thought public surveillance and participation excellent.

"Would you like some more coffee?" she asked. "I have to attend a meeting in about forty minutes, but we could go down and have some coffee first. I had a very quick, rather skimpy lunch, and my meeting is likely to run late, so I could use a snack now."

By then I had taken so many notes that I needed a break, and so I readily agreed to a coffee expedition. Waltraud hunted through the papers on her desk and extricated a folder. She left instructions with Fräulein W., and we walked toward the staircase.

"I'd rather walk down, wouldn't you?" she asked, so I told her about my constant problems with the *Paternoster*. "Awful thing!" she admitted.

"We are lucky that this Schöneberg Borough Hall is so large," she said. "I suppose if we were to accept the division of Berlin as final, we should have to build a West Berlin city hall, but meanwhile we keep on making do."

"Do you think the city government will ever accept the division as final?" I asked.

"Politically it would be difficult," she said, "but I am less optimistic than many of my associates. The trend in the past decade since the Wall has been in the direction of permanent division. The Wall itself was only a final gesture; it symbolized a division which already existed."

We began our descent of the shallow steps, and she continued: "What worries me is that an entire generation in East Berlin, in the G.D.R. has never know anything but communism. I wonder whether they are growing up less critical, with less expectation of personal freedom than their parents? And on both sides of the Wall, half the population has never lived in a united Germany, a united Berlin. Perhaps they will begin to think of the division as normal and simply accept it."

I told her that I could not think that.

"Well," she said, "we can at least hope for tactical arrangements, some easing of tension, some accommodation which allows visiting and greater trade, but I am a hard-liner on one point, the point of personal and political freedom. We Germans know too intimately what dictatorship is. We cannot compromise on freedom, not after Hitler." She turned to me and smiled, embarrassed by her intensity. "Come, let's have that coffee!"

9

Eric

During the first postwar years all four sectors of Berlin remained devastated and impoverished. The Soviet sector had suffered the most intensive damage because it included the congested mid-town boroughs and the main government buildings, but in the years before the blockade all Berlin was a rubble heap peopled by gaunt women and children and by a very few elderly or crippled men. In those years Berlin, West and East, was a dismal, depressing city. After the blockade, Marshall Plan dollars and Bonn D-marks began to pour into West Berlin. The rubble gradually disappeared; houses, factories and shops sprang up; the Kurfürstendamm asserted its leadership in fashion and vitality; and the contrast between bustling, prosperous, brightly lit West Berlin and the drab, still rubble-strewn streets of East Berlin was stark. For more than a decade reconstruction, prosperity and well-being ended at the sector border.

However, the people living east of the Wall are also Berliners, and they too are intolerant of disorder and of poverty. More slowly than in the Western sectors but as inexorably, the East Berliners also carried away rubble and began the reconstruction of their neighborhoods. Visiting East Berlin between 1953 and 1965 I noticed the painfully gradual changes. Then the pace increased. The grim Leningrad architecture of the Stalin Allee, now renamed for Karl Marx, gave way to the lighter, more cheerful German stone and glass. Modern apartment blocks, shopping centers, even rebuilt churches and public buildings gradually altered the landscape and the atmosphere. The Catholic Cathedral, St. Hedwig's, was restored with Western money. The East Berlin government rebuilt the state theater and the opera house and began the reconstruction of the lower Wilhelmstrasse, which had been almost totally flattened during the war. East Berliners slowly blossomed into colors and more modern fashions; shop windows, especially those near the sector border and along

108

the Karl Marx Allee, displayed more merchandise more attractively. By 1970 the contrast with West Berlin remained sharp, and East Berlin was still relatively drab, relatively Spartan, but it was far more modern, more prosperous and more cheerful than it had been just a few years before. East Berlin has changed slowly, but progress seems to be gathering momentum, at least as far as appearance and atmosphere are concerned.

One aspect, however, has changed very little over the years, and that is the procedure of getting into and out of the Eastern sector. Concrete tank traps, solidly constructed watch towers, and efficient death strips patrolled by guards armed with high-powered rifles and machine pistols have replaced the casual, improvised barbed wire of the early days of the Wall. The methods of checking passports, of supervising the flow of visitors at the crossings have become more smoothly professional; border guards and customs officials have grown generally less hostile, and more of them seem able to speak English or French to accommodate bewildered tourists. Nevertheless, the overall atmosphere of crossing from one world into another, moreover into a world from which return is not guaranteed, has remained unchanged.

Rattling along in the rather dingy car of the *S-Bahn,* Berlin's city railway, watching the last miles of West Berlin slip past the dusty window, feeling the vibration as the train clatters across the bridge over the Spree and penetrates beyond the Wall, and observing the sudden explosion of placards, the omnipresent and grimly armed guards on patrol along the river, and the relatively empty streets, I always catch my breath and square my shoulders against the impact.

There are two routes by which the non-German can enter East Berlin: one the famous Checkpoint Charlie, through which sightseeing buses, visitors in private cars, and pedestrians pass; the other, the Friedrichstrasse railway station, which one reaches by *S-Bahn.* In recent years I have preferred not to travel into the East with a car and so I usually go over by *S-Bahn.*

The entire *S-Bahn* network in West as well as East Berlin belongs to East Berlin. The maintenance workers, ticket clerks, and train crews are employed by an East Berlin authority, and so the atmosphere even in West Berlin's *S-Bahn* stations is that of the East. The stations lack the sparkling cheerfulness of the pastel tiled subway stations. The kiosks selling newspapers and chocolate bars are dingy and uninviting. The uniforms of the employees are drab and almost colorless and shapeless. Even the passengers seem furtive and reserved, as though embarrassed to be patronizing an East Berlin railway.

The first time I travelled into East Berlin by *S-Bahn*—in 1964—the trains were still very old ones. They had undoubtedly been swept and probably hosed, but they looked grimy. In those days there were very few West Berliners on the train. My friend Sigrid explained that her fellow students, then still firmly anticommunist, refused to use the communist-owned line.

"We never travel on it, especially not at night, especially not women students alone. The trains go on past the Wannsee [at the edge of the Western sector of Berlin bordering on the G.D.R.] right into the Soviet Zone."

At that time the thought of ending inadvertently in the Soviet Zone was frightening to most West Berliners.

It was summer, as it most often is when I am in Berlin, and many other academic people were visiting the city. Several of the young people waiting at the West Berlin *S-Bahn* station "Zoo" were obviously students— Scandinavians, French, English and a few Americans. Some carried knapsacks with a Union Jack or Danish cross painted on the back. Most were young men in jeans or shorts. There were a few earnest young women wearing sunglasses with cameras bouncing against their bosoms. Most of the other passengers were elderly women carrying shopping bags bulging with fruit or with gift-wrapped packages, the inevitable bunch of flowers protruding from the top. These were probably West Germans on their way to visit sisters, brothers, or perhaps children living in the East.

I bought a return ticket from the grumpy elderly woman clerk in the hall below, climbed aboard the venerable escalator and was slowly transported to the platform above. I had only a few minutes to wait until the dark red train bearing the sign "Friedrichstrasse" appeared from the west. I got into a nonsmoking car and found an empty seat on one of the wooden benches, carefully avoiding the places marked reserved for the injured or sickly. A stout woman in her sixties took the seat next to me, and I noticed a tow-headed doll and a teddy bear sticking out of the top of her capacious shopping bag.

The car was almost silent. Only two female students across the aisle whispered and giggled. The other passengers seemed tense and almost sullen. I looked out the smeary window at the buildings and parks of West Berlin, at the brightness and prosperity which we were leaving behind. We stopped at the Tiergarten and in the Hansa development. A few passengers got on; no one got off. We made a final stop in the Western sector and then rattled noisily across the railway bridge into the East. On our right I could see the shell of the old Reichstag building, the barbed wire, the watch towers and the guards. We rolled on into the

Eastern sector. The streets had a deserted, depressed look, empty of traffic and virtually empty of pedestrians. Many buildings were still badly damaged. Their walls bore pockmarks testifying to artillery fire as well as gigantic posters proclaiming the joy of the Free German Youth, the achievement of production norms or loyalty to Comrade Ulbricht.

The train plunged into the dark interior of the Friedrichstrasse terminal. The walls were a dull grey, the panes of glass near the ceiling dim with dust. Guards carrying rifles patrolled on a catwalk overhead. The passengers surged herdlike toward a flight of stairs, and I followed. On the floor below large signs directed West Germans in one direction, foreigners in another. I followed the handful of students and one or two tourists into the hall for foreigners. We lined up casually and one after the other surrendered our passports to a uniformed guard seated behind a high desk. He handed me a numbered white card. Passing through a narrow gate into the body of the hall, I found a place at one of the scattered tables and opened my handbag. I had been warned of the regulation which requires all visitors to declare the exact amount of money they have with them and so I had brought only ten marks and some change. It was easy to count. I filled in the exact amount on the white printed form, signed it, and then exchanged five of my marks for five East marks at the counter.

On this day there was only a short delay before my number, the number printed on the white currency declaration form, was called out. Presumably officials in a back room check the passports against lists of suspected agents or smugglers or refugees, then return the approved passports to a window at the far end of the hall. There the guard announced four or five numbers over a public address system, and those of us summoned again took our places in line, filed past his window and retrieved our passports.

The next step was customs inspection. In recent years this procedure has become more relaxed, but at that time it was still rigorous and exact. Each bag or knapsack, every handbag had to be presented and examined. The discovery of secreted currency above the amount declared would mean immediate arrest. Western newspapers and books were strictly prohibited. Gifts for East Berliners had to be declared. I waited patiently while the Danish student ahead of me submitted to a meticulous search of his knapsack and wallet. I had nothing with me except a handbag, which I placed on the counter for inspection.

"What's this?" the inspector asked, taking out a paperback.

"Just a mystery," I explained. I had very carefully avoided choosing anything political.

"You can't take that into East Berlin," the official said. "It is imperialist propaganda."

"It is a very harmless book," I insisted. "Look," I held it up, " it is by Agatha Christie. Last time I was in East Berlin I saw that one of your larger theaters was showing an Agatha Christie film. If it is all right to see her films, it must be all right to read her books."

He wavered and said, "Well, I should confiscate it."

"I am right in the middle of it!" I exclaimed.

"Why did you bring it with you?" he asked. "You're not going to give it to anyone in East Berlin, are you?"

I assured him that I would not. "I just like to have something to read on the train or while I sit in a café."

"Well," he said, "you must promise me not to leave it in East Berlin and not to bring any Western books the next time you come."

I readily agreed and moved on past the barrier clutching my rescued book. I glanced at my watch and saw that I was a little early. I was supposed to meet Eric for lunch at exactly noon, and it was just a quarter to twelve. It was a bright, sunny day, and so I decided to stroll for a few minutes along the Friedrichstrasse. Despite the mid-summer brilliance, the street seemed drab and drained of color. The aged tram that turned off the main street and ran beside the canal was dingy yellow and rattled morosely. I too turned off and walked alongside the canal, passing prison-like barracks of dark grey stone. There were almost no people in the street, and those I met hurried by, their eyes downcast. I walked as far as the famous Pergamon museum, decided to return alone to visit it, turned, and walked briskly back to where Eric and I were to meet.

I entered the main waiting hall of the railway station precisely as the great clock proclaimed noon. I walked slowly across the open space of the hall, threading my way among preoccupied and luggage-burdened travellers toward the florist's stall opposite the entrance. Despite the warmth of the day I was wearing my wine-red tweed suit with a few wild flowers pinned to the lapel. I displayed discreet interest in an elderly couple who appeared to have mislaid their train tickets; I smiled at a harried young mother carrying an infant and leading a weeping toddler; I glanced only surreptitiously at the small cluster of people standing near the florist's. A stout, sturdy man who could only have been a peasant, a travel-weary old couple and two teen-aged boys were all I saw. I looked away, scanning the row of ticket windows, then back toward the stall, and noticed a slim young man in blue walking purposefully across the hall.

He was about thirty, I thought, with dark blond, very straight hair. His features were regular and rather sharp. He was of middle height and very spare, almost gaunt. The suit was obviously off the rack, of middle quality worsted and much too heavy for the warm weather. The toes of his shoes were embarrassingly pointed, but the shoes were polished to an impressive gloss. The young man glanced at the flowers on my lapel, at my clothes and shoes and smiled tentatively. I smiled and walked directly toward him.

"Frau Doctor?" he asked, and I nodded and extended my hand. He introduced himself as Eric and congratulated me on my punctuality. "Shall we have lunch right away or would you like to drive around a while? You must tell me exactly what you would like to see and what kind of people you want to meet."

That was my first meeting with Eric. A year before I had written the East German government explaining that I planned to write a book about Berlin and asking whether they would arrange for me to visit some schools, hospitals, factories and farms. I received a friendly answer assuring me that the arrangements would be made, and, after a further exchange of letters, we agreed on the day and time and place of my meeting with their representative. They had asked how they could recognize me and what I would wear. I had committed myself to the red suit; they suggested the flowers. Both precautions had been unnecessary. I would have recognized Eric as a member of the species "official" in any crowd, and he certainly had no difficulty recognizing me among a gathering of East German travellers, certainly not in those days when my shoes, my clothes, and my make-up shouted Western to the most uninformed observer.

Since then I have returned periodically to East Berlin, and I usually meet Eric. He has changed over the years as East Germany has changed. He has grown more relaxed, more confident, less dogmatic and far less rigid. That first year I found him prickly. He was entirely literal-minded, very quick to take offense. His manner was formally correct and conventional. I had the impression that he had memorized a set of rules for the entertainment of lady visitors, and I was sure he thought of me as a lady visitor rather than as a professional woman or female scholar. In my limited experience no one can be as belatedly bourgeois as a representative of a proletarian domocracy. He would offer me flowers or conduct me to the ballet or try to buy me a gift, not so much because he thought I would like flowers or enjoy the ballet or appreciate a gift as because it said on page thirteen of his manual that this was the correct behavior. From time to time he would recite a little joke which he had memorized, having learned after our first meeting that I liked to laugh and frequently indulged in quips. He obviously was most anxious to secure promotion, and he was certainly conscientious and correct, but there were times when I could gladly have shaken him just to see whether he was stuffed, and I was always glad to escape him at the end of a day of touring and interviewing.

In more recent years he has become a little less stuffed, a little more human. These days he sometimes risks a spontaneous joke, occasionally even about communism and the G.D.R. He has grown mellower and more sophisticated, and I find his company less strenuous. On our first meeting he was at his most wooden and unbending.

That first day he had arranged an extensive program for me. We began by driving slowly toward the Alexanderplatz, which was just being cleared. Only a scattering of shops and the new House of Teachers occupied the fringes of the empty square. We did not stop. Instead we drove on to the Karl Marx Allee, glancing right and left at the modern shops and cafés and restaurants.

"We shall come back," Eric assured me, "but right now I want to give you an overall impression."

We drove out along the Frankurter Allee, passing older apartment houses and department stores. He took me to one of the newer housing projects just off the Frankfurter Allee, and we walked around its periphery. These were tall, ugly buildings with narrow windows still in the Russian style, but they were new and clean, and there were playgrounds overflowing with laughing, shouting children.

We had lunch at a lakeside restaurant. The food was copious if indifferent, the service courteous if casual, but the view was superb and the Austrian wine quite drinkable. I remember that in those years East Berlin coffee was still weak and tasteless, probably *ersatz*. After lunch we drove around the city to a student home and to the university; there we walked through the massive library and past several construction sites where housing and public buildings were going up. Later we parked the car and strolled along the fashionable part of the Karl Marx Allee, browsing in one shop after another. In a bookstore Eric insisted on buying several volumes for me, cheap editions but useful.

At about five we stopped at the Opera Café in the newly reconstructed Crown Princess's Palace, then one of East Berlin's few elegant restaurants. Eric explained that all restaurants and cafés were classified according to price in classes I through IV.

"Our top-class restaurants are largely for entertaining foreign visitors, diplomats and trade missions, and they charge luxury prices. Very few East Berliners can afford to eat in a place like this," he said, obviously proud of the plush and glass interior.

"Is that good socialism?" I asked and regretted it. His answer was a very long and obviously memorized treatise on the equality of inequality. I concentrated on my apéritif and looked around at our fellow guests, who appeared to be, as Eric had said, foreigners, probably from East European countries.

Over the second sherry Eric asked me what kind of people I would like to meet and what I would like to see in East Berlin, and I gave him my list. We made plans for further meetings and for an excursion or two into East Germany.

"I thought I'd take you to the Berlin City Hall, the famous red *Rathaus,* for dinner," he suggested. He signaled for the waiter in what seemed to me a most uncomradely manner. I thought that perhaps he was self-conscious in unwontedly luxurious surroundings. He paid the bill, and we walked down the curved staircase and out into the small park.

"These will interest you," Eric announced proudly, pointing to a series of stone busts dotted along the path. "We have repaired them and put them back up!"

I walked up to one after the other of the busts and was astounded to discover my old friends Scharnhorst and Gneisenau as well as Marshal Blücher.

"But they are militarists!" I said, not quite believing my eyes.

"Not any more," Eric said with perfect seriousness.

Berlin's old *Rathaus* is indeed red. It is constructed of deep red stone and has the forbidding, brooding look of a fortress. At that time most of the surrounding buildings were in ruins and much of the area was simply empty. It was evening, and there were even fewer cars than during the day. For blocks around the neighborhood seemed desolate and eerie.

Inside the rathskeller, however, the atmosphere was cheerful and cheering. Red brick warmed by suffused light, rounded arches and tables of seasoned wood created a mellow, relaxed haven from the austerity outside.

"I think I should go and comb my hair and redo my make-up," I suggested.

Eric smiled stiffly and shook his head. "Oh no, here in our socialist city that sort of thing isn't necessary," he said and began to lead me toward a table.

I tapped him lightly on the shoulder and as he turned, startled that I had something to say, I explained carefully:

"Eric, if your government is going to assign you to escort female visitors, you had better learn that when a woman says that she must comb her hair or repair her make-up, usually it is necessary."

He flushed a deeper red than the red brick walls and hesitated. I guessed that he had been instructed not to let me out of his sight, and obviously he could not come with me to the ladies' dressing room. On the other hand, he could hardly refuse to let me go. While he debated with himself I turned back, found a woman attendant at the cloak room and asked her for directions, strenuously suppressing a giggle.

We drank an excellent Hungarian red wine with dinner, and we ate venison with cranberries. Here the service was relaxed and friendly, the clientele largely German. This too was a luxury restaurant, but it seemed to be patronized by the East German political and technological hierarchy.

I learned almost nothing personal about Eric during that first encounter. Over dinner he told me that he had studied economics, that his family came from one of the eastern provinces, that his father was killed during the war, and that is about all. His conversation was stiffly polite and always guarded. He interspersed descriptions of housing projects or explanations of planned reconstruction with short sermons on Marxism-Leninism, which he seemed to recite by rote. His personal likes and dislikes, his hobbies and interests, his values and idiosyncrasies remained unstated.

Although the day was interesting, it was also strenuous, and I was grateful when he dropped me at the Friedrichstrasse station and we said good-bye. There were very few people crossing at that late evening hour, and so it was only a matter of minutes before my passport was returned to me and I was allowed to cross the customs hall and on into the station itself. I climbed the stairs to the platform labeled "Trains to the West," entered the waiting train and soon was rattling back into West Berlin. To this day I always sigh a little and relax when the train clatters across the Spree.

That was the year that I was spending the summer at the Adam von Trott House, the Lutheran students' residence, on the Wannsee. I could have stayed on the *S-Bahn* all the way to Wannsee, but instead I got off at the Zoo, descended the steep stairs into the gaiety and lights and bustle of West Berlin, strolled over to the Kurfürstendamm for a late cup of real coffee at one of the sidewalk cafés, luxuriating in the vitality of the scene. Then I took a bus and was home by midnight.

That first meeting with Eric took place during the summer of 1964. Since then we have met virtually every year, usually several times, but to this day I cannot say that I know Eric as I know Sigrid, whom I also met that summer, or as I know any of my West Berlin friends. Eric remains merely an official. However friendly he is when we are together, he is always obviously on duty. His behavior has gradually grown more relaxed, his attitude toward me and to his work seems less rigid, but I still know far less about him than he knows about me. Only occasionally, in an un-guarded instant, can I glimpse a facet of the real Eric.

But he has been very helpful to me, and I should be ungrateful if I complained too much of his reserve. He painstakingly arranged a variety of interviews with an excellent cross section of East Berliners. He intro-duced me to many aspects of East Berlin life, from housing projects and day nurseries to nightclubs and the zoo. He supplied me with statistical reports, books and brochures, and he was tireless in driving me around Berlin and out into the country.

One of the first people he took me to visit was a retired dancer who lived in a small apartment on the Karl Marx Allee. I had been told that only party functionaries and technocrats could rent these apartments, and so I was not prepared for Irene. We knocked on the door of the third floor apartment, and a few moments later the door opened and a minute figure in black greeted us.

Irene was in her mid-sixties with wispy hair of faded blond streaked with grey. She was scarcely five feet tall and could not have weighed a hundred pounds. The black jersey tunic over black tights emphasized her slimness and fragility. Wide dreamy eyes peered out of an elfin face under the irregular fringe of hair. She blinked and nodded as Eric introduced me and then with a swift, birdlike movement, she swept us both inside.

The living room was moderately large but seemed cluttered. An im-mense wardrobe, modern but massive, dominated one wall, and there seemed to be a profusion of couches, chairs and cabinets. An easel, stool, and painting gear stood in front of the window. Notebooks, sketch books, and other books were strewn over the couches and chairs. A striking mod-ern painting hung on the far wall. The remaining walls were hung with Chinese watercolors, etchings, and prints. The curtains fluttering at the window were of bright orange and rust with splashes of yellow and green. One of the couches echoed that precise shade of yellow, another was rust. It was a colorful, crowded, and yet also austere room, quite individual and rather overpowering. It certainly reflected relative affluence, even though the quality of the fabrics and furniture did not match the flair.

"Come in," Irene invited. "Shall I get you some tea or would you like mineral water or some fruit juice?" It was a warm mid-morning so I opted for fruit juice, and Eric readily agreed. She nodded, birdlike, and disappeared.

"She is a party member," Eric said. "She got an activist medal for service last year, and she is very proud of it."

Irene bounced back into the room carrying a small tray with three glasses of apple juice.

"I'm glad you chose this," she said. "I am on a diet."

"Surely not to lose weight?" I asked, astounded. She nodded.

"Oh, yes. I am just finishing a fasting cure, and I've lost fourteen pounds," she said proudly.

"Did you need to lose weight? You are so slim," I said, thinking that skinny would be a more accurate word.

"It is purifying," she said. "I like to keep myself spiritual and not material. Every now and then I fast. This time I ate absolutely nothing and drank only mineral water and fruit juice for seventeen days."

"Isn't that dangerous?" I asked.

"Well, naturally one has to be quiet during that period. I rested, played records, and read most of the time, and, of course, I meditated," she explained soberly.

"But if you are a communist, Miss Irene, what do you meditate about?" I asked. "Surely not on God or religion?"

"I meditate on beautiful thoughts, on truth and on spirit. Even if one is a dialectical materialist, one can believe in spirit!" she said with sovereign semantic originality.

I avoided looking at Eric, and she went on, "I find that making a fasting cure is excellent for the health. It keeps me young and vital. Right now I am a little weak, of course, but tomorrow I shall start to eat just a little, perhaps some rice with fruit or a custard, and, in a few days, I shall feel splendid. At my age it is very good to keep slim, and of course I can dance better when I am down to minimum weight."

"Do you still dance?" I asked.

"Oh, yes, when I am not fasting. I give lessons one day a week at the children's home, where I used to teach full time, and I also teach a few private pupils here in my home. This is a two-bedroom flat, and so I have one of the rooms arranged as a dance studio. It is rather small, but I have a bar and a large mirror and the floor is rather good."

We talked a little about dancing, and she told me that she had been the pupil of a famous dancer. She danced professionally for several years and then opened her own dance studio.

"I was a communist even then," she said. "I wasn't content just to earn a living or even to express myself artistically. I wanted to be useful to working-class women, and so I organized special after-work classes with gymnastics and reducing exercises as well as creative dancing. I had

special low rates for working women. They loved the dancing. It helped
keep them healthy and gave them an outlet for their creative energy.
The older women had as much fun as the children when we put on our
recitals. They helped make the costumes for the children and design and
paint the scenery."

I asked whether she had remained in Germany during the nazi time
and she said yes.

"I had never been active in the political work of the party. Technically
I was only a fellow traveller. I was called in by the Gestapo once or twice
and questioned, but they were always polite." She shrugged, "I suppose
they thought I was harmless. They warned me to stay out of politics, and
so I did. I was allowed to continue to teach dancing, and I did so all
through the war."

"In Berlin?" I asked, and she nodded. "Were you bombed out?" I asked.

"Entirely!" she said. "I had a large studio apartment with wonderful
high ceilings and a splendid wood floor right in downtown Berlin, but it
was totally destroyed. I lost everything, so of course I could no longer
teach."

"Not without a studio," I said. "What did you do?"

"You will laugh, but I got a job singing and dancing in a cabaret. It
was not a very high-class cabaret, and I did not much enjoy it, but it was
a living. I found a furnished room and later shared a flat with one of the
other women in our show."

She laughed, "What times we had! The building the cabaret was in was
bombed three times, but was only partially damaged each time, so we
were always able to sweep out the broken glass, clean up the rubble and
keep the show open. After the war things were even worse: sometimes
there was no heat; often the electricity was cut off, and we had to play
with candles or lanterns. No one had any money, so we were paid in kind,
that is with flour, vegetables, and potatoes and once in a while a little
coffee or a bar of soap. Some of the customers bought their tickets with
food, you see, because the currency was worthless. Sometimes we were
hungry, and we were usually cold. Our costumes were in tatters, and it
was almost impossible to get make-up or dancing shoes or even light
bulbs and hammers and nails to make the scenery!"

"I remember going to cabarets in those years," I said, "and the audience
froze too, but we could wear winter coats and heavy sweaters under them.
You had to dance and sing in flimsy costumes. It must have been awful."

"It was, and most of us had colds or sore throats most of the winter. I
finally got pneumonia and had to quit, but by then local government was
more or less back in operation, and, as soon as I was well, I was able to

get a job teaching dancing in a children's home. My doctor helped me get the job because he said stage dancing or cabaret work was too strenuous for me."

"You were lucky," I said.

"Very, because at least the home was heated, and I had regular, daytime hours and could get enough sleep. I was awfully run down. The school job was part of the civil service, which meant that I would get a decent pension when I retired."

I asked her about the home, and she explained that it was a home for orphans and neglected children.

"It is in one of our prettier suburbs. We house about five hundred children, infants up to eighteen years. We have our own school and even an open-air theater where we put on dance festivals and reviews."

"You sound as though you enjoyed it," I said.

"I loved it," she said, "although it was very strenuous work. I had I don't know how many classes. Mornings I taught the little ones, three to six years old. I insisted on no more than ten in a class, you see, so I had to teach class after class all morning, but I enjoyed it and the children learned. They were terrific! You should have seen those tiny ones in our recitals.

"Afternoons I took the older children, seven to fourteen, and evenings I had a few private pupils, girls with special talent whom I taught free. One of my former pupils is with the state ballet now, and I am very proud of her. Several others teach dancing."

"How long did you teach at the home?" I asked.

"Until I was sixty, which is four years ago. By then I was eligible to retire, and I found that I was very tired. It was getting to be too much for me." She smiled shyly. "I miss the children, even though I still teach a few. I enjoyed getting the recitals and dance festivals together. I loved the excitement and the pleasure the children had in showing their skills and talents to their parents and friends. We gave prizes and special awards for top pupils, and youngsters with professional talent had a chance to go on to ballet school."

"You don't look as though you were bored by your retirement, though," I said.

"Oh, no! I miss the rush and excitement. But I also enjoy the rest and especially the leisure to do a little sketching and painting, and now I have time to travel a little. This past spring I visited the Black Sea, and next year I want to go to Scandinavia. I am old enough to get a travel visa."

"I take it that your pension is adequate," I said.

"I am very lucky," she said. "As a member of what we call the intelligentsia I get sixty per cent of my former salary plus 118 marks a month. That is quite generous, and I can supplement it by giving private lessons, so I am quite well off. One must be, you know, to live in the Karl Marx Allee."

"Is the rent here high?" I asked.

"By East German standards, very high. Rent here in East Berlin is normally very low, but I pay over a hundred marks a month for three rooms."

"That seems very little to me," I confessed.

Eric explained; "Our rents are fixed in relation to average incomes. We set rent rates according to what people can afford to pay, not according to the cost of the building or its maintenance and certainly not what the market will bear. I'll take you to some low-rent apartments later."

"This is a convenient place to live," Irene said. "I confess that I miss the big rooms and high ceilings of my prewar apartment, but for an older person, a small, modern apartment is a blessing. I do most of my own cleaning and cooking, and this is easy to care for. I also appreciate the elevator and the shops, all in a row right down the block. The Allee is a pleasant street to stroll on too. I enjoy window-shopping and then sitting for an hour or so on sunny days in one of the parks or at a sidewalk café, and, of course, it is a convenient address for my friends to visit. The subway station is right at the corner, and there are good bus connections. It is perfect for a retired woman living alone."

"I can see that you like living in Berlin," I said. "Are you a native Berliner?"

"Absolutely *waschecht!*" she said. "My mother was an actress, my father a journalist, and both were born in Berlin. That's rare! I grew up in East Berlin in a suburban district. I started studying dancing when I was seven. I've danced and taught in Berlin all my life, and I can't imagine living anywhere else. I've visited Paris and London and Rome, and I loved them all, but I am a Berliner. I feel really at home only here, and now that I am retired, I intend to get the most out of Berlin. That's one reason why I fast, to keep healthy so that I can enjoy living more and longer."

We thanked her, wished her well, and said good-bye. She waved gracefully from her apartment door as we disappeared down the stairs.

"It's only the third floor," Eric had said. "It's quicker to walk down."

As we walked to the car, he asked how I had liked Irene. "I'm afraid she's a little peculiar," he confessed.

"She's eccentric, but then some artistic people are. I liked her," I said.

"She's an old maid," he said. "Imagine! Fasting for three weeks and

meditation. I suppose she's one of these silly intellectuals who flock after
Eastern religions." He frowned disapprovingly.

"A crypto-Buddhist?" I asked.

"Probably," he answered seriously, opening the car door for me. "But
she's an old woman," he said, sliding into the driver's seat. "It doesn't
matter what she thinks."

"She's only sixty-four," I said. "That's not old these days."

"No, but we only care what young people think, and our young people
are all rational."

"You mean atheists? All of them?" I asked.

"Most," he nodded with satisfaction. "At least all the intelligent ones
are. The few Christians can go their way, they won't amount to anything.
In another generation religion will be wiped out."

"But surely people still go to church here in East Germany. I know the
state supports the theological faculties and collects and distributes the
Church tax."

"For the time being," he admitted. "There is no point in upsetting a
minority of sentimental, ignorant people when they will die out anyway.
We concentrate on educating young people scientifically."

"Where are we going now?" I asked, as he turned off the Karl Marx
Allee, and we found ourselves in a neighborhood of old, partly bombed-
out houses. The rubble had been cleared away, but many buildings were
empty shells; some had a corner or one wall missing.

"I thought you would like to see another older woman living on a
pension, but this time a poor one," he suggested.

I agreed, and he pulled up in front of a dingy red-stone, four-story
house, the last of a row. Next to it was an empty lot where one or two
bombed-out remnants had obviously been cleared away. Three small boys
played with a beach ball. A scrawny, striped cat darted across the lot and
climbed the far wall.

Eric pushed open a heavy door, and we almost fell into the dark hall.
The odor which engulfed us seemed to be compounded of old, imper-
fectly cleaned wood, generations of coal or coke fires, stale cooking, poor
plumbing and male cats. I rank myself second to none in my affection for
cats, but I also suffer from a cleanliness-is-next-to-Godliness upbringing.
I swallowed hard and followed the intrepid Eric up the creaking, dingy
staircase. It was dark as well as grimy as we crossed the second-floor land-
ing. I almost tripped over a bucket and a mop propped against the wall.
"Someone gallantly trying to reverse the trend of decades," I thought.

Eric knocked on the door of the second-floor rear flat. The door opened, and, when he had explained who we were to an unseen, high-pitched female voice, the door swung open, and we were admitted. We entered a large room, a combination kitchen, living room, and bedroom. A gigantic, old-fashioned coal stove filled most of one wall. There was a small coke stove in one corner, a lumpy couch covered with an old army blanket along the far wall, a cupboard once painted white, a round table covered with a much-mended off-white cloth with a faded red fringe and a few plain wooden chairs.

The woman, who offered us coffee but gratefully accepted our refusal, was about seventy, of middle height, with a lumpy, shapeless figure and a grey, perhaps unwashed complexion. Her grey hair was greasy and unkempt. She wore a faded green-and-white checked cotton dress and shabby grey-black shoes. Her attitude was defeated, plaintive, and self-pitying.

We asked Hilda about her flat, and she told us that she paid forty marks a month for the one large room and two cubby holes.

"I use the one, not more than a large closet really, for my clothes and for storage, and my nephew has a couch in the other. His room has no window so we leave the door to this room open at night. I sleep here on the couch."

"Do you cook on that big stove?" I asked, thinking that it must use a tremendous lot of coal.

"No, it would be too expensive," she said. "I have a little hot plate and we make do with that. I'm old; I don't need much to eat; and my nephew gets his hot meal at work at noon. At night I just boil some *wurst* and sauerkraut or some potatoes or we eat cold food. Herb is satisfied with bread and cheese most nights as long as he gets his beer."

She explained that Herb works in the nearby slaughterhouse.

"He's a bit wanting," she said. "He never had any training, but he has enough sense to earn a bit. He gives me ten marks a week."

"I suppose his money helps," I suggested.

"A lot," she said. "I get only 145 marks a month as pension. Of course, food is cheap, ordinary food like bread and potatoes, but now butter is dear. I can afford only half a pound of butter a week, and we never have real coffee. The good stuff costs forty marks a pound. We use *ersatz*. Of course, some things are free for retired people, like going to the doctor and getting medicines."

She picked up rimless glasses from the wicker sewing basket on the stove and showed them to me.

"I got these free," she said proudly, "and Herb gets a check-up at the plant and has all kinds of insurance."

I asked my usual question about whether she was a Berliner. She said that she came from Silesia.

"My parents moved to Berlin, though, when I was thirteen. I didn't like it here at first. I guess I was shy and homesick. I quit school as soon as they'd let me, but I hadn't learned a trade, so I had to work as a housemaid. That's not a bad life, and sometimes I could save my money. It all went in the war, though."

"Have you always worked as a maid?" I asked.

"No, ma'am," she said. "I got married when I was twenty, and my husband took me to the Rhineland to live. I used to go out to work two or three mornings just to help out. My Fritz worked in a factory and made pretty good money, but he died of cancer in 1935, and I came back to Berlin."

"Did you marry again?" I asked.

"Well, not to say marry," she said. "I had a friend, and we took a flat together. He worked as a waiter and made good money, and we fixed up our place real nice. I had some good laces and linens, solid, heavy furniture and real crystal. In 1942 my friend was drafted even though he was over forty. He was killed in Russia in 1943, and the same year our flat was bombed out and everything destroyed."

"Where did you go?" I asked.

"Well, by then I was working full time as a cleaning woman in one of the city government buildings. One of the bosses there said that the concierge of the building where he lived had just died. He got me the job, and I moved into the basement flat there. That was nice," she said nostalgically, "but in 1944 it was bombed too. I didn't mind that so much. I didn't have anything more to lose."

"Was the whole building destroyed?" I asked.

"Pretty near," she said. "All the top floors were gone. After they cleared it up a bit, we found most of the first floor was still standing. After we got the rubble and smoke out of the cellar and white-washed the walls, I was able to move back into my flat. Of course, the windows were out, but I patched them up with boards and canvas. It was cold in the winter, and it wasn't fancy, but it was a place to live, and in Berlin in 1944–45 that was pretty good."

"Did you stay there until the end of the war?" I asked.

"I stayed until 1950 because even after the war I couldn't find another place to live, not anything I could afford anyway. In 1950 the government said the old house was dangerous and had to be torn down. I had to get out, so they had to find me a place to live."

"Did they find this for you?" I asked.

She nodded. "They have a housing office. I told the woman there how much I make and she sent me to look at three or four flats. They weren't much, but then I couldn't afford much. There was one nicer than this, but it cost fifty marks. See, then I didn't have my nephew with me. He came to me three years ago, after his mother died."

"Do you plan to stay on here?" I asked. "Couldn't you apply for one of the new apartments?"

"I could, I guess, but the new apartments are mostly for people with children. It's only right. Besides, I've moved so many times, I'm a little tired. This place isn't very fancy, but it's cheap, and it's a roof over my head. I'm an old woman; I don't think I'll bother moving again. I only worry about what will happen to Herb when I go. He works, but he can't really look after himself." She shrugged with weary acceptance.

We thanked her and left feeling depressed.

"One more before lunch?" Eric queried, and blinked like a puzzled owl when I giggled and nodded. We got into the car and he drove about five minutes and drew up in front of a large, modern school.

"This building was just finished," he explained. "In fact, it's not all finished inside, but it's been in partial use since September. It's a trade school and has up-to-date labs and workshops and kitchens—quite a showpiece."

"Are we going to tour it?" I asked.

"Not today. Some time if you like, but I want to introduce a girl who works here as a secretary."

He led the way into the building and down a brightly lit corridor. The hall still smelled of fresh concrete and new paint. Eric knocked at a glass-paneled door marked "Records," opened it and went in.

"Fräulein Herta?" he asked, and a buxom young woman in a tight but dazzlingly white blouse and dark blue skirt rose from her desk and smiled at us. She wore her light brown hair pulled back tight in a pony-tail; her fresh complexion was free of make-up. She bounced enthusiastically toward us, extending her hand.

Eric introduced us and said that Herta was an active member of the Free German Youth. She found chairs for us, and we sat and talked with her for a while. Herta was then twenty-two. She lived alone in a small flat near the school.

"I used to have just a furnished room, but my landlady was a grouch. She wouldn't let me cook, and she complained when I did my laundry. It was awful, but I was lucky: I found a tiny place of my own. It's only one room, you know. I don't even have a bath, just a toilet. I have to bathe in a laundry tub in the kitchen, but I have a very modern kitchen with a refrigerator and an electric stove and sparkling white cupboards. I'm very proud of it!"

"Do you like to cook?" I asked.

"Oh, yes, I love it, but I'm not always home evenings. I work with the F.D.J. several evenings a week. I'm a group leader for young apprentices, and that takes not only time but a lot of thought. Girls always have problems! You know how they are, and they pop into my flat now and then to weep on my shoulder or complain or just to talk. Half the time I don't know what to tell them, but I make coffee or cocoa for them and listen. I guess that helps.

"But cooking I do weekends, and then I invite a couple of girl-friends in for a big dinner, and we go dancing afterwards. That's fun. Of course, some weekends we take a steamer on the lakes or get on the subway or bus and go out into the country, or we take our bicycles and picnic lunches."

"Only girls?" I asked.

She shook her head. "I haven't got a boyfriend," she said. "I had a friend, but he was transferred to Dresden. I wasn't really in love with him. I think I'm too young to be serious about a boy. I don't want to get married for a while yet. I dance with boys, and I suppose I'd like to meet someone nice, but I don't want to settle down for years yet."

"You enjoy your work?" I asked.

"I like being independent," she said. "It's fun, too, working in a brand new school, and my boss is nice. She's only in her thirties and very lively and cheerful and easy to work for."

Herta explained that she had attended the Basic School until she was fourteen; then she went to a commercial school for two years to learn shorthand and typing.

"I've been working since I was sixteen," she said. "I began as a stenographer earning 280 marks a month. Now after six years' experience, I am a secretary and earn 500 marks. That's gross, you know. After deductions for taxes and insurance I take home 390 marks. That's pretty good for a young woman," she said with satisfaction.

She said she pays seventy marks a month rent. "It's in an old building, but I have a nice big room, and they've made a modern kitchen for me. I'm buying my furniture a little at a time. I bought a nice couch, which I pay for on the installment plan. It will take me two years to pay that off; then I can think about what else I want to buy."

"Can you live well on your income?" I asked.

"Oh, yes. I have over three hundred marks a month after I pay my rent. Food is cheap except for things like coffee and imported fruits and alcohol. I walk to work and have lunch here at the school cafeteria, so I have quite a bit to spend on clothing and on my apartment. My vacations are very cheap. I can go to F.D.J. vacation homes on the Baltic or in the Hartz mountains or go with one of our group tours to the Eastern countries."

"How about entertainment and hobbies?" I asked, and she said that she was a member of an amateur theatrical group and that kept her very busy.

"I love the theater and am very much interested in the new films, especially Czech and Polish and French. I also like the opera and ballet. Our F.D.J. club gets tickets at reduced rates. And I like to play tennis and go swimming. I gain weight very easily as you can see, so I have to get enough exercise!"

She told me that she works seven and a half hours a day, five days a week. "Here in the G.D.R. everyone is entitled to at least eighteen days' vacation a year and up to thirty days depending on one's income. In addition, we get up to six weeks' sick leave a year at ninety per cent of our salary."

"Suppose you have a serious illness and are away longer than six weeks?" I asked.

"Then we get fifty per cent of our salary for a whole year, and of course, our health insurance pays for hospitalization and medical care."

"Suppose you had a baby?" I asked.

"Any woman, married or not, who has a child is entitled to fourteen weeks' maternity leave at full pay and, of course, longer if there are complications and she is not well. Did you know that every working woman is entitled to one day off a month in addition to her annual leave?"

"Yes," I said. "They have that in West Germany, too. I think it's a good idea. What do you do with yours?"

"Well, I'm disgustingly robust. I don't need mine to sit with my feet up and drink tea, so I sleep late and then go shopping, get my hair done and see a film. It's wonderful having a weekday off when every one else is working, and the hairdresser's and other shops aren't crowded! Of course, a lot of girls are grateful to have the day just to rest, and married women who work usually do their house-cleaning or laundry."

I asked whether she was planning to stay in Berlin, and she said she would not like to live anywhere else.

"I guess I could have got a job in Dresden when my friend moved there, but somehow I can't imagine living anywhere but Berlin. Everything is here. And I like the people, especially the young girls I work with."

We thanked her and said good-bye. Eric glanced at his massive watch and asked where I'd like to have lunch. He mentioned some of the more elegant East Berlin hotels and restaurants, but I said I should like to eat in a *Kneipe,* a typical Berlin neighborhood pub.

He said, "I know just the one," and we hurried to the car.

We drove for about fifteen minutes and found ourselves in a residential part of the city which had survived the bombing with only light damage. The houses, heavy grey stone, stood in long rows. Each had four stone steps, high, wide windows and grated basement ones, each was four or five stories high. Apparently only the corner house had been bombed, and in its place, a square, squat two-story building had been built to house the *Kneipe.*

"It's modern!" I said with disappointment.

"Not inside," Eric assured me. "They saved the big mirror and the Wilhelmine furniture and prints."

He led me to the door. He was right. Buff-colored walls, dark wood paneling and heavy wooden tables and chairs created an illusion of age. A stag's antlers hung over the bar and old-fashioned faded prints decorated the walls. Most of the patrons were men, some in shirt sleeves, but there were two families with small children and a few couples. It was past noon, and most tables were full. We were lucky to find a small table at the back.

"Not much of a menu," Eric said, handing me a single typed sheet. He ordered schnapps as an apéritif while I read the simple menu. A stout, sturdy woman with greying hair and a clean but stained white uniform took our order.

"Can you eat *Eisbein?*" Eric asked. "It's their speciality."

Eisbein is a Berlin specialty. It is pig's knuckle, usually served with a mountain of mashed potatoes, sauerkraut, dark bread and beer. I am told that it is delicious, but it is one of the things that I cannot eat.

"The *Würstchen* are always good," he suggested, "or the wiener schnitzel. It seems funny to have that in Berlin, but it's good here."

I chose the schnitzel, and Eric ordered *Eisbein* and beer.

"Well," he said, when the waitress brought our chilled schnapps, "Here is to your book!"

I thanked him and sipped. "What have you planned for the afternoon?" I asked.

"If you don't mind, I think I'll leave you on your own for a while. I ought to go back to my office to check my mail and make a few phone calls. I can drop you on the Karl Marx Allee to window-shop and meet you at about four at the Hotel Berolina for coffee. We have an appointment at five with someone who will interest you, I think."

The food when it arrived was served on heavy-duty white crockery, the knives and forks were steel, the napkins a shiny paper, but the waitress smiled kindly and set down the heavy plates carefully and gently. They were piled high, and the food was delicious. I seldom drink beer and almost never at noon because it makes me sleepy, but beer was the only possible drink at a *Kneipe,* and it too was delicious. We ate slowly and quietly, both a little tired from all our questioning and listening. I listened gratefully and passively to the giggles of three little girls, to the robust laughter of a group of heavy-set working men.

"Man!" one of them cried, "they'll never win! They haven't got a chance with Schmidt out of the game!" I knew they were talking about soccer. Our waitress brought them a new round of beer and schnapps, and one of them patted her sturdy arm. "Thanks, *Oma* [Grandma]" he said.

"*Oma,* indeed!" she said in mock annoyance and flounced away.

After lunch Eric drove me to the Karl Marx Allee. It was not yet two. I had more than two hours, and it was a bright, sunny day. I decided that this was a good opportunity to check the prices and quality of some of the goods offered by the chic shops along the avenue.

Slowly I wandered along the Allee, browsing. I entered a very smart shop with glass walls and counters dedicated to home decoration. Fabrics, candles, table linens and glassware were arranged with restraint and taste. Some of the things were very atractive, but there was a limited selection and the prices were high.

Next I visited an obviously exclusive boutique and asked to see dresses in my size. A rather stiff, middle-aged woman in black brought several afternoon dresses for me to inspect.

"This one is from Paris," she said and mentioned a famous couturier. I had seen almost the same model in West Berlin. The price here was about twenty-five per cent higher. The dresses were attractive, but the selection was limited, and the prices very high by Western standards. I guessed that only top-level functionaries or foreign visitors could afford them. I saw nothing that tempted me. I found the styles, although pretty, just a little too conventional, too unimaginative. They seemed to lack flair and individuality.

I thanked the saleswoman and strolled out and up the avenue. I checked the prices of men's and women's shoes. Again, there was a lack of range in both style and price. The quality seemed good, the styles dull and conventional. Utterly absent were the very cheap, mass-produced shoes which abound in West Berlin department stores, insubstantial slippers and sandals which come in a dazzling variety of colors, forms, and styles and appeal to young girls who love style and variety but are limited by a small budget. Absent too were the shoes of international luxury quality which ornament the chic Kurfürstendamm shops. In those days I usually paid thirty to thirty-five dollars for my Bally shoes in West Berlin. I saw no women's shoes in East Berlin for more than twenty dollars, and, obviously, there was nothing up to the Bally standard. On the other hand, in West Berlin I had seen colorful summer standals for three or four dollars, and there was nothing here that cheap.

Next I found a hairdresser and went in to inquire about prices. Here again were none of the luxury and little of the beauty mystique of the chic Western salon. The rooms were overcrowded and utilitarian, a little dingy although undoubtedly hygienic. The proprietor himself came to speak to me, and he smiled warmly.

"*Ach,*" he said after we had chatted for a while, "it is so hard to get help and supplies. Hairdressers are private enterprise, you know, not state-owned, and the schools encourage their pupils to train for state-owned industries. Many youngsters don't want to enter private enterprise, so there just aren't enough apprentices. I also find it hard to get hair dyes and lotions and good quality shampoos. You see, in a socialist economy necessities come first. Luxuries like beauty items have a low priority." He continued, "Of course, that's logical. I accept that in principle, but this is my livelihood and sometimes it is depressing."

I found the prices roughly similar to those of an average hairdresser's in the West and far lower than in the United States or England. A plain shampoo and set, for example, cost about a dollar, a woman's haircut about twenty-five cents, a permanent wave only three dollars.

I left the harassed hairdresser and continued my stroll. I passed two film theaters, one showing the Agatha Christie mystery film I had mentioned to the customs guard, the other a West German film. Later, when I asked Eric why they showed Western films in East Berlin, he said the mystery was harmless and that the West German film portrayed the decadence of life among the *nouveau riche* and was instructive.

In shop after shop I came to about the same conclusion. The shops were full of all kinds of goods, the quality was generally good, the prices medium to high. Imported clothes and luxuries were scarce and extremely expensive. What was missing was range, variety and individuality. Young East Berlin girls were dressed in clean, crisp dresses of decent quality, but most of them were in navy blue, tan or dusty green. One year almost every young woman I met on the street was wearing a navy-blue nylon raincoat because that year the factories had made navy-blue nylon raincoats.

West Berlin abounds in large department stores which specialize in very low cost goods, something like discount houses in America. Goods in every size and style and color overflow the counters: cosmetics, nylon stockings, lingerie, hair ornaments and wigs, costume jewelry, sandals and scarves and handbags, house dresses, aprons and children's clothing, toys and housewares and luggage, everything from hairpins and measuring spoons to electric mixers and bicycles. Some of the merchandise is frankly shoddy. A ten-cent toy or a three-dollar house dress does not pretend to quality or high fashion, but the abundance of choice, the variety of color and style, the genuinely low prices appeal to very young shoppers, to newly married couples or to families with many children. Many sophisticated shoppers pride themselves on the occasional bargain they uncover in one of the *Warenhäuser*. If I want a measuring cup or an egg beater, I go to a *Warenhaus*.

There is nothing quite like this in the East. If an East Berlin schoolgirl wants to buy a hair ribbon or a pair of summer sandals, she must buy one of substantial quality and pay a substantial price. On the other hand, if her mother wants a sophisticated, high-fashion dress, she may not find what she wants, and, if she does, the price will be exorbitant. The little boutiques which feature copies or copies of copies of couturier fashion are also missing. The mother may find a dress in her price range, but chances are it will be housewifely and solid and most of her friends will be wearing the same model in precisely the same color.

It was a warm day, and I found all that looking and asking and note-taking rather wearing, so even though it was only three-thirty, I decided to go directly to the Berolina. Until the completion of the new hotel in the Alexanderplatz, the Berolina was East Berlin's only sophisticated international hotel. It was finished in 1954 and, I am told, has 750 beds. It boasts that each room has a private bath. The Berolina caters especially to foreign dignitaries and travelling athletic teams. Sightseeing buses from West Berlin stop there so the passengers can get refreshments, and the parking lot usually flaunts a few West German Mercedes cars as well as several Volkswagens.

I went first to the ladies' room to wash away some of the dust and heat, afraid that later Eric might insist it was not necessary. As I brushed my well-cut hair and then carefully applied my French cosmetics and scent, I noticed the envious sniff of the dark woman next to me. She was perhaps forty, her hair was neither shaped nor tinted, and she wore no make-up. Her complexion looked as though she had simply washed it in cold water and harsh soap for forty years.

We smiled at each other, and she asked, "Are you French?"

I walked back to the lobby to wait for Eric. Benches and low tables stood in disciplined rows, but most of them were full. I walked slowly and found one empty place. Luckily I had bought a newspaper, and so I scanned the headlines. Three little boys probably from one of the Eastern republics of the Soviet Union were having a game with the electronically automatic doors. Apparently they had never seen doors which opened without being pushed. They came in at one side, rushed around, went out the other, and then kept running around and around, giggling and pushing a little, fascinated with Berlin's technology.

Eric arrived very promptly at four, a little breathless, and he apologized because I had been waiting. Then we drove off to another of Berlin's many districts. We passed a secondary shopping center with smaller shops and department stores and a cluster of restaurants and pubs. After fifteen or twenty minutes we pulled up in front of a prewar, middle-class apartment house. There had been little bombing in the immediate neighborhood, and this house seemed entirely unscathed.

We walked up to the second or third floor and Eric knocked on the door of the front apartment. A very old woman opened it and asked us in. She was small and dressed in dark blue with a white lace collar. She wore her gleaming white hair in a loose bun. Her hands were thin and showed her age, but they were well cared for, and she wore two impressive diamond rings and a delicate diamond-studed silver watch.

Mrs. Schüler invited us into the living room which was furnished in the dark, heavy style of the 1930s. She had baked a pound cake, and she served tea elegantly on a silver tray with fragile Dresden cups and saucers.

"I thought you might like China tea," she said. "One gets it so rarely here. My daughter in England sends it to me."

I accepted my cup and thanked her.

"My elder daughter was lucky enough to escape," she explained. "You see, I married a Jew. I am not Jewish. My father was a Berlin surgeon who took a brilliant young Jewish doctor into practice with him very long ago. Goodness! Very long ago indeed! We were married before the First World War. Eventually my husband succeeded to my father's practice, and he became quite well known. We had a fabulous life here in Berlin during the twenties. We knew so many artists and writers; we went to the theater and had our box at the opera, our season tickets at the symphony. It was a sad time, of course, but a brilliant and exciting time." She sighed.

"We had two girls. The elder one, Erika, read an ad for a servant girl in the London *Times* in the spring of 1939. Imagine! She answered it, they accepted her, and she went to England in July 1939, just in time. She had to go on working as a housemaid for three years to justify her visa, but, of course, then they couldn't send her back and wouldn't because she was half Jewish."

"She wasn't interned?" I asked.

"No. She had to register, of course, but as a *Mischling*, a half-Jewess, she had a special status, and she was only twenty when she left here."

"And she stayed after the war?" I asked.

"She got a better job after 1942, and later she married an Austrian refugee living in England, a psychiatrist. He has a good practice in London and they live in the country near by. She is happy and well and they have three children. She telephones me every two weeks. It only costs ten shillings, imagine!"

"Is your other daughter here in Berlin?"

"Yes. Hannah is two years younger than Erika. She had a hard time during the war, but she survived. Of course, as half-Jews neither of the girls had been allowed to attend the Gymnasium. Erika went to trade school to learn to be a lab technician, intending to work for her father. Hannah wanted to be a writer. She had no formal education—she just finished Basic School—but we had plenty of books at home, and she read avidly."

"What happened to her during the war?" I asked.

"She was conscripted for forced labor, as the *Mischling* children were. Her work was hard, and the hours were long but not as bad as some. She had to clean out railroad cars. It was very uncomfortable in the winter because the cars weren't heated while they worked in them, and you can guess how cold and windy railroad yards can be, how icy. She ruined her hands, poor thing, and her complexion got all rough and dry. It aged her, but she survived, and as I said, so many didn't, so we were grateful."

"And later?" I asked.

"Well, right after the war she got a job with the government. She was one of the few accredited antinazis, so even though she didn't have a degree or even her *Abitur*, she was taken into the civil service. She got married in 1950 and now has two children."

"Did she ever write as she'd wanted?"

"As a matter of fact, she does write. After her first child was born she began writing children's stories. She has done three or four children's books, and they are very successful. I think she still hopes to write a serious novel some day, but not yet. Perhaps when the children are grown."

"Were your daughters brought in up the Jewish religion?" I asked.

She shook her head. "No, my husband belonged to a Jewish congregation, but he was not active and he did not insist that the girls be Jewish. If we had had a son, that might have been different, but he thought it would be better to have the girls brought up in my religion, thinking girls are closer to the mother. They are Protestant, though I must say we have never been very churchy people. I still belong to the Church, mind you, and sometimes I go, but the girls weren't brought up strictly. However, it turned out to be lucky for them that they'd been baptized. No one could accuse the nazis of being Christian, but baptized half-Jews were a little safer."

"Your husband?" I asked tentatively.

"He survived too, which is a minor miracle. He was arrested, of course. He was not only a Jew but technically a practicing Jew. Naturally, he was among those rounded up, and he was sent to a concentration camp, but we had many friends in Berlin, and some of them were nazis. Does it surprise you that nazi officials had Jewish friends?"

I said no, not really.

"Or," she added, "that Jews had nazi friends? But life isn't like a textbook—people don't live by definition. There were nazis and nazis, just as there were Jews and Jews."

"Of course," I agreed.

"Well, one of our nazi friends happened to be the state's attorney. Actually, his mother was our friend. She had been my husband's patient for many years and still came to him long after Jewish doctors were forbidden to treat Aryans. Many did, as you know. They came at night or pretended to be coming to play bridge with me."

I nodded. "And the other way around," I added. "I have a woman friend in Munich who is a physician. She and her husband treated Jews and half-Jews secretly all through the war, or until their Jewish patients escaped or disappeared."

"That happened here too," she said. "Well, when my husband was sent to the K.Z. my younger daughter went to see the nazi state's attorney. She pleaded with him; he agreed to intervene; and within a few weeks my husband was released. Of course, he was forbidden to practice medicine, and he was kept under surveillance, but he was safe."

"He lived through the war?" I asked.

"Oh, yes. He lived until just ten years ago, when he died of heart disease. We were both lucky. We weren't even bombed out."

I asked whether she still had many friends in Berlin and whether she went to the theater and to concerts.

"I am an old women," she said. "I am eighty-five, and so most of my friends are either dead or abroad or in the West. I have always had a few younger friends. I have my daughters and their children. Hannah lives close by, and so I see her and the children frequently. Once in a while I go to a matinee, but usually I prefer a quiet stroll through the park and a cup of tea in a café, or tea at home with friends.

"I don't know whether Berlin isn't as gay as it once was or whether I am just too old, but still I have a good life."

I asked whether she received a pension.

"Oh, yes, an ample one. A retired doctor gets 600 marks a month. As a doctor's widow I am entitled to 300, but as a victim of nazism, I get an additional 160, which brings the total to 460, which is very generous. It is more than enough for an old woman! I pay only 64 marks a month for rent because this is an old building, but I have three rooms, plus kitchen and bath. I live very comfortably. A woman comes in to do my heavy housework twice a week, and my daughter takes out my laundry and helps with my shopping. I cook for myself."

"The pound cake is delicious," I said truthfully.

"I like to bake once in a while, especially if my grandchildren are coming to see me."

"Is there still a Jewish community in East Berlin?" I asked.

She nodded. "There is a remnant. Naturally, since I never belonged to the congregation, I am not in close touch with them, but I know a few of my husband's old friends, or rather their sons and grandsons. They keep in touch. The present rabbi used to be the cantor in the old days. He still visits me occasionally. He escaped to Denmark in 1938 and then in 1940 to Sweden. He came back in 1945.

"It's a small community. It was once very powerful in business and in the arts, but today it is only a fragment. Still, some survived, and they maintain their identity as Jews and as Berliners."

When we left her, we were both feeling a little tired and a little subdued. Eric said that he hoped I was not too tired for one more appointment.

"So late?" I said. It was well after six.

"We are invited somewhere for an early supper," he explained. "I'll see that we break away early enough to get you to the Friedrichstrasse at a decent hour. You'll find these people very interesting."

Instead of driving back toward the center of town, he turned east and drove toward the outskirts of the city. In a quarter of an hour we found

ourselves in one of those districts of Berlin which, although part of the
city, seem like the separate small towns they once were. This one had
a central square with an *S-Bahn* station, an old inn, some shops, and a
pub. Only the *S-Bahn* and the tram line proclaimed it part of the metropolis.

Eric turned off the main street and pulled up before a four-story
house in a side street. We entered a narrow, dark, but clean-smelling hall
and climbed well-scrubbed steps to the second floor. Eric knocked at the
door on the left, and it opened. A small wiry man threw his arms around
Eric and slapped him on the back.

"Well, boy, how are you? Welcome, welcome! Marti is waiting for you.
It's been too long. Come in," he said all in one breath. Then he turned
to greet me, and Eric introduced Rudi. Rudi shook my hand vigorously
and led me into the living room.

Marti came bustling out from the kitchen drying her hands on her
ample, checked apron. She was a little taller than Rudi, plump but
firm, with sandy hair streaked with gray. She was about sixty, I thought.
When she smiled, her blue eyes sparkled and her cheeks grew pink and
she still had a young girl's dimples. She too shook my hand and made
me welcome.

"Supper is all ready!" she announced. "I'll bring it right out. Eric, can
you open the wine for us?"

He nodded and followed her into the kitchen. I had a chance to notice
a photograph of Lenin in a dark beret on one wall, and Ernst Thälmann's on the opposite wall next to a group photograph. Rudi intercepted my glance.

"Thälmann," he said, and walked over to the photos. "Look," he said,
pointing to the group photograph, "this is me with the beret right next
to him. We were all comrades together in the Kiel Uprising. Didn't Eric
tell you?" I shook my head. "Ah, he wanted to surprise you. I'm an old
Spartacist, one of the few left."

I studied the photograph, and there indeed was a very young Rudi,
perhaps nineteen or twenty at the time but basically unchanged. Now
his face was deeply lined, but he had stayed lean and he was very tan
for a notherner. I glanced around the apartment. Rudi invited me to
sit on the elderly plush overstuffed sofa. There were no signs of luxury.
The room was small, and I later learned that there was one small bedroom, a bath with no hot water, and a very old-fashioned kitchen.

Marti came back bearing a large wooden tray laden with cold cuts.
Eric followed carrying the opened wine bottle. Marti set out the plates
of cold meat and cheese and black bread on an oval table in front of

the sofa. I noticed that an old-fashioned ceiling lamp shaded with fringed linen hung over the table.

"Now, what did I forget?" Marti inquired, surveying her table. "Ah, margarine and mustard and the glasses!" She darted back into the kitchen.

"And pepper and salt," her husband called after her.

"But our guests would like a schnapps before supper, surely," he suggested, and Eric agreed. Rudi produced slim schnapps glasses from a corner cupboard, then went into the kitchen to procure the chilled bottle. Marti brought in the missing items and swept off her apron, stuffing it behind her as she sank into a square-backed upholstered chair. Rudi judiciously poured white liquor into four minature glasses.

"To our American visitor!" he toasted, and his wife beamed and raised her glass.

"We don't see many Americans," she said. "We used to, before the war, before Hitler. I always liked them."

"We used to know some Americans in Moscow," her husband said, and he explained that they had fled Germany in 1933 and lived in the Soviet Union until the end of the war.

As we began the simple supper Rudi told me a little about their life in the emigration to Russia.

"We were homesick, of course, and we found the climate harsh, but there were other Germans and Austrians there. Our Soviet comrades found work for us both so we could earn our living. Of course, we didn't live there as we do here," he said, gesturing at the apartment, which to him seemed luxurious and large, "but we lived, which is more than we might have done in nazi Germany."

"They were hard years," Marti said, "but we were younger, and we also had good friends. I worked in a factory during the war—hard work, long hours, low pay, but we workers all felt we were helping to defeat Hitler and fascism. Rudi and I lived in one room in a big apartment we shared with seven other émigrés. There was no central heating and seldom hot water. Fuel was scarce during the war years and food—" she shrugged. "Well, we didn't starve."

"Beans and soup and tea and sometimes bread," Rudi said, remembering.

"Good tea!" Marti added, "and cabbage. I hate cabbage!" she grinned and shuddered, "but we Germans are spoiled. It was good for us to live simply for a few years. The worst part, for me, was the fear when the fascists were advancing on Moscow. They got very close," she said.

"You both came back in 1945?" I asked.

"Right at the end of the war," Rudi explained. "Things were pretty bad here then, but Marti and I were classified as victims of fascism so we had preference in finding apartments, in rationing and in jobs. I worked for the Russians as an interpreter for the first year and then as the schools began to reopen, I applied for a job in my own profession. I'm a gym instructor."

That, I thought, explained the lean hardness of his face and body.

"Did you teach in a public school?" I asked.

"I taught in a special sports school, a sort of college to train athletes and gym teachers," he said, "but I retired three years ago. Mind you, I still work out regularly. I belong to the local men's athletic group and we meet twice a week at our district Sports Hall."

"Rudi won a medal for parallel bars in 1964," Marti said proudly, "and his school has a cabinet full of awards that his teams won while he was training them."

After dinner we drank hot, strong tea, and Rudi poured a postprandial schnapps for each of us. He eagerly accepted my offer of an English cigarette. I should have liked to have offered him the almost full pack, but I sensed that he would be offended. I was amazed that such old party faithfuls, veterans of the emigration to Moscow, should be living in such simple circumstances. The apartment was comfortable, but it was anything but luxurious. When I went to wash before starting my journey back to the West, I passed through the kitchen and noticed the old-fashioned stove, the immense bucket of water heating on a back burner.

"We have no water heater," Marti explained as she led me through. "After I cook I always heat a bucketful for the dishes and for our evening wash. Do you want some for your hands?" she asked, but I declined.

The towels were clean but worn thin; the bath had a plain wooden floor, untiled and uncarpeted; the tub was the old iron sort with huge claw feet, but inside it was a small yellow plastic laundry tub.

"We bathe in that," she said. "It takes less hot water! But most often we wash in cold water to save fuel."

Eric and I left just after supper, having thanked our host and hostess sincerely for an interesting evening. Rudi and Marti were charming, warm-hearted, and obviously honest people. I regretted that I had not met them on my own, that I had not been able to ask them a few of the frank questions that had come to mind, because I thought had I been alone I might have received some frank and enlightening answers.

"Could you come back on Saturday?" Eric asked as he pulled up near the Friedrichstrasse railway station. "I have some tickets for a good Soviet film I thought you might like to see."

I agreed to meet him on Saturday at two. Saturday was a beautiful day. We had a pleasant drive and then, since the film was one of those fashionable epics that last for many hours, we had to content ourselves with a snack instead of dinner. The film, largely documentary, concerned the German invasion of Russia during the summer and fall of 1941, concentrating on the advance of Army Group Center toward Moscow. I was amused and impressed that the Soviet script-writers had managed to hang onto a precarious balance between antifascism and patriotism to Mother Russia on the one hand and official friendliness to their gallant East German comrades on the other. Individual German soldiers were portrayed as average, normal, likable human beings, victims, along with the Russians, of the fascist tyranny. Only the Hitler government, the nazi elite, were depicted as brutal or as the enemy.

The film used an obvious but effective device of demonstrating the Wehrmacht advance by showing in scene after scene road signs reading "200 Kilometers to Moscow," "140 Kilometers to Moscow," then "60" and finally "35." At the final signpost the Germans dug in, the snow began to fall flake by flake, gust by gust, then relentlessly falling snow inexorably obliterated the signpost itself and with it German hope of taking Moscow, of victory.

When the film had reached its inevitable end, Eric and I blinked after the prolonged darkness, smiled vacantly at each other, and staggered out of the theater.

"Let's go to the pub next door for a drink," Eric suggested.

Since we had only sandwiches at four, we each consumed a bowl of hot, pungent Hungarian goulash soup with black bread. Afterwards I ordered a dry, white wine, but Eric chose schnapps. Usually abstemious, this evening he seemed to hunger and thirst for alcohol, perhaps for oblivion. I sipped my wine judiciously and watchfully and asked what he had thought of the film. Just as judiciously at first, he discussed its technical merits, the photography, the mixture of Wehrmacht documentaries with fictional segments, but then after the third or fourth schnapps, he interrupted himself.

"Damn it all!" he pounded the table. "Just think. Thirty kilometers to the Kremlin! Actually inside the Moscow suburbs. We almost made it!"

"You did, didn't you?" I said quietly and let him drink. So much, I thought, for our beloved Soviet socialist brothers.

I have seen Eric many times since that evening, and I have gradually learned a little about him. He was married a few years ago and now has a little girl and lives in the suburbs of East Berlin. Sometimes he confides a fragment of his past, a lesser fragment of his genuine viewpoint, but I have never learned as much about my communist comrade as after that Soviet war film. Whenever he becomes obnoxiously didactic, pedantically reciting Marxism-Leninism to me at great length, I remember that involuntary "We almost made it!" and grin.

10

Dorothy

One of the peculiarities of Berlin is the way the streets are named. Like most cities Berlin has its share of streets named after monarchs, generals, and historic battles, its sprinkling of avenues honoring the constitution and the republic, but not for Berlin such prosaic locations as the corner of Sixteenth Street and Avenue Q. In Berlin each neighborhood seems to have a theme, a leitmotif from which the names of its streets derive. Hyacinth, Gardenia and Tulip Streets, for instance, reveal to the initiate that they lie adjacent to the botanical gardens. Where but in scholarly-minded Berlin would you find entire neighborhoods of streets named for physicists, mathematicians and historians?

Therefore I was not surprised to find myself driving along Copernicus Street past Galileo and Newton Streets one May morning on my way to attend oral examinations at a West Berlin Gymnasium. The street names seemed in harmony with the academic occasion and perfectly typical of Berlin.

I drew up in front of a two-story, sprawling modern building, easily found a parking place, and walked toward the entrance. A tall, slim woman in her early thirties came briskly toward me. Her light brown hair was combed neatly into a soft twist, her serious grey eyes were direct and friendly. Her dress, a soft grey jersey which flowed as she walked, was discreet and understated but in the latest fashion.

She smiled tentatively, and I introduced myself.

"Oh, good," she said, extending a hand. "You are just in time for my discussion class before the examinations. I am Dorothy H."

We shook hands, and she led me back up the steps and into the building.

"Our school is quite new," she said, "just three years old. It's not just a Gymnasium, you know. The *Realschule* [commercial high school,

141

grades 7–10] classes meet in this part of the building. Our Gymnasium classes are held upstairs."

She walked ahead of me to the staircase. A bell rang, and scores of young people poured out into the corridors when we were halfway to the next floor. At first glance, they seemed like adolescents anywhere in the Western world, but as I looked more closely, I noticed a difference. Indeed there were some young males with beards and long hair, but relatively few, and most of these seemed costumed for a period play. They looked more like cavaliers and young knights than like hippies or revolutionaries. Bearded or shaved, dressed in modern flamboyant style or in conservative greys or blues, most of the boys looked freshly laundered and well groomed, and the girls were neat and very vital. Even the inevitable noise they made moving from room to room seemed a disciplined, cheerful noise.

Dorothy pushed open a classroom door and let me go ahead of her. I entered a small room containing ten or twelve oblong tables, each with two chairs arranged irregularly about the room. There was a large globe, plants lined the windowsills, and on the walls hung the usual maps of Germany, of Western Europe and of the world. A bulletin board covered with clippings and political cartoons and charts of governmental structure hung near the door.

"This is a class of seventeen- and eighteen-year-olds," Dorothy told me. "They will be taking their exams for the *Abitur* next year. We give political science in the last two years of the Gymnasium."

I asked how often they met, and she said every day for a forty-five-minute period.

"They are really enthusiastic, and, of course, they love discussions. You will see," she assured me as the young people began to troop in and settle themselves at the tables. Dorothy and I shared a table at the window side of the room.

The discussion that day was rather technical. Apparently the pupils had been reading about the process of drafting the federal government's budget. The class had divided into committees, each charged with the study of the budget of a single ministry. Now they pooled their information and observations. They asked each other sophisticated and penetrating questions and carried on the discussion with relatively little intervention from Dorothy. They were certainly interested, and I counted sixteen of the twenty pupils who either asked a question or voluntarily offered a comment during the period. The atmosphere of the class was serious and scholarly but also relaxed and happy. The pupils expressed a variety of viewpoints and often disagreed emphatically and articulately but always with courtesy, frequently with humor. The arguments were often interrupted with laughter.

When the bell rang I was surprised that the time had gone so quickly. I complimented Dorothy on her class.

"They are a good group, but then they are all aware that next year will be a challenge for them, that then they will have to think on their feet and prove that they can do independent research. They are quite serious about it. This is the year when most of them grow up, when they face up to the imminent encounter with the *Abitur*."

We gathered our handbags and notebooks, and she led me down the hall. The examination room was a large classroom in which the oblong tables had been arranged to form a large *U*. At the center of the *U*'s opening was a single table with one chair. Teachers filed in, chatting and laughing. A small, grey-haired purposeful woman began distributing folders to each faculty member. Dorothy presented me to Dr. L., the school's principal, who shook hands and invited me to sit next to her at the head of the table. She gave me a folder and explained that it contained the entire school record of each of the candidates to be heard.

"You see," she said as she took out a mimeographed sheet and showed it to me, "these are the grades of Miss W., the first candidate, from the time she entered the Gymnasium."

I looked over the list and saw that the grades were for all subjects in grades seven through thirteen.

"These are the evaluations of her teachers in the past three years, and this is the most relevant to today's exam, the evaluations of her German teachers. You'll find a set like this for each pupil."

I began to leaf through the folder. Judging by the record, Miss W. seemed about a *B*-student. I thought it would be interesting to hear how well she would do in the oral examination.

"Here she is," Dorothy whispered. "The young woman with her is the German literature teacher."

The teacher patted her charge on the shoulder and took her place at the end of the *U*. The pupil, a small, dark girl of about nineteen, wearing a shapeless green woolen dress, looking as though she had not slept and had consumed too much coffee, took her place behind the candidate's desk.

"You may sit," the principal told her, and rather self-consciously she did. "You may smoke, Miss W. There is an ash tray."

The young woman said that she did not smoke.

"All right, ladies and gentlemen," the principal began. "I think that we might get underway. Our first candidate is a pupil of Miss G.'s. Sophie, will you introduce her please?"

Sophie G. stood and gave her pupil's name, age, and class. "Miss W. will be examined on three plays, one by Shaw, one by Schiller, and one by Hauptmann."

She handed the girl a folded slip which Miss W. opened and read. She sat staring at the questions for a full minute while male and female teachers leafed through their grade folders, lit cigarettes, and settled themselves more comfortably in their wooden, straight-backed chairs.

"All right, Marie?" Miss G. asked. Marie smiled and nodded. She read the question aloud: "Compare the character of St. Joan in Shaw's play to that portrayed in Schiller's."

"All right, Marie. What do you think?" her teacher led.

Slowly at first and then gradually more confidently, more articulately, the young woman marshalled her facts and her impressions and soon she was coming to grips with the essentials of the question. After about ten minutes, she paused and looked at Miss G., who then interjected a specific question. The candidate answered, and her teacher threw two or three short questions, which she also dealt with skillfully. Miss G. turned to the principal and asked whether she had a question for the candidate. Dr. L. produced a very general *pro forma* question and then asked whether any other faculty members wished to pose questions. One or two did, and then the principal glanced at her watch.

"I think our time is up," she said. "Thank you, Miss W."

The candidate thanked the principal and the faculty and went out accompanied by her literature teacher. The teachers at the table relaxed and chatted briefly until the next candidate appeared. In each case, the pupil was sponsored by the teacher of the subject in which he was to be examined. Each pupil had been instructed to prepare in a particular area; for example, Miss. W. had been told to read five or six specific plays in preparation. Each candidate was questioned for about twenty minutes.

The bell rang at noon just as the board was finishing its examination of the third candidate.

"We shall break for lunch," Dr. L. announced, and we all stood up gratefully and began to drift out of the room.

"There's a little café down the street where we could have lunch quietly, if you'd like," Dorothy suggested, and I accepted with alacrity.

"It's easier to answer your questions there," she said, "than with twenty colleagues leaning over our shoulders and gossiping in our ears."

We hurried down the stairs and out of the building into the late spring sunlight. The café was unpretentious, but it was clean and cheerful and quiet. Dorothy ordered *Würstchen* and a small glass of beer. I asked for scrambled eggs and a glass of Moselle.

"Today I was off duty," Dorothy said. "Tomorrow I have two boys scheduled to be grilled."

"Does that make you nervous?" I asked.

"Not as nervous as it makes them, but darned near! As I said, we begin coaching our pupils the year before, preparing them as much as we can to answer questions ad lib, to stand up and defend their views, to arrive at independent opinions, and we always think we have done very well until about a week before the orals. Then we all get cold feet, teachers and pupils, and go into a tailspin."

"But naturally you don't let them know," I said.

"Oh, of course not. At least, we try not to. They take a lot of mothering the last year, but it is surprising how grown up they are when it is all over, as though they had been transmuted."

"Forged like steel," I suggested and she nodded.

"This whole process of the examinations for the *Abitur* is a little hard on them, but on the whole, they seem to thrive, and most of them even like it. It's a challenge, a kind of proving oneself, and when they have passed it shows that they are capable of going on to do independent scholarly work."

I asked whether most candidates would pass, and she nodded confidently.

"Oh, yes, the large majority will pass the first time around. Those who really don't have the ability or the interest have long since been weeded out. About fourteen per cent of the youngsters who enter the Gymnasium ask to be transferred after the first semester, and I should say that only about half of the entering pupils stay on to complete their *Abiturs*.* By and large those who stay to take the exams have a fairly good idea that they will pass, and as I said, we coach and encourage them for a good two years before."

"How many examinations does each candidate take?" I asked as the waitress brought our lunch.

"Four written examinations," she said. "German, mathematics and one foreign language are compulsory for all pupils. About ninety per cent of the youngsters choose English as their first foreign language. Then there is a fourth written examination in a specialized subject varying with the type of school."

---

* According to the office of the Berlin Senator for Education approximately 24% of Berlin's seventh-grade pupils begin Gymnasium; 11.5% complete the *Abitur*.

"You mean in a humanistic school the fourth exam would be in Greek or Latin, while in a technical school it would be in one of the sciences?" I asked.

"Yes, and in others it would be in social science or economics, in a second and third language, or perhaps in music or art."

"The student has to pass these before taking the oral examination?" I asked.

"Yes. In fact, before the orals each pupil is assigned a preliminary grade, a composite of his score in the written exams and an average of his grades for the past three years in each subject. He need only take the oral if his grade is not clearcut or if it is unsatisfactory."

"In other words if he has a definite "2" or "3" he can omit the oral?" *
I asked.

She nodded, carefully cutting her sausage and spearing a slice.

"Yes, but so many are borderline cases, and we prefer to give them every chance to pull up their averages if there is any chance of it. Pupils take four oral exams: in German, in one language, in social science, and in an elective such as science or art or music."

"You don't give all the examinations during the final month, do you?"

"No. The pupils take some of the written exams a whole year, some a semester, before the finals. We are beginning a new system in Berlin which allows gifted and ambitious youngsters to take their entire battery of tests at the end of the twelfth Gymnasium year instead of waiting until the thirteenth year. If they pass, they may go right on to the university. I am all in favor of that."

"Yes, so am I," I said. "I am all in favor of individuality."

"Some of the so-called reforms seem silly to me," she admitted, "but this one I approve of. There has been some discussion of taking the final Gymnasium year, that is the thirteenth school year, and incorporating it with the first two university years into a new institution called a college. I can see that the first two university years could be separated from advanced study, but I am not sure what would happen to the *Abitur.*"

"From the point of view of age grouping it might be good," I said tentatively.

"Yes, possibly," she said. "Most thirteen-year pupils are nineteen. That is quite grown up for a secondary school, and the twenty- and twenty-one-year-olds are rather young for the university. Yes, from that point of view it might be good, and it would enable the university to insist on a matric-

* German grades range from 1 to 5 or 6. The highest grade, "1" corresponds to *A+* in an American school and is exceptional. A grade of "5" is unsatisfactory.

ulation exam at the end of the three college years before a student could
go on to advanced study."

"The universities would be centers of research and of advanced scientific, scholarly study," I said. "It sounds sensible."

"That does, but some proposals are dangerous, I think. I am not a diehard," she said, "but I am no friend of levelling in education, and I am
afraid that too many of our German educationists and politicians who
play politics with education are trying to make a sacred cow out of
democracy."

"Are you thinking about the comprehensive schools?" I asked.

"Yes. Well, in the first place, as you know, Berlin has postponed the
division of pupils until the end of the sixth school year. In the other
West German *Länder* children divide into the three basic branches at the
end of the fourth school year when they are ten or eleven. In the fifth
year some enter the Gymnasium, some the commercial school, and the
rest go to higher classes of the *Volksschule* and then into apprenticeships
or trade schools."

"In West Germany about half the children in the fifth year are in
Volksschulen, aren't they?" I asked.

"About that," she said. "In Berlin we keep the children in the Basic
School for two more years, but in the fifth and sixth grades we begin a
foreign language and include some specialized courses."

"Do you find the extension of the Basic School a disadvantage to children who later go on to the Gymnasium?" I asked.

"In general, yes. Of course, even in the Basic School we divide the
children into ability groups so the democratization of keeping them in
the same building is more apparent than real, and the new system does
give some youngsters who had not thought of going to the Gymnasium a
chance to see whether they might enjoy languages and more serious
academic subjects. The Basic School does not have the professional atmosphere of a Gymnasium. The fifth and sixth grades there are not up
to a Gymnasium's academic standards. My own opinion is that more is
lost than gained by flattening out education."

"Then you must oppose the new comprehensive schools?" I asked.

"Utterly!" she said. "I am no social snob. I think that any child of
whatever background who has the ability and the interest should be encouraged to stretch himself to his limits, but I also believe that the modern, technological world demands more, not less, excellence and, perhaps,
unfortunately, more, not less, earlier not later, specialization."

"Do you think children can be sorted out into academic and nonacademic types at twelve or ten?" I asked. "Aren't some late-bloomers?"

"Some are, of course, and I don't advocate an entirely rigid system. There should be ample opportunity for late-bloomers to switch over to an academic track when they discover their natural bent, but we could do that through extra classes, summer school, special coaching. The late-bloomers are a small minority. The overwhelming majority of children do sort themselves out by the end of the fourth school year. I believe in a system with maximum flexibility but also maximum challenge and opportunity for the gifted child.

"You know," she went on, "failure to challenge a bright child can blunt his intellectual curiosity and destroy his interest in school. I think it is time that we began offering our eleven- and twelve-years-olds more, not less, intellectual stimulation, more, not less, creative education. I think the genuinely modern trend is toward more individuality. This doctrinaire idea of lumping all children together to attempt to make them equal in my opinion is the opposite of progressive, but it certainly seems to be the present trend in Germany."

"I have a theory," I said, "that egalitarianism in education appeals to two kinds of people: on the one hand to the leveller, who consciously or unconsciously resents the supposed social or economic superiority of the intellectual class, and on the other to the generous-minded but naive intellectual who wishes to share what he considers the obvious superiority of his way of life with everyone or at least with as many people as possible."

"And that, if you like, is intellectual snobbishness!" Dorothy commented.

"Exactly," I said. "The implication is clearly that a technical or commercial or manual education is inferior, that manual work is demeaning."

"Which is both mistaken and misguided, and as I said before, anything but progressive or modern," Dorothy said.

"A very bourgeois attitude," I said.

"Well, goodness!" Dorothy said. "I am as bourgeois as anyone can be. Both my parents were Gymnasium teachers. In fact, my mother still teaches. I'm sure that my grandparents believed that manual work was less dignified than an intellectual profession. At one time perhaps my parents believed it, but certainly my mother no longer does and I never did. Society needs all kinds of talents and all kinds of skills, and surely any skill should be respected. Surely it is more progressive, more democratic to accord every citizen dignity regardless of the kind of work he does, to acknowledge individual differences in taste and temperament as

Fig. 9. One of the new West Berlin comprehensive schools (photo by Landesbildstelle, West Berlin)

Fig. 10. Girls at the Martin Buber comprehensive school, West Berlin (photo by Landesbildstelle, West Berlin)

well as in intellectual endowment and to try to give each child the kind of education which suits him as an individual."

"Oh, I agree with you," I said. "I think it is a basic misconception to view the public school system as a machine for the fabrication of intellectuals. Granted that a highly technological and affluent society needs more scientists and professional people than a backward or agrarian society, there is still a limit to the number of doctors, lawyers, and scholars who can be absorbed, and nothing is worse, I think, than a surplus of unemployed and unemployable intellectuals or semi-intellectuals."

"The condition in many of the developing nations," Dorothy suggested. "Yes, and today all professions demand greater specialization than ever, better quality education than ever, so in my opinion it is more urgent to start children on separate tracks earlier, not later."

"Do most of your colleagues agree with you?" I asked as the waitress served our coffee.

"Goodness no!" she said and laughed. "Did you ever see three teachers, especially three German teachers, three *Berlin* teachers who did agree on anything? We are a garrulous profession, and hairsplitting is our favorite pastime."

"Almost as bad as professors," I said.

"My dear, quite as bad! It's our professional disease. Whenever two or more of us gather together it is a *Kaffee Klatsch!* Chatter, chatter, chatter! I'm as bad as the rest, I admit it."

"Me, too," I said sadly.

Dorothy grinned, "I suppose it's international. We Germans are just used to thinking we are the world's worst or most of everything. In some ways I think we are the world's silliest nation."

"I would argue with you about first place," I said.

"In some ways Americans and Germans are much alike," she said. "We are both insecure. The British and French don't go in for this soul-searching and breast-beating. I have the impression that if the British discover that they are not very good at some profession or skill, they conclude that it must be rather vulgar to be good at it."

"Skills like exporting more than one imports?" I suggested uncharitably.

"Exactly. We Germans are one extreme or the other. Either our way is not only the best but the only conceivable way, or else everything we have done is wrong and we must rush to copy some foreign nation, nowadays America. So many of our educators simply accept without question any theory or practice that originates in America. We are trying to out-Dewey Dewey."

"You've taught in America, haven't you?" I asked.

"Yes. I spent a year in a small town in New York State as an exchange teacher. I enjoyed it, and I liked the Americans. I sincerely think we Germans can learn a lot from them, but to be frank, chiefly from their mistakes."

"But you probably won't," I said gloomily.

"No, of course not," Dorothy said. "We shall insist on making the same mistakes and being German, we shall make them very thoroughly. I am no fanatical nationalist," she added. "I think that we can learn from many nations and especially from America, but I have never believed in slavish imitation, not even before my year in New York."

She absently stirred her coffee. "I do see that in the last quarter of the twentieth century an academic education cannot be the privilege of a closed caste. Of course not. And I can see the social and political danger of cloistering our Gymnasium pupils, sheltering them from the real world so that they become *Weltfremd,* unworldly, unrealistic and perhaps snobbish."

"Do you have answers to these problems?" I asked.

"No," she answered frankly. "But I do not think any educational system is perfect. Every system creates some problems, but I think one must have a hierarchy of priorities."

"First things first," I said. "What do you put first?"

"Producing educated people. I think other goals such as social engineering have to take a secondary place. Don't misunderstand me. I am a socialist, that is I belong to the S.P.D., but I cannot think it is the primary job of the school system to serve a doctrinaire theory of abstract equality. In the first place, there is no equality. Children are different. In the second, society needs young people with widely different, basically different skills. Realistically speaking, society needs only a small percentage of scholars and scientists and artists, a somewhat larger but still limited number of doctors, lawyers, and chemists, but it needs a whole assortment of technicians, office workers, and skilled workers. It is simply an economic and social necessity that most schools must educate computer programmers, nurses, stenographers, and electricians. I think we should try to make all of our youngsters happy, healthy, and good citizens, of course, but primarily we must educate them to the best of their individual ability and according to their individual tastes and interests."

"And if a few choose the wrong path?" I asked.

"An educational system can be geared to the needs of the majority and to the needs of society and also provide some loopholes to protect the minority," she said. "The commercial and trade schools should not be inferior; they should be different. There is no reason why a pupil at a good trade school should not be taught to think logically and even creatively, no reason why pupils with broader interests can't choose an academic elective like higher mathematics or a science or language."

"In other words, you are suggesting the upgrading of the commercial and trade schools rather than the levelling down of the Gymnasia?" I said.

"Exactly," she nodded. "I am not suggesting the introduction of Latin and Greek or calculus as required courses or adding electives at the expense of a sound trade-training but simply offering courses pupils really want as extras. Then, should the pupil discover latent academic talent or interest, it would be easier for him to transfer to a Gymnasium."

"He would already have some credits?"

"And some background," she said. "It also makes it easier for him if he chooses the second way of evening school."

"I understand that in Berlin you have two kinds of academic evening schools, one to complete the *Realschule,* and the other to qualify for the *Abitur.*"

"Yes," Dorothy said, "so you see the pupil who, at grade five or seven, chooses the *Realschule,* or trade school, is not choosing a dead end. Either choice can lead eventually to a university if he persists."

"I notice you say 'he,' " I said, and she smiled.

"Awful, isn't it? But one does for convenience and out of old habit. Actually in Berlin we do relatively well by our girls. About half the pupils in Berlin's public Gymnasia are girls. In the Federal Republic the figure is only about a third girls."

"Berlin has always been more progressive than other German cities," I said, signaling the waitress for our check.

As we strolled back toward the school I asked Dorothy what she thought of the trend in West Germany toward all-day schools. Traditionally German children have gone to school only until one or two P.M. but the new system, which is winning widespread acceptance in the Federal Republic, will keep children in school until four or even five P.M. Judging from her views on the comprehensive school, I guessed that Dorothy would oppose the all-day school, and she did.

"I understand the reasons for it," she said. "Knowledge is expanding so there is more for youngsters to learn and therefore some educators think we have to add courses and more hours to the curriculum. My view on that is that we are not here to stuff heads with knowledge but to teach young people to think and to find out facts for themselves. Besides, there is a limit to what a child can learn in one day or one year, and leisure time is part of growing, part of learning."

I said I thought that was especially true in learning a language. "One can only learn so many new words a day, and one must rest a little in between."

"Exactly. It's true of mathematics and science too. Learning is a growing, not a cramming, process, it has to be organic."

"The other reason for the all-day school is to provide supervision for the children of mothers who work until five or to provide a safe and interesting recreation area for city children who would otherwise have to play in the streets. What about that?" I asked.

"Awful!" Dorothy exclaimed. "I think it is dreadful to organize children from morning to night, to march them around in group formation. It is bad enough that we have so many organization men in our society, but organization children would be a nightmare. A child needs privacy, and he needs to choose his own friends and cronies. He should not always be pushed together with the same twenty or thirty children who happen to have been assigned to his school class.

"I believe in maximum freedom for children and maximum individuality as I said before. If a segment of children need after-school supervision, then let it be voluntary, let it be away from the school and the school atmosphere, and let it reflect maximum individual choice."

"You mean in neighborhood youth centers?" I asked.

"Youth centers, parks, gymnasiums, that sort of thing. There are also voluntary youth organizations like Boy Scouts that can help. Of course, there could be some after-school clubs, sports certain days a week, but not assigned as part of the required school day. Why should children who do have supervision at home and who have cultural and recreational facilities available to them be locked into a regimented, collectivist program?"

I wondered what would happen to the child who studies music and who practices after school or to the girl who takes ballet lessons or the young person who likes to paint or fool around in a chemistry laboratory in the basement. Those activities would be relegated to evenings and weekends, and perhaps much of it would go by the board.

"Along with much of the child's individuality," Dorothy said. "Creative children need to be alone to read, to walk, to think. We Germans once prided ourselves on being a nation of thinkers and poets. Potential poets and thinkers would be stifled by all-day, everyday enforced companionship."

"Mass man," I suggested, and she nodded. She glanced at her watch.

"We have about twenty minutes before the next examination. Would you like to walk around the block before I take you in to meet some colleagues?"

I agreed, and we walked on past the school entrance.

"That's my car," Dorothy said, pointing to a dark blue Volkswagen parked at the curb.

"Do you drive to work every day?" I asked.

"Yes. I live clear on the other side of town, and there is no really direct subway or bus line. Besides, I like to drive home after work; it gives me a chance to relax and sort out what I've done during the day, what I plan to do the next day."

"Do you live with your parents?" I asked.

"No. I went away to boarding school to West Germany and then to Munich University and after that I felt I wanted to live on my own. I was engaged for a year or so before I went to America."

"But no longer?" I asked.

"No. Naturally my fiancé did not want me to accept the exchange award. He wanted me to stay and get married, but I was awfully interested in seeing something of the world, and I wasn't ready to settle down. When I came back," she shrugged.

"He had met someone else," I suggested, and she nodded. "They do," I said.

"I suppose," Dorothy admitted, "that if I had really wanted to marry him I would have stayed. Just the same, it hurt me very much. You see, he wrote to me that whole year while I was away, and he never mentioned another woman, never broke off the engagement."

"They do that too," I said.

"When I came back to Berlin three years ago, I started to teach here in this new school. There were new colleagues, new pupils, a new building to get used to. I had to hunt for an apartment and furnish it. I bought the car and began to explore corners of Berlin. I made a few friends and looked up some old ones, but on the whole, I live very quietly."

"And you are not engaged again or planning to be?"

"I think I should like to marry, but I am not in a hurry. There is someone who takes me to the theater or to a concert once in a while. He is very nice but, frankly, a little dull. He teaches literature and writes poetry and lives with his mother."

"Don't marry him," I said, and she laughed and assured me that she would not.

"The trouble with teaching," she said, "is that one has so little free time. Evenings I always have to prepare for the next day and sometimes grade papers as well, and weekends I like to read to keep up to date, and I have shopping and laundry and cleaning to do. I visit my mother, who is fun, most Sundays. We often go to concerts or for long walks. She is planning to retire next year, and she can't decide whether to go to my sister in Bavaria or stay here in Berlin. She loves Berlin. It would be hard for her to leave."

"You would miss her," I said.

"Yes, but my sister Edith complains that she misses her too, and I suspect she wants her as a baby-sitter. Edith has three small children."

"And you may marry," I said.

"I might if I ever had time to get about a bit more and meet people, but the only time I am really free is in the summer holiday, and so far the only people I've met on holidays have been other female teachers."

"Some day," I said.

"Perhaps. But meanwhile I have an interesting job, a comfortable salary with all the emoluments, a pleasant apartment and, all in all, a very good life."

"And you enjoy living in Berlin?" I asked.

"I love it. I enjoyed school in Bavaria, and I had a wonderful time at Munich University, but I was always glad to come home during the holidays. Berlin is perfect for teachers. We have the best of both worlds: we can enjoy living in Berlin, and we also get long enough vacations so that we don't become claustrophobic."

"So you plan to stay?" I asked.

"Oh, yes. Of course, I'd go abroad for another year if I got the chance, and I like to travel, but I would not like to live anywhere else. Berlin is very special," she said.

We had circled the block and arrived back at the school entrance.

"Come along," Dorothy suggested. "You'll probably want to wash up and then I'll introduce you to some other teachers. The principal has invited us both to have coffee with her afterwards."

I followed her up the shallow stone steps, impressed with her independence, her detachment, with her vitality and self-assurance. "She knows who and what she is," I thought. "She is Dorothy, she is a Gymnasium teacher, and she is a Berliner, and she is very happy about being all three."

"If we hurry," she said, "we can have a quick cup of coffee in my office before the examination!"

11

Sister Catharine

Catharine, swathed from head to knee in stiff, sterile white, head bandaged, hands gloved, face masked, reporting for duty as Senior Theater Sister at the door of the operating room of one of West Berlin's smaller hospitals, is a formidable presence, almost unrecognizable as the exuberant, cheerful young woman I knew in Greece. I met Catharine very far from Berlin when she was off duty. The small, plump figure, squeezed precariously into a bright green mini-bikini, stretched out on the hot sands of an Ionian island, gave no hint of on-duty severity and dignity. When she stands, Catharine is perhaps five feet four. Her face with its broad, sloping cheek bones, its smooth, tawny skin framed by heavy dark hair, her subtly slanted amber-colored eyes gave me no reason to suppose that she was a Berliner. Her mother, more draped than dressed in black, her greying black hair bound in thick braids twisted around her head, sat regally under the family beach umbrella. Perched on a straight-backed beach chair pouring iced tea from a thermos flask for her basking daughter, she looked like a benign but archaic mother goddess.

I had seen them each day for three days and each time we met we all greeted each other politely in our few words of Greek. On the third day as I sat on my small terrace playing with my kittens, Electra and Orestes, the two women passed and I overheard a few words of German. "German?" I asked a puzzled Electra, and decided they must be some sort of East European refugees who had settled in Germany. Later that day, though, I met them again and this time we spoke German.

"We're Berliners," Catharine told me as her mother silently poured ice tea. "Oh, we're Russians too, but now we are Berliners. I am a nurse, a theater sister, and we live in West Berlin."

For the two or more weeks Catharine and her mother Nichola stayed on the island I seldom saw Catharine wearing anything but a bikini. Her

157

mother wore alternately a copious and decorous one-piece black bathing
suit or her robelike black dress. I saw them only once in the evening.
Mornings I met Catharine for an early swim and afternoons I often
stopped to have tea with them—under their striped umbrella.

"There are a good many Russians in Berlin, Frau Doctor," Nichola
told me.

"I know there are Russian Orthodox churches," I said.

"Three," she said. "It is through the church that Catharine has grown
up speaking Russian. We have many friends in the congregation and we
spend many Russian evenings together."

"I grew up in Berlin," Catharine said, "but in a little Russian corner
of Berlin. Of course at school I knew German children, and later at the
hospital most of my friends were Berliners, but my closest friends have
always been children of Mama's friends."

Nichola nodded, "*Ja,* we Russians like to keep our sense of community,
our identity, and we like the children not to forget their mother tongue.
Naturally we hope that our children will marry within the community to
preserve their religion as well as their culture."

"Not me, *Mamuschka.* I won't marry."

"*Ach,* you're young yet, you can't know," her mother said.

"I'm over thirty," Catharine asserted, "and I have no time for men.
Besides, I enjoy my life as it is. Why, I have everything. An interesting
job, a good salary, a lovely apartment and a darling Mama. What more
could a man give me? He could only disturb our peaceful, pleasant life."

Nichola smiled. "Children, Catharine, but you still have time and I
admit most of the men available aren't much. Perhaps some day?" She
shrugged, a tired, patient gesture.

Over our iced tea, served in tall glasses accompanied by small almond
biscuits brought in a tin from Berlin, Nichola told me that she had been
born in Leningrad in 1901.

"My family was a respectable, middle-class family. My father was a
lawyer. When my teachers at school suggested that I had a promising
voice and should study music, my parents were a little hesitant. They
knew my grandparents would object, and, of course, they did. They
thought a singing career meant the opera, and that was the stage and
unheard of for a respectable girl."

"Did you convince them?" I asked.

"My father was a great music lover and very enlightened. He talked
them into accepting the idea that concert singing was perfectly respectable
and he assured them I would sing mainly Church music. So I studied
voice, but then the revolution happened."

"You would have been sixteen in 1917," I said.

She nodded. "I'd had only a few months of voice lessons. Already my teachers were promising me that I would be a singer, but the Bolshevik revolution swept all that away."

"Your family fled?" I asked.

"My father was shot by the Bolsheviks during the first bloody weeks. He was a class enemy, you understand. My mother took me and the younger children to her sister in the provinces. I tried to persuade Mama to escape to the West somewhere while it was still possible, but she refused to leave. Her parents were too old to leave. Grandma had a weak heart, and my little sister was too young. But my mother urged me to go. She gave me some of her jewelry, sewed it into the seams of my dresses and told me to try to get to Berlin. She and Papa had once visited Berlin, and she knew the Germans loved music. 'You can go on with your singing there,' she said, and so I joined some of our family's friends who were going to try to escape, and, well, we made it."

"You got safely to Berlin?" I asked.

"Yes, all of us, but what a Berlin! Well, you can imagine what Berlin in 1918 was like. The Germans had had their own small revolution, and there was still unrest. Berlin was a defeated capital, a hungry, desolate city. Worst for us, there were no jobs. Thousands of returned veterans were out of work. What jobs there were, were of course for them, not for an untrained schoolgirl who knew almost no German."

"But Mama was lucky," Catharine interjected. "We are always lucky, Mama and I. Almost."

Nichola nodded. "*Ja, Ja.* By accident I met a German couple, middle-aged, who owned a small business firm. They had lost their son in the war and they more or less took me under their wing—treated me almost like a daughter. They hired me even though I knew next to nothing. They helped me with my German, they taught me about office routine, and finally the wife taught me bookkeeping. After a few years I became fairly competent and I was truly earning my salary. I was very grateful, but I was also sad because obviously I had to give up my dream to become a singer."

"I suppose you had no time during the early years to practice," I began.

"No time, no money for lessons and not much energy. Besides, where could I have sung? You can't bellow operatic arias or, worse, scales and exercises when you live in a furnished room. You'd soon find yourself on the street."

"But you did sing, Mama," Catharine objected.

"*Ach,* in church!" Nichola admitted. "Yes, of course. I sang in church in our marvellous choir, and that was a blessing."

"You still sing there," Catharine added. "Mama still has a beautiful voice."

"Our church has always been a great blessing to us, especially to me during those early days. Not just spiritually, but as a center of life for many uprooted Russian *émigrés.* Those were bad years for us, learning every week, every month, of more deaths at home. Shootings, starvation, disease, and then the many who simply disappeared, some on the trek through Siberia to the Far East, some during the civil war, some just . . ." she threw up her hands, "just gone."

"You did get news, then?" I asked.

"Sometimes someone had a letter, sometimes a new refugee arrived. Sometimes a German traveller or a sailor from a ship would bring us messages. We were all hungry for every scrap of news, and we huddled together, sharing every tidbit, offering comfort to those who had heard nothing or heard the worst. None of us was quite alone."

"Mama met Papa through the Church," Catharine explained.

"We met quite early," Nicholas said, "and since we both came from Leningrad and I had known his mother from our church at home, we became good friends right away. We wanted to marry, but neither of us could afford to think of marriage those first years. Sasha was determined that he would have his own business, so we both worked and saved. I saved for our household, Sasha for the business. I was thirty before we married and thirty-three when our son was born."

"But we had a nice life, Mama, before the war."

"We had a comfortable home," Nichola said. "My husband's small business prospered. Of course he worked very hard, and we always lived frugally. When the nazis came to power we were not happy. We had fled Russia to escape dictatorship, but then as Russians we were used to tyranny. We were sad about the loss of freedom in Germany. We were grateful to the Germans for taking us in. The Germans, the Berliners, seem hard on the surface. They are not as warm, as affectionate, as demonstrative as we, not until you know them. Then they are good friends, though. So many Germans were good to us. I mourned for Germany, but we kept quiet."

"You didn't think of emigrating again?" I asked.

"No, we had invested so many years in building the business, in buying our apartment and making it comfortable. Besides, we still had a pleasant life. Our apartment was never luxurious, but it was, well, civilized. We had a few nice things, and we were a happy family. By then we had two children, good children; we were free to practice our religion and meet with our friends. Under Hitler, even if you weren't a nazi or a party supporter, as long as you weren't Jewish or communist, as long as you lived quietly and didn't mix in politics, you could live a private life, you could keep your culture, your religion. We could not have done that back in Soviet Russia."

"Did your husband go into service?"

"No, not exactly," she said. "By 1940 we had to close down the business because we'd depended on imports. Besides when manpower began getting scarce, as you know, all nonessential businesses were closed. My husband was too old for active duty, but he was assigned to the War Department as a kind of business manager in the department of supply. He didn't mind the work. I went back to work, too, as women were asked to in those years. I found a job as bookkeeper in a firm involved with war production. Luck, too, because by 1945 I had a responsible job and a good salary."

"Your husband died?" I asked.

"Papa was killed," Catharine said.

"Yes, one evening on the way home from the office, where he'd been working overtime, there was a raid. I suppose he must have heard the warnings while he was at the office, but he kept on working. He must have been on his way to a shelter when the bombs began falling. He was killed outright."

"Awful," I said.

"*Na, ja,* it happened to so many," she said. "I still remember the look on the Red Cross woman's face when she found me with the children in our neighborhood shelter and told me. Catharine was about eight then; Gregor was ten or eleven."

"Was your apartment building bombed?" I asked.

"No, our whole block was spared, although blocks right and left of us were demolished. I kept on with my job. I kept the children with me, even though they wanted to evacuate them to the country. At least if anything happened, we would be together; I would know."

"*Mamuschka* was a *Trümmer Frau* after the war," Catharine said.

Nichola nodded. "My bookkeeping job lasted until 1945. After that, my boss tried to shift to consumer goods, but there weren't many goods of any kind. He didn't want to fire me, but business was very bad. He had to reduce my working days to two a week and cut my salary. It didn't matter. There was nothing to buy with money anyway."

"I still remember the watery soup and pasty bread," Catharine said.

"Once in a while we had some potatoes and we were usually lucky enough to have tea. The tea kept me going, but I lost thirty pounds and I suppose I looked like a scarecrow. The children were like sticks."

"So you worked with the rubble crews?" I asked.

"*Ja,* three or four days a week I tied a black *babushka* around my hair, put on my oldest dress and sorted bricks and rubble. Oh, how hard I scrubbed my hands and nails and my hair on Saturday night so that I'd be decent for church! But we only had cold water and almost no soap."

"You always looked spic and span, Mama, for church and when you went to the office," Catharine said. "I remember the rubble. In the next block it was piled as high as the third-floor balcony!"

"*Ja,*" Nichola said, "I never thought we would get it cleared up or that Berlin would ever be a beautiful city again."

"Did you go back to working full time when the economy began to revive?" I asked.

"Yes. By about 1947 things started to pick up, and within a year or so I was working full time, but it took several years before my family and I could really begin to live comfortably. Those first years we had to supplement my salary by selling something once in a while."

"I remember that I cried when you had to sell the ring that Papa gave you. We even sold our living-room rug, but we have a nice one now, haven't we, *Mamusch?*"

"But you sent the children to school?" I asked.

"Somehow we managed. Gregor had a scholarship at a private Gymnasium and later he went on to the Free University. He is Doctor Gregor now: he has a fine job in one of the commercial banks in West Berlin."

"Does he live with you?" I asked.

"Gregor is married," Catharine answered.

"He married a pretty Russian girl from our church, and I am now a grandma. They live near by and still go to our church, so we are still a happy family."

"And Catharine?" I asked.

"I went to a public Gymnasium," Catharine said. "Ever since I was a little girl I'd wanted to study medicine. During the war when we children played Red Cross, I always wanted to be the doctor, never a nurse. At school I loved chemistry and biology and got good grades."

"Good! She won a prize. She was the best in her school in biology. She should have gone to medical school. We would have managed," Nichola insisted.

"How would we have managed, Mama? By having you work and scrimp and save while I sat five or six or ten years in a library or lab? I

Fig. 11. Nurses off duty at the Free University's clinic (photo by Landesbildstelle, West Berlin)

couldn't let you do that. I remember too well those years you shovelled and hauled rubble. I couldn't let you do it!" Catharine insisted.

"She wouldn't," Nicholas said to me and smiled sadly. "Well, perhaps I was too worn out to have taken it for ten years, but I do wish I could have."

"We're happy now, Mama, and I like my job. I decided that if I had to become a nurse I would at least become a specialist. I would be a very good nurse. And I am, I think. Anyway, the hospital seems to like me."

"Like you!" her mother said. "They made you a Theater Sister at twenty-seven. That shows they respect and trust you."

"Junior Theater Sister," Catharine corrected. "I became Senior only last year, but you see, Frau Doctor, I've been working and earning some kind of salary for ten years. It was only a pittance at first, but now I do quite well. If I'd studied medicine, I probably would still not be financially independent."

"It is not a question of money, Catharine," her mother said, "so I shall not be so vulgar as to remind you what your income as an M.D. might be ten years from now."

Catharine giggled, "No, don't!" and kissed her on the cheek. "Money isn't everything, but after you've been poor for years the way we were after the war and while Gregor was at the university, it is very satisfying to have a comfortable income, to be able to refurnish the apartment, to go out to the opera once in a while and wear pretty clothes, to afford a vacation in Greece, don't you think?"

I agreed.

The next morning when I came out of the water after an early swim I found Catharine playing with the kitten Electra on the sand. Electra, of course, pretended that she had no idea that I was there.

"This is a dear little kitten!" Catharine said as Electra climbed up and slid inside an up-turned beach umbrella.

"Dear?" I said. "She's a little horror! She is always leading Orestes into situations that I have to rescue him from. She climbs to the roof or up a tree; he climbs after her. She climbs down; he howls!"

Catharine laughed, "Ah, that's why you named them so! I thought she was Electra because of her color. She is a lovely amber."

"That too," I admitted, scooping Electra out of the umbrella. "You know Greek?" I asked.

Catharine nodded. "You forget, I wanted to study medicine."

"You seem so very happy," I said tentatively.

Catharine nodded vigorously. "Yes, I am, and I do see that I might not have been nearly so happy as a doctor. It is a very hard life, and I would have had very little time for my private life, for Mama and for reading and music and for Church. Yes, I agree. Things probably work out as they should. I think I would have been a good doctor! But I am a very good nurse. Some day I shall be a supervisor."

"Will you stay in Berlin?" I asked.

"I think so," she said. "There are Orthodox congregations in other cities. We have many friends in Munich, for instance, and it would be pleasant to live in Munich. Sometimes I think it would be heavenly to live in a city where we could drive out into the country weekends, maybe even have a little cottage somewhere. Sometimes the tension in Berlin is almost more than I can take and I think I shall have to get out. But I don't. I don't suppose we shall."

"But you like living in Berlin?"

"Oh, we all do, we Russians. Berlin is cosmopolitan, it's alive, it's tolerant. I think I would feel homesick anywhere else."

I heard Orestes meowing and went off to rescue him, but that evening I met Catharine and her mother strolling in the village and invited them to have a cool drink at a waterfront café.

"Aren't these children appalling!" Nichola whispered, obviously referring to the Scandinavian and English young people in faded jeans and sloppy shirts.

"They look undernourished," I said, knowing that many of them lived on bread and Cokes or coffee and slept on the beach.

Nichola sniffed. "Foolish children! They think they are communists, some of them, or at least they call themselves communists. I wonder what they think would happen to them with their long hair and beards if the real, grown-up communists took over their countries? They are playing games with politics, and it's too dangerous for that!"

"You are interested in politics?" I asked.

"Mama is, as you see," Catharine answered. "I haven't time."

"But you vote," her mother said. "I insist that both my children vote," she assured me. "How they vote is their business, but citizens must vote. I escaped from Russia; I lived through Hitler and the war. I don't want to live through another dictatorship or war. It's logical. If good citizens don't vote, if they're too busy to take an interest in politics, which means an interest in what is happening in the community, then ruthless, ambitious men or lunatics and fanatics will be able to take over."

"I think it's good that Mama is active," Catharine said.

"I am, you know," Nichola said. "Now that I no longer work, I am a member of a C.D.U. women's group, and I find it highly interesting. Who knows? Some day I might even be a candidate."

Catharine admitted that she does not always vote for her mother's party. "Sometimes I just don't agree with them!" she said. "But usually I do. I certainly am not fond of Mr. Brandt's *Ost Politik*."

"Well, we *émigrés* couldn't approve, could we?" Nichola asked. "I had such hopes for your Mr. Nixon," she said and sighed. "But still, we do have faith in the United States, and I have faith in Europe. However much I worry, and these days I do, I can't believe that we are going to be so foolish as to sell Berlin and Europe out to the communists. We have all been through so much, we *émigrés*, we Berliners. We can't give in now."

12

Dr. Luise

The doctor's waiting room was a narrow oblong with chairs arranged along the walls around a long, narrow center table strewn with magazines. It was a dimly lighted room, decorated in browns and beige, a little dingy but spotlessly clean and comfortable. I took my place in the only remaining chair and began looking over some notes I had just made. The waiting patients were as unpretentious as the room. A stout old woman in drab grey read a tabloid. Beside her a thin and rigidly upright old woman in black knitted furiously with some thick purple wool. A twenty-year-old shop girl or stenographer, crisply efficient in a white blouse and short navy-blue skirt, leafed through a film magazine. A middle-aged workman, dressed in clean tan slacks and an open-necked white shirt, fingered his pipe and eyed the "No smoking" sign. A very young mother, obviously expecting a new child within weeks, tried to amuse a sickly and irritable two-year-old, pointing out photographs of animals and children in a slick travel magazine.

From time to time the doctor's assistant, a tall, slim young woman in a white nylon uniform, appeared at the inner door to call out the next patient's name. One by one the patients disappeared into the inner office, to reappear after five or ten or fifteen minutes, nod a general *"Auf Wiedersehen"* and leave. As the final patient, the stout old woman, trudged out heavily, I glanced at my watch. It was almost eight o'clock. Just then the doctor herself appeared, sighed with relief and weariness and held out a cordial hand.

Luise is a tall, athletic-looking woman. Her eyes are blue, her hair sandy turning grey, and she has the fresh complexion that often accompanies that coloring. At first glance one might think her Scotch rather than middle German. She wore down-to-earth brown tweeds under a crumpled white professional coat; her shoes were low-heeled brown Oxfords. She is not masculine or brusque, but rather a competent, motherly woman, attractive in a vague, distracted way as though she seldom gives thought to her appearance, but her features are good and her expression kind. Her voice is reassuring as well as commanding; she is decidedly a doctor to inspire confidence in a fearful patient.

"Well, Miss Anne," she said. "It is good to see you again. I heard from Hannah, my housekeeper, who heard it from her sister, Eleanor's housekeeper, that you were in Berlin again. I was delighted when you telephoned, and hoped it wasn't just because you have a sore throat!"

"No," I said. "I'd hoped to visit you in any case. In fact, if you'll let me, I'd like to get around to doing that interview with you that we have put off for so long." She agreed. "But after dinner!" she commanded. "First we'll look at that throat, then we'll relax, and later we'll work. Now come along," and she led the way into her examining room.

It looked exactly like any other doctor's examining room. The standard fixtures were not new, but the porcelain and steel gleamed with high polish. She motioned me to a straight-backed chair, scrubbed her hands, and then extracted a spatula and a small flashlight from the instrument cabinet.

"Let's have a look," she said briskly. "No, that's not strep. Allergy, I'd guess. Have you been sneezing?" I admitted that I had, but not badly. "If it doesn't bother you too badly, I think I shall not prescribe any medication for the allergy. Some cures do more harm than the disease." She mixed some brownish crystals in a glass of warm water. "Here, gargle with this; that should ease the discomfort." When I'd finished, she washed her hands again, took off the soiled white coat and hung it on a hook on the door and led me back through the waiting room to her private apartment.

The living room, too, was all in browns and tans, its lived-in, comfortable shabbiness set off by a few elegant, probably authentic ancient Greek vases and jars.

"Sherry will taste foul after that iodine stuff. Can I give you some whisky? Good for the throat." I thanked her and agreed. I did not have to add, "water and no ice" because obviously there was neither ice nor soda. Her bar consisted of three or four bottles and a row of glasses standing on top of a bookcase. She handed me my drink, with a casual *"Prost,"* and we sat down to talk.

She eased into a deep leather chair. I took the guest's seat of honor on the low couch. "I don't suppose you want a cigarette with that throat?" she asked, tentatively holding out a silver box. I said no, and so she took one and lit it. "I know I shouldn't, it's a bad example for the patients, but I never smoke in front of them. Besides, I am so busy that I seldom have time to sit down and relax with a cigarette, and I make it a rule not to smoke unless I can. That keeps the total down."

I sipped a little whisky and we talked idly for a while about current Berlin politics. Something she said prompted me to ask, "Doctor Luise, didn't you once tell me that you used to be a communist?"

"Well, the next thing to it," she said. "When I was a girl I was pretty radical. I never actually joined the K.P.D. [German Communist Party], but I flirted with the idea for a time. I often attended communist public meetings and rallies."

"Were you a convinced Marxist?" I asked.

"I don't think I was very ideological," she reflected. "It's hard to remember accurately just what I believed before 1933. That's a long time ago and I was very young, but I think I thought then that only the communists were sufficiently united and tough enough to keep Hitler from coming to power, and whatever I was it wasn't a nazi."

"I can understand that," I said. "Was your family radical or very active politically?"

She laughed. "Goodness, no! They were as bourgeois as they come and provincial to boot. My father and grandfather were doctors, my mother's people owned a small but locally well-known brewery. We were a typical small-town middle-class family; our town had a population of only five thousand people and it was right in the middle of the Brandenburg plain."

"Were your parents very conventional, then?" I asked. "Did they object when you wanted to study medicine?"

"Oh, no, far from it. Both my mother and father were amazingly progressive. I suppose you'd call them old-fashioned liberals. Anyway they both firmly believed in education for women, and I was lucky that our town had built a modern Gymnasium, which opened its doors the very year I was ready to enter. The curriculum emphasized German instead of classical or foreign languages, and so the school was called a 'Reform *Real* Gymnasium.'"

"You liked school?" I asked.

"I loved it! I seem to remember that we had very lively, interesting teachers and I always did very well in school. I knew before I got my *Abitur* that I wanted to study medicine, but I couldn't decide which university to attend. My father thought I should see as much of the world as possible before settling down to my career, and so he suggested that I attend not one but several universities. One could do that easily in those days—spend a semester here, a semester there. Papa said he didn't care where he sent the money, as long as I was happy, and so I attended Freiburg, Marburg, Greifswald, Innsbruck and Berlin. I don't have an alma mater, just a whole tribe of aunts.

"Papa didn't have a lot of money to send me. A small-town doctor, however skillful, didn't make enough in those days to allow for frills in the budget. In each town I lived in cheap furnished rooms, usually with grouchy landladies who resented female students and who wouldn't permit any laundering or cooking in the rooms. I sent my dirty clothes home for my mother to wash, and I ate the traditional student's lunch: thick pea soup, frankfurters and bread. It cost fifty pfennige, about twelve cents. It was cheap, nourishing and good."

"It all sounds like fun," I said and she nodded.

"I enjoyed all the universities and all the towns I lived in, but I absolutely loved Berlin. Berlin was fabulous in those days. It was exciting, I suppose, for everyone, but for a young student straight from the provinces, it was heaven. I fell in love with it, poor though I was. I used to do without lunch twice every week and wait long hours in line to buy standing-room tickets for a few cents for the theater or the opera. I had to stand in the highest gallery, but I saw every new production.

"When I passed my medical school and state exams, I looked around for an opening for an intern in a Berlin hospital, and luckily I found one in the Moabit City Hospital. Interns were not paid salaries in those days, but I got room and board and Papa still sent me a small allowance, so when I had a free evening I could still go to the theater. It was a marvellous year, and, incidentally, I also learned a good deal about medicine."

"You were lucky," I said.

"I was," she admitted. "It was a good beginning; but after that the carefree years were over.

"I finished interning during the depths of the depression when there were few jobs available in any profession and still fewer for women. In medicine a female doctor was, as a rule, considered only for an appointment that male doctors had rejected as uninteresting or unpleasant."

"Like what?" I asked.

"Oh, duty in tuberculosis sanitoriums or in insane asylums. Since I hoped eventually to specialize in pediatrics I was fortunate to find a position in the pediatric section of a tuberculosis asylum.

"It was hard and sometimes heartbreaking work because many of our patients came from poorer sections of the city, and we caught them too late, but, again, I learned a lot. Then the war came, and suddenly there was a shortage of doctors. Virtually all the male doctors except the elderly and the sickly were called for military service. Women doctors were in demand. It was nice to be wanted. Suddenly I found that I had a choice of positions. I became medical consultant to a city home for neglected children, the post I still occupy. A year later my cousin, who is also a doctor, was called up for military duty, and I took over this practice for him. After the war he decided to move to West Germany and so I have kept the practice.

"Our children's home was bombed out during the war, totally demolished, but we were able to get all the children out without having any of them suffer anything worse than abrasions and, of course, fright. We found an inconvenient old building to move into, hoping it would be temporary, but of course we then couldn't find anything better, not with all the bombing going on all over Berlin. We were still there when the war ended; and we found ourselves in the Russian sector."

"How did you feel about the Russians and communism then?" I asked.

"We naturally found ourselves under Soviet rule. Almost immediately the communist authorities dismissed the director of the home, along with all of the top staff, and replaced them with Communist Party functionaries. Although these new appointees were party hacks who knew nothing about medicine or, for that matter, about children, they interfered in medical and educational matters at every turn. The government issued regulations and directives and sent us tons of forms to fill in. Life turned into a bureaucratic nightmare. Most of the rest of us on the staff began to find it unbearable."

"Were you able to leave?" I asked.

"Not overnight," she said. "It is not so simple to move a whole building full of children without official help. We planned it carefully and, of course, secretly. At about the time that a split between the governments of East and West Berlin seemed imminent we decided we must move. In those days many ministries and offices were moving from East to West Berlin. I suppose the Russians didn't like it, but they didn't prevent it, and they didn't prevent us.

"We moved into our temporary home toward the end of 1948, hoping as soon as possible to find or build a more suitable home. There was such a backlog of construction, so many homes and apartments and hospitals and schools that urgently needed to be built in West Berlin, that we were not able to move into our new quarters until 1968."

"Twenty years," I said.

"That was a long time to wait, but we now have a beautiful center. Our architect is one of the most famous in West Berlin, and our facilities are modern and scientific in every way, as well as bright and cheerful and pleasing to the eye. Instead of one large building to house the children, we now have a village of small cottages. The children are divided into groups of eight, all of staggered ages from fourteen days to fifteen or sixteen years to form a family. Each family lives with its house-mother in one of the separate, small houses. There is a medium-sized administration building, which contains my offices and an infirmary, and there is a small reception center to house new arrivals until they can be processed and assigned to a family. All these buildings group around a garden, lawns and playgrounds. It is all very pleasant, and we believe we achieve happier results with the children in such surroundings."

"It sounds lovely," I said.

"I think it is," Luise said. "I hope you'll be able to come out and have a look around some day soon."

A few minutes before, Hannah had appeared, noticed that the Frau Doctor was deep in conversation and nodded mutely. Now Luise glanced at the Victorian clock on the bookcase and pulled herself out of the deep chair. "I'm sorry to starve you this way! It is late for dinner. I am sure you are more than ready to eat." I agreed that I was ready, and she showed me the way to the small dining room.

Dinner was simple and healthful as befits a physician's table, but there was a tempting and calorific berry pie for dessert, served with heaped whipped cream.

"This is delicious," I said, "but when I think of the calories!"

Luise laughed. "Well, me too, but don't think of the calories. Think of them tomorrow and eat oranges."

"I will," I said. "Your Hannah is a marvellous cook."

"She is, and a good deal more," Luise said rising. "Come, let's have our coffee in the living room."

We resettled in our comfortable chairs, and Hannah brought in the coffee tray. Luise poured cognac into cordial glasses and raised her glass.

"Berlin," she mused. "Do we have unique medical problems? It is hard to be sure about cause and effect or uniqueness, but we have a few problems which seem to be specifically the result of our Berlin situation.

"In the first place, there is the obvious fact that a divided city requires double the social, educational, and health facilities. We need two of everything, one East, one West. That goes for schools, clinics, courts, hospitals, prisons, everything. The uncertainty has the effect of postponing needed construction. Organizations keep on using provisional or inadequate or antiquated facilities year after year because they don't want to invest in costly new buildings if reunification is possible."

"Does the division of the city affect your children's home directly?" I asked.

"In our particular case we experienced some personal tragedies because of the Wall. Many of our children come from East Berlin families, or from broken homes in which one of the parents lives in the East. The Wall meant final separation. It is tragic for a child to be totally separated even from a bad parent.

"My private practice reflects some of the special social problems of postwar Berlin. For example, Berlin is a city of old people. The percentage of the population over fifty, and especially over sixty, is abnormally high. Among my patients, more than half are over sixty, and a disproportionate number are women. As you know, in the over-forty-five age bracket in all Germany, but especially in Berlin, there is a dramatic shortage of men."

I nodded. "Yes I know that the regiments recruited from Berlin, Potsdam, and the surrounding area suffered extraordinarily heavy casualties in the war and that after the war the Russians rounded up every able-bodied male over eighteen they could catch for forced labor in the U.S.S.R. as reparation in kind."

"Quite true," Luise said. "They recruited most ruthlessly in Berlin, West and East. Consequently, almost all young and healthy Berlin males were either impressed or they escaped, usually to West Germany. Relatively few of either category returned."

"I've seen the statistics," I said.

"In consequence, we have far too many middle-aged and older women who live alone. These are women of various social origins, but all of them have had very hard lives. They lived through the depression, the nazi period, the long years of bombing. They experienced the death in battle of sons or husbands or fathers, perhaps of the men they might have married. They lived on into the postwar years to clean up the rubble.

"It was the women of Berlin who literally picked up the pieces. You remember them, the *Trümmer Frauen,* the rubble women?" she asked.

"I remember vividly," I said.

"Well," Luise said, "then you know that quite literally, it was the women who began the rebuilding of Berlin."

I nodded.

"They rebuilt Berlin, but tore themselves down doing it. They worked long hours in the heat or cold, inadequately dressed, underfed, earning a pittance. Many of them lived in the shell of a bombed-out house, in a cellar or air-raid shelter, unheated except by a sad little coal stove

Fig. 12. *Trümmer Frauen* in 1941 (photo by Landesbildstelle, West Berlin)

fuelled by a few briquets of coke a day. Those who had something left to sell, jewelry, paintings, rugs, radios, coats, shoes, could buy food or fuel on the black market. Otherwise they did without and starved and shivered."

"I remember," I said.

"Unless they were young and pretty, in which case they had other resources. I treated many young women in those days, some of them mothers of small children, widows or wives of missing P.O.W.s as well as young girls, who took to the streets to earn cigarettes or chocolate bars to trade for food or coke in the black market. Lord knows how many mothers fed their families this way during those years. The damage was not only physical, and it couldn't all be cured by antibiotics."

"Do you see medical results now?" I asked.

"All of these women, the *Trümmer Frauen* and the Fräuleins, wore themselves out, exhausted themselves physically and emotionally, and many of them suffer for it now, especially if they still live alone, and so many do.

"Many men came back from the war or from prison camp so shattered emotionally or physically that they couldn't work, at least not to normal capacity, for years. Other men were forbidden to work, those who had held any kind of middle- or high-level post before 1945 as well as Nazi Party members. In such cases the return of the husband meant even greater burdens for the woman, who had to continue to work to support another person, and deal with an injured personality."

"Some men never recovered, I suppose," I said.

"Some didn't," she said. "I have known other cases where the man recovered his health and much of his equilibrium and with the return of prosperity was gradually able to succeed in his business or profession or craft, gradually increase the family income to the point of affluence, and then he divorced his wife. In the past several years I have seen many instances of the breaking up of marriages of long standing, both partners in their late fifties or sixties. This is a very new phenomenon for Berlin, especially for lower-middle and middle-middle class families. Formerly the men of these classes were too conventional and too poor to afford a divorce or even to afford a mistress. Recently there has been an easing of moral restraint coupled with a rise in living standards. Lower- and middle-income level people have gradually come to think that luxuries are neither immoral nor beyond their grasp, and one of the luxuries middle-aged men now grasp for is young girls, very often their secretaries. This leaves a fifty- or sixty-year-old divorced woman, a long marriage and a hard life behind her, worn out, probably old for

Fig. 13. A woman cleaning her doorstep in a working-class neighborhood, West Berlin (photo by Landesbildstelle, West Berlin)

her years, perhaps in poor health, alone. Even her children are likely to be away in the G.D.R. or West Germany. It is a serious and a very sad medical problem, one of the side effects of economic and social progress."

"Like air pollution?" I asked, and she said, "Exactly."

I asked her some questions about her profession and found her especially concerned about the medical schools. "I have a very good opinion of the younger members of my profession, including the women. I find that their university training has been solid, especially in the theoretical area. However, I think the course of study is too long. Obviously there have been so many new discoveries in medicine that knowledge has proliferated beyond what we thought possible when I was a student. It seemed only natural to keep adding courses to the curriculum to include some of this new knowledge, but this has meant additional semesters and years. This is socially undesirable. It ridiculously prolongs the emotional, social adolescence of students.

"In the case of a woman medical student you can see the obvious complications. Will she wait until she finishes her studies and her internship, perhaps two years of specialization, before she marries? Medicine is not a discipline a woman can pursue with her left hand. It requires the lion's share of her time and energy and concentration. Or will she marry and perhaps have children, interrupting her studies? In that case she may be forty before she qualifies. Either choice is imperfect and, I think, undesirable."

"Is there a solution?" I asked.

"Solution? I am not sure, of course, but I tend to believe that the course of study could be shortened. Under the present system our young doctors are theoretically excellent, their university training has been splendid, and yet, I find them often hopeless in dealing with real, live patients. They tend to view them as textbook cases rather than as people. I suppose they have simply spent too many years in labs and lecture halls and have become *Weltfremd,* strangers to the world. Some young doctors are shy and self-conscious; others cool and aloof. Rarely do you find one who knows how to reassure a frightened patient or comfort a dying one, who can deal with pain and emotional shock, or who can relate humanely to worried or bereaved parents or spouses, and all of that is as much a part of a doctor's profession as prescribing the right pill or knowing where to cut."

"As a layman, I think perhaps more so," I said.

"I think medical students should gain experience in dealing with people earlier in their development. Perhaps they could work in hospitals as aides during summers, or something of that sort. We could add post-

graduate summer courses, weekend seminars and closed-circuit TV programs. Even doctors who have been practicing for long years need updating and refresher aids because of the deluge of new discoveries. No
matter how long you keep a young person tied to the university, much
of what he learns will be obsolete or obsolescent before he has practiced
a few years. Medical school should be sound on fundamentals, of course,
as it always was, but it should not try to cram all available current knowledge into the student before he gets out into the field. It is impossible,
and, as I said, the side effects are worse than the cure."

"It's way out of my field of competence," I said, "but I certainly agree
that what you say makes sense."

"I suppose you want to know about my politics?" she asked. "I don't
think I have any these days."

"Well," I said, "I would like to know whether you belong to a political
party or go to meetings or vote."

"No," she said. "I don't belong to a party nor am I at all active. I
don't have time. Most doctors don't. I don't attend meetings or rallies
or even watch television debates, but I am still interested in politics
and I read the newspapers and magazines carefully. I don't consider myself a member of any party and do not vote consistently. The only thing
I am sure of, after my experience in the Soviet sector, is that I am not a
communist. I believe in social reform, in social progress, of course, but
I am no longer convinced that state control and central planning are
the best ways to achieve it. This is another case where the cure may be
worse than the disease. I think the state probably must help, but the
widest latitude possible should be left to the individual and to private
organizations.

"But, as I say, I have little time to dabble in politics. What free time
I find I devote to my hobby. I collect in a modest way. I am especially
interested in ancient Greek pottery and sculpture. I go to exhibits, lectures, auctions, and I spend every summer in Greece somewhere. Last
summer I was in Crete.

"Religion? I am a Church member, Evangelical. I do not think it
unscientific to believe in God, as many doctors do. But, like politics, I
have little time for organized religion. I belong to a congregation and
pay my Church tax, but I almost never attend service and I am not active in any of the Evangelical organizations.

"As you can see, I have a modest, middle-sized, middle-class practice,
and I make a modest, middle-level income for a general practitioner. I
also have a retainer from the children's home, and so I live comfortably
and pleasantly. Most of my comfort is thanks to my housekeeper, Han-

nah. She has been with me for almost twenty years. Our friend Eleanor
knew that I needed someone and sent her Marthe's sister along to me. I
bless Eleanor every day of my life! Hannah is a treasure. She is almost my
age, that is, over fifty, and she is absolutely devoted. She takes the irregular, uncertain life of a doctor in her stride and is never fussed if she
has to serve me coffee at five A.M. or dinner at close to midnight. She is
used to having me called out in the middle of the soup, having to warm
up the meat course later. She grumbles, of course, if some delicacy is
spoiled, but she never grumbles with me, only with circumstances.

"Salary? She gets about 400 marks a month plus her room and board
and a few fringe benefits. She has a full-month's vacation each year when
she faithfully visits the Bavarian Alps. She has a completely free hand
in the apartment. She plans the menus, does the shopping, pays the bills.
She even answers the telephone and enters appointments for patients in
the book.

"I also have an office assistant, Lise, a young girl of twenty-one, who
is married to a good-looking policeman. She earns 500 marks a month,
works forty-five hours a week and has Wednesday afternoons free. As you
could see, Lise is a pleasant, sensible girl.

"Berlin? With my jaundiced view of the Soviet government I have
not been an optimist about reunification. The Russians knew exactly
what they wanted: a divided Germany; and the Stalinist Ulbricht regime was certainly not going to compromise with the West Berliners or
with Bonn. I saw no solution. However, in recent years I have grown
more optimistic. I am still not sure that either the Russians or the East
Germans will compromise, but now I think we can hold out. West Berlin
is doing very well, surprisingly so as an isolated half-city cut off from its
hinterland and from the Federal Republic. We are thriving economically,
and our morale is high. As long as the Federal Republic and the Allies
continue to support us, and as long as they make it clear to the East
that they continue to support us, we can hold out."

"By now, I guess you are a real Berliner," I said.

"Well," she admitted, "I'm not a native Berliner but I'm a Branden-
burger, and that's the closest thing. I've lived here so long and lived
through so much that I couldn't imagine living anywhere else or being
anything but a Berliner. Stay in Berlin? Oh yes, my work is here. I
enjoy my visits to Greece, but I am always glad to get back. I still enjoy Berlin almost as much as I did when I was a young medical student,
even though these days I don't have time for much but work. Berlin
has changed too, of course, but it's still Berlin. As long as it is, I suppose
I'll stay."

13

Hans

Hans is one of the lucky East Berliners who live in an attractive, modern apartment. He belongs to a co-operative building society, a kind of mutual self-help organization of citizens who want new apartments and are prepared to contribute their skills and labor.

"There is still a long waiting list for the apartments available through the housing office," Hans told me. "My fiancée and I want to get married next spring. She lives at home with her mother, who has no room for us. Besides, who wants to live with his in-laws? Not me, especially not when we're first married. I had only a furnished room before I moved in here. Liz and I couldn't have lived there, so I had to find an apartment or build one. I built one, or helped."

Hans, twenty-nine, is a skilled machinist who works in a paint factory in East Berlin.

"There's not much a machinist can do in building houses," he said, "but all of us who belong to the group help out evenings after work and weekends with the unskilled labor. Those with skills, of course, like carpenters or electricians, contribute their skills. I helped with the common elbow grease all through last summer when the evenings were long and we could work until nine at night. When the building was standing, I worked on the installation of plumbing, the heating system, and the indoor painting. Naturally, it takes longer to build a house that way in off-hours and weekends, but we had a lot of fun too."

I asked where the co-operative got its capital, and he explained that each member pays a certain amount into the fund each month.

"The co-op money is handled by a state bank," he said, "and each of us pays according to the size apartment he is going to have. Naturally, we all had to pay in for a couple of years before we had enough to buy
180

our basic supplies and begin building. Now me, for instance, I joined about three years ago."

I asked him whether he had been engaged when he joined the co-operative.

"No, I wasn't. I put in for a one-room apartment and paid at that rate, but when I got engaged a year ago, I increased the payments to cover a two-and-a-half-room apartment. Of course, no bachelor gets a new apartment that large if he intends to live alone!"

"When are you planning to marry?" I asked.

He grinned. "When we have enough furniture," he said. "Of course, Elizabeth's idea of what is enough is not quite the same as mine. I think we could do without a few things for the first few months, but she wants to have everything just so before she moves in, and, of course, our mothers both agree with her." He shrugged his shoulders philosophically.

"But you are already living here?" I asked.

He nodded. "We have no bedroom furniture yet. I sleep on the couch. We've ordered a double bed and dresser, and we pay a few marks each week on it. As you see, we don't yet have a rug for the living room, but my folks gave us the china cabinet and some chairs and Elizabeth's mother made the curtains for the whole place. Liz and I had already bought the couch, those two armchairs and the table, so we're doing pretty well. What I mean is, they're paid for. We'd save up and paid cash. We like it that way. I'm paying off the refrigerator and stove and Liz's grandma is giving us china and silverware, not whole sets, of course, but enough to begin with."

"Have you got linens?" I asked. "Towels and sheets and tablecloths?"

"Yes. Liz has been collecting and saving and she's finally set the date. We're getting married next June. That's almost a year off, and we've been engaged almost a year, but it takes a long while to save up and buy everything you need even for a small apartment, and, as I said, Liz wants to do things right. We're even having a church wedding."

"Is that unusual among your friends?" I asked.

"Fairly. The government likes people to have state weddings and, of course, anyone who is ambitious goes along with the trend, but Elizabeth and I are both church members and so are our families, so we decided to go ahead and have the wedding in church. Liz already has the material for her dress, and she's going to wear her grandmother's veil that somehow survived the war."

"A real wedding, then?" I asked.

"The works!" he said. "White dress, veil, but only one bridesmaid, my youngest sister. We can't afford a big wedding, and we'd rather spend money on our flat. Our families will get together to arrange the reception, just an informal affair at my parents' house. It'll be simple, no fuss or show, but both Liz and I think it's important to do things right, especially now."

"Do you go to church?" I asked.

"I'm afraid I don't go very often. Liz and her mother go regularly, but I seem to get there only on holidays or when there's some special service. You know how it is when you're a young bachelor. You like to go out Saturday nights, and then it's hard to get up on Sundays, and since we began building the apartment house, I've spent most of my weekends working here. But after we get married, I expect Liz will reform me."

We were sitting in the newly painted, half-furnished living room of the new apartment. Hans had offered me coffee, but he had warned me that he was not very good at making it.

"Besides that, all I've got is beer, and luckily a couple of glasses!" he said, and so we were drinking beer.

"Elizabeth has had a pretty hard life," he said. "Her father was a nazi. Mine was a capitalist; that's bad enough!"

"Was he a prominent nazi," I asked, "or just a follower?"

"Sort of a middle-sized nazi," Hans explained. "Not a *Gauleiter* or anything like that, but a kind of local bigwig. He was one of the old party members, the kind who joined before 1933, the kind the communists especially dislike. He was killed in the war, and her mother never joined the party. In fact, her mother never left the Church all through the nazi time. Elizabeth was born in the same month her father was killed in 1944. She was the baby. She has two older brothers. The mother had a tough time after the war as the widow of a party member."

"Did they lose all their property?" I asked.

"Property, bank account and pension," he said. "Liz's mother went back to live with her mother, who was also a widow. Liz's grandfather was a doctor, and he was killed on active duty as a medical officer in the East. Her grandma looked after the three kids while her mother went out to work as a *Trümmer Frau,* collecting rubble. That was pretty hard for a middle-class woman. She did it for over a year, winter and summer. There was very little food and never enough fuel those first years. In 1947 she found a job working in a school cafeteria. That was hard work too, long hours of standing, but at least it was warm in the school and sometimes there was a little leftover food to take home."

"Hard years," I said.

"Hard for everyone, of course," Hans said. "Liz's mother works in a doctor's office now. She doesn't earn much, but the work is much lighter, and she enjoys it."

"What do the two brothers do?" I asked.

"Well, as children of a nazi, naturally, they couldn't go to a university, but both of them went to trade school and are skilled workers like me. They earn good money and help their mother out a little."

"And Liz?" I asked.

"She's a lab technician. She works in the same plant I do. That's how we met. Here's her picture," he said and handed me a small photograph in a red leather frame. Elizabeth is a pretty girl with fluffy blond hair and small, precise features.

"She's lovely," I said. "She's not bitter about not being able to study at the university?"

"Oh, no," he said. "What's the use? She would like to have studied medicine or chemistry, but she enjoys her job, and we think we will have a full and interesting life. A profession isn't everything."

"How did you happen to become a machinist?" I asked. "Was it because your father was a capitalist?"

He grinned. "As a matter of fact, I would like to have gone into industrial management myself. I had pretty good grades at school, and, if I had waited, I would have been permitted to go to the university because by now the regulations have eased. My dad was in management. I was kidding when I said he was a capitalist. He was no Krupp, but he worked for heavy industry before the war, and he owned a few shares and some property. During the war he was an officer, so all around he ranked as a class enemy. After the war he was barred from management, and my older brothers and sisters were not allowed to go to the university."

"Your father is still alive?" I asked.

"Yes, luckily. We are a big family. I have five older brothers and sisters and two younger sisters, eight of us in all. My dad was a P.O.W. in Russia, and he served for five years in a Siberian labor camp. He didn't get back to Berlin until 1950. My mother had a pretty rough time."

"I can imagine," I said. "Could he work at all when he got back?"

"Not for a while, of course. He wasn't allowed to work in management, and he wasn't strong enough to do any physical work. Besides, he hadn't been trained. By 1951 or 1952 he was well enough to do light, physical work, but he was untrained, and he earned very little."

"But things are better now?" I asked.

"Oh, a lot. In the first place, the regulations are more liberal. Dad is working in management again, and my older brothers and sisters are all working. Like me they all went to trade school and became apprentices and have skilled jobs and earn good money. Three are already married. My youngest sister, the one who is going to be Liz's bridesmaid, wants to be a chemist, and she will be allowed to go to the university."

"You could study nights, couldn't you?" I asked.

"I could, but during the past year, I've been busy planning for the apartment and for our wedding. Maybe later, after we're settled. For the moment Liz and I are content."

"Do your parents live in Berlin?" I asked.

"Yes. We have been very lucky. We still have our house. We lived in a residential section that was only lightly bombed. Our house was damaged a little, but not badly. Later, when the Russians invaded the city, our house was chopped up by artillery fire, but it was still standing in May 1945. The windows were all out, the roof was caved in, and only the basement was habitable, but that was lucky. If more of the house had been usable, we might have lost it. As it was, my mother was allowed to live in the basement. After my dad got back, he and my older brothers began clearing up the mess and rebuilding. Some of our friends helped too, and gradually we got the house back in shape. During the bad years, we were able to rent out some of the rooms, and that helped a lot. Now that some of us are living away from home, my parents rent out the upper floor."

I asked a few questions about his work, and he said that he is a trade-union member.

"Everyone belongs and some meetings are obligatory," he said, "but I am not very active. There is a certain amount of pressure for workers to join in some of the evening activities, and so I belong to one of the plant's bowling teams, but, frankly, I think it is a nuisance. I'm not an enthusiastic bowler, and I'd rather spend my evenings with my own friends."

"Are there a lot of planned activities?" I asked.

"*Ach,* too many!" he said. "Union meetings, sports, outings, special films or lectures or exhibits. A man hardly has time to go out with his girl or to be on his own or with his own friends. Of course, that's the idea. They like to keep the workers busy and keep them in groups."

"But, on the whole, things are better?" I asked.

"Oh, lots better," he said, pouring more beer into our glasses. "For one thing, we are down to a seven-and-a-half-hour day. I work from seven-thirty until four and get a half hour for lunch plus two fifteen-minute breaks morning and afternoon. I get twenty days' vacation a year, plus all the usual sick leave, health insurance, and so on."

"Do you get lunch at the plant?" I asked, having learned that most Berliners do.

"Yes. Our cafeteria isn't great, but it's not too bad. I pay a mark for a hot meal, including dessert. It's not fancy, and, of course, if I want beer or coffee, that's extra, but the food is decent and filling."

"You don't have a car yet, do you?" I asked.

He grinned. "What do you think I am, a capitalist? Liz and I both have bicycles, but I usually take the subway to work. I get it right on the next corner, and it only costs five cents, that is, twenty pfennige. The plant is six stations away, so I'm there in twenty minutes, and I only have a block to walk from the subway exit. Not bad."

"Do you cook for yourself evenings?" I asked.

"I can't cook!" he said. "Sometimes I warm a can of soup or boil some frankfurters, but usually I just eat cold cuts or make a sandwich at night with a glass of beer. Once in a while Liz comes over and cooks for me or else we go out to eat. Sundays I eat with my parents or with her mother."

"Where do you shop?" I asked.

"Oh, that's very convenient," he said. "There is a market right on the corner near the subway stairs. I stop in there mornings on my way to work and leave my order and then in the evening I stop by and pick it up. Housewives who work do that too. It's marvellous."

We talked a little more about his work, and he explained that the paint factory was one of the relatively few privately owned enterprises in East Berlin.

"Almost all large-scale industry is public," he explained. "Big concerns are almost all V.E.B.'s, that is government-owned firms. Some small businesses are co-operatives like our apartment house. I have a friend, for instance, who drives a taxi. He belongs to a taxi co-op. They have seven taxis, ten drivers, a manager and a couple of mechanics. The men own the business as equal partners."

"What kind of private businesses are there?" I asked, remembering that a hairdresser had told me that his shop was privately owned.

"Usually they are very small scale like local shops. Some larger businesses are semiprivate. The government owns fifty-one per cent of the stock, the old owner or partners forty-nine per cent. A very few, like my paint plant, are entirely private, but they have a hard time. Profits are drastically taxed, and so there is never enough profit to reinvest in expansion or research and development. It is hard for private firms to compete with public firms."

I asked him what hobbies he enjoys when he is not busy working on his apartment.

"Liz and I both sail," he said, "and we like to ride our bicycles out to one or another of the Berlin lakes and sail or walk or just have a picnic. We think we'll probably go up to the Baltic Sea for our honeymoon and spend two or three weeks sailing."

I asked whether he and Elizabeth often went to the theater, and he said they were enthusiasts.

"Mind you, Liz and I are quiet people. We don't go out very often. Most evenings we prefer to read and listen to music, but now and then we like the theater or a good film or concert. Sometimes I wish we were in West Berlin! The quality of the theater here in the East is excellent. I'm not complaining about that, but there are too few theaters, too few performances for the people who want to see them, and the choice of plays is so narrow, so restricted. I like the classical theater, but here they show the same handful of plays over and over. There are very few new ones, and most of those are dry and dull, or at least Liz and I think so. They're so didactic and moralistic!"

"What about films?" I asked.

"Same thing," he said. "There aren't nearly enough cinemas. Three or four big film theaters downtown and a few small ones sprinkled over the neighborhoods—not nearly enough for a big, metropolitan city. If we want to see a film over the weekend, I have to buy the tickets weeks in advance. There is only one cabaret and only a few nightclubs, and they are expensive, geared to foreign visitors and West Germans. Besides, even the nightclubs are dull and they close at midnight.

"That's the worst of socialism!" he said with exasperation. "It is puritanical and damned dull! When I think of what Berlin used to be, how exciting my father says it was before the war, and then think how provincial it is now, I get depressed. Downtown Berlin is dead by eleven at night, even on Saturdays. Most of the time it's better to stay at home and listen to Bach and read a book, except that the books are also dull. They are one-sided and dogmatic." He sighed.

"It's true that we are liberalized. We no longer live under terror. We no longer have to work excessively hard or do without necessities or even comforts. Life is a lot better than it was, and I am not ungrateful, but, my God, it is dull!"

He laughed at his own vehemence and seemed cheerful about his complaint, but I could see that he also meant it.

"But you are not unhappy?" I asked.

"I am not content!" he said, "but no, not unhappy. I am grateful too. We've come a long way in the past ten years, and whether you like the system or not, you can't help having a feeling of accomplishment, of achievement." He glanced around at the half-furnished room and smiled. "It gives you a pretty good feeling to be moving into a flat that you helped finish yourself, in an apartment house you helped to build. I pay only $15.00 a month for maintenance. We all chip in on the work of cutting the lawns, shovelling snow, cleaning the halls. It makes you feel as though the house is yours, if you know what I mean, and you also save money."

He poured the last of the beer into our glasses. "Besides, I have my family and Elizabeth, and maybe our children will have a more interesting life with more opportunities. When you think back to Berlin in 1945, things could be a lot worse. We're pretty lucky, all things considered." He sipped the last of his beer thoughtfully. "Still, it's damned dull!"

14

Eva

As I walked into Eva's back room I was engulfed in a wave of nostalgia. It smelled and looked like Berlin in the 1950s. "West Berlin in the 1950s," I amended, "East Berlin in the 1960s." The odors of sawn wood, fresh plaster, paints and turpentine mixed with that of recently poured concrete.

"Disaster area!" Eva said and smiled and apologized for the mess. "As you see, we are decorating. The shop was too small, so I'm adding the old storeroom to the shop area, and we've just built this annex to use for an office and for storage. I needed the space."

A tall, blond painter in a paint-streaked white coat and canvas cap tramped up from the basement, wished us good morning, hoisted two heavy cases of merchandise and carried them down to the basement.

"They have to take all the stock out, of course," Eva explained. "We're storing it in the cellar at the moment. As soon as we get these shelves in here finished and painted, I can stock this room and then they can begin decorating inside in the shop."

"Will you have to close the shop?" I asked.

"Oh, yes, but I want to keep the time to a minimum, so we're doing all this first." She reached under the canvas covering a wooden desk and fished out a yellow plastic folder. "Here is the sketch of what the shop will look like after it's finished. I want it to be cheerful. It will have low counters, lots of glass, bright colors and subtle lighting. There will be darling little chairs for the customers and a small desk so they can try out the pens or look at cards. Right now it's dreadful," she said and giggled, pointing at the cartons stacked in irregular piles on the floor, on cabinets, on the desk, to the once-white canvas draped over the office furniture, paint dribbles on the floor, a ladder leaning against the newly installed shelves.

188

"But in two weeks it will be beautiful! I can hardly wait to see it, and I am sure that I shall do a lot more business, that it will prove worth the investment."

"Is it very expensive?" I asked.

"Well," she said, cocking her head on one side, considering, "it costs a lot less than it would in West Germany and it's easier to get it done. You always have to wait so long to get workmen in West Germany, and yet I find these Berliners more reliable, more skillful and certainly more cheerful and good-natured. They do everything. Now painters are not expected to cart boxes away, but they willingly do it just to be nice!"

"You are a woman alone," I said, and mentally added, a little woman who looks frilly and fragile.

"Yes, but I was a woman in West Germany and younger, and work-men were never so obliging. Berliners are more relaxed. They're not afraid they're going to lose their dignity if they help you. They're not afraid you are trying to take advantage of them. It's different here. There's a lot less hostility between workers and employers, I find."

"Less class-consciousness," I suggested and she nodded.

"I like it," she said. "I have to employ people, and so I'm dependent on them. I don't want to play the boss or order people around. I'm grate-ful if the work gets done, and surely it's much pleasanter for us all if we're friendly?"

"I certainly think so," I said.

"You're an American, you're used to it. I'm from a small West German provincial city where things are more cramped, more rigid. Berlin's in-formality seems strange to me, but very nice."

She pulled the canvas covering from two wooden, straight-backed chairs and uncovered a corner of an old, roll-top desk. "Here," she said. "These chairs aren't very fancy or very comfortable either, but I guess we can make do with them, and you can take notes on this corner. It's clean!"

I thanked her and pulled out my notebook and ball-point pen. "I sup-pose you borrow money to finance redecorating?" I asked.

"Oh," she said. "You have probably been talking to Senate officials who have told you how easy it is for small businesses to get loans in West Berlin! Well, it's true that the Senate guarantees bank loans to small businesses for construction or expansion, but that doesn't make it easy to borrow."

"Easier, surely?"

"Well, I suppose so, but banks still demand collateral as security for their loans, and in a business like mine there is no collateral. I don't own the building, I only lease, so I can't offer that as collateral. I own the business, but that represents only the stock and equipment, and in the case of a middle-sized stationery shop, that isn't nearly enough. We have a rapid turnover. I never have a large inventory, so it wasn't all that easy to borrow and I didn't qualify for the special low-interest loan. I had to make a normal, commercial transaction and I shall have to pay full interest." *

"But you think it will be worth it?"

"Oh, I hope so! It's always a risk, but I think there is enough demand so that the expansion will pay. I shall have to pay about 280 marks more interest on the loan over a five-year period than if I'd qualified for the Senate loan, but that isn't too bad, and frankly, I somehow prefer dealing with a private bank, maybe because I am an entrepreneur myself, a capitalist, however small the scale. I never like dealing with the government. Bureaucrats can be stiff and petty, don't you think?"

"Often," I said.

"Do you know, the decorating firm started work within two weeks after we'd signed the contract? That is what I call enterprising! But I understand that there isn't as much work now as there used to be; money is a little scarcer, so the contractors are eager for work."

She reached under a tarpaulin and pulled out a bottle. "I apologize for not being able to offer you coffee, but you can see why I can't! Can I give you a schnapps?"

It was early in the day for spirits, but I appreciated the embarrassment of a German businesswoman unable to offer hospitality to a guest or colleague. Naturally I said, "Yes, thank you."

Eva fished again and conjured up two small glasses and a roll of paper towels. "They're perfectly clean," she assured me, rubbing the glasses with a towel. She handed me a glass filled with clear schnapps.

"Thank you. May I drink to the success of your venture?"

"Thank you!" she said raising her glass, "and to your visit."

"*Prosit!*" a painter chimed in good-naturedly, bending to lift two more cases. Eva blushed and looked a little sheepish, apparently dubious about the propriety of serving schnapps in the morning.

"Do you mind if I ask questions about yourself?" I asked.

"But no! That's what you're here for. I expect you want to know where I come from, whether I'm married, that sort of thing?" I said yes, and she continued, "I come from Regensburg in the Palatinate; do you know it? It's famous for the boys' choir in the cathedral."

* The West Berlin Senate guarantees bank loans to qualified small businesses at the special rate of 3½%.

"I've been to Regensburg and to the cathedral," I said, "and of course I know the Regensburg boys' choir."

"It's a pretty town," she said. "I was born there and went to school there. I don't have an *Abitur,* just a certificate from a commercial high school. I was an apprentice in bookkeeping, and when I qualified I worked for a year or so in a small office to gain experience. Then I got a better job in a larger firm, and I met my husband who was the office manager.

"I married after a few months," she said, "but I kept my job for about two years longer; then my son, Rudi, was born. Rudi is six now." She stopped for a sip.

"Just after Rudi was born my husband was transferred to the firm's office in Passau, and so we moved there. It's a charming town on the confluence of the Inn and the Danube, and we found a lovely apartment but were never happy there." She shrugged. "The usual reason. My husband became more and more distant, spent more and more evenings away from home. He grew irritable and absent-minded. Well, you understand. We decided to get a divorce."

"You are not Catholic?" I asked.

"No, and I don't think it's good for a small child to grow up in a home that is divided and unhappy. I thought it would be better for Rudi to be away from his father and away from Passau, which is a small, provincial town where people would gossip."

I said that I thought she was probably right.

"I liked Passau. It's a pretty, colorful little town with its crooked, steep medieval streets, its broad squares, its archways and cathedral, but I was growing restless. I decided that colorful antiquity was fine for tourists with cameras, but what I wanted was a clean, modern city with broad streets, bright, chic shops and worldly, broad-minded people. I toyed with the idea of moving to Munich or perhaps to Düsseldorf.

"Then one day I walked with the baby carriage to the post office. I suppose I'd passed the poster out front a thousand times, but I'd never paid attention to it. This time I noticed that it was one of those bright, amusing, 'Come to Berlin' posters, the kind that invite young people to make their futures in Berlin."

"I've seen them all over West Germany," I said.

"Well, it said that there were brochures about moving to Berlin at the town hall, so off I went and got one. The brochure listed all the financial and tax advantages of moving to Berlin. It promised help in finding and financing an apartment, in starting a business."

"And you decided to come?"

"Well, more or less. I packed up and took the train to Regensburg

Fig. 14. Strollers on the Kurfürstendamm, West Berlin (photo by author)

first. I wanted to leave Rudi with my mother and talk over my decision with my old boss, who has a good business head."

"Good idea," I said. "Did he advise you to try Berlin?"

She nodded. "He even offered to lend me money! I came to Berlin alone to have a look around, and I loved it! I went to the City Hall to inquire about the plan for immigrants, and they couldn't have been nicer. When I said before that I don't usually like bureaucrats, I didn't mean them. They were so helpful.

"The people at the economics office gave me all kinds of information about businesses that were available and bank loans. I just told them that I was twenty-seven and divorced, that I had a small boy, and what kind of training and experience I had, and they gave me advice. The housing office gave me a list of apartments and I went around looking at them."

"You had decided to make the move, then?"

"Oh yes. As I said, I fell in love with Berlin. I found a small apartment in one of the new housing projects way out in Lichtefelde. I hesitated about taking an apartment so far away from downtown Berlin, but I thought it was a marvellous location for Rudi. The project is surrounded by trees and lawns. There is a forest only a block or so away. The area is almost rural. There is also a brand new kindergarten and primary school just a block away, with no street to cross. I visited the school and talked with some teachers. I watched the children playing, and I thought it was ideal. I also realized that in a neighborhood with a lot of young children it would be easy to find a young mother to look after Rudi while I'm at work, so I took the apartment."

"Do you have very far to come to work?"

"Well, meanwhile I've learned that no place in Berlin is very far. The subways are excellent and we have a station right on our corner, so I'm here within a half hour."

"Do you like the apartment?"

"It's small, but it's very convenient. We have a small living room, only one bedroom and an absolutely tiny kitchen and bath, but there's a lovely balcony that overlooks the forest, which makes up for a lot. However, Rudi is growing. He really needs a bedroom!"

"Soon he'll need a place to do his homework," I said.

Eva nodded, "Of course, and a place for his toys and books! So far I've been pleased that the place is small, because I do my own cleaning and cooking. I shop on the way home and take my laundry to the laundromat at the shopping center. A small place has been a blessing. But I've put my name down for a larger apartment in our project and as soon as one becomes available, we'll move. I don't want to move out of the neighborhood.

"Rudi is six now and goes to the primary school, so he has a lot of school friends. I also have a marvellous woman who takes care of him after school and on Saturdays. She lives in a private house just down the block from us. They have a big, old-fashioned garden, where Rudi and her two children play. Sometimes she takes them to the playground, where they play on the swings and slides. She's much better with small children than I am. She is firm but very patient and affectionate. I'm afraid I'm often snappish and nervous after a day at work. Well," she shrugged, "businesswomen and women alone have worries."

"We do," I said and she smiled.

"Yes, well, you are a professional woman. You understand how it is. I am a trained bookkeeper. I know I wouldn't starve if I failed in business. I could always get a job and support my boy, but I don't want to fail! I enjoy my business. I like being independent. It's a challenge! It's wearing. It's sometimes hard on the nerves, but I'd hate to have to give it up!"

"Do you think you would keep your business if you remarried?"

"*Ach!* Marriage. I don't know. I've been so busy just getting started that I haven't had time or energy even to think about it, much less to make friendships with men. Running a small business is no nine-to-five job. I am always busy, and when I am not busy I am tired. When I have free time, I want to spend it with Rudi."

She paused and reflected. "Actually, I should like to remarry because I'd like to have another child, but after my first experience, after having felt so miserable and helpless in Passau and feeling, however tired and burdened I am, so independent, so useful here in Berlin, it would be difficult for me to marry. It would be very hard for me to trust a man again, but, if I did, I think I should insist on carrying on with my business. If I married again, it would have to be to the kind of man who would understand that, a man who would want me to be independent.

"But not now! Not yet, for goodness' sake! Now I have to pay off this loan, get my business on its feet. Right now I shall have to think about plowing every mark of profit back into the business. That's the difference when one is the boss! An employee can spend what he earns. I have to expand my inventory, spend money for advertising."

"Does your former husband help?"

"Under German law he would have to help support Rudi even if I didn't want him to, but I use the money he sends only for the boy. I buy him clothes and toys and I put some aside each month for his education later."

"Have you always been in this shop since you came to Berlin?" I asked. "And what made you decide on a stationery shop?"

"I had no particular idea when I came here what sort of small business I wanted to invest in, or, indeed, what I could afford, but I knew that it would have to be something that didn't require too much initial capital or much specialized knowledge. For instance, you have to know something about catering to run a restaurant."

"Of course," I said.

"Well, while I was looking around, I took a job as a bookkeeper, and it happened to be in a stationery store."

"Oh, I see."

"As soon as I'd rented the apartment and arranged to start work, I flew to Regensburg to get Rudi and my things; then I came back and settled in. I worked in this small shop in Wilmersdorf for about six months and pretty well got the hang of the business. I found I liked it. Just then the owner had a severe heart attack and decided to retire. He offered me the business. I thought it over, consulted a lawyer and the economics people and said yes. That was five years ago."

"Did you prosper?"

"Reasonably," she said, "and I learned a good deal about the stationery trade, but I realized that I couldn't expect to do much business in that neighborhood. After a year or two I began looking around for something more promising, and finally, about three and a half years ago, I found this shop. It's in a quiet side street so the rent isn't prohibitive, but it's very close to the Kurfürstendamm, so I think there are all kinds of opportunities. After I've made the shop more attractive, more noticeable, I think I shall have lots more business."

"You handle commercial business as well as social, don't you?"

"Oh, yes. We are classified as a middle-sized enterprise because of the volume of sales. I supply many firms with stationery wholesale."

I asked how many people she employed and she groaned.

"That is my real problem! Girls! Oh, it's easy enough to find sales girls, but good ones are scarce. So many young girls are not the least bit interested in their jobs. They only work so that they can earn money for clothes, for wigs or costume jewelry, or nowadays to take trips to Spain! They spend their money faster than they make it, and they are not interested in the future, certainly not in my future! They are careless about orders, they are slow and often rude in serving customers, and they are not worth their salaries!"

"Can't you find older women?"

"I try, but I also need someone with qualifications. I want someone with at least the intermediate diploma from a commercial high school, and qualified girls and women are scarce."

"Are you looking for a girl?"

"I am, but I have to be very careful before I decide. Hiring an employee in West Berlin or West Germany is no casual undertaking. There are so many laws to protect employees, you know, and they are costly creatures!"

"Health insurance, social security, that sort of thing?"

"All of those! If I hire a girl straight out of school, someone less than eighteen, she is entitled to four weeks' annual vacation! If she's over eighteen, a beginner gets two weeks' vacation; experienced shop girls get up to three weeks. Then there's sick leave. A clerk is entitled to up to six weeks' sick leave. During that time I'd have to pay her full salary and also pay for a replacement. That can work a real hardship on a small business, though it might not seem so. It makes me think twice about hiring a young married woman, I tell you!"

"Or a much older woman, I'd imagine. As the employer you have to pay a share of the old age and health insurance, too."

"I do. A sales clerk is entitled to retire with a partial pension at sixty, and many married women or widows with a pension choose to do that. Otherwise she can retire with a full pension at sixty-five. I think that's fine. I think health insurance is fine. I know I should pay my share, and of course I do it, but in return I'd like to get a willing and competent worker. The problem seems to be that the more benefits a worker receives, the more security he or she has, the less need he seems to feel to earn his right to work. He doesn't seem to see that unless I stay in business and make at least a modest profit, he wouldn't have any of the benefits. If I go bankrupt, I won't even be able to pay taxes to help with the government's share of all the benefits."

"Do your girls seem to think that shopkeepers are rich?"

"The silly ones at least think I am richer than they are, but they don't realize how much it costs to stay in business, how little personal profit my son and I receive from the business. They certainly don't realize how hard I have to work and how many worries I have."

"It sounds as though the life of the small businesswoman isn't easy. Do you regret your decision to strike out and become an entrepreneur? After all, you've had to borrow money. You must always be under pressure, and, as you say, you're unlikely to get rich."

"I didn't do it to get rich, and I really love it, however much I complain. It is a strain, but I enjoy the challenge. I like it much better than working for someone else. My kind of shop is fun. I sell to pleasant, interesting people. I'm lucky to be in a delightful neighborhood, and I think Berlin is wonderful. I like my apartment; I'm impressed with Rudi's school and with the opportunities here for children, for their education and recreation. I like the city and the people! No, all in all, I'm glad I came and glad I made the leap into private enterprise, however insecure it is."

"The insecurity of the city doesn't bother you?"

"Not really. Maybe because I'm too busy to worry? But I just enjoy the atmosphere. I regret that I almost never have a chance to take advantage of the cultural opportunities. I almost never go to the theater or even to a film. But later, when Rudi is older, I'll take him to museums and to concerts and to decent films on Saturdays or Sundays. Now I sometimes take him to the zoo or on a boat trip around the lakes. It's a wonderful city for children."

"All that outweighs the worry?"

"It doesn't really, but average people like me, like my neighbors, live in their daily life. I like my home, my work. I'm happy the way my child is growing up. When I have a few minutes to spare or sometimes when I go to see a customer or salesman, I walk along the Kurfürstendamm or down one of the interesting side streets. I browse in the shop windows. I stop to buy a paperback book or a pair of pantyhose and chat with fellow shopkeepers. I stop at a sidewalk café for a quarter of an hour to take a coffee-break and just watch the people walking by, the tourists, the foreign workers, and the Berliners. People live from minute to minute, from day to day, not really from crisis to crisis, and in Berlin the minutes are fun. After living in a provincial town with narrow streets and narrower people, I am grateful for every minute, for every day in Berlin. It's so alive! And I feel so alive here. It was worth coming, whatever happens, and I hope my son will be able to grow up here. Just think, Rudi will be a Berliner!"

15

Axel Springer

The building that houses the giant Axel Springer publishing firm is nineteen stories high, a skyscraper for Berlin. It is an impressive modern building in stone and glass. Blocks away I could see the story-high letters which spell out "Axel Springer Verlag" across the full width of the nineteenth floor.

"He's a big man," my middle-aged taxi driver told me. "Our students and radicals don't like him, but he knows what's what. Over there," he gestured with his thumb in the direction of the Wall just yards away, "they hate him, and that says a lot."

He held up his right arm and shook it so that the sleeve of his coat slid back. "See that? That watch? It's from him."

"From Springer?" I asked.

"*Ja,* sure, the day he opened that new building of his he gave a big reception. Everyone was invited. Champagne, sandwiches, everything, and you know what he did? He gave every taxi driver in West Berlin a watch. A good watch, too, maybe not the most expensive in the world, but just the same, think of it!"

"Every taxi driver?" I asked, amazed.

"*Jawohl!*" he said. "I told you. He's a big man. He's always doing things like that. He's made a fortune, but he gives a lot away too. I think he's a great guy, and not just because he gave me a watch."

I pushed open the plate-glass door and walked across the open space of the entrance hall. Modern and sober without being austere, the atmosphere hushed but relaxed and friendly, Axel Springer's publishing house radiates success, efficiency, and power. The elderly man at the reception desk greeted me politely and showed me to the elevator rows.

"Take this elevator," he suggested. "Nineteenth floor."

I thanked him and pressed the button marked nineteen. Two diminu-
198

tive girls in their early twenties, both carrying sheafs of papers, entered the elevator and smiled politely. One of them pressed buttons six and seven. A thick-set young man in conventional dark blue, carrying a heavy briefcase, walked in importantly and pressed eleven. The door closed, and we rose silently to six. As the small blond clerk walked out and waved back to her friend, I caught a glimpse of the corridor. Later my impression was confirmed that eighteen floors of the building are efficiently modern, cheerful, discreetly luxurious but basically utilitarian. The nineteenth floor was a different world, certainly a different century.

Axel Springer's personal world is not one of plastic tile and fluorescent lights, of cool, efficient fuctionalism. Neither is it one of obvious opulence or vulgar display. There are efficiency and opulence, but both are disciplined by restraint. I stepped out of the elevator into an atmosphere of deep piled carpets and walnut paneling. A discreet receptionist told me that I was expected and led me down a softly lit corridor to the door at the far end. Here I was greeted by a still more discreet and very attractive secretary and ushered into an inner office.

Ernst Cramer, Axel Springer's chief of staff, rose from behind a large, unpretentious desk, smiled and walked toward me, hand outstretched. He asked his secretary whether the coffee was ready, noting with pleasure that I had arrived exactly at ten. "Quite Prussian," he said with obvious approbation. I nodded, accepting the compliment.

The stately secretary brought in a tray, and Ernst served coffee in classical white cups. As we drank our coffee, we talked about my interview with Mr. Springer.

At exactly ten-fifteen an inner door opened and Axel Springer bowed slightly, introduced himself, and invited me into his personal office. He is a tall, elegant-looking man, rather like a good-natured, well-tailored Viking. He was dressed in what I later learned is virtually his uniform, closely fitted grey flannel, probably bespoken in Savile Row. His hair is blond, slightly greying, his eyes Scandinavian blue, his manner negligently graceful, deceptively unbusinesslike. He looks younger than his age, boyish. Only occasionally does a spark of intensity betray the fact that he is a fiercely dedicated person, someone to be taken very seriously.

We sat comfortably in his wood-paneled office with its wall-wide plate-glass window overlooking the city. "Now," he said, "what would you like to know?" I said, "Everything!" and he promised to begin at the beginning.

"The beginning," he began, "was in 1912, when I was born in Altona, which at that time was part of Schleswig-Holstein. Now it is part of Hamburg."

I said I thought he looked like a Viking, and he laughed. "One of my grandfathers was Danish, and I have always had a great affection for all the Scandinavian peoples, especially the Danes. Did you know that there are about five hundred Danes living in Berlin? They have their own Danish Lutheran church, and sometimes I like to attend service there just to feel at home.

"My father was a publisher. He owned a small publishing house in Hamburg, so I grew up in the business. He was known as an antinazi, and so, like all antinazi publishers, he was forced to close. We had a pretty thin time of it, especially during the war, but we survived.

"I was lucky," he went on. "I never had to join any of the nazi organizations, and I never served in the army or anywhere in the government. That was difficult during the war, but we managed. I took all kinds of odd jobs. Once I even worked as an usher in the movies, but that was better than working for the nazis.

"Sometimes, of course, we got discouraged, but my mother was wonderful. She used to keep a photograph of the entire nazi cabinet, and whenever I got very pessimistic about the state of Germany and of the world, whenever I was afraid that maybe the nazis would actually win the war, she would hold up the photograph and make me look at it. 'Look, my son,' she would say, 'is this what the rulers of the world look like?' and I would laugh and say no, and then she'd laugh and say, 'Well, they won't be the rulers of the world!' Of course she was right.

"Sometimes now I get discouraged about the Wall, about those people over there," he gestured to the wide window. "Then I remember my mother and her photograph and think of Ulbricht's face and tell myself that the rulers of the world don't look like that either."

I said that in our age one couldn't be too sure. I asked when he had begun his own publishing career.

"Even when I was a boy, and especially when I grew furious with the nazis, I used to dream of having a mammoth publishing business, and my mother always encouraged me. Right after the war I applied to the British authorities for a publishing license. Hamburg was in the British Zone, of course, and all publishing was licensed by the occupation powers in those days."

I said that I remembered, having worked in Berlin with the United States Military Government after the war. "As a matter of fact, I was with the American office which was in charge of the press and films."

"Ah," he said, "then you know how it was. It stood me in good stead, of course, that my father had been closed down by the nazis and that I had never worked for that crowd. I think I was one of the first to get a license."

"Of course," I said, and I asked whether he then began to publish one of the papers that made him famous.

"No, not right away. I began publishing in 1946. My first publication was a magazine which later was called *Kristall,* an illustrated magazine which you may remember. I rather liked it, but it was a bit too highbrow to be commercially successful. It had loyal readers but not enough of them."

"Often the way," I said. "When did you start your more popular publications?"

"In 1948 I began to publish a paper I called the Hamburger *Abendblatt.* At that time there were six newspapers in Hamburg. Within a year my *Abendblatt* had the top circulation."

I asked him what the secret was, and he said that he had always thought that German newspapers were too dull and pedantic.

"They aim over the heads of their readers and they bore them! I wanted a paper like British and Scandinavian papers, one which emphasized human interest, which separated fact from opinion."

"Didn't German newspapers do that?" I asked.

"No, dear lady, they preached. Some of them still preach. My papers express opinions but in editorials or signed commentaries, not in the news items.

"Apparently the public liked the human approach. We tried to make even politicians human by writing about their personal lives, their families, their hobbies, and not just their stuffy public statements.

"I hope we have been successful in a deeper sense. Before 1933 the newspapers in Germany almost unanimously opposed the nazis. Socialists, and conservative and middle-of-the-road democrats all published newspapers, and all of them urged their readers to vote against the Nazi Party, and what did the public do? It read its antinazi newspapers day in and day out and voted nazi. My conclusion was that the newspapers had little influence because they didn't really speak the same language as their readers, they didn't communicate. I was determined that my papers would, and I believe they do."

In 1952, he told me, he learned that the British occupation authority wanted to sell its official German language newspaper, *Die Welt.*

"Until then," he explained, "most newspapers in Hamburg were the organs of one or another of the political parties, S.P.D., C.D.U., and so on. The British wanted *Die Welt* to be unattached to any one party, to be independent. The only kind of newspaper I wanted to run was a politically independent one, and by 1952 I was sufficiently independent financially as well to be in a position to make a bid for the paper."

"*Die Welt* is rather different in style from your more popular papers, isn't it? Did you change your journalistic philosophy?"

"No, I think of *Die Welt* as a paper for the elected, that is, the decision-makers, and my other papers for the voters, but I think all my papers are human and not stuffy."

I told him that I enjoy *Die Welt* and always read it when I am in Germany. "How did you get to Berlin from Hamburg?"

"Well, do you remember that when Willy Brandt was Governing Mayor he began to encourage West German business firms to move to Berlin? He wanted to bolster the economy and the morale of the city. I visited West Berlin, talked to the mayor, and decided that I would move my entire office to Berlin, not just establish a branch office here. I looked around for a site, found this, thought it perfect and bought it."

"Did you like building your headquarters right on the sector border?" I asked.

"There is no better place for a newspaper publisher to have his office!" He got up and walked over to the window. He waved an arm elegantly in the direction of the street below. I went to the window and looked down at the Wall, which ran along the east side of the street. A VOPO in the nearby watch tower trained powerful field glasses in our direction. Three guards marched purposefully between rows of barbed wire, two carrying rifles, one a machine pistol.

"They travel in threes now," he said. "Two might more easily conspire to cross over."

"Some of them still do get over, don't they?" I asked, knowing that many who flee to the West are young border guards.

"Some," he said. He pointed straight ahead to a cluster of tank traps and large placards. "That's Checkpoint Charlie, there before the Wall curves east. It is a good reminder living on top of this. Right there, on the other side of that Wall, Russia begins."

He turned and smiled ironically. "They call it the German Democratic Republic. It's neither democratic nor German. If the Russians pulled out their twenty divisions tomorrow, the regime over there would be overthrown in a matter of hours. If you ask me, there are more genuine communists in West Berlin and West Germany than in the whole of East Germany."

He walked back to his desk, and I slipped into a straight chair near the window.

"You will think it is no wonder our students and leftists think I'm the world's worst reactionary. Whenever West Berlin students go on strike, they come and picket my building. Sometimes they even throw bombs. To them I typify the repressive bourgeois society they are trying to destroy. To them any anticommunist is *ipso facto* counterrevolutionary and an outdated Cold Warrior."

He relaxed into the chair behind his desk. "In reality I am anything but an extremist. I like to think of myself as a radical of the center."

We both grinned, he with self-deprecation.

"Well, it's true. I have consistently opposed any kind of totalitarianism, fascist or communist. My father opposed the nazis from the beginning, and our whole family suffered for it. Even as a young man I accepted deprivation because I opposed them too. I still oppose fascism or military dictatorships wherever I find them as well as all forms of communism.

"I am worried that many of these young people who accuse me of reaction and fascism seem to be antisemitic, and antisemitism is one of the things I have consistently fought against. Our young radicals say they are only anti-Zionist, not racists, but there are definite antisemitic overtones in Moscow's attitude. There is no question that thousands of Jews have been fleeing from Poland in recent months because of antisemitism there. Our young radicals say they support the Arabs in the Middle East for purely political reasons, but I suspect that some genuine antisemitism creeps in."

He asked me whether I knew that his publishing house was built on the site of the old Ullstein *Verlag*. I said that I had heard that he had bought out Ullstein.

He nodded. "It was a famous and prestigious Jewish house before the nazis came to power, and we are their heir. I think that imposes a duty on us to fight antisemitism in every form, and it also gives a religious foundation to our house."

He went on thoughtfully:

"I am not one of those Germans who believe in breast-beating, but on the other hand, I do not believe in running away from national responsibility. I think that we Germans do have guilt to expiate, and, in relation to the Jews, I believe that we can help expiate it by supporting Israel. I have always been a strong advocate of aid to Israel and have endorsed every move of the Bonn government to seek reconciliation with the Jews, both through paying compensation to individual victims or their heirs and through friendship with Israel. I am rather proud that my building stands directly over the old Jerusalem Street."

"You oppose antisemitism and communism," I began. He interrupted and amended, "I oppose totalitarianism in all forms." I indicated my

acceptance of the amendment and went on, "Do you consider yourself a
fiscal conservative? Do you oppose socialism?"

He paused and reflected. "I suppose you would call me a fiscal conservative if you mean that I support a sound currency and oppose inflation, but I certainly favor what we in West Germany call the social
market economy in the Erhard tradition. I believe in free enterprise, in
maximum economic freedom, not because I am a capitalist but because
it works; I also support every possible humane provision for social welfare, so in that sense I am no enemy of our Social Democrats."

I made a few notes and then asked about his views on foreign policy.
"I know you are a strong friend of the United States and of the Atlantic
Alliance."

"Oh, yes," he said. "I support greater unity within Europe but always
within the framework of co-operation with the United States. This makes
me unpopular with the radical students, who think every defense of the
United States is a sign of imperialist war-mongering, but I am used to
that. I find it a little harder to defend myself against the newer critics of
your country who worry about statements by such Americans as Senators
Mansfield and Fulbright calling for the withdrawal of U.S. troops from
Europe, who fear that America is no longer willing or able to defend
freedom in Europe. Every time any American politician makes a speech
like that, our West German press plays it up. I think they overemphasize
the importance of the demands, but there is no question that West German confidence in America is less than it was."

I asked whether this lessening confidence was recent and whether it
had some connection with Willy Brandt's *Ost Politik*.

"I think it goes back to the Wall," he said. "There has been a slow but
basic change in the thinking of many Social Democrats since the Wall.
You asked me before whether I was antisocialist. I have never been an
enemy of the S.P.D. I have always had many close friends in the Berlin
socialist party, including Willy Brandt when he was Governing Mayor. I
respected them and trusted them. I freely acknowledge the historic role
of the S.P.D. in raising the dignity and the living standard of the working
man. I have always been a friend of German trade unionism. I am certainly aware of the vital role the S.P.D. leaders in Berlin played after
1945 in keeping the city free. They put on a gallant fight, as you know, to
keep the communists from taking over their party and the trade unions.

"These men have been my friends. I had grown used to the fact that
socialists like them had long since rejected Marxism—if they had ever
accepted it. They still believed in social reform but not in Marxism, and,

like me, they believed by the 1950s that Marxism as an ideology was dead. We thought it was buried for good when both our S.P.D. and the British Labour Party repudiated the doctrine of nationalization of industry."

I agreed and said that I too had believed that in the 1950s.

"But now, you see, we have a new generation of young socialists who are espousing a kind of neo-Marxism, and the tragedy is that some of the older socialists who had long since discarded Marxist views are jumping on the neo-Marxist bandwagon, whether because they have changed their ideas or just to keep in step with the younger generation, I don't know."

"You said you thought this change had something to do with the Wall?" I asked.

"I think it has. I think many genuinely anticommunist Berlin socialists were shocked and shattered by the failure of your President Kennedy to take a stand against the building of the Wall. Many of our high-ranking socialists knew that Allied Intelligence had warned the American authorities over and over that the East Germans were planning a new move against Berlin, but at the Vienna conference with the Soviets, J.F.K. not only did not oppose the idea vigorously, he seemed to acquiesce. That is, he showed that he sympathized with the East German regime over the mounting loss of refugees, and the Russians apparently interpreted this as acceptance of their plan or of Ulbricht's plan.

"Well, the Wall was the first shock. The Americans sat on their hands and contented themselves with mild reproaches, and many disillusioned socialists concluded that the United States was no longer prepared to back up its commitment to defend freedom in Berlin or in Europe with anything more than words, and so they began to look elsewhere for security. They decided that since they couldn't stand alone against the East they had best seek rapproachement, and hence the Brandt *Ost Politik,* a policy of seeking understanding, of accommodation."

"Poor us," I said and grinned. "Is everything our fault?"

"No, no, *gnädige* Frau, centainly not," he assured me chivalrously.

"Isn't there," I asked tentatively, "a natural tendency among left-of-center politicians to take an optimistic view of human nature generally and of left-wing nature in particular? *Pas d'ennemi à gauche. . . .*"

"You mean the convergence theory?"

"Yes," I said, "and the optimistic hope that the post-Ulbricht regime in East Germany will gradually grow less pedantic, less Stalinist."

He agreed that this element exists. "They really believe, apparently, that, because the communist world is no longer monolithic, communism itself is softening and is less dangerous and therefore one can deal with the lesser communist states. Young socialists hold up Yugoslavia as a model of socialism without Soviet domination, conveniently forgetting the recent experience in Czechoslovakia.

"These left-wing socialists criticize me because I object to our courting the communist government in Poland. They want to know why I favor reparations to Israel but refuse to acknowledge our moral debt to the Poles, who also suffered from nazi crimes. This is typically muddle-headed liberal thinking, isn't it? On the one hand, they do not see that to make overtures of friendship to the present dictatorial government in Poland would be like showering friendliness on the present Czech regime. It would not show friendship to the Polish or Czech people, who know their governments are repressive. On the other hand, our liberal friends gush over every Eastern potentate, bestowing brotherly kisses on each cheek, and try to outdo each other in gestures of conciliation, while they revile and anathematize the Greek colonels, Franco, and the South Africans. I oppose all dictatorships, but I am consistent. These left-wing liberals measure with a double standard."

I asked him whether he thought this kind of thinking represented a danger for Berlin. He nodded gravely.

"I'm afraid that it might. I am no friend of Willy Brandt's *Ost Politik*. I know that he and the S.P.D. have assured the German people that they will continue to hold out for adequate guarantees for West Berlin, that their new friendship treaty with Moscow includes an acceptable Berlin agreement guaranteed by the four powers. Brandt insists that the agreement insures adequate provision for West Berlin's cultural, economic, and legal ties with West Germany, but in my view this is not enough to guarantee West Berlin's freedom. Our political tie with the Federal Republic should also be assured, and I am very dubious whether the East will ever agree to this. The Brandt people tend to soft-pedal the question, and I fear that this is a dangerous portent for West Berlin.

"As far as I can see, this so-called *détente* is nothing but a series of concessions to the East, and the net result is that the G.D.R. has won international respectability in return for a few sops. It is true that West Berliners can now visit East Berlin under specified restrictions a limited number of times a year, but can East Berliners visit us? The Wall still stands. East Germany is still an armed fortress, and the VOPOs at the border still shoot real bullets at escaping refugees. As long as human beings are killed week in, week out, trying to escape from the 'German Democratic Republic,' I cannot believe in Brandt's *détente*."

We talked a little about the future. I asked him whether he was optimistic about the long-range possibility for the reunification of Berlin and of Germany and he assured me that he was.

"It was no accident that I built my publishing house in the exact geographic center of Berlin. I built it there with an eye to the future because some day I expect Berlin to be reunified. I expect Germany to be reunified."

I asked when and he said, "I believe it, definitely, but I cannot say when."

"Five years?" I asked and he shook his head. "Ten years?" He smiled and again refused to predict.

"Fifty years?" I asked and he laughed and said, "Yes, absolutely. You see, I believe in the United States. I realize that America is suffering severe and profound problems, economic, social, political, and I can foresee that she will have to go through a long period of crisis. Obviously, there are difficult times ahead for our American ally, but I firmly believe in the untapped reservoir of strength in America—physical, political, and moral strength."

I said I hoped that he was right, then asked what he thought of the strength of the Soviet Union.

He said that he thought the new generation of Soviet leadership was cynical. "They are no longer sincere Marxists. They are materialists, but not dialectical materialists. They are affluent, opportunistic, and conformist. As you know, in a bureaucratic and repressive system the people who come to the top are usually not the most brilliant and certainly not those with the most integrity; they are the organization men, the opportunists; and these are the most easily corrupted. Many of the elite in the U.S.S.R. are men with a price, and this just may hold out a hope to the West."

"On the whole, would you describe yourself as optimistic, Herr Springer?" I asked, having noticed, I had thought, an underlying sadness pervading all his energy and thrust.

"Yes and no, *gnädige* Frau. I think I am constitutionally optimistic, and in the long run I do have faith both in American strength and resolution and in the inevitability of German reunification, but I am not blind to the problems in our civilization. There is more wrong with the situation in West Berlin and West Germany than just the party in power. We are undergoing a basic moral crisis. The young people are partly right when they complain that ours is a sick society."

"You mean morally sick?" I asked.

He nodded. "I mean things like the epidemic of nudity and pornography and sadism, like increasing violence and crime, loss of respect for law and for religion. West Berlin has become more licentious in the past few years than it was during the Weimar days."

"And we know where that led," I said.

"Do you know there are sex shops in West Berlin?" he asked.

"I saw one," I admitted. "It was on a side street just off the Kurfürsten-damm. What do they sell? Do you know?"

He laughed and disclaimed knowledge. "Didn't you go in, *Gnädigste?*"

"Certainly not," I said.

"No scientific curiosity!"

I said that I was too old for such curiosity, and he agreed that he was too. "But people are making money out of this orgy of pornography, and this sort of thing, silly though it is, does undermine public morality."

"But you don't agree with the leftist youngsters that capitalism is the cause?" I asked.

"Not in the sense they mean it, but in another sense it contributes to the cause. Free enterprise produces affluence, and I believe that affluence in many cases produces boredom and cynicism. Here," he said, and shuffled through some papers on his desk and handed me a cartoon. It showed a young girl with hair streaming over her face, peace beads hanging down her front confronting an obviously conventional and bourgeois middle-aged man. The man, her father, asks, "But, my dear, what have I failed to give you?" The girl answers, "Perhaps poverty."

I looked at the cartoon and laughed.

"We have failed our young people," Springer continued. "We have given them too much luxury, and we have made their lives dull. We have failed to give them challenge, excitement and goals for living, and in consequence they are spoiled, bored and demoralized. No wonder they rebel."

"Is there any solution?" I asked.

"Religion," he said. "We have fallen away from God in the West. There are more Christians over there in the East than here in the West. Christianity, as you know, has always flourished under persecution, not in affluence. Western civilization was founded on religion, and, when faith is undermined, so is the whole fabric of civilization."

"Don't you get discouraged?" I asked.

"Sometimes I get very badly discouraged. I believe that we in the West must return to God, to basic morality, to the fundamental truths of our civilization, or we shall be destroyed, but I am far from sure that we shall do so. Sometimes I am sure that we are facing the end of our civilization, its final dissolution. Certainly we are in the midst of a grave crisis."

We were silent for a moment, and then he said:

"Sometimes I feel isolated and then I remember that Martin Luther, whom I greatly admire, was also often close to despair, that he felt lonely and isolated in his later years. I keep his picture on my wall to remind me that, in one of his dark moods, Luther said that if he knew that the world were going to end the next morning, he would still plant his apple tree today.''

I smiled in recognition because I too had grown up with legends of Brother Martin.

"So," he said, and smiled warmly, "I plant apple trees."

"You plant them successfully," I said glancing around. "You have a green thumb."

He said, "So did Martin Luther." He consulted his watch and suggested that we go in to lunch. "I should like to show you our library and clubroom," he said, rising and ushering me to the door. We walked across a carpeted corridor and into a long and spacious room paneled in soft, mellow pine and lined with books.

He told me that the books, mostly old and some of them precious, had been donated by a member of his staff. Ernst later explained that Mr. Springer conceived of the library and lounge as a club for all Berlin journalists. Any of them can use the library or have drinks or lunch in the dining room.

"After all, since a conservative is one who affirms basic truths, who believes in continuity, this nineteenth floor is my personal affirmation of continuity, of tradition, especially of Prussian tradition."

He showed me several paintings, most of which were works of the court painter of Frederick II. "Most of his works are in the Charlottenburg Palace, but I was lucky enough to be able to purchase a few others."

The huge chandelier, the vases and candlesticks were uniformly of the eighteenth century. The small portrait of Frederick the Great, Old Fritz, the immense one of Otto von Bismarck dominating the room from its place of honor over the mantel, proclaimed the Springer commitment as well as his classical taste.

He led me over to a window-table spread with a snow-white cloth sparkling with polished silver and clear crystal.

"Welcome, Frau von Lewinski," he said and smiled and bowed slightly, holding the table so that I could slide behind it to the bench. I thanked him. "A gentle room," I said.

His aides Claus Dieter and Ernst joined us, greeted me and sat down. Mr. Springer suggested steak and chose a light red wine. The waiter offered us rolls, and, when I refused, Springer commented:

"Ah, you avoid bread too. I never eat it. It's poison." He told me that he kept to a stringent, almost Spartan diet. "Lean meats, fruits and vegetables, low starch, and as a rule, very little alcohol. I enjoy a good

Burgundy or Moselle wine, of course, but when I am working, I stick to light, dry wine, and very little, especially at lunch."

Claus Dieter asked whether I had been over to East Berlin on this visit. I said that I had. "I was trying to take photographs for the book and for lectures, but the weather was so bad that I had to give it up."

"Raining?" he asked.

"Pouring," I said, "and awfully cold for this time of year. I only had a light raincoat and nearly froze."

"Pretty hard to concentrate on photography when you're freezing and the rain is pouring down your face," Ernst said.

"Impossible," I said, "and besides, I was trying to get shots of people, people shopping, people strolling, and there weren't many people."

"Not in the rain," Mr. Springer said. "Not even the East Berliners are Spartan enough to stroll in a cold rain."

"Not even when I want to photograph them!" I said. "Besides, people look so grim and drawn on a rainy day. All the pictures I did get make the city look grey, the people miserable."

"East Berlin is grey, Frau Doctor," Claus Dieter commented.

"Not that grey!" I protested.

"Next time you go over," Mr. Springer suggested, "be sure to have a look at the new housing projects just on the other side of the Wall facing our publishing house. They are some of the most attractive apartments they have done, and we think they built them because of us. So many visitors come to our *Verlag* and look down at what they can see of East Berlin from our nineteenth floor that they have built showcase apartments exactly where they can be seen from here."

"To some extent all East Berlin is a showcase," Ernst said, and Springer nodded in agreement.

"Oh yes, East Berlin is dull compared to West Berlin, but if you travel from the rest of the country in East Germany to East Berlin, you will think it is paradise. Chemnitz, for instance, is unbelievably depressing. The entire city is one color, grey."

"Compared to Chemnitz," Ernst said, "East Berlin is a Potemkin village."

We ordered fruit and coffee, and I asked whether the average East Berliner knew about Axel Springer. "I know the government over there knows about you."

All three men laughed, and Ernst said, "Knows! He is their bête noire."

Springer nodded and said that the East Berlin television station had produced a series of five two-hour programs about him called "*Ich,* Axel

Caesar Springer," portraying him as a power-greedy ogre, the all-powerful czar of the West German media.

"West Berlin TV also did a long series about me which they called 'Three Days in the Life of Axel Springer,' and, of course, a lot of East Berliners saw that. They always watch our TV, as you know, so by now I am quite well known over there."

"A household word," I said. "But do they believe you are an ogre or do they take that with a grain of salt?"

"In my opinion the average East Berliner takes most propaganda with several grains of salt. In the first place, the Berliner is sophisticated, cosmopolitan, not a country bumpkin, and, in the second, he has access to West Berlin radio and television, so he has a basis of comparison which Europeans farther east lack.

"About me in particular—well I had an experience which showed that at least some of them disbelieve the propaganda. Not very long ago when I was visiting my home near the Danish border, I was driving along a country road, and I saw two elderly women. They were typical old-fashioned old ladies with white hair and flowered hats, and there they were, trudging along a dusty country road miles from the nearest farm or village. I stopped my car and offered them a lift. They hesitated and then one of them said, 'Oh, aren't you Axel Springer?' I admitted I was, and she said, 'I recognized you from the TV program.' They immediately got into the car and I drove them to where they were staying. I found they were from East Germany, and, since they were over sixty-five, they were permitted to visit relatives in the West. They had both seen the propaganda film about me on Eastern TV, but they assured me that they hadn't believed a word. In fact, the propaganda had backfired and after also having seen the West Berlin film on me they thought of me as rather a hero. They were delighted when I drove right up in front of the house where they were staying."

As soon as we had finished lunch, Axel Springer excused himself. Ernst offered to take me around the building. "If you need photographs, we have an excellent collection downstairs in our library." We went down in the elevator, and he introduced me to a helpful librarian, and soon I was sitting at a small, modern desk examining stacks of press photographs of Berlin.

During that entire visit to Berlin the people in the Springer office went out of their way to be helpful to me. They arranged interviews with people I wanted to see; they suggested others whom I might want to see. They supplied data and articles and publications. Several times they invited me to stop by at Springer House for coffee. They telephoned almost every day with news or suggestions.

Early one morning Ernst stopped at my hotel on his way to the office and caught me in the lobby just as I was going out with my camera.

"Come have some coffee with me," he suggested, and we went to the hotel's breakfast room. He told me that Mr. Springer was giving a reception that evening for the West German Association of Women Entrepreneurs, and he invited me to come.

"You know, there are a lot of independent businesswomen in Germany," he said. "Some of them own little neighborhood shops, some run middle-sized businesses, and some are full-scale industrial managers. There are women from all kinds of businesses, from fashion and cosmetics to heavy industry, and they come from all over West Germany. We thought it might be fun for you."

I said I thought it might too.

"About six," he said. "There'll be lots of champagne!"

There was lots of champagne, liberally served by a platoon of very young, very smart waiters. The discreet reception room, the library and clubroom all overflowed with business women, festively dressed. The few men scattered about the room looked mildly embarrassed and utterly overwhelmed.

I found a sheltered place at the far end of the room almost under the Bismarck portrait. I leaned against one of the broad windows which looked down nineteen stories to the Wall. Several of the businesswomen came over in twos or threes to peer down at the Wall. They seemed to take it for granted that I was a Berliner because they asked me to point out landmarks. Dutifully, but amused and delighted with my small deception, I indicated Checkpoint Charlie, the Prussian museum, the Friedrichstrasse.

"It must be sad to live in Berlin," a small-boned woman said in a Rhineland accent.

"But exciting," her taller, ampler friend added.

Just then an aide turned on the microphone across the room, and Axel Springer made a little speech to welcome his guests. He was charming and flirtatious, and the women seemed to enjoy it.

"He's so good-looking!" the little Rhinelander said. "Like a Viking," her friend commented.

"Like a good-natured, boyish Viking," I amended, and they agreed and applauded his speech.

Ernst located me easily in the crowd because he and I seemed to be taller than most of the guests.

"It was fun," I told him and thanked him for inviting me.

"Well," he said, "the champagne was good."

"Marvellous!" I agreed, and we immediately found a waiter with full glasses.

"He does this all the time, you know," Ernst explained. "Almost every conference or convention that meets in Berlin is invited here for a reception, about one a week."

"But that must cost a fortune!" I said, and he agreed that it cost quite a bit.

"He gives away a lot of money too," he said. I told him I had heard about the watches. "He gave an organ to the Danish Lutheran Church not very long ago, and you may have heard about the library he built in Jerusalem. It is one of the most modern libraries in the world. He thinks of it as a kind of personal reparation from an individual German to the Jewish people."

"He is deeply committed to that idea, isn't he?" I asked.

"He is deeply involved with Israel," Ernst said. "We visited there for the opening of the library last year, and it was obvious how much involved he was. We took along some work to do, planning to get it done on the plane on the way out, but he said he was too keyed up, too excited about visiting Israel to be able to concentrate on extraneous work. All the time we were there, I kept reminding him of the work in my briefcase, and he kept putting me off, saying, 'Not now, not here!' Finally, on the plane returning to Germany he breathed a deep sigh and said, 'All right, bring out the work,' and we cleared it up in a couple of hours. On the way to Israel or while he was there, he was too much absorbed to be able to think of anything else."

"Is he always so emotional, so intense?" I asked.

"He has a lot of temperament," Ernst said.

"He appears so casual," I said, but I was not really deceived.

"That is his style. He never gives the impression of being businesslike or efficient. He is charming, offhand and leisurely, as you have seen. He will chatter, tell anecdotes, gossip and joke for almost an hour without ever coming to the point of a business conference and then suddenly, in the last five minutes, he will zero in on the point and mop up all the business, usually very shrewdly. He can accomplish as much in those final five minutes as most businessmen could in the full hour."

"Like a cat," I said with approbation, and Ernst agreed, knowing by then that I liked cats.

"He pounces, you mean. Exactly, and right on target."

"Yes," I said, musing, "I was not misled by his nonchalance. He is a formidable person. I am glad that he likes us."

"Americans, you mean?"

"Yes," I said.

"He is very sincere about that. Did I tell you that he ran into Mayor Schütz at the Berlin reception for the N.A.T.O. commander, General Andrew J. Goodpastor, and Schütz was ribbing him about his opposition to the left-wing students. He said, 'Tell me, Herr Springer, don't you like any intellectuals at all?' Springer answered, 'Yes, of course, when they are in uniform.' Of course, he meant General Goodpastor, who is very bright. He has been a very loyal supporter of President Nixon."

Just before I left Berlin I again visited the Springer building and again found my way to the nineteenth floor. The day was gloriously sunny, and so we had an excellent view as we looked out of one of the windows on the opposite side of the building from those facing Checkpoint Charlie. Axel Springer pointed over to the East to a cluster of obviously new and very modern buildings which from that distance looked like a Christmas village.

"That is the Alexanderplatz," he said. I recognized it even in miniature. "Now look at the television tower. It is one of the highest towers in the world and, of course, our Eastern brethren are very proud of it. Now look carefully at the silver sphere."

The tower is a tall, slim column capped with a gigantic silver sphere. "You can see that the sphere is studded. Now watch what happens when the sun comes out from behind that cloud." We watched, and as the sun emerged, a huge silver cross glowed from the sphere. It was the sun reflecting on two horizontal and two vertical rows of studs.

"The East Germans didn't intend that, of course," Springer said and grinned. "We call it the Pope's revenge."

I laughed and reflected that the unplanned silver cross shining audaciously from their proud television tower is just one thorn in the flesh of the East German government. Their near neighbor Axel Springer is a more irritating one.

Axel Caesar Springer is an enemy to be reckoned with. He has certainly achieved his early ambition to establish a mammoth publishing house. The restrained opulence of the nineteen-story modern building erected exactly at the edge of the communist Wall, exactly at the center of Berlin, straddling the old Jerusalem Strasse, proclaims both the Springer ideology and Springer power. From the popular tabloids to the serious *Die Welt,* Springer newspapers blanket West Germany and West Berlin. Not only have they mass circulation but they are read by

Fig. 15. The Wall, with a view of East Berlin's television tower showing the reflection of a cross: "The Pope's Revenge" (photo by Landesbildstelle, West Berlin)

a loyal following. The voice of Axel Springer may not be decisive but it is always heard.

Axel Springer, anachronistic romantic to liberals, repressive symbol of reaction to young radicals, comforting voice of stability and continuity to millions of ordinary German newspaper readers, stubborn defender of a cause grown unfashionable, digs in, smiles elegantly, and continues to fire journalistic salvos. I was impressed with the man's intensity and stature, with his Lutheran and conservative sense of stewardship. Whether he is the ogre, the power-hungry press czar he is painted by his enemies, or the benevolent, freedom-loving first lord of the West German press, he is someone to be taken seriously, and certainly he is fascinating.

He is also a Berliner, like so many Berliners by adoption. He and his impressive new building have become symbols of the city, his publications the voice of at least one segment of the city's population. Whether one admires or fears, patronizes or praises, one cannot ignore Axel Springer and West Berlin. All Berlin would be far less colorful without him.

16

Sister Hedwig

"A day nursery?" Eric said and nodded. "Yes, a day nursery would be a very good idea. We take the education of children very seriously here in East Berlin, and we begin with the very small children. Yes, I'll look up a good day nursery for you."

True to his word, on my next visit to East Berlin, Eric greeted me with the news that we were on our way to the pride of all East Berlin day nurseries. We drove up to a spic-and-span modern structure, a glass and pastel-yellow concrete oblong set in a shady garden adjacent to a modern school and playground. Eric escorted me as far as the door, told me that I was expected and promised to fetch me in two hours for lunch.

As I rang the bell I noticed three baby carriages and a stroller lined up in a kind of concrete baby-carriage parking lot to the right of the entrance. A slim, starched young woman in a uniform like that of a student nurse admitted me, smiled and led me to a sunny, antiseptic waiting room. The walls, tiled floor, the fragile-looking modern furniture were all bright yellow; the curtains were yellow with green and orange stripes. It was blindingly cheerful.

I scarcely had time to observe this when a middle-sized, firmly plump, rosy woman of about thirty-five bounded into the room. She wore the traditional white of the registered nurse, but there was nothing starchy about her personality. She beamed at me and exuded overwhelming maternal warmth.

"Good morning!" she said emphatically. "I am Sister Hedwig, the matron here. I should like to show you around myself."

I introduced myself, we shook hands and she promptly swept me out of the room and down the corridor. I felt a bit dazed, almost drowned in the backwash of her energy and efficiency.

Evidently believing in first things first and that even an infant army

217

marches on its stomach, she conducted me to the kitchens. As I would have guessed, it was a gleaming, sterile theater of operations, all stainless steel and sparkling porcelain. A dainty young nurse was carefully measuring milk into steaming bottles. She did not look up or interrupt her work as we entered.

"*Na*, Sister Catherine!" Hedwig announced, "Here is a visitor from America come to see how we take care of our babies."

Precisely filling a bottle and capping it, Sister Catherine set down her huge saucepan of milk, turned and smiled.

"Good morning," she said. "Forgive me for not shaking hands, but I have to keep sterile. I am doing the bottles for the infants."

Matron beamed and reassured her. She pointed out the giant steel vats of pea soup simmering on the stove. A row of ceramic soup bowls, each with a child's name painted on it, stood waiting for the hot soup.

We said good-bye to Sister Catherine, and Sister Hedwig led me along a corridor, up a flight of stairs, and out onto the broad balcony which ran the full length of the back of the two-story building. It was a covered balcony like a loggia. A line of miniature cots and prams stood side by side; in them about a dozen infants slept in the sun. A small blond student nurse sat in a low chair placidly knitting. She stood stiffly when she saw us, and the matron whispered an introduction.

"This," she said softly, sweeping a rounded arm in a broad gesture, "is where our smallest ones take their rest on sunny days. The bigger ones have cots and deck chairs downstairs on the terrace."

We went back indoors and entered the first room on the right. This was a square room painted bright yellow. Twelve or fourteen small children sat on low stools around a single round table in the center of the room. A grey-haired, kindly nurse (the nurses in charge of classes are kindergarten teachers, not registered nurses but dressed in nurses' uniforms) and a fresh-faced probationer hovered over the children watching and helping them with their drawing or craft work. With a gesture, Sister Hedwig motioned them to go on with their work and not pay attention to us. She showed me the blackboards, a bulletin board gaily decorated with bright-colored paper animals, and a collection of toddlers' toys and tricycles. There was even an old-fashioned rocking horse. The room and all its equipment were spic-and-span and cheerful.

In the next room a single young nurse, her wiry red hair escaping untidily from her pert cap, was reading a story to a group of about ten plump, rosy-faced children of perhaps four or five. She grinned up at us, we waved and smiled, and she continued reading. As we arrived at the third room, a short, squarely built maid in a grey uniform was just setting down a heavy steel tray covered with bowls of steaming soup. Ten children sat primly in their circle, hands folded on the yellow table in front of them, and waited silently for their lunch. Their tall, athletic nurse poured hot cocoa from a huge pitcher into each child's ceramic mug.

"We have a birthday child today, Matron!" the nurse announced brightly. "Claudia, tell us all how old you are."

A slender girl with straight blond hair falling to her shoulders blushed and stammered, "Four years old." Sister Hedwig and I wished her a happy birthday. The class nurse led her charges in singing happy birthday to Claudia. By then each child had a bowl of soup and a mug of cocoa in front of him but none had begun to eat. All then sat perfectly still, hands folded.

"Before you begin your lunch, children," Sister Hedwig said, "why don't you sing a nice song for the *Tante* who has come all the way from America to see you?"

Ten pairs of blue eyes widened and stared at me, and ten small faces blushed and smiled shyly.

"Let's sing the song about the little bird," the class nurse suggested, and she began it for them. The young voices piped softly, almost inaudibly. Afterwards the girls tittered self-consciously.

"Now, children," the nurse said, "you may begin your lunch and afterwards there is a special treat. Claudia's mother left us a birthday cake, and we'll all have some!"

"Sweet children, aren't they?" the matron said as she led me down the corridor. Too sweet, I thought, saddened. She threw open a door revealing a sparkling white-tiled room lined with minature washbasins and shower stalls and spotless green-and-white towels hanging in an orderly row.

"The washroom," she said, "and here next door is the little room for the potties, where the nurses bring the small babies to be trained. The toddlers are escorted in shifts after their lunch."

She explained that each nurse brought all her charges at once and set each on its pot all in a row.

"Whether the children want to or not?" I couldn't help asking.

"They want to," she smiled. "You see, we have most of our children from a very young age, and they are trained in regular habits. We bring them all here at regular intervals. It is rarely necessary to bring an individual child between times unless the child is sick."

She took me into the examining room, which is used by the medical supervisor on her weekly visits. Colorful wall charts recorded the growth and weight of the children.

"Doctor examines each child once a week, and, of course, she is available in case of emergency. Sister Catherine and I are registered nurses, so we can handle small things like sniffles or first aid. We get a few bumps and cuts, of course, but rarely anything serious. We take very good care of our children, and they are all well-fed and healthy."

She pulled a card out of a file drawer and showed it to me.

"This is Claudia's card—the little girl who has the birthday today. You see here the record of her weight and height, the dates of her shots, and notations about any little sicknesses or upsets. She came to us when she was three months and now she is four years old, so we have a complete record of her development."

"Does the doctor advise about diet and nutrition?" I asked, examining Claudia's card and handing it back.

"Oh, yes," she said. "She lays down the general rules, and Sister Catherine draws up the weekly menus. Naturally, if any child has an allergy or digestive trouble, Doctor recommends special foods. If the child requires something very special, the parents usually bring it. We had one little girl, for instance, who couldn't digest milk. Her papa brought three jars of yogurt every morning when he left Dolly with us."

Hedwig rose and led me down the hall to her own office. This was also yellow and modern, but it was spacious and a little less clinically austere than the other rooms. Hedwig directed me to an almost comfortable chair and disappeared to order coffee. I glanced out of the picture window behind her desk at the playground and the elementary school in the background. Several young children were climbing on a jungle gym, others were digging in a sandbox and two dashed up and down on tricycles. They certainly seemed healthly, but they were all amazingly quiet.

"Are those your children playing out there?" I asked as Hedwig reappeared, "or do they belong to the elementary school?"

"Some of each," she replied. "Our four- and five-year-olds play there. We can use their junior swimming pool, too, during certain hours. Most of our babies go on to that school, and many of them already have older brothers or sisters there, so when they have to leave us, they feel quite at home and secure.

"Yes, our children get wholesome food, expert medical attention, lots of exercise and not only loving supervision but professional teaching." She pointed to a huge chart on the wall beside her desk. "You see here a chart which predicts the normal development of the child, the exact age in weeks or months at which he should develop certain skills, at first just physical skills, like smiling or turning over or sitting up and later mental skills, like recognizing words, distinguishing colors or numbers or letters."

She took a large orange-colored card from a file drawer and held it out to me. "Here is Claudia's development chart. You can see that our nurses have tested her, observed her every week since she came here, noting her progress in terms of the norm." She studied the card. "Our Claudia seems just about average, maybe a tiny bit slow but well within the normal range."

"Do you use these measurements to alert the doctor to possible physical disability or retardation?" I asked.

"Yes, that's the major reason for them. If a child is slow in developing, we show his card to the doctor, and then she keeps the child under observation and perhaps spots a hearing defect, weak eyes or even something more serious like epilepsy or cerebral palsy."

"What happens if you locate a severe handicap?" I asked.

"That depends on how serious it is," she said judiciously. "Mild epilepsy, minor hearing defects, slight retardation we can deal with. The doctor would call in the parents and recommend treatment by medication and therapy. Our girls can carry out simple therapy, exercises and so on, and we can administer medication in mild cases. In severe cases the child has to be transferred to a special school. We have schools for the deaf, for example, for disabled and severely retarded children."

"What do you do," I asked, "if the child seems physically normal but just slow or lazy?"

"Many children are," she said, again beaming. "In that case our girls give the child special attention, encourage him, work with him. If he is physically flabby, for instance, his nurse will teach him special exercises, calisthenics, and we will probably call in his parents and show them the exercises and ask them to work with the child evenings and weekends. We do much the same thing if the child is mentally slow. We call in the parents and show them little games they can play with him to teach him skills; we ask them to encourage the child to achieve his norm, to bring him up to his proper level. No normal child here is allowed to be slack and lazy or to fall behind the class. All children who can, learn early to fulfill their norms."

"Forgive me for asking," I said, "but doesn't that kind of pressure tend to make your children nervous and tense?"

Undauntedly cheerful, she beamed and said, "But no, the opposite. It gives them a feeling of security to know we care that much about them, and, when they achieve their goals, when they fulfill their norms, they feel accepted, and that increases their self-esteem."

"Doesn't that much emphasis on achievement tend to make them highly competitive?" I asked, thinking of the socialist ideal.

"But no," Sister Hedwig replied. "We are aware of that danger, you see, and so we emphasize the group spirit; we encourage the child to achieve in order to be a full-fledged member of the group, to co-operate, to support the team. Our babies grow into healthy-minded, constructive, co-operative little citizens, and, of course, they have a great deal of fun along with their development."

"I could see," I said, "that your nurses are affectionate and gentle."

"Oh, yes, they're especially screened. I would only take on a girl who really loves children. Naturally, all our girls have professional qualifications. Two of us are registered nurses, both with postgraduate training in pediatrics; all the others have graduated from a special school for training nursery school teachers. Here we have one attendant for every five children. That is the ideal, of course, and not every nursery school attains it."

"You are well equipped," I said.

She nodded. "Yes, well I must admit that we are a model nursery. Not every nursery in the G.D.R. is brand new. Some have to make use of old buildings, private houses or church basements, and not many have the equipment, the shaded gardens and playgrounds that we have, but ours is the ideal, the aim. Nevertheless I think that small children are better cared for even in an imperfect nursery school than at home."

"Even if the mother doesn't work?" I asked.

She nodded emphatically. "In the G.D.R. most young mothers do work. You know that an employed woman is entitled to fourteen weeks at full pay as maternity leave? She usually stops work about six weeks before the baby is due. That leaves her about eight weeks free after the delivery and, by then, most young women are glad to turn the babies over to us and go back to work."

"Don't some young mothers want to nurse their children?" I asked.

Hedwig waved aside such instinctual considerations. "Most of them would rather earn money to pay for a television set. Besides, we consider nursing old-fashioned and unscientific. Surely a sterile bottle with scientifically planned formula is healthier for a child?"

I smiled politely but made no comment.

"Mothers are not always good for children," she continued, "and grandmothers are even worse. Most of them know nothing about child development or psychology. Let's be frank; some of them are not even fond of children and have no patience with them. Our girls would not have chosen this profession if they had not loved children and enjoyed working with them."

"Do young mothers have to return to work after eight weeks?" I asked.

"Oh, no. There is no compulsion, but, as I said, most young couples are trying to pay for their furniture or they simply need two salaries in order to live comfortably. If a young woman is highly trained, it is uneconomical as well as boring for her to stay at home. We hope that eventually we shall have enough modern, well-equipped, professionally staffed nurseries so that every baby can enter one at eight weeks. Just now, of course, there is a shortage, and so there is a waiting list."

We had finished our coffee, and a glance at my watch told me that Eric would probably be waiting for me outside to drive me to lunch. I thanked Sister Hedwig and told her my visit had been instructive. She walked with me to the door, whispering now because the children were resting after their lunch.

She pointed to the carriages and strollers parked outside the front door.

"The mommies or sometimes the daddies drop their babies here on their way to work any time between six and eight in the morning. Then they stop back in the evening, often after they've done their shopping, pick up baby and carriage and wheel them home."

I nodded and she continued, "Such lucky mommies! They can go off to work knowing their babies are in a lovely nursery all day, cared for, fed and loved, and then they can have them evenings and all weekend just to play with. We do all the work, and they have much of the joy. Really, our mommies are quite spoiled."

She smiled broadly, exuding managerial maternity. I smiled and shook her extended hand.

"*Na,*" she said, challenging, "if you had a little baby, wouldn't you be happy to have him here with us?"

I hesitated, smiled, and replied, "Your nursery is certainly very cheerful and very well-planned."

I thanked her and hurried down the path to the waiting car.

17

Gerd

Gerd was waiting when I hurried to our rendezvous under the big clock in front of West Berlin's Zoo railway station. The hands of the clock pointed to three minutes after five, and I had arranged to meet him at five. The street in front of the station was crowded with rush-hour commuters dashing for the big yellow buses, darting into the station to catch the *S-Bahn* or down the wide steps to the *U-Bahn*. Energetic young workers, smartly dressed office girls, sedate older men and women milled around, apparently waiting for friends or spouses, but directly under the clock stood only one person, a neatly dressed young man. He looked at me questioningly, appraising my dress and my shoes, obviously European. He looked doubtful, but I smiled and held out my hand, and he grinned and shook it.

"Gerd?" I asked and he nodded. I introduced myself. "I know you want to get home," I said, "so why don't we have coffee right here at the station café?" He agreed, and so we climbed the steps to the café, which overlooks the broad square.

"Shall we find a window-table?" I asked and Gerd agreed.

"I've grown up in Berlin," he said, "but I still get a kick out of watching the Berliners. They're fun to watch, so alive!"

My glance at Gerd was smiling but also appraising. His suit was dark navy, and it was carefully pressed; his white shirt was impeccable despite the warmth of the day. His shoes polished to a deep gloss; his face shone and his brown hair was cut very short. The face was broad, the nose short, the eyes a deep, serious blue. Nothing that he wore was expensive. All of it seemed to be mass-produced, off the rack, but it had been carefully if conventionally selected, tenderly cared for, and it was proudly worn. His grin was frank, open and warm-hearted. He was, I knew, exactly eighteen, but he seemed younger.

224

"Funny the union boss picking me," he was saying. "Will people in America who read your book be interested in me?" I said I thought they would.

"But I'm just an apprentice!" he said. "I mean, I'm not a very interesting guy, just sort of ordinary."

I said, "I hope you are typical, but I don't believe you're ordinary."

"Well," he said and shrugged philosophically, "you ask me things, and I'll tell you and then you can decide." I said I would, but just then a trim young waitress trudged up to the table in the heavy footgear that was fashionable that year. She blinked artificial eyelashes at us, and we ordered a pot of coffee and a Coke.

"Cake?" I asked, knowing that he had been working all day and was probably used to eating early.

"Please," he said, nodding, and ordered something with a lot of whipped cream.

"Now," I suggested, "tell me how you decided to become an apprentice. You work for the Berlin Electrical Works [B.E.W.A.G.], don't you?"

Gerd nodded. "I've been with them since I started my apprenticeship. That was two years ago, when I was sixteen. I went to a commercial high school and received my intermediate diploma when I was sixteen. During the last two years at school my class was visited by all kinds of speakers, union men, skilled mechanics, electricians, government officials, businessmen. Each of them told us about the opportunities and requirements of different skills, different fields. Sometimes they showed films, sometimes our teachers took us on tours of factories or offices. Sometimes we'd spend a whole morning, even a whole day, at a big foundry or factory. We'd tour the works, talk with skilled workers and foremen and with young apprentices; we'd have lunch with the workers and then hear a talk by a boss or union leader after lunch. It was fun. One day we toured an ice cream plant, and they let us eat as much as we wanted."

We both grinned, and I knew I had been right about him. "Did your teacher advise you in making your decision?" I asked.

"Oh, sure, and there was also a special guidance counsellor who looked over our records and gave some of us tests to see what skills and likes and dislikes we had. The school doctor examined us too, because of course there are some professions you can't qualify for unless you have good eyesight or are especially strong. Did you know you have to be very healthy to qualify to be a cook in a restaurant? I can see a steelworker or a miner, but a cook?"

"It's hard work," I said. "Long hours over a hot stove and working under pressure."

"I know, that's what my mother said."

"Did you want to be a cook?"

"No, but a friend of mine did, and the union turned him down."

"Did you have trouble making a decision?"

"No, I always knew that I was interested in electricity, ever since I was a kid. Some of my friends couldn't decide, and their parents had to come to school to talk it over with the teacher and counsellor, but most of us had made up our minds by the middle of our last school year. When you decide and the teacher and counsellor and your parents agree, then you sign up on a list. You have to be approved by the industry you've chosen and by the union involved, because both the management and the union share in training you."

"You were sure right away?"

"I was sure about the electricity part, but what I really wanted to do was to be an engineer. On the other hand, though, I liked the idea of being independent as soon as possible. Going to the Technical University would mean I'd be dependent on my folks for years and years, and I didn't like that idea. I talked with the electrical workers' union representative, and he assured me that there was plenty of opportunity to get ahead in the electrical field. Once I finish my apprenticeship I can go to nightschool to get into either management or into engineering."

"Do you plan to do that?"

He nodded sagely. "Eventually. But when I first qualify I think I'm going to take a year or two just to enjoy my independence—maybe take a trip abroad somewhere on my holidays."

The waitress arrived with our order. "It may seem a little thing," he said, eagerly taking up his fork, "but having grown up in a large family in a small, city apartment, where, even though there was always enough money for the necessities, there was never much left over for the little extras that make life fun like this," he pointed his fork at the cake piled high with a mountain of cream, "it seems very important to me to earn my own money. It will be heaven to be able to go out with my friends and walk into a café or restaurant and order whatever I want, to take out a pretty girl and be able to ask her where she would like to go! I know those things are not important, and that after I've done them for a year or so I'll want something more substantial, but right now I'm eager for them."

I thought he was almost too sensible for such a young man. "How soon will you finish your apprenticeship?" I asked.

"One more year," he said. "The apprenticeship lasts for three years.

I'm just finishing the second year. The program is pretty good, I think. The whole apprenticeship program is supervised by the Berlin Senate and also by the trade unions. They keep us all under their wing. They see that we're not exploited, that our health is looked after, that we work only the legally permitted number of hours and so on, and also that the standards of the professions are maintained."

"How many days a week do you work at the plant?"

"Three days," he said. "Mondays and Thursdays I go to school from eight to one-fifteen. Tuesdays I go to work at the usual time, that is at seven-fifteen, but when we finish at three I go to classes right there at the plant until five. The union runs those."

"So three days a week you work from seven-fifteen until three? What kind of work do you do?"

"Well, the first year all apprentices are assigned to a kind of a flying squadron. We have an orientation program first, of course, but then we're assigned to a supervisor who parcels us out to the various departments. We are sent out to fill in for men who are absent or on vacation all over the Berlin electrical system—that means anywhere in West Berlin. By the time we finish the first year we should have worked in all branches of the industry and learned a little about all phases of the work."

"That sounds good," I said. "What do you do in the second year?"

"In my particular case, I've been assigned to one aspect of the work, and I visit all our member plants in turn to work in this area. Now next year, they'll teach us a little about management, about the organization of the firm, and we'll also be sent out on a bus tour of electrical plants throughout West Germany."

"Do you have to pass an examination at the end?"

"Oh, yes. We have to pass a written exam at school and a practical exam given by the union. If we pass, we're guaranteed a year's employment by B.E.W.A.G. at the normal salary for a beginning, qualified worker."

"What is your life like at the plant? Do you enjoy your work? Do you have fun?"

"Oh, we have lots of fun. I wasn't sure whether to choose a large or a small industry, but I finally decided on a large one because there's more opportunity, more variety in the work; but a kid does get kind of lost in B.E.W.A.G., which has about six thousand employees. I'm a pretty small fish in a pretty big ocean! But we apprentices stick together. We always meet for lunch at the cafeteria, and we have our own recreation room, where we play cards or games or just meet and talk when we're not busy. We can even give parties there after work, say for the birthday or engagement of one of the fellows."

"Do you go out together after work?"

"Oh, sure, and the union organizes outings and sports for us. There's a bowling league and football, that kind of thing. What's nice, too, is that we go back to our old school for our theory classes, so we keep in touch with people from our old class who've chosen other fields. We still see them twice a week, and that makes us feel at home. We're not quite shoved out into the world on our own."

"You enjoy the atmosphere at the plant? Do the older men help you?"

"Yes, they're all helpful. Most of them are very patient and teach us as much as they can. The B.E.W.A.G. plants are modern and bright, and the food is pretty good. We apprentices get a decent lunch free, always a hot dish and dessert. It's not fancy but it's good and there's lots of it!"

"That reminds me," I said, "would you like another piece of cake?"

"Oh, I don't want to be greedy," he said.

"If you've been at work since seven this morning you've earned it, and you must be starved," I said signalling our waitress.

"I'm always starved!" he said. He told the young woman what kind of *torte* he would like. She shook her head at the greed of the male sex but trudged off to fetch the calorific cake.

"Do you go away from Berlin when you get your vacation?" I asked.

"Usually," he said. "I am entitled to twenty working days. My mother and sister and I generally try to arrange our vacations for the same weeks and go off together."

"You said you came from a large family. Are there other brothers and sisters?'

"No, I meant that my mother and sister and I used to live with my uncle, Mom's brother, and his family. That was before we found an apartment. They were all nice; I like my uncle and aunt and cousins; but it was pretty crowded and we sort of got in each other's way. Mom and Helge and I came over from the East, you know."

"From East Berlin?"

"Yes. Helge and I were born in the country, in a village in Brandenburg. We lived there when Helge and I were small. Then my mother moved to East Berlin and got a divorce from our father, and after that we came to West Berlin to live with our uncle. I guess I was about seven and Helge was three."

"Is your father still in the East?"

"Yes. We still get letters from him. Helge and I are under the protection of the Senator for Youth and Sport because our father lives in the East. You see, the divorce court in East Berlin ordered Papa to pay fifty marks a month for each of us children. He puts it into an account in Mama's name in a bank in East Berlin. Until the Wall, Mom used to go over each month to collect it. She couldn't take the money out. That was illegal, but she was allowed to buy any goods listed as surplus and bring them back for us."

"Now what happens to the money?"

"Papa still pays it into the bank, and it is accumulating for us. The Senator is the trustee for the account, and he's trying to work out some kind of agreement with the East Berlin authorities to transfer the money. Papa only has to pay my money another year, until I finish my apprenticeship. He has to pay for Helge for four more years."

"You said that your mother works," I began.

He nodded. "She's a secretary for an accounting firm. She works five days a week, so Helge and I have to help out with the shopping and housework. We have a nice apartment now, large, old-fashioned rooms but a modernized kitchen."

"Do you mind doing housework?"

"No. I like to cook. I'm not a gourmet chef, you know, but I can broil a steak or fry eggs. Helge and I each do the cooking one evening a week, and we do the washing up every night. I don't much like that, but we do it together and it's not too bad."

The waitress brought Gerd's cake and he thanked her and dived into it. "This is better than my cooking," he said, grinning.

"It's better than mine," I admitted. "Do you and your friends go out a lot? I shouldn't think you'd be able to stay out late if you have to be at work by seven."

"Three mornings," he said. "Yes, that's pretty early. I have to leave the house a little after six, so you're right, I don't go out much during the week, but there are Friday and Saturday evenings and all day Sunday. I belong to our church's young people's group. We meet once a week, and we organize dances and plays. We wrote and produced a cabaret last year. That was fun. We play ping pong or darts, sit around and drink coffee and talk."

"Protestant Church, Gerd?" I asked and he nodded.

"We're all Lutherans and we all belong to the Church and pay our Church tax, but I'm afraid I never go to service, anyway not often. I think our pastor is a terrible bore, anyway for me. His sermons seem to be aimed at morons and he only talks in generalities. He never seems to say anything to me, if you know what I mean. I don't think he's interested in young people."

"But you go once in a while?"

"Oh, well, my mother and sister go and they drag me along now and then. Of course I go on Easter or Christmas and I don't want to lose contact with the Church. When I get married and have children I want the kids to be brought up as Christians. I think it's important for a family."

Once again I reflected how mature Gerd seemed to be for an eighteen-year-old and wondered whether it was because he had been brought up without a father and had thought of himself as the man in the family. There have been so many German families without fathers, I thought.

Gerd was telling me that he also spent an occasional evening at the neighborhood youth club in Schöneberg. "It's in a cellar room, and they have it fixed up with tables and a dance floor, good-looking posters on the walls. It's groovy! They have all the latest records, but I'm getting a little old for the club."

"How old are the members?"

"Fifteen to eighteen, and most of the girls are only fifteen or sixteen, and they're pretty silly. Girls that age are, well, silly is the only word I can think of, they're so unnatural and vain. They deck themselves out in clothes too old for their age and they paint themselves and glue on inch-long eyelashes. They look ridiculous. And they puff away on cigarettes to make everyone think they're grown up and worldly."

I smiled. "You don't approve of cigarettes? Or just not for girls?"

"They're not healthy. Most of us boys don't smoke because we're all involved in one sport or another. I'm on our school's rowing team and I still like to play soccer once in a while. Besides, why should I want to ruin my lungs? But it's worse for the young girls. They're too young, and they don't even know how to smoke."

I laughed and said that obviously he didn't have a girl-friend at the club.

"No, I dance with them because I like to dance, but I don't take them out. There are one or two girls at church that I go out with now and then, but I don't want to get serious about a girl. When I do choose someone, I want a nice, sensible girl, someone quiet who likes the same things I do and who'd like to get married and have a nice home, but right now I'm in no hurry to settle down."

"Are any of the young men you went to school with married or engaged?"

"A few," he said, "and I don't think it's a good idea at all. Some boys marry when they are still apprentices, more get married the minute they finish their three years, and I think it's foolish. If young people marry before they're really ready to settle down, it doesn't work out. Gosh, a fellow and girl eighteen or nineteen are still kids! They think marriage is going to be fun, all dancing and movies and love. They want to be able to go out a couple of times a week the way they did before they were married, and they find they have to use the money to pay for the furniture or the TV set. Then they usually have a baby and it's worse. They have even less money for themselves, even less free time. Then they are really stuck in their small apartment, or at least the wife is.

"If the boy is still immature he's likely to take off with the fellows he used to run around with, go out with the boys once or twice a week, spend money he can't afford or maybe get involved with other girls while the young wife sits at home bored and angry." He shook his head, "I've seen it happen a couple of times. It's no fun for the boy and it's certainly not fair to the girl."

"You are sensible!" I said.

He grinned and shrugged. "Well, I have a mother who was divorced, and I have a younger sister. I like women. When I do get married I want a good marriage. I won't go out with any girl too often until I'm ready to be serious, and that won't be until I'm twenty-five or so. I want to travel a little and save a little money first."

We talked a while about marriage and families, and then I asked whether he was interested in politics. I was not surprised by his answer.

"I think politics is fun! I've always been interested in politics. I'm not sure that I'll join a party, and I'm not a member of the party's youth group, but I think of myself as an S.P.D. follower. I think I'd vote S.P.D. because I like the way the party has governed Berlin. I think they've done a very good job here. I'm no expert on foreign affairs or economics so I can't really judge their performance in Bonn, but Berlin is more important to me and I can judge that."

"Are your friends interested in politics?"

"*Ach,*" he said, "all of them are, even the girls. We all read the papers, watch political programs on TV and talk about important issues. I think that even twelve- or thirteen-year-old kids in West Berlin are usually interested in political issues and are pretty well informed. Here we grow up surrounded by politics. It comes as naturally to us as breathing."

"Girls too?"

"Oh, not the silly ones at the club, but serious girls, yes. I know several girls who know as much or more about political questions as boys, but they're usually shy about expressing their views. They read, though, and they're interested."

"Do you think women should be involved in politics? Would you want to marry a girl who was active in a party or club?"

"Sure. I think women are very sensible people. I think we could use more common sense in government. And yes, I do like girls who are serious, who are interested in more things than just what they look like or what they are going to wear or what they can buy. I think it would be terrific to have a wife who was active, as long as politics didn't take all her time. As you noticed, I also like to eat, so I hope she'd have some time to cook. But I don't want a girl to be just a *Hausfrau*."

Naturally I asked him whether he and his friends sympathized with the radical students, and I was not surprised by his answer.

"No, Frau Doctor. I don't think anyone who has come from the East can sympathize with them very much. I know that many of them say they are not communists, others that they are not the Soviet or East German kind of communist, but in trying to undermine Western society, overthrow Western government, they are playing into the hands of the communists, the real communists.

"No, I can't approve of anything that strengthens the position of the East. I'm not one of those communist-haters who think all Soviets are brutes and that everything east of the Wall is bad. I know that there are a lot of decent individuals who are communists over there. We have an uncle who is some kind of minor official in East Berlin, and he's a pretty nice guy. We meet him sometimes when we are on vacation in Austria or Rumania.

"I also believe that some aspects of life are better in the East than in the West. I think, for instance, that the East German school system is excellent. It emphasizes achievement and intelligence, and I think that is good. Their technical training is good, too, more intensive than ours but probably narrower.

"There are good things about the East, and after all the East Germans are our own people. We can't hate them, but we don't have to make their mistakes or throw away the good things that we have here.

"I told you my mother works for an accounting firm? Well, their office is just overlooking the Wall. She can see over the Wall from her desk; she can watch the VOPOs patrol with their rifles and machine guns and dogs. There is a watchtower a couple of hundred feet down the Wall, and she often looks out to see the VOPO in the tower staring at her through his field glasses, or at least it looks that way. She says it is very depressing, and she'll be glad when her firm moves to another office this year."

"I don't blame her," I said.

"Do you know what we West Berliners do on Christmas Eve? Most families open their presents at about five and have a small meal. Then at about seven people begin to drift out into the streets, individuals, families, whole groups of people. They drive or walk to the Wall carrying Christmas trees and candles, and then they place their trees or candles in jars or bottles along the Wall. People whose houses or apartments or offices border on the Wall put candles in their windows so that the whole boundary of West Berlin becomes a blaze of lights.

"I'm no fanatic. I think I'm anything but, and most of the time I manage like everyone else to forget about the Wall, forget about the division of the city, about the threat of the future, but every now and then I can't help remembering.

"No," he said, "I wouldn't want to have to live in the East, and I'd hate to see us swallowed by the East, and so I haven't much patience with irresponsible people who undermine our position. On the other hand, I'm not pessimistic. I think there are many people in East Berlin who still believe in freedom. Think of the students at Humboldt University who circulated petitions supporting the Czechs, and did you know that a bunch of working-class boys in the East beat up a policeman because they thought he was brutal? Those are good signs! So who knows? Perhaps in another generation things will change. I hope so. Meanwhile, though, we'll have to keep our own irresponsible left from destroying us!"

"Are you optimistic about that?" I asked.

He grinned, "I guess I am generally an optimist, but yes, I think so. I think we young workers are a pretty sensible and generally mature bunch, and we're the majority. The radicals are only a small minority, even among the students. Most young men and women from eighteen to twenty-five or thirty are working, paying taxes, carrying the burden of society. I think we have the strength and the common sense to keep a handful of wild ones in line. Anyway, I hope so because I love Berlin and I want to go on living here."

18

Walter

"That mountain country down in Bavaria and Austria is pretty country, I don't deny that," Walter said. "For some reason or other I always seem to go there on my vacation. The people are decent, honest, straightforward fellows, not like those blowhard Rhinelanders, but to tell you the truth, I don't understand half of what they say. Those mountain folks have a dialect you could cut with a knife."

Walter also had a dialect, straight from the streets of Berlin. I grinned at my mental image of his attempt to converse with a mountaineer.

"Bavarians take some getting used to," I said.

Walter smiled, "Well, ma'am, you've lived down there a good while, but West Berliners like me, workingmen with only two or three weeks off a year, we don't get much of a chance to get used to them. I've just about gotten used to 'jo' for 'ja' when it's time to come home. Not that I ever mind that part."

"Coming home?"

He took a long, slow pull on his pipe. "Funny, isn't it, but as much as I look forward to those three weeks in August and as glad as I am to get away, I'm gladder to come back. Mountains make a nice change and try-ing to figure out a strange dialect is sort of fun, but it's not like home.

"Talk about nationalists, I'm no nationalist. Why I can't even believe that those show-offs from Düsseldorf and Cologne are real Germans. They throw their weight around and push everybody about just because they have money. Where'd they get their money, I'd like to know. Black Mar-ket, most of them. Elbows, that's what they've got.

"No, I don't much blame foreigners, even Austrians, for muttering about the rude German tourists if they mean those Rhineland get-rich-quickers, but those people are foreigners to me too. No," he added judiciously, "give me Berliners every time."

234

"Why do you like them?" I asked.

"Berliners?" He raised an eyebrow. "Well, it's hard to say exactly, but I think it's because they don't ask questions." He broke off and laughed, "No offence. I mean, they don't ask curious questions like 'Where do you come from?' or 'Are you married?' or 'What's your religion?' Berliners just accept you as you are, take you as they find you. You can be married or divorced, Catholic or Protestant or, for all they care, Buddhist. You can be from Silesia or the Ukraine, have no education or six degrees—they just take you as you are. I like that."

"Cosmopolitan," I suggested.

"I guess so. They're big-city people, not hicks. They don't snoop; they're not critical and they're not snobs. They're just human and friendly and at the same time they leave you your freedom. God! I couldn't stand to live in one of those villages where everybody knows everybody else's business and tries to run it!"

"Do you come from a village?" I asked.

He shook his head. "I was born in Cottbus in the Old Mark, Brandenburg. That's a pretty big town, but no world city, like Berlin. My people were of the working class, and we lived in a clean, respectable working-class neighborhood. We were always self-respecting folk, but the depression of the 1930s hit us pretty hard. I had the bad luck to get out of school right in the depth of the depression."

"Had you been to trade school?" I asked.

He shook his head. "I was a real hard-luck kid," he said. "I just went to the *Volksschule*. There were no jobs those days even for experienced, skilled men, certainly none for a kid without either experience or skills. I was one of the millions of unemployed all through my teens.

"Well, you can see, ma'am, why a good many working-class people supported Hitler. I never did, mind you, but he made jobs and he provided training. I'd be unjust if I didn't give them credit, the nazis. Maybe it was rearmament and maybe it led to war, but it took us off the streets. I not only got my first job, but they put me into a training program."

"What kind of training?" I asked.

"Aircraft maintenance," he said. "I worked for the Luftwaffe. Matter of fact," he added proudly, "I was on the team that worked on our very first jet planes. That was fun. A real challenge. Something brand new."

"What happened when the war came?" I asked.

"Well, we were all sort of reservists," he said. "I was just absorbed into the Luftwaffe as a noncom, but I kept on with the same work, only in uniform. We repaired and refitted planes. I didn't see much of the war," he shrugged almost regretfully. "Oh, we moved around from one airfield to another, but it was always the same work, usually the same team, and almost always far behind the lines."

"So you never got into combat?" I asked.

"I wasn't even taken prisoner," he said. "When the war ended I was in what became the Russian Zone, but I wasn't even drafted for reconstruction work. Don't ask me why. But I was out of work. All I knew how to do, all I'd ever learned, was how to repair planes, and back in 1945 it looked as if Germany would never have any planes to repair again!"

"What did you do?"

"Well, first I got myself to East Berlin. I mean, I'd done odd jobs now and then in the Zone, but there was no real work. In East Berlin I went on getting odd jobs. I bided my time, and in 1950 I crossed over into West Berlin. That wasn't any trick in those days, only, like everybody else, I had to come over with just what I could carry in my pockets."

"Didn't you have friends here in the West? People you could have brought your belongings to gradually?" I asked.

"Well, I knew I had some old Luftwaffe buddies somewhere here, but I had to find them. No, I just came. I stayed at a cheap hotel, an inn, for a few days until I could locate my pals; then they asked me to stay with them until I got on my feet."

"Could you find a job right away?" I asked, guessing that he had come over to the West without much money.

"Not legally," he said. "You see, before I could get a permit to work in West Berlin, I had to be processed as a refugee. I needed to get an official residence permit first, and all that took time, but meanwhile I needed to earn money."

"What did you do?"

"Worked black, like a lot of fellows," he said as he carefully emptied and then refilled his pipe. "I got odd jobs, usually delivering goods in a small van, that sort of thing. Always nonunion, casual jobs where they weren't too fussy about papers. The pay was poor, of course, and any minute I might have been caught and sent back."

"You had to eat," I said. "How long did that go on?"

"Until 1953, when my papers finally came through." He grinned. "Well, you know governments and papers! Always takes time. They don't want you to starve; they're just slow."

"What kind of job did you get then? There still weren't many airplanes to service."

"Not for a brand new refugee, anyway. Besides, I'd been out of the trade too long. No, I got a job delivering drugs for a pharmaceutical factory. The money was decent, but I was a little worried about the future. There was no pension with that job."

"Could you find something better?" I asked.

"I looked around, and in 1956 I got taken on as a driver at the City Hall in Schöneberg. That's a city job, so now I do get credit toward a pension."

"Whom did you drive?" I asked.

"Oh, we drove those big black Mercedes cars—the ones with the official plates. We drive big-shot visitors, guests of the Senate, and city officials when they don't have their own cars with them. It's fun, and pretty interesting sometimes. Once I drove General Clay. I've got a photograph home of him standing next to my car."

"Are you in the photo?" I asked.

"Yes, indeed. I'm standing right there. I enjoyed that kind of driving," he said, "but I had to stop on account of my heart. You have to pass a physical exam every year to be a City Hall driver. Well, that's only natural. Imagine if I were to have a heart attack while I was driving some V.I.P., or if some driver couldn't see well or hear properly!"

"Was that long ago?" I asked.

"About four years back," he said. "The doc said I couldn't drive any more, but I was still young enough to work, too young to retire, so they found me some light work." He told me that he now worked as an information clerk directing visitors to the proper offices in the labyrinthine City Hall.

"That's pretty interesting," he said. "I miss getting around the city, but I see some interesting visitors. The pay's not much, but there are advantages to working for the city."

I discovered that while his job does not rank as part of the actual civil service, it still carries many of the benefits of a civil service appointment. Employees like Walter are classified, and they move from class ten up to class one according to years of service. Salary, vacation days and other benefits rise proportionately.

"I used to work forty-five hours a week," he said, "but now it's down to forty. Sometimes I have to work Saturdays, but usually not. I get thirty-three days of annual leave, that is, thirty-three working days, so that amounts to quite a vacation." He explained that all employees who are older than forty are entitled to a minimum of twenty-seven days' leave, and then they earn additional days with each year of employment.

"My health is pretty good. I have to take it easy on account of my heart, but so far it hasn't bothered me much. Touch wood! If I should get sick, I'm entitled to six months' sick leave because I've worked for the city longer than ten years. Those who've worked less are entitled to four months' sick leave."

I told him I thought that was generous.

"I can retire at sixty-two," he said, "but if my health holds out, I'll keep working until I'm sixty-five. At sixty-five, my pension will amount to seventy-five per cent of the average of my last two years' salary. Naturally, if my heart should act up and the doctors should certify that I'm not fit to work, I could retire earlier and get almost the full amount."

I asked whether city employees usually belonged to a trade union, and he said most of them did.

"It's not compulsory," he said, "but in fact most of us are members. I've always belonged because I think the union does a lot for us and it's only right to pay my share, but I've never been an active member. I pay my dues and I wish them well, but I guess I'm too lazy! I'm not active in politics either. I'm interested. I read the papers, listen to news on the radio, and I talk over political problems with my cronies, but I never go to a party rally or a political meeting. Funny, isn't it? You'd think working here in the midst of politics, right in the City Hall, seeing politicians of all parties every day, I'd be more interested. Maybe I see too much of them, not that I don't like them. They're all very considerate and pleasant gentlemen, but when I get home at night, I just want to forget about them all."

I said I could understand that. "Do you vote, Walter?"

"Oh, sure, I always vote, and so far I've always voted for the same party, but I'm not a party member. I'd feel free to vote for another party if it seemed right. I always make up my mind just before the election. I listen to the candidates, read what they have to say and then decide."

I asked whether he thought he'd vote for his usual party in the next federal election.

"Gosh, I don't know!" he said. "Who knows what can happen before then? The whole world might change. I'll wait and see."

"Another beer?" I asked.

"No, thank you, ma'am, two beers after work is my limit."

"I don't want to keep you too long," I apologized. "Your wife may have your supper waiting."

"No wife, ma'am. I'm a bachelor—never been married. I live in a small flat all alone, and by now I've grown used to it. I like living alone." He said that he had once been engaged. "While I was in the Air Force. We hoped to be married after the war. Somehow I kept getting moved around

too much those last years of the war for us to think of settling down, but
we had all kinds of plans for when the war was over." He shrugged. "I
guess we both knew it wouldn't work out."

"What happened?" I asked, wondering whether I should.

"She died. Her family decided to try to get from East Germany to the
West before the Red Army moved in, and Elly was just one of the ones
that didn't make it. Well, as you know, a couple of million Germans just
didn't make it. What's a miracle is that so many millions did. Think of
the streams of refugees from Russia, from the Sudetenland, from East
Prussia and the Oder-Neisse lands, millions, all crowding the roads. What
with the bombing, the artillery, disease and exposure, it's a wonder so
many got over safely. Elly didn't. Her brother told me."

I tried to say I was sorry, but he brushed it off. "Oh, that was long ago.
She wasn't a pretty girl, you know, but she was gentle and quiet. I somehow never got engaged to another woman. I guess I was poor for too long,
and by the time I had a steady job and a little security I was over forty
and was too used to living alone. As I said, I sort of like it."

I asked about his apartment, and he said it was in an old building.
"Prewar, and not really modernized, so the rent is cheap. It has a great
big balcony where I raise mushrooms and have a kind of roof garden.
That's my hobby. My dream ever since I got to West Berlin has been to
have one of those weekend gardens on the outskirts of the city—a little
strip of garden with a small hut or cabin, where I could spend quiet weekends and raise vegetables and flowers."

"I know them," I said. "Can't you put your name on a list?"

"No use," he said. "The gardens under rent control are reserved for
families with children, and the control-free ones are too expensive for
people in my bracket. Now that West Berliners can't have cottages in the
country or get away weekends, everybody and his brother wants one of
those weekend gardens. I'm afraid for me it's just a pipe dream, like having a sailboat or owning my own house. Not for the likes of me!"

"But you enjoy your flat, you say. How do you spend your evenings and
weekends?"

"Oh, I putter about. I used to do a lot of weekend fishing. I liked that,
but these last years the lakes are so crowded on weekends you practically
have to stand in line to cast a fly. It's no fun. Too bad—we have some
lovely lakes. The fishing used to be great, but now it's really not worth
hauling my gear out on a bus. I'd rather stay at home and read or watch
sports on TV. I love the Olympics; I guess everyone does, but I also watch
football and skiing in winter and ice hockey."

"Do you like music?" I asked.

He grinned, "If you mean that rock noise, no! Can't abide it. I like nice quiet music, though, especially as background when I read."

I asked about his reading and he looked sheepish. "Kid stuff, I guess, but I like to read about space exploration and rockets, science fiction, that sort of thing. I guess it's because I still love planes and flying even though I can no longer work on engines. Gosh, how I'd love to see one of the rocket launchings at Cape Kennedy! I watch every space flight on TV. That's exciting."

I asked about friends, and he said he still had quite a few old comrades from Luftwaffe days. "We meet one evening a week in our regular pub and drink a few beers, talk about politics, about the future and the old days. Sometimes we play cards. Even the married fellows can get out one night a week. Some of the others meet more often; sometimes we bowl or go to a football game."

"What do you and your friends think of the students, of the trouble at the universities?" I asked.

"Oh!" he said. "Do you really want to know? You should be a mouse under the table when the boys get on that subject!"

"Can I be?" I asked. "I mean, do you think I could meet some of your friends and listen to their views?"

"Well, sure, if you wouldn't mind meeting us in a pub. I mean, it's just an ordinary workingman's pub, but it's a family place, perfectly respectable. Matter of fact, a few of us will be getting together tomorrow after supper, a mixed group, not just Luftwaffe."

He assured me that I would be welcome and gave me the address. I said that I would be there at eight. We walked slowly back to the City Hall, where I'd left my car. I thanked him for letting me interview him; we shook hands ceremoniously, and I waved, "Until tomorrow!"

The pub was exactly as I had imagined it, clean, modern, respectable. A bar ran along one wall. The rest of the square room was filled with square and rectangular tables, colorful with bright yellow cloths. A small radio behind the bar played the quieter sort of popular music, German and American. About half of the tables were occupied, a few by couples or by groups including housewifely women, most by men drinking beer, chatting or playing cards.

As I entered most of the patrons looked up as though it was unusual to see a woman alone. Walter rose from behind a large table at the back of the room and walked forward to meet me. He was wearing a dignified, dark suit, a white shirt and a very conservative, striped tie. His shoes were polished to a bright shine.

"You're just on time, Frau Doctor," he said smiling, and he led me to his table. "These are all the men of our little group." They half-rose and smiled as I nodded and took the chair one of them pulled out for me. Walter introduced me.

"What can we get you to drink?" the oldest man of the group asked.

"You are all drinking beer," I said. "I shall have beer too."

"Oh, no," the older man said, "not beer for a lady professor! You must have wine."

I tried to protest, but he insisted, and so I said I would drink a light Moselle. "Fräulein," he called, and an elderly waitress came over to the table. "A quarter liter of Moselle for the lady."

Walter introduced each man in turn: Georg, the oldest, Hans who seemed to be a kind of boss, Heinrich, Willi, Werner and Paul. Each smiled to acknowledge the introduction; some bowed.

"Walter tells us you want to hear our opinions for your book," Hans said.

"On the students? On the *radicalinskis*? Not fit to print!" another said, and his friends laughed.

"Why us?" the older Georg asked. "We are only workers, not very important people."

"You are Berliners, and my book is about Berliners," I explained.

"Ha!" Werner said, "we're not even Berliners!"

"I am!" Heinrich protested. "*Waschecht*, baptized with Spree water!"

"Then you're the only one," Derner retorted.

"Me!" Paul said. "I'm from Silesia, and everyone knows . . ."

Two or three of his friends chimed in, "*Ja, ja,* that the best Berliners come from Breslau."

"Anyway, the noisiest ones," someone muttered.

"But why us, *gnädige* Frau," Georg persisted.

"Because you are workers," I said, "and because you do come from different places." I asked where each came from: Georg and Walter from Mark Brandenburg, Werner from Pomerania, Willi from East Prussia, Paul from Silesia, Hans from Hamburg; only Heinrich was a born Berliner.

"I think you're a very good cross-section," I said. "Probably a typical mixture of Berliners."

"For people our age, *gnädige* Frau," Hans said. "Nowadays we don't get many people in from the provinces, certainly not the Eastern provinces."

"We get a few," someone suggested.

"A dribble," Georg said, "like those two VOPOs that got over last week. Where were they from? Pomerania?"

"Luckily we don't get many Saxons." They all laughed.

"You don't like Saxons?" I asked. "Because of Ulbricht?"

"Did you ever hear such an accent?"

"Such a voice! Squeak! Squeak! Squawk!"

"No, Frau Doctor," Georg was explaining, "the Berliners never liked Saxons even before Ulbricht. We call them 'coffee Saxons,' meaning they drink their coffee sweet."

Hans added, "That means they talk sweet, but you can't trust them. They're hypocrites."

Paul nodded, "*Ja,* it's true. When you read that one of the border guards shot to kill, you can bet it was a Saxon."

"Even VOPOs don't really want to kill their fellow Germans. Most guards aim over the heads of the refugees," someone interjected.

Georg continued, "We say the Berliner says what he thinks, the Silesian has long ears, but the Saxon . . ." He shrugged, "No good!"

Just then the waitress arrived with my Moselle, and several of the men were ready to order refills for their beer mugs. The men told me a little about their work, their background and their politics, and before long they were talking about the subject I find comes up most frequently with all classes of men of the middle to older generation when they are relaxing with friends, especially if they have drunk a few glasses of beer—the war.

"We sure were scared of the Russkys, but as individual people they aren't bad, most of them," Heinrich was saying. "I went into the navy back in 1944, when I was eighteen. Silly time to go into the navy when we hardly had any ships! I was trained as a machinist, but there wasn't any work for me, so a bunch of us were transferred to the infantry and retrained for three months.

"I was assigned to a company of new recruits, mostly kids of seventeen or eighteen," he said. "I was the old man in the outfit because I was nineteen by then. We were sent to the front somewhere near Danzig and were in combat for only a few days when damn near the whole outfit was wiped out. I was lucky. I was wounded badly enough to be shipped to a hospital further west, near Stettin, but not badly enough really to be sick. They let me out in time to try to escape to the West before the Russians arrived. You should have seen the mess! The roads were crowded with refugees and troops, everyone trying to get as far west as they could. I didn't want to be taken prisoner by the Russians.

"I'd got only as far as Mecklenburg when the Red Army caught up with us. I cut off from the stream of people and hid in the woods. In fact, I got lost somewhere out there in the woods. There must have been thousands of foot soldiers hiding out, lost and hungry. We didn't even know when the war ended!"

"How did you get food?" I asked.

"Oh, at farms, when there was anything. At one farm I got a piece of an old tablecloth to make a white arm band to show that I wanted to surrender. Most of us had thrown away our guns and ammo. I was trying to walk to Berlin where I lived."

"Did you make it?" I asked.

"Not quite. I was almost there when a Russian soldier came pounding along on a horse. He stopped and reached inside his jacket, I thought for a gun. I was sure I'd had it! Instead he grinned at me and tossed me a pack of cigarettes. A few miles farther on I ran into a whole bunch of Americans who had been liberated from a P.O.W. camp. They took me along with them into Berlin, where I gave myself up."

"You were lucky," Werner said. "I was in the artillery, in France first, later in the East. We were at Smolensk when our front collapsed. We were shunted down to Yugoslavia and then Austria and ended up in Czechoslovakia. Fifty thousand of us were taken prisoner by the Czechs. They had no rations for prisoners. We marched three days without a bite of food. On the third day we found some potatoes lying in a field and cooked them. We ate our horses, hunted snails to cook and stewed pine cones."

"You survived," Hans said.

"The Czechs hated us, though. My outfit especially, because we were S.S. troops. Man! I hadn't enlisted in the S.S.! I was an artillery man, but in the last year of the war I was just transferred to the S.S. No one asked me whether I liked it. Anyway, a lot of died on the march, a lot more later when we worked in the Soviet Union down near the Turkish border. We built roads and helped to build a factory and some men worked in mines. I was lucky. The Soviets found out that I'd been a tailor's apprentice before I'd been drafted, so they put me to work making uniforms. I worked overtime for the officers and got little gifts of food, wine and cigarettes.

"By summer 1946, only a handful of my comrades were still fit for work, and the lot of us were dirty, skinny and unshaved. We got a new camp commander, who was a pretty decent guy. He took one look at us and sent for medical officers. I guess they said we were unfit for work because by the next day we were on trucks to Moscow, and soon after we were in Frankfort on the Oder for mustering out. By October 1946, I was back in Berlin hunting for my mother."

"Bombed out?" one of the older men asked.

"We had lived near the Tiergarten when I went away," Werner said.
"Our whole neighborhood just wasn't there any more. It was just blotted
out. There were signs up on some of the ruins saying "Family Muller" or
"Family Schulz" or "G. Winter moved to . . ." and then the address, but
I couldn't even find the place where our apartment house had stood."

"How did you locate your family?" I asked.

"Red Cross," he said. "It took several days to trace my mom, and when
I turned up at the tiny basement flat she was living in, she hardly recognized me. I guess I looked pretty awful."

"We all did, those days, especially if we'd been working in labor
camps," Willi said. "Uniforms in rags and falling off because we were so
skinny, long hair, beards, grimy. Who'd recognize us?"

"Not even our mothers!" someone said, and they all laughed.

"I hardly recognized her," Werner said. "She was a pretty sad sight too.
First thing she told me was that my younger brother, Gus, was missing in
Russia. My oldest brother Karl, had been killed in Russia, as a matter of
fact at Stalingrad, in 1943. I think the worst thing for me was that my
sister, my little sister Anny, had died while she was expecting a baby.
Mom said she just starved to death, but I guess it was from never being
warm enough, from overwork and from the shock, too."

"Shock?" Hans asked. "Russians?"

Werner nodded. "Mongolians. Mom had been raped too. Well, most
women were, unless they were barricaded somewhere. Sis they caught on
her way home from work. A bunch of them, God knows how many,
dragged her into a bombed-out building. She never knew whose child it
was."

"You never told us that, Werner," Paul said quietly.

Werner shook his head. "I never told anyone. Even Mom and I never
talked about Anny, not for years. Mom had put her pictures away. She
kept them. She still has them all locked away somewhere, but I guess she
couldn't look at them. Anny'd been engaged to a nice guy in the navy.
He was killed in the last months of the war."

"You feel worse about the women," Hans said. "My mother and sister
were killed in an air raid, in fact in the famous one."

"Hamburg?" someone asked, and he nodded.

"That was almost as bad as the raids on Dresden," he said. "Fire
bombs. They were burned up. A whole section of the city was burned up.
My other sister, Lisa, was a nurse with the army in Italy, right near the
front. She came back safely."

"I was a lot luckier than most of you, I guess," Paul said. "I came from a family of ten children. I was the youngest, and we all came back. Not one of us was killed or even died on the trek."

"I was luckier than that," Georg said. "I wasn't even in the army! I worked for the railroads, and I was a little old for military service. You remember Goebbels used to say that 'wheels must roll for victory'? Well, anyone working with wheels could get deferred if his work was essential and he was old enough. I just sat out the war."

"Where?" Hans asked, "in Berlin? That was no picnic!"

"Berlin was no picnic, and certainly trying to keep the trains running in spite of the bombings wasn't easy, but it was a darn sight better than what I was doing," Willi said. "Do you know I was in service from the first day of the war in 1939 until the last day in 1945? And I was in the damned Labor Service before that! Couldn't call my soul my own, if I had a soul in those days, which I doubt."

"You were in the Luftwaffe, weren't you?" Werner asked.

"At first I was; later they transferred me to the infantry. I served in Poland, then in France and finally in Russia. I was lucky in one way, though. I got wounded just before the collapse, so I was in the hospital when the war ended and I didn't have to be a P.O.W. or do labor service. No more uniforms for me. I wouldn't even be a Boy Scout leader or sing in the choir in church. I hate uniforms, all uniforms. I even growl when I see a postman!"

The others laughed. "All I can say is, however bad it was to lose the war, we were lucky we didn't win it. Do you realize that if we'd won, most of us would still be in the Army of Occupation in Russia? How would you like that?" Willi asked.

"Here!" Walter broke in. "What are we depressing this lady with our gloomy war talk for?"

"Quite right," someone agreed.

"She doesn't want to hear about labor camps and bombings!"

"No, *gnädige* Frau, we apologize, and surely you need some more wine?" Hans said. He signalled the waitress.

"What the Frau Doctor wanted to know was what we think about the students," Walter explained.

"*Ach!* That's even gloomier!" Heinrich said and they laughed.

"We're not reactionaries, *gnädige* Frau," Hans said. "I think we're all socialists, always have been."

"Ninety-eight per cent of the men at my plant are trade-union members," Paul said, "and I'd say most of those usually vote S.P.D. On the other hand, relatively few are active either in the union or in politics. We have about a hundred and fifty men at the plant, and I'd say about twenty are fairly active in the party, including me. I'm a regular member and I'm active in our local group."

"We're all interested in politics, aren't we?" Hans asked and everyone nodded or said *"Ja!"*

"We certainly all vote," Heinrich said.

"Yes, and we keep informed about what's going on over there," Paul said, making the usual over-the-shoulder gesture to indicate East Berlin or East Germany.

"Most of us have relatives living over there," Werner said.

"I have," Paul said, "and I have relatives in the Polish-occupied area, too. I'm still saving up my marks, hoping that someday we can go back. Willy Brandt and his treaties don't worry me!"

"He's a Silesian," Heinrich said. "They never give up."

I asked whether Paul had seen his Eastern relatives since the war, and he nodded. "My aunt, my mother's sister, has been here a couple of times. She's over sixty and can travel to the West, but of course her children and grandchildren can't because they're still productive."

"They might stay," Werner said. "She goes back because they are there."

"Whenever she visits West Berlin the Berlin Senate pays all her expenses while she's here," Paul told me. "They pay the fare from the East German border, Frankfort on the Oder, and each Eastern visitor also receives pocket money and a gift package."

"I didn't know that," I said.

"Ja," Walter said. "Caritas and the Evangelical Church also give them gifts."

"And the Red Cross," someone added.

"Every Eastern visitor," Paul said, "and the visitors' bureau here helps them find their relatives if they've lost contact, or find a place to live; it even helps with theater tickets and tours of the city. I don't know whether you remember Franz Neumann, the old S.P.D. county leader? Well, he always looked after my aunt especially and saw that she got medical and dental care while she was here."

"We look after our Eastern friends who come here," Hans said. "The propaganda over there is so distorted, so heavy-handed that we like to show them while they're here that we have a progressive and social-minded government too!"

"Better than theirs," Paul said.

"I like to watch East Berlin TV," Heinrich said, and several others agreed that they did too.

"What programs do you watch especially?" I asked.

"Everything, particularly the news and political shows to learn what the party line is for the week," Heinrich said.

"I watch the ceremonies," Willi said. "They're so corny, so square!"

"Like warmed-over Nazi *kitsch,* so sentimental and phony," someone contributed.

"But the kids over there have never heard of anything else. They look a generation behind the times when you see them, the girls with their braids, the boys with their shining faces, the young women without make-up, with dowdy dresses," Heinrich said.

"The workers over there know better," Werner said. "They're not taken in by all the propaganda. I work in a big garage, and we have affiliates in East Berlin too. Of course now the East Berlin garage belongs to the state, but I still know some of the workers. They write, and we send packages. We have forty-seven colleagues over there. We used to send packages from the firm at Christmas until one year seventy packages didn't arrive. Now we send them individually and mail them in half a dozen different post offices, and we send them throughout the year, not just at Christmas. Most of them get there."

"Do your friends over there need packages?" I asked.

Werner nodded, "You'd be surprised. They have enough food, but there are still a lot of things they can't get or can't afford."

"You said the workers were dissatisfied," I began.

"They don't like the way promotions are given for docility, the way pay is scaled according to productivity."

"Piecework," Paul said. "The worst kind of reactionary measure to any trade-union man."

"Workers have many advantages over there," Werner went on. "They have excellent recreational facilities, sports, outings and vacation homes. They offer the children a lot. The schools are good, and there are beautiful summer camps, but everyone knows the price and they are not taken in."

"No one could be taken in by the kind of propaganda the East Berlin TV hands out. They lay it on with a trowel," Heinrich said.

"Did you ever see Arthur Schnitzler's program?" Paul asked. "He's the East German Goebbels and about as subtle."

"We all watch him," Heinrich said. "He's fun."

"He pictures the Westerners as all devils."

"We call him the black Schnitzler."

We ordered still more beer and wine and the talk bubbled on. I asked about their opinion of Bonn and they variously responded:

"For Bonn we Berliners are a charity case."

"Bonners are too far away, they don't understand the East."

"Bonners graciously fly to Berlin now and then, but they don't drive in, they don't have to wait in line at the crossings, they don't experience the controls, the humiliations, the delays."

"The Bundestag! It should meet here every four weeks."

"This *détente* is *quatsch*—nonsense!"

"I am a socialist; I used to like Willy Brandt, but the idea that you can win concessions from the Russians by appeasing them is pure nonsense."

"We're not warmongers, not hawks, *gnädige* Frau; in fact, it's because we want peace that we believe as we do."

"*Ach,* we know the Russians! We've lived too close to them too long not to know them. We know the Russian doesn't want war. He just wants to get as much as he can by growling."

"I'm not saying I object to recognizing the G.D.R. It's there. What's the use of pretending it isn't?"

"No, and I don't object to acknowledging the Oder-Neisse Line," Hans said and then ducked as Paul and Willi pretended to throw their mugs at him. "No, really, we've lost the Eastern provinces, and that's that. There's no point sticking our heads in the sand like ostriches. That's just recognizing reality and pacifying the fears of the Poles, but I object to any concession which bargains away Berlin's rights."

"Salami tactics—cutting off a slice at a time," someone said.

"I don't blame the U.S., Frau Doctor," Paul said, "for thinking that it has problems which are closer to home and more acute than Berlin. Cuba is a lot nearer. No, if there's blame, then it's Bonn's."

"We've been very lucky here in West Berlin," Hans said. "We have really free elections. We've had a humane, progressive government. We have a high standard of living. I guess we have no right to complain. It's just that we all get tense and a little irritable being shut in."

"You walk a few miles and bang! You bump into barbed wire."

"You want to get out for your vacation and you have to drive across the G.D.R. That always gives me the willies. I'm scared stiff every time I drive through that I'll get a flat or a ticket. I know they won't do anything to me. It's not a sensible fear, but I'm scared just the same."

"We're all a little afraid and nervous about the future, but we stay," Hans said.

"You might think, *gnädige* Frau, that because we're only workers we haven't much to lose, we haven't a very big stake. None of us makes a lot of money. There's not one of us who can ever hope to own a house, even the smallest, cheapest house."

"A house? What are we? Capitalists?"

"We make good wages, we have all kinds of social programs, health insurance, old-age pensions and recreation centers, but we're relatively poor, all of us, and yet I think it is the workers who have the most to lose. I think it's the workers in the East who are the worst off. The intellectuals are fine. They have a good life."

"Fine? They put them in insane asylums in Russia!"

"Good place for some of them, Heini," and they all laughed.

"But the workers have a drab, dull life with nothing to look forward to. The worst part about life over there is its dullness, and, if you ask me, it's dullest of all for the factory worker."

"Well," someone said, "I suppose life over there isn't very good for anyone, even party hacks. I have a cousin in Brandenburg who is a minor party official, and it seems to me he's always worried."

"Oh, well, children, there's no use in our worrying. We don't make policy, and we can't really change anything."

"We can vote."

"Oh, we do vote."

"You still haven't told me what you think of the students," I said, and they all roared.

"Well, actually we have, you know," Hans said. I admitted that they had.

"We pay for their universities and their stipends." Werner said. "When you stop to think about it, it's always the people in the low- and middle-income levels who pay the bulk of the taxes. Now, I believe in freedom. I think our students should have freedom, but I don't think they should use their freedom to destroy ours."

"Especially not when they're living on the fat of the land on our tax money," Paul said. "When we were their age we were trudging through the snow or mud getting shot at."

"Maybe that's what's wrong with them. Maybe they're bored. Maybe what they really need is adventure, a little danger, and so they try to stir it up?" Heinrich suggested.

"I'll give 'em adventure!" Willi said, and they laughed.

"What they need," Hans said, "is more experience with real life."

"What they need is hard work."

"Discipline."

"There, you see, we do sound like hard hats. Is that what you call them? But we are not ogres. We don't hate the students because they are more fortunate than we were," Hans began.

"Fortunate! They don't know how lucky they are."

"But that's it. They don't. They can't know. They didn't live through the depression, through the Hitler time, through the war. They didn't fight in Russia or work in a labor camp or rebuild Berlin out of the rubble. How can they know?"

"They can look at the Wall."

"*Ja, ja,* but we see it with different eyes. Our eyes have already seen so much. We have all been through so much. Maybe we have all been through too much to have been very good parents? Maybe we were worn out before we began? Who knows? Anyway, we can't blame them for not being us, can we?"

"What will the Frau Doctor think of us!" Georg said. "Arguing, shouting. She'll think we're narrow-minded, opinionated fanatics."

"She'll think we're bores," Heinrich said and I protested.

"She'll think we're Berliners," Paul said.

"We all have big mouths." They laughed.

"Guilty as charged," Hans said. "Well, we all do have opinions, and we all care. I guess that's not so very bad. After all, it's more than just our city. It's more than just everything we've gone through. It's the way we live, the way we spend our free time; it's everything we care about. I guess we do get a little emotional about it."

"Don't apologize," Paul said, touching him on the shoulder. "We'd be worse, not better, if we couldn't get excited."

Indeed, Berliners always seem to have opinions and they always seem to care.

I thanked Walter and his friends. Hans and Heinrich were going in my direction and so they walked with me to the subway.

"Big mouths, that's Berliners," Heinrich said.

19

Pastor Carl

Suddenly, as though in answer to a silent signal, Carl and I broke into a run. We rushed headlong, laughing like schoolchildren, down a narrow track through the wood, leaping over rocks and tree roots, darting around prickly bushes, until we landed at the narrow, rocky brook at the foot of the hill. Breathless, we both stooped to splash cooling water on our faces, then collapsed on convenient rocks.

"If you broke our thermos," Carl began.

"No, no! It's safe," I assured him, slipping my tote bag from my shoulder and reaching inside.

Carl laughed again. "Couple of kids!" he said and began to unpack his rucksack. "All right here?" he asked and pulled out a small, plaid blanket and spread it under the trees.

"Good," I said and began to set out flasks and cups. "I needed that run," I said. "I'd been in Bonn too long. I had to get unstuffed."

"They are a bunch of stuffed owls down there, aren't they?"

"Awful!" I said, understating. "Fruit juice or coffee first?"

"Save the fruit juice for later when we're thirsty from walking," he suggested. He began prying open packages of sandwiches. "What's here? Chicken, I think, and ham and cheese. Thick ones with good dark bread. My mother did us proud.

"I needed the run too," he said, "because I've been in West Berlin too long. Not that Berlin is stuffy. God, no! But you get a little stir-crazy here. You feel shut in, confined."

"A lot of Berliners have told me that," I said. "No wonder!"

"Good thing we have the Grunewald and the lakes," he said, looking around. Far in the distance we heard someone whistling, but otherwise there was silence, and we saw no sign of people in any direction, sheltered as we were by the small hill. "There are thousands of Berliners tramping through this forest this minute, most of them having a picnic under some tree, the lucky ones by a stream, and yet you and I feel alone, isolated, private. If we Berliners didn't have a big forest to get lost in, a place to feel free and away from everything, I don't think we could have held out this long."

"Perhaps not," I said.

"Did you ever take one of those little steamers around the city which thread in and out of the lakes and canals?" Carl asked. I nodded. "Of course people who can afford it have yachts or small boats. They can sail for hours on West Berlin lakes."

"It's dangerous, though," I suggested. "Don't some of them drift over into East Berlin or into G.D.R.?"

"Sometimes. Usually, the East guards just send them back. Of course there's always a danger of losing the boat: the East Germans might confiscate it."

"Less fun," I said.

"Still, we're lucky," he said, pausing between sandwiches to stretch out under the tree. "Cigarette?" he offered. "You've only had one today. You're under your quota."

"No thanks, I'll have it later. I'm hungry!" I said, reaching for a second sandwich.

"Why should you be hungry?" he asked. "I did all the work! Did you preach a sermon? No! All you did was sit there with my mother and listen. You didn't even have to take notes!" He lit his cigarette and then added, "I wasn't a bore, was I?"

"Anything but," I assured him. "You were very lively and challenging. Very Prussian," I added. "The full armor of the Lord, and all that."

Carl grinned. "What did you expect me to be—Italian or Zulu?"

"Very Prussian," I answered. "I was impressed with your congregation. Lots of young people, and not all female, which I might have anticipated."

He gestured as though to toss a small rock at me. "Are you about to cast the first stone?" I inquired, and he laughed.

"But you see, even the Church keys people up. Hold on! Fight the good fight! Learn to live with conflict! It's all very strenuous for the poor Berliner. Sometimes he needs to escape, to forget that he lives in a vault, walled in, to forget that he must always be vigilant and tough, and just get away!" He sighed. "For that we have Sundays and the Grunewald, and I thank God."

He leaned back, his head against the trunk of the tall fir tree, letting his cigarette dangle from his hand, and breathed in deeply. "Berlin air!

I swear that if someone took me up in a helicopter and flew me in circles blindfolded for hours and then let me parachute into the Grunewald I would know the minute I landed that I was in Berlin. Berlin air really is unique."

"I think so too," I said. "To me it is a little like Attic air, exhilarating, like a very dry champagne."

"Attic air is dry and warm," Carl said, remembering. "Berlin air is cool. It smells like firs and pines and sandy soil and lakes. I love Greece. I like Italy and Bavaria. I enjoy wandering through Burgundy or exploring Norwegian fjords. I'd love to visit the States or the Far East or Africa. But whenever I am away from Berlin too long, no matter how lovely I find the place I'm visiting, however pleasant the people, I always get homesick for Berlin. To me there's something very special about Berlin and about Berliners."

"Are you *waschecht*?" I asked.

"Baptized with Spree water!" he boasted. "My father's family came from Leipzig and my mother's from Silesia, but they were both born in Berlin, so that makes me entirely *waschecht*."

"But you've spent a lot of time outside Berlin, haven't you? At school, during the war, afterwards?" I asked.

"I went to a boarding school in West Germany when I was fourteen, largely so that I wouldn't have to be active in the Hitler Youth. My father, who was a musician and so not officially political, was always strongly antinazi. He was a deeply religious but still an unorthodox man, a Bach expert. He objected to my being turned into a trained seal, as he said, so he sent me off to the country, where I'd be less conspicuous."

"Was your mother politically active?" I asked, thinking of the fragile and elegant woman who had sat next to me at church that morning.

Carl shook his head. "No, except to the extent that she was always involved in relief work, in raising funds for orphans, and arranging outings for old people. She was always a humane person, a gentle person. She is also sophisticated. We had many friends who were Jewish, foreign, left wing, and otherwise undesirable in nazi eyes."

"If your father was a professional musician, you naturally would have," I said.

"Of course, that is until the nazis forced them to leave the country or arrested them.

"I think my father was glad to get me out of Berlin. I looked a little too much like the ideal nazi boy. He probably thought it would go to my head. It can, you know. It's heady stuff."

"I do know," I said and easily imagined Carl at fourteen, blond, big for his age, probably radiant with enthusiasm and vitality. He was very like that at forty, except that the war and the postwar horrors had swept away naïveté and gullibility. I could appreciate his father's concern.

"Were you religious in those days?" I asked.

"Not especially," he said. "Oh, I believed in God and I guess I was conventionally religious. I loved the music. Not only our Protestant Bach but also all those glorious Catholic baroque and pre-Reformation Masses. I played the organ, and I think my family thought I'd turn out to be a musician."

"Do you still play?" I asked.

"Oh, just for fun. After all it's pretty hard to carry a pipe organ around during a war, so I got out of practice."

"When did you go into the army?" I asked.

"Right out of Gymnasium," he said. "Let's see, that was in 1942, probably in July. I remember that I finished my basic training and was sent to the Eastern Front in time for that beastly winter."

"Stalingrad winter," I mused and he nodded. "But you were sent to the Moscow front, weren't you? I seem to remember that you served under Henning von Tresckow."

"Indeed I did, but not at first. My group of reserves almost got sent south to Stalingrad. The High Command shifted a lot of troops south that fall. Relatively speaking, I guess we were lucky. They sure were glad to see us when we arrived in front of Moscow, raw though we were."

"Fall, 1942," I said, remembering. "The Germans had suffered devastating losses by then. They must have been glad to see recruits!"

Carl nodded grimly. "By then we'd lost something like two million men on the Russian front, counting wounded and missing."

"You arrived in time for the Soviet winter offensive, I take it?"

"My baptism by fire," he said, "and pretty sobering it was, but we managed to hold on. They didn't pry us loose. Not that winter. It wasn't all bad. Not even on the Eastern Front. If I had to fight in Russia, I'm glad it was with the Ninth Infantry. They were a great bunch. They called the Ninth the Counts' Infantry because we had to many titles, but of course we also had sons of some of the most able professional and business families, healthy farm boys and a substantial underpinning of Berlin working-class youngsters."

"Berliners mostly?" I asked.

"Berliners, Potsdamers, Brandenburgers," he said. "It was a terrific outfit. When I joined them they had already fought their way from the

Bug in Poland to the suburbs of Moscow. They were in the spearhead of Army Group Center and they darned near took Moscow. After I joined them we did less advancing."

"*Post hoc?*" I murmured, and he grinned.

"Maybe. I think Stalingrad may have had something to do with it too."

"And Hitler," I conceded.

"Lord, Anne, you don't need me to tell you about the Ninth! You must have a dozen friends who were officers, and I was only an enlisted man!"

"How many officers came back, Carl?" I asked.

He thought for a while. "You know of the dozen or so I can remember from those first two or three months, I can think of only three who survived, one because he was transferred to the West in 1943, two because, like me, they were wounded and evacuated from the front. Not only did the Red Army gradually push us back, straight across Russia and Poland into Germany and on to Berlin, but we also suffered losses from the Gestapo after the twentieth of July."

I nodded. "A number of your officers were implicated in the plot. I suppose all of them were investigated. Were you involved?"

"No. As I said, I was just a kid and an enlisted man, although by 1944 I was lucky enough to be serving on Tresckow's personal staff at Central Army Group Headquarters. I guess I hero-worshipped him. I was only a uniformed office boy, but I was constantly in and out of the general's office, carrying papers, answering telephones. I had a pretty good idea of what was going on and who was involved, but luckily the Gestapo considered me a nobody and only questioned me casually. A lot of officers I knew, some who knew my family before the war, were arrested and some were executed. The worst, of course, was Tresckow's suicide."

"As you said, you admired him. It must have been a shock."

"Strange isn't it, that in the middle of a war, surrounded by death, the unexpected death of one man should still be a shock, but it is. It was," Carl said.

"Did you consider yourself an antinazi by then?" I asked.

"Frankly, I hadn't had much time to consider myself anything. An enlisted man at headquarters on the Eastern Front was kept pretty busy. I didn't have much chance to read or much time to indulge in bull sessions, and, as much as I liked the men in our outfit, in those days you had to know a man very well before you'd talk politics with him, especially opposition politics."

"It was easier for officers," I suggested.

"For professional officers," he said. "Many of them had known each other since military academy days, some since childhood if they came from military families. They knew who their friends were and whom they could trust, but, for a draftee among other draftees, it was a very different ball game. By and large, I kept my mouth shut. But I listened and watched and drew conclusions. After Tresckow's death, after the investigation and the trials, when details of the plot came out I made up my mind in a hurry."

"Were people at your headquarters frightened during the investigation?" I asked.

"I'm not sure," he said. "I was too stunned and later too miserable because of the failure, because of the executions, because of what might have been, to be frightenend. Besides, at the front we were kept busy by the Russians, and by July and August 1944 we knew that there wasn't much hope. If I was frightened it was a dull, anesthetized fright. I guess by then we were punch drunk. We just kept on working each day, slugging away, hopelessly."

"You were never a prisoner?" I asked.

"I was one of the lucky ones," he said. "I got close enough to the shooting to catch a piece of shrapnel in January 1945, so I was sent back to Berlin and later to West Germany. I was in a hospital in Hanover when the British took the town, and so technically I became a British P.O.W., but as soon as I was released from the hospital the British released me too."

"Your parents?" I asked. "Were they in Berlin all during the war?"

"My father had a weak lung, and so he wasn't called up, not even for the Home Army. He gave concerts for the troops and he worked for the Red Cross. My mother worked part time for the Red Cross until things got really bad. By the end of 1943 both parents were working six days a week and all kinds of hours."

"What did they do?" I asked.

"You'll have to ask Mama for the details, but they did things like evacuate children, identify air-raid victims, find temporary housing for people who were bombed out and help veterans find families who had been forced to move. They kept right on doing it after the war, until my father got too ill."

"He survived the war, then?" I asked.

"My mother said he seemed to thrive on the work, but the postwar years were too much for him. Our house and the Red Cross office were never really warm. There wasn't enough fuel. Nine hundred calories isn't enough food for anyone, but for a lung patient it's a death sentence. For Dad it was exactly that. In 1947 the Red Cross finally arranged to send him to the Alps, but by then it was too late. He died about a month after he left Berlin."

"Had you come back to Berlin?" I asked.

"I didn't dare, and my parents begged me not to because of the Soviet labor draft. I didn't want to add to their worries and I certainly didn't want to get rounded up and have to spend two to five or more years building roads or working in mines in the Soviet Union. I'd already spent enough time there."

"Did you settle in the West?"

"When I got out of uniform, I went to my mother's sister Sophie, who was a widow of a Rhineland industrialist. She was living quietly in Marburg, and so I entered the university there. I was fortunate enough to see my father before he died. When he left Berlin, I hitchhiked to the village in the Alps where he was staying, and we had a good, long visit."

"I'm glad," I said. "Did you know then that you wanted to enter the ministry?"

Carl shook his head, "No. For the first two years at Marburg I just dabbled. I loved music but I decided that I didn't have enough talent to be a musician. I thought of studying music history, of teaching or being a critic, but I wasn't sure. I took a lot of philosophy courses and I enjoyed those. I like literature, and I was active in one of the political clubs on campus. I was a Jack-of-all-trades, and I just couldn't decide."

"What made you decide? Do you remember?" I asked.

"Do we ever really know why?" he asked. "I think Tresckow had a lot to do with it."

"His politics," I asked, "or his death?"

"Both, I think. After I got back from the front, I began reading anything I could get my hands on about the resistance. I talked with people, asked questions. I wasn't surprised to discover that some of my father's friends had been involved, at least at the periphery and that one of my officers who survived had been deeply involved. He came out of it alive only because he happened to be in the hospital all through the months of the investigation and trials."

"Was this what made you decide to enter the Church?" I asked.

"I'd always been a Christian of sorts, but I began to realize that these men, men like Moltke and Yorck and Klaus von Stauffenberg, had a deeper and more vital view of Christianity than anything I'd ever imagined." He paused and reflected, "Of course, I should have known through Bach, but perhaps I'd been simply too callow before the war. I found that I was also beginning to see more dimensions in Bach!"

"I can see that it wasn't just a flight to otherworldiness," I said, and he grinned and lazily reached for another sandwich.

"No. I'm afraid I'm not very ascetic. It wasn't any kind of flight, even though the world seemed a grim and unpromising place for a young German back in the late 1940s. I wasn't looking for solace or anesthesia, I was looking, if you like, for a new commitment, for something to dedicate myself to, for an arena in which to be useful. I know it sounds pompous to put it into words, but I wanted to find some way to let people know about the men of the resistance, about their ideas." He stopped. "I told you it would sound pompous."

"Words do," I agreed, "but I know what you mean. I feel the same way. It's why I teach and write books."

"People would think we were batty or else had a high opinion of our worth and influence of we told them," Carl said.

"I suppose so," I said, "but I suppose it would have sounded just as pompous when Moltke and Yorck first said it, or for that matter, Luther or Paul."

"I also thought that after the war the Germans would need the Church. I knew they needed God, but I thought they'd also need the temporal institution, and they'd need young pastors who had been through the war, served on the front, men who had shared the experiences of returning veterans and could understand their desperation, their sense of shame or guilt, perhaps of rage."

I nodded. "I'm sure that was true. Have you found it so?"

"Yes and no," Carl said. "Most of my work has been with young people who never experienced the war, but of course they were scarred by it. My first assignment was as assistant pastor in a waterfront parish in Hamburg, a pretty rough neighborhood."

"Good experience," I said. "Did you enjoy it?"

"I loved it. I was anything but spiritual and I certainly didn't have a chance to use any of the fancy theology I'd learned at the seminary, but I enjoyed every day. Naturally as the assistant, I had charge of the kids, especially of the Confirmation Classes. All I can say about trying to cram Dr. Martin Luther's Small Catechism into teen-aged sons of dock workers and sailors it that it is a good thing God happened to recruit a six-foot-four assistant pastor!"

I laughed. "Did you intimidate them?"

"No, but I tried. At least they didn't intimidate me."

"Did you teach them any spiritual truths?"

"Once in a while, surprisingly. It was like feeding pills to cats, if you know what that is. Most of the time they escaped and evaded, but now and then I'd slip one down."

"Hard work," I said.

"Very, but then basic training isn't supposed to be easy and I certainly learned a lot. Looking back, I realize that I came from a very conventional, even prim home. Both parents were quiet, gentle people, musical, artistic, tolerant, and I was sent to a private school for children of similar backgrounds. It wasn't until I got into the army that I began to run into people of different backgrounds, but even there I landed on staff duty at headquarters and that was relatively sheltered, especially in the Ninth: I learned more than enough about death and dying but not much more about living, about everyday life along the waterfront, for instance, about family fights and drunken fathers and unpaid bills, about prostitution, venereal disease and unwanted babies." He paused.

"In the army I knew about these things as statistics, but I don't think I ever expected to encounter them in my congregation. I mean, suddenly the Bible word harlot was no longer a word, or even some starving Russian girl. It was Helga in my Confirmation Class and probably Helga's mother."

"Could you help them?" I asked.

He shrugged. "Well, I got them to the clinic. I once suggested to Helga that I could help her with her school work so that she would pass and be able to qualify for trade school, but she simpered and waggled her hips at me. At least that put me in my place!"

"After Hamburg?" I asked.

"I stayed on the waterfront a little more than two years; then I was transferred to a suburban, middle-class parish; but that was less interesting. It was near enough to a seminary so that I could take a couple of courses, and the church had a fairly decent organ so I could catch up on my music; it wasn't a bad experience for two years. After that I was invited to come to Berlin."

"Had you always planned that?" I asked.

"Oh, yes. I'm a Berliner. I hoped to be called to a Berlin parish eventually, but I hadn't expected to be asked to work at the bishop's office. That is really fun. I'm in a kind of public relations work, planning Church radio and television programs, organizing public lectures or concerts. I can use my music background; I meet fascinating people; and I very often work with young people; so I'm doing exactly what I enjoy."

"Lucky!" I said. "But you also preach sermons?"

"Only when the regular pastors are away or sick," he said. "I'm filling in for Pastor Müller for six weeks while he takes a good rest in Bavaria. He had a bad case of flu this winter and never quite recovered, so the church sent him to the mountains. I enjoy preaching now and then, and eventually I'm sure I'll enjoy settling down with my own congregation, but right now I prefer what I'm doing."

"I'm very glad that you're here in Berlin," I said. "I'm going to exploit you by asking you for all kinds of information about the Evangelical Church. Do you mind?"

"Delighted!" he said. "When and where would you like to start? Tomorrow? No, give me tomorrow to organize things. We'll start Tuesday. Would you like to interview the bishop?"

"I'd like to shake hands with the bishop," I said, "but I'd rather interview someone I wouldn't be afraid to bother."

Carl agreed. Almost simultaneously we looked at our watches and decided that we should pack up and get on with our Sunday walk. "My mother expects us between four and five for tea," he reminded me, "and we'll have all summer to talk about the Church in Germany." As it turned out we needed all summer.

Carl was as good as his word. Monday evening he telephoned to report that he had arranged an appointment for me on Tuesday morning at nine at the main office of the Berlin Lutheran Diocese. As I walked to the subway I passed streams of Berliners making their way from outlying districts to the center of town, to offices and shops, bustling as always and yet seemingly relaxed and cheerful. A short, heavy-set man stood aside to let me go first to buy my ticket. A plump matron smiled and showed me which staircase to take.

Just as I arrived at the platform the subway train swooshed discreetly into the station. "Krumme Lanke, all aboard," a disembodied female voice commanded. I easily found a seat since the stream of traffic was moving in the opposite direction, and once again I marvelled at the cleanliness and silence of Berlin subways. Just before we arrived at Dahlem the subway emerged from underground and became a surface railway. We were now in the spacious suburbs, a region of elegant houses, green gardens and tall trees.

At Dahlem, the subway stop which serves the Free University, I got out, together with several young men and women carrying books and briefcases. I strolled along familiar streets, admiring the attractive villas, the colorful, carefully landscaped gardens, remembering that before the war many officers of Germany's High Command and General

Staff had lived in this neighborhood. Now, I supposed, affluent professional and business people owned the houses. Some of the larger houses bore brass signs proclaiming them institutes or research centers of the Free University.

Faraday Way is just a few blocks from the Free University. Across from the diocesan office stands a tall, red-brick church, famous during the nazi years for the sermons of Martin Niemöller. I walked up the steps of the modern house and thought how unlike a bishop's palace it was but how well in keeping with Prussian Protestantism. Inside, the decor was sober and dignified.

The receptionist was blond and very young. A student, I guessed, summer job, possibly a pastor's daughter. She smiled and swiftly conducted me to an inner office, where a tall, gaunt man rose to greet me. He was dark and wore a dark, clerical suit. I judged him to be in his middle or late forties. He was a serious, intense man temperamentally unlike the ebullient Carl.

We shook hands and he asked me not to use his official title of Bishop's Deputy. "Call me pastor, if you like, or just mister. We Berliners shy away from titles, and frankly I believe that there is no title higher than pastor. By calling I am a pastor; the other title is just administrative."

I agreed, and he invited me to sit opposite him. "When I was appointed to this post I chose this office for its French doors." He pointed toward the doors, which opened onto a cool and fragrant garden. "In the spring the office is flooded with the scent of lilacs, and this time of year, in high summer, we have a dozen varieties of roses. Whenever I feel stale from too much concentration or just from boring routine, or when I grow depressed with the state of the world, I look out into the garden and breathe in the aroma of lilacs or roses, or I take a stroll up and down to sort out my ideas."

"It's lovely," I acknowledged, "and I had just been reflecting how modest this building is for a bishop's see."

The pastor laughed. "You see, it depends on what you consider luxury. Now," he continued, "just what is it you would like to know about the Evangelical Church in Germany?"

I told him that I already knew some of the basic statistics about the Church, that for instance in the Federal Republic in 1970 twenty-eight and a half million people officially belonged to the Evangelical Church, and twenty-five million were registered as Roman Catholics. "I know, too that there is a controversy raging over the Church tax."

He nodded. "There is indeed. I suppose it is only natural that there should be because, you see, Church members in West Germany pay a

total of one billion dollars a year in Church taxes. Opponents claim
that between 1953 and 1967 the annual income of the Evangelical
Church from the tax rose 439 per cent, while the average wage increased
only 150 per cent."

"I can see why some people object," I said. "I've read that the F.D.P.
has declared official opposition to the Church tax. How much does the
West Berlin Church gain from the tax?"

"In 1968 in West Berlin the Evangelical Church received 106 million D-marks and the Catholics 17.4 million D-marks."

"Have many people withdrawn their Church membership to avoid
paying the tax?" I asked, and again he nodded.

"Membership has been declining steadily. Withdrawals exceeded new
members for the first time in 1963. In 1967 the excess of withdrawals over
new members reached 14,000 and, not surprisingly, the largest proportion of withdrawals was in Berlin."

"You mean, you expect greater disaffection, perhaps greater religious
scepticism in large cities?"

"Usually," he said. "Church attendance is traditionally smaller in
large cities and among young people than in small cities and rural
areas. In recent years Church attendance has been declining steadily. In
1962 we estimated that about 45 per cent of the Church members in
the Federal Republic attended services regularly. By 1966 the figure was
down to 39 per cent and in 1969 we reckon 37 per cent."

"The figures sound depressing," I said. "Are you personally pessimistic
about the future?"

"I hope you won't think that I'm a facile optimist, but I think that
we are losing our nominal Christians, people who only attended church
because it was socially acceptable. We are losing young people who used
to attend because of parental pressure and now in these more permissive
times are asserting their independence. These either were never convinced Christians or, if they were, will return to the Church when they
feel they can do it of their own volition as adults. Many young people
do drift back after they marry and begin to raise a family."

"Even hippies and revolutionaries," I said.

"But of course we have hippies and revolutionaries within the Church,"
he said.

"Jesus freaks?" I asked.

"Some," he said. "Jesus is very in with some young radicals as you
know."

"But are they in the established Church?" I asked.

"Some," he repeated, and he told me a little about the congress of the Evangelical Church in Stuttgart in 1969. "There was a time when I was considered a radical in the Church," he said. "Then I gradually found that I was considered just a bit left of center, and by now I am a middle-of-the-roader. I haven't changed, or at least I don't think so. I've grown older, so perhaps I have changed a little, but the climate within the Church has changed radically, and just within the past ten or fifteen years."

"But from what you say, the young people are not satisfied with the Church, liberalized though it is."

"Apparently not," he concluded. "They certainly made some very vocal complaints against the Establishment at Stuttgart. Of course some of the young people proved themselves radical in another direction. They are radical evangelicals demanding a return to a more scripturally oriented church. Most of our young people, however, are quiet and compromising."

"Establishmentarians," I said.

"Basically the majority usually are, I think, but at Stuttgart the radicals demanded that the Church become more activist in social problems, that we contribute more to developing nations, work more to preserve the environment and to foster the growth of a more democratic social order. Their slogan seemed to be that the Church should accept the Sermon on the Mount as its active, secular platform." He smiled reminiscently. "Some of our stuffier clergymen were quite shocked!"

"Dare one say that the Sanhedrin perhaps was shocked also?" I said.

"Certainly, and while I felt that the shock was probably salutary, I also noted that there was not much evidence that these youngsters were about to become meek in order to inherit the earth."

"Alas, no!" I said. "Is the Church taking steps to win over young people, the moderates or semirevolutionaries?"

"We are certainly trying to encourage more young people to become active in the Church and to assume responsibility for leadership. For example, in 1971 Bishop Kurt Scharf was instrumental in having the voting age for Church members reduced from twenty-one to eighteen. In West Berlin we have 159 Evangelical congregations, each of which elects from four to fifteen elders to assist the pastor in running the church. Each congregation also elects delegates to the Berlin Church Council, which assists in running the diocese. Previously these elections were held during the regular Sunday service so that only those who attended church could vote. We estimated that normally only about five per cent of the eligible members actually voted in the elections. In 1971 all congregations throughout West Berlin held elections on the same day, and the polls were kept open from eight in the morning until six in the evening so that any member who was interested could arrange to vote."

"Did that help?" I asked.

"It's a little too early to be sure of the effect, but certainly more people voted than usual, and we hope that the younger members of the congregation will accept the change as evidence of our interest in encouraging them to participate."

"I understand that the Stuttgart congress marked the official withdrawal of the East German churches from the E.K.D.," I said.

"At one time the E.K.D., the Evangelical Church in Germany, was a reality. Not so many years ago the E.K.D. was the only genuine all-German organization," the pastor said.

"I remember that when Otto Dibelius was Bishop of Berlin he actually governed the whole diocese, including East Berlin," I said.

He nodded. "Yes indeed. The diocese of Berlin includes not only all Berlin but also the surrounding province of Brandenburg, which is entirely within the G.D.R. In a sense the concept of German unity was preserved in the person of the bishop."

"Certainly in the person of Bishop Dibelius," I said and he smiled wryly.

"If you remember, the East German Church sent delegates to the annual Church meetings and occasionally, when the East German authorities happened to be in a friendly mood, we even held E.K.D. congresses in East Germany."

"I also remember the days when Bishop Dibelius regularly conducted services and held meetings in East Berlin."

"I remember too," the pastor said. "When Willy Brandt was mayor, he and his family often attended Sunday service in East Berlin to hear the bishop preach. In the days when the East was accusing the Federal Republic and the Western Allies of causing the continuing disunity of Germany, when they were championing the slogan of unification, of course they encouraged gestures of unity."

"Even from the Church," I said.

"Even from the Church; but after 1957, when they began to espouse the doctrine of separation, they changed their slogans and their policy toward the E.K.D. The Soviets and East Germans began demanding recognition of the sovereignty of the G.D.R., and so they fostered the concept of two German churches, East and West. How could there be two German states but only one German Church?"

"Did they prevent meetings in the East?" I asked.

"The first measure they took was to try to cut off Western financial support for the East German churches. They calculated that, without money from the West, the Evangelical Church in East Germany would either have to curtail its activities drastically, perhaps close most of the churches, or else accept subsidies from the communist government and so become a captive, tame Church."

"There were already too few pastors in East Germany, weren't there?" I asked, remembering past conversations in the East.

"Many of our pastors were killed during the war, serving as chaplains at the front. Many who entered Soviet P.O.W. camps with their troops never came back. Others fled to the West while it was still possible," he explained.

"It must be difficult to recruit young men for the ministry in the East," I suggested.

"Very difficult," he agreed. "After all, most children grow up attending the public schools, where they are systematically taught atheism. Their teachers and textbooks ridicule religion, and only the bravest and most dedicated Christian parents send their children to Sunday School or teach them the Bible at home."

"The communists don't actually interfere with the operation of the churches in the East, do they?" I asked, remembering photographs of party chiefs with bishops at Christmas.

"If you mean that they don't forbid the holding of Sunday services or prevent citizens from attending, they don't. Some churches remain open and pastors may preach, although of course, they have to be very careful about what they preach," he said.

"As under the nazis," I suggested.

"Exactly," he said. "A pastor may preach and he may visit his parishioners, but if he visits members of his congregation who never attend to urge them to come to church he can be arrested for disturbing the peace. All missionary or evangelical activity is illegal. Church membership has dropped drastically, Church attendance is low, recruitment to the ministry is pitifully inadequate, and yet, you know, some of us believe that this is not all bad. Conventional Christians have dropped away, but perhaps we have only lost the dead wood. Those who remain loyal are genuine Christians."

"Yes, I've heard several Christians say that," I said. "The big question is whether enough genuine Christians will be able to hold out, whether there are at least a few young people recruited to the Church each year. Are there?"

"Some," he said, "and those who come are deeply committed. Enough?" He shrugged. "Only history will tell us that. We can only trust the Lord, who assured us that the gates of Hell will not prevail against His Church. Meanwhile, we hang on and watch and pray."

"But as you said, the communist policy towards the Church fluctuates."

"Yes. We have already lived through several phases. Naturally all party members and important government officials have withdrawn from the Church. Any young person with serious political ambition, or indeed any serious worldly ambition, must still leave the Church, but the state puts no direct pressure on average citizens to withdraw. In fact, the opposite. In East Germany an individual may retain his Church membership but refuse to pay the Church tax. Many do that."

"I understand that about two-thirds of the people in the G.D.R. still officially belong to the Church. That is a lot," I said.

"Yes, but as I said, the great majority are not active. The state and the party plan all kinds of activities on Sundays—sports events, meetings, outings—especially for young people so that they cannot attend church," he explained.

"Do they still prevent young people who have been confirmed from attending a university?" I asked.

"They are a little less stringent, and so are the churches. As you know, all youngsters in the East must join the Free German Youth, but they are not required to remain members. Those who do, go through a 'Youth Dedication' ceremony, consecrating them to socialism and to the state. In order to attend universities a young person must have gone through this ceremony."

"But the churches, especially the Catholic Church, excommunicated any young person who participated in the dedication. Do they still?" I asked.

"In principle," he said. "We Protestants say that a young person who participates in the ceremony cannot be confirmed, while the communists say that a youngster who has been confirmed cannot participate."

"But in practice?" I asked.

"In practice, most pastors advise their members to follow their own consciences. Even most Catholic priests grant absolution to young men and women who have gone through the ceremony and then ask to be reinstated, and most of our ministers encourage their young members to postpone confirmation until after the Dedication."

"So in this way the individual avoids direct confrontation?" I asked.

"During the early postwar years, it was psychologically easier for East Germans to hold out, to refuse to compromise. Many of them believed that the communist government was only temporary, a product of the Soviet occupation, and that eventually it could be overthrown. Others hoped to escape to the West, and so they considered their day-to-day life in the East as only a stopgap. Since the Wall, however, most have had to accept and learn to live with the harsh reality that at least for their lifetimes the communist regime will endure and that they probably cannot escape." He shrugged. "The average citizen must cope with worldly realities as he sees them. He must think of earning his living, of his children's future. He needn't become a communist and certainly not an atheist, but he must deal with the communists in terms of their power and his own weakness."

I nodded. "And so he and you must compromise."

"We hope that we are compromising only with the forms, with the externals, but by now about ninety per cent of East German young people participate in the Dedication. That still leaves ten per cent who do not, and that is rather substantial considering the price."

"It is," I admitted. "Would you say that official East German policy has become less militantly antireligious in recent years? Has the thaw had any substantial influence in this sphere?"

"Yes, and no," he said. "As I said, East German policy regarding the Church fluctuates. After an initial phase of rather aggressive atheism, the S.E.D. Party leaders began to pose as friends of the Church, especially of the Evangelical Church as a symbol of the German unity they espoused."

"Before 1957?" I asked.

He nodded. "I don't know whether you remember the All-German Evangelical Congress that was held in both East and West Berlin in 1951, but the S.E.D. used it as a showcase for their demands for German unity. The opening session met in East Berlin's St. Mary's Church, and many prominent East German officials attended. Wilhelm Pieck was photographed sitting next to Bishop Dibelius. Placards all over East Berlin exploited the theme of Germans at one table."

"But that phase didn't last?" I asked.

"Not long at all. A new era of conflict began the very next year with a wave of arrests of pastors. In 1952 many clergymen, especially the younger ones, fled to the West. Events such as the Hungarian revolt in 1956, which sparked outbursts of sympathy among East Germans, especially among university students, and in which Christian groups were necessarily involved and the West German adherence to N.A.T.O., intensified the hostility and added to the atmosphere of repression."

"Yes," I said, "I remember the years when bishops Dibelius and Hans Lilje were described as N.A.T.O. bishops."

"In headline after headline in *Neues Deutschland*," he said. "And of course the churches in general were accused of being pro-Western, bourgeois, and warmongers."

"But more recently, hasn't there been a softening of attitude?"

"In a sense," he said. "As I said before, the government in the East now espouses the doctrine of two German states, and inside their German state they are trying to establish friendlier relations with an East German church, trying to make it a tame church. Naturally they do not want to let the Church become too powerful or too influential, but they seem to believe that allowing it to survive may syphon off some dissident feeling."

"Something like allowing parties other than the S.E.D. to continue and to share in the coalition?" I suggested.

"Yes, very like that," he said, "and sincere Christians differ in their view of the correct response to this. Some insist that we must remain adamant and uncorrupted, that we should not compromise; others think we should compromise in anything nonessential in order to survive."

"It sounds like the controversy inside the early Christian Church during the Roman persecutions," I said, and he agreed.

"It is difficult to know which side is right," he said, "but as I started to say, the East German authorities have succeeded in their goal of dividing the Church. They have made it increasingly difficult for us to maintain even the form of unity between the Eastern and Western branches of the E.K.D., but at the Stuttgart meeting the split became formal and final."

"The East seceded?" I asked.

"Yes. The forty-two East German delegates formally withdrew from the meeting and announced the establishment of a separate East German League of Evangelical Churches. That marked only the formal burial. The patient had been dead for some time."

"But you seem not entirely pessimistic," I said.

"I am far from optimistic, even about the West," he commented. "Not only is Church attendance down in the Federal Republic and official withdrawals on the increase, but even those who attend church seem less religious, more sceptical, more worldly and materialistic. Fewer Church members each year bother to be married in church."

"Many no longer bother to be married," I said.

"Exactly, and fewer members care whether the Church approves or disapproves of divorce. The soaring divorce rate is not confined to agnostics. Our public schools in the West teach religion; our government collects the Church tax to support the work of the churches. Officially, West Berlin and West Germany are Christian societies, and yet are we Christian? Less and less, I should say."

"But there are signs of vitality?" I asked.

"Oh yes, some. As I said, I think that in the West as in the East the dropping away of nominal Christians is probably beneficial, a pruning of the vine. The inner strength, the spirituality of those who remain is greater, and, as I said, although we have fewer young people in church and fewer recruits to the ministry, those we have are genuinely dedicated."

"Not all bad, then," I said. "And Berlin?" I asked.

"*Ach,* Berlin! *Na, ja.* The Berliner in general is not materialistic to the degree the West German is, but he is worldly in another sense. He is sceptical, ironical, realistic. He is independent and likes to make up his own mind. He is irreverent and unimpressed with rank or display. A parish full of Berliners is not a flock of lambs!"

"Isn't that good?" I asked.

"I think it is excellent. When a Berliner is a Christian he is a sincere and profound Christian. They are always a minority in any society but they exist even in Berlin and I am delighted to have the opportunity to work with them and for them. I hope to stay in Berlin as long as there is work for me here."

"Even if it is sometimes depressing?" I asked.

"It is usually depressing," he said, "but then, as I said before, I have the lilacs and the roses to cheer me. Berlin is very lovely, not a pretty city, not romantic or ancient, but very green. The gardens, the parks, the forests and lakes are quite beautiful. We are very lucky."

He stood and took me by the elbow. "Come, I will show you around our offices and get Martha to round up some booklets and statistics for you; then we shall come back and have coffee in the garden. You know what the Berliner says about problems? In fifty years it will all be over. So will we, dear lady, so today let us work and sniff the roses, enjoy the beauty—and have a cup of steaming coffee!"

It was another bright sunny day and as usual I had been rushing. I felt warm and rather worn and I was grateful when I arrived at the quiet little café and found a table in the shade. I realized that I was early for my appointment with Carl and so I ordered coffee and settled down to read a relaxing novel. The waiter brought my coffee and I had read only a few pages when I saw Carl, large and bearlike, unclerical in a sports jacket and light trousers, loping along towards the café. He saw me, grinned and waved and rushed in to shake my hand.

"I'm not late, am I?" he asked, dismayed when he noticed my coffee.

"No," I assured him, making room for him on a chair piled with my briefcase and some books. "I was very early and very thirsty."

He smiled, reassured, and sat down. "Well, how are the appointments?"

"Good," I said and thanked him again for arranging them. "I'll let you see my notes when I type them up," I promised.

"I brought you a new list of people and places you might like to see," he said and reached into an inner pocket to extract a paper. The waiter returned. "Have you ever drunk Moselle and Herva?" he asked.

"Something like a *Gespritzener?*" I asked.

"Something, only very fresh. You'll like it. People drink it a lot in Berlin," he said and ordered two. "I thought we might go to an early film and have something to eat at one of the student pubs later. No good going to one of their co-ops too early; the crowd does not arrive until after eight."

"What kind of film shall we see?" I asked.

"I read three or four reviews," Carl said. "There are at least two showing in this neighborhood which are very in, and I suppose it is more or less our duty to see them."

I laughed. "Need we do our duty when we're off duty?"

"Of course not," he said, "not even in Prussian Berlin, but I thought perhaps you'd like to see one of the chic films." He mentioned the titles, and we both agreed that some time we would like to see them. "Only thing is," he said, "there's always a big line waiting to get in to anything that famous."

"Do you know one that isn't chic but that we'd enjoy?" I asked and was not surprised when he suggested a light comedy which was showing at one of the smaller theaters in a side street.

"Besides, it's cheaper," he added.

"From what I've been hearing about the Church tax, I'd have thought you clergymen were rolling in D-marks," I submitted.

"I hope you noticed our plush palaces and luxurious offices," he said.

"Not guilty on that score, certainly. Every office I've seen has been frugally furnished and is utilitarian in the extreme. No baroque marble, no rococo cherubs, just lots of wooden desks and straight-backed chairs. But you do have an enormous budget. I suppose most of it goes to support schools and hospitals and to pay salaries," I said.

"The Church in West Germany and West Berlin runs a lot more than churches, as you know. We have all kinds of activities from day nurseries and schools through adult-education centers, hospitals, vacation homes and old-age homes, youth clubs, overseas exchange programs, social services, radio and TV programs and housing projects."

"I've noticed," I said. "Here in the West a great many social and economic activities are run by the Church that are taken care of by the state in the East and by separate charitable foundations in America."

"Ah, here comes our Moselle. I hope you like it." Carl thanked the waiter and raised his glass.

"*Prost!*" I said and sipped. "It's pleasant indeed." He smiled and I took another sip. "Do you approve a state-collected Church tax? I know that some clergymen don't."

"Yes, I do. I realize that some conservatives, or rather libertarians, disapprove because they believe that the Church should be more independent of the state, whereas some leftists disapprove because basically they disapprove of religion or, at least, of state-sponsored religion. They would prefer to see the state carry out our nonsacerdotal functions. In other words, both the centralists and the extreme anticentralists oppose the tax, but I'm a middle-of-the-roader on this issue."

"You don't believe in total separation of Church and state then?" I asked.

"I believe that neither institution should interfere in the realm of the other, but on the other hand, I believe both are pillars of society and should work together to maintain a moral and humane social order. I don't think the state should run the Church, but under our system it doesn't. The state collects the tax and hands over the money according to a rigid formula to the two denominations to spend and administer." He reached for cigarettes and offered me one. "How's your quota doing?"

"Fourth today," I said, reaching for one.

"You converts to Prussianism put us *waschecht* Berliners to shame!" he said laughing and lit the cigarette. "I haven't had many today," he said. "I can't afford many. Church tax or no!"

"Isn't there a danger with a large budget that the Church will grow too institutionalized, too bureaucratic?" I asked and he nodded vigorously.

"Absolutely, but there's always some danger. In my view it would be worse if most of that money were retained by the state and the federal government were to take over our social functions. That would lead to even more bureaucracy and to greater concentration of power."

"What about voluntary contributions and separate, private fundations?" I asked.

"Theoretically I would approve," he said, "but as a matter of practical politics, I'm afraid it wouldn't work. Don't forget, here in Lutheran Germany we have a tradition of paternalism. On the one hand, our people are accustomed to receiving services, to being provided for. On the other, our middle class is not accustomed, as is yours in the States, to being required to volunteer their services or contribute their money. They do contribute their money, but through taxation."

"Wouldn't they through a tax-incentive program?" I asked.

"I hope they would eventually, but it might take several years to train them, and meanwhile the services have to be performed and paid for," he said.

"Of course," I reflected, "it is in the tradition of the antinazi resistance that Church and state should not be entirely separated, that it is the duty of the government to help make the social order Christian."

"Absolutely," Carl said. "Well, you know as much about the Kreisau people as I do, especially about Moltke and Yorck."

"I know that they were Lutherans," I said, "and that they believed that much of the cruelty and moral irresponsibility of the nazi era was the result of the gradual loss of religious faith, the loss of the influence of the Church."

"The founders of the C.D.U. thought the same thing," Carl said. "Adenauer and his friends firmly believed that Germany's only hope for moral recovery was the strengthening of religion in public life. The Christian Democrats, and at the time many socialists agreed, advocated participation by the churches in public education. The early West German political leaders worked closely with the clergy, especially with the Catholic hierarchy."

"It was said," I commented, "that Cardinal Frings was the real chancellor."

"*Eminence grise* at least," Carl contributed, "and I'd be less than honest if I said that as a Protestant pastor I always approved in general of the influence of the Catholic clergy on Bonn. Sometimes I have disapproved strenuously in specific cases, and yet on the whole I prefer a government which is influenced by Christianity than one which follows only the dictates of immediate self-interest. Under Adenauer West Germany became officially a Christian country, and even though this obviously did not transform the bulk of Germans overnight into saints I still support the idea."

"Germans did seem to flock to the Church after the war," I said. "I suppose that was natural. The Church was a symbol of continuity; it was one institution which had endured through the centuries, unlike any of the German governments."

Carl nodded. "Refugees from the Eastern provinces, people whose houses had been bombed, and children separated from parents could feel reassured by the familiar liturgy and music of the Church. It was home and a link with home."

"It was a link with their childhood, with their traditions, with their past," I suggested. "It also offered comfort, especially to those with a burden of guilt, to the desperate."

"Guilt was a staggering burden during those early postwar years," Carl said. "Knowing that the nazis were brutes and that one's Jewish neighbors disappeared, that whispers of opposition resulted in middle-of-the-night visits from the Gestapo is one thing. The merciless exposure of the details of torture, of extermination, was something else. Day after day the Allied-controlled radio and the licensed press assaulted our psyches with new evidence of nazi crimes, new statistics, more revolting photographs."

"Psychologically that must have been more shattering even than the bombing and the physical dislocation," I said.

Carl nodded. "I think it was, and especially for the average, simple citizen who had believed in and supported the nazis."

"Yes, of course," I said. "My friends of the resistance tell me that they feel guilty because they failed, because they didn't do enough soon enough to prevent Hitler from coming to power, to prevent the war from breaking out, but that kind of guilt is nothing compared to that of people who actually were nazis, I'd suppose."

"Objectively speaking," Carl said, "but your friends probably have tender consciences and I'm not so sure about the little activists. Still, many of these minor nazis or average citizens who voted for the Nazi Party were basically naive, even idealistic, and these were genuinely shocked and horrified by the exposure of the details of the nazi crimes and they lacked the spiritual reserves of your more sophisticated friends. People like that simply collapsed morally. They lost their faith in their ideals, in their country, in themselves. Some of these we were able to win for the Church. Anyway, during the postwar years many average people came to church."

"I have the impression that many young people who wished to identify with some nonnazi, antinazi idea looked to the Christian churches during those early years," I said, "especially when the story of the resistance movement began to be known. Young people, however cynical, need heroes, and they could find heroism in men like Stauffenberg and Moltke and in the Scholl family. Surely Moltke's letters and Inge Scholl's poetry must have influenced a generation of young people, as they did you and me."

"I think that was true for a while," Carl said. "Certainly we had a wave of recruitment in the clergy in the postwar years and the churches were full, but apparently this spiritual upsurge hasn't lasted. Today Church tax receipts, as you said, are up, Church attendance is down. Critics on both the right and left oppose the Church tax, and many educators and politicians oppose teaching religion in the schools. The Church is on the defensive, and even within itself it is divided."

"Part of a general leftward drift?" I asked, sipping the last of my wine.

Carl nodded and glanced at his watch. "That film doesn't start until six-fifteen," he said. "We have time for another drink if you'd like."

"If you'd like," I said, and he signalled the waiter.

"The German miracle did its share," Carl suggested. "In part, the average German simply used up all his energy, all his concentration, his entire personality in working for the material reconstruction of the nation and of his individual life. He began to live solely for the rebuilding of his home, of his business or profession, of his town. Whole families lived, worked, struggled and planned only to buy a bicycle, to furnish an apartment and then to buy a car. Later they slaved to buy a luxurious car, to own furs and jewelry and send their children to the right schools, to take trips abroad. God didn't take a back seat to mammon—He was pushed right out of the car!"

I said that I agreed entirely. "I can understand that children growing up in that acquisitive, materialistic environment couldn't be expected to be very spiritual or even basically moral."

"No," Carl said, "nor can you really expect them to love and respect their parents, however many material luxuries they shower on them."

"I have a young friend who confided to me that she is unable to love her parents for exactly that reason and because they are conventional churchgoers, loveless, spiritless, nominal Christians; the young woman refuses to attend church, although she is basically a very sensitive and spiritual person," I said. "I find that tragic, for the parents as well as for the young woman."

"Any kind of cripple is tragic," Carl said, "and moral, spiritual atrophy is probably the worst form of crippling there is. Germany these days is full of that kind of cripple."

"Not only Germany," I said.

"This era of materialism and affluence impinges on religion in another area," Carl said, "in the area of information. Not only has there been an explosion of technical knowledge, not only do more people go to school longer than ever before, but more people than ever are bombarded with facts, with information and with misinformation than ever in history. Not just the ever-present television, but films, illustrated magazines, radio, records and tapes. The mind and senses of a child growing up today are constantly assaulted. It's no wonder if he grows confused as well as sophisticated."

I nodded. "Certainly the TV-educated child has a high standard of professionalism. He expects his teachers and pastors to entertain him as well as his electronic baby-sitter. I've noticed with college students in the

States that those who watch TV a great deal often develop a layer of false sophistication. They think that they know something because they have seen it on television. They don't realize or want to realize that you acquire knowledge only by intellectual effort. Worse, they believe that they have experienced something, war for instance, or love or death, because they have seen a picture of it. It makes them rather weird and very pathetic. If you like, that's another form of crippling."

"It would be," Carl said, "and this surface sophistication makes it very difficult to get through to the real person under the glossy, hard exterior. The average person today acquires a veneer of scepticism; he has been exposed to a kind of pop-enlightenment—Sunday supplement courses in evolution, sex education and Freudian psychology.

"Grown men and women seem to pride themselves on not believing in Adam and Eve and the apple, on not believing in a God like a dear old grandpa! Some of them will tell you with a perfectly straight face, 'Well, we have seen a film on TV about the Pleistocene age, so how can we be expected to go to church?' I'm serious!" he said.

"And the situation is serious. At the beginning of the century, average men and women were by and large credulous. It was the intellectual class that was sceptical. Now, average men and women are still credulous but they believe in what they fondly call science, and only the intellectuals and nuclear physicists and astronomers come to church," Carl said.

"It is true," I said, "that we Lutherans have become very highbrow, very philosophical. I think you and I and people we know are Christians because they have read Marx and Darwin and Freud and then gone on to Buber and Heidegger and Tillich. Our God is Tillich's God, beyond the God of monotheism, but, my dear, you can't translate that into popular theology. And these former Christians who are hung up on doubts about Adam and Eve and the Pleistocene era seem to be looking for an excuse not to believe. Were they ever Christians?"

"No, of course not, not in any deep, spiritual sense, but the Church doesn't exist only for the saints! And you are right, I think. We have become too highbrow. Many of our pastors are intellectual snobs who preach over the heads of all but an intellectual elite."

"What do we need," I asked, "knee-slapping gospel songs, emotional revivalism?"

"I don't know, but Jesus didn't preach abstruse theology, and he didn't preach to the scholars of his day but to the simplest people. The gospel isn't theology; it's a down-to-earth, very human message. Somehow, that is what we have to get across. Somehow we have to penetrate the hard gloss of pseudoscepticism, shake up the complacent, smug philistines,

Fig. 16. Working-class neighborhood pub, West Berlin (photo by Landesbildstelle, West Berlin)

make them realize that they are human, that they have minds, real minds which can be used, which are not mere file cards, that they have hearts and feelings and a personality, not just a bankbook and a social security card, that it does matter what their children think of them, what kind of marriages and homes they have, whether they are capable of loving."

"How?" I asked quietly.

"How?" he grinned. "Man! If I knew that I'd be elected dictator next week, or anyway, bishop." He looked at his watch. "I tell you what, let's pay this nice man and stroll slowly to the theater. We can solve the 'how' over a bottle of red wine after we see the film."

20

Pastor Ruth

"Aren't we lucky it didn't pour like this while we were tramping through the Grunewald?" Carl said.

"I'm lucky that you're driving me to this appointment!" I said. "I'd drown if I tried to walk from a subway stop, and you know how hard it is to find a taxi in a downpour!" The rain was streaming down so hard that Carl could hardly see the road. He slowed the old, blue Volkswagen to a crawl and leaned forward, his nose almost against the glass.

"A deluge!" he said. "If it keeps up like this, I think I ought to come back for you. As you said, you'd never reach the subway without getting drenched and I doubt that you'd find a cab."

I shook my head. "No, Carl. You have work to do. I can ask Pastor Ruth to telephone for a taxi. Besides, it will let up."

"You're sure?" he asked. "I could come back in an hour and a half or so. Poor old Bluetooth may be on her last legs, but she jogs along and she's better than drowning."

I assured him that I would manage.

"This is as close as I can get," he said, "but if you duck under those trees and make a dash for it you won't get too wet."

"Thanks," I said, squeezing out and holding my notebook against my chest. "See you Sunday!" I called and ran. Naturally neither Carl nor I ever have an umbrella. The trees sheltered me and I arrived at the austere modern office building only a little damp. A glance at the announcement board told me that the office I wanted was on the third floor. I found Pastor Ruth's office at the end of a long, dim corridor.

The woman who responded to my knock was a tall, sturdy, serious-looking woman probably in her late forties. Her two-piece blue jersey dress was simply cut and without adornment. Her black leather shoes were of good quality and well polished but practical and modest rather than fashionable. She wore no make-up, not even lipstick, but her grey-ing dark hair was well shaped and framed her face like a cap.

She smiled and welcomed me with a brisk handshake. "Come in!" she said and motioned me to a straight-backed, wooden chair. The office was a small cubicle, modern, cheerful and rather bare. There were no vases of summer flowers, no potted plants. No paintings decorated the walls, no figurines or *objets d'art* relieved the austerity. Not even an ash tray embellished the desk, only piles of papers, stacks of books and an appoint-ment book.

"We're rather new here," Pastor Ruth explained, "and I am so busy rushing from one meeting to another that I haven't done much to make my office attractive. Besides," she added ruefully, "I am just not talented that way. To be perfectly honest, I don't much notice decoration."

"I don't either when I'm working," I admitted.

"My room at home is something else," she said. "When I am off duty, I like a warm, relaxing atmosphere. When I'm working I prefer no distrac-tions, and if I'm too comfortable I'm likely to get lazy!"

I laughed, not quite able to picture the brisk, energetic Pastor Ruth as lazy.

"Now, what would you like to know?" she asked. "Probably first of all how rare a bird I am? How many female pastors there are?" I nodded. "Well, I looked that up for you. Of the 16,190 Evangelical pastors in the Federal Republic, including West Berlin, only 330 are women." [1970]

"Not many," I said, but she assured me the number is growing and the status of women pastors is improving.

"Especially in Berlin," she explained. "There is a lot of prejudice against women as actual heads of parishes. In the Lutheran Church we have had women deaconesses for a long time. People accept them, and therefore they more readily accept a woman as an assistant pastor or as an official in one of the Church's social services. A woman pastor running a school or an orphanage or a hospital is usually accepted, but when it comes to a woman in the pulpit," she shrugged, "well, the Pauline doc-trine is very strong."

"But there are women who run parishes, aren't there?" I asked, remem-bering a very impressive woman pastor I had met the year before.

"Yes, and as I said, our situation is especially good in Berlin. In Ham-burg, Hanover, Bavaria, Brunswick and Lippe there is not a single woman in charge of a parish, but in West Berlin we have twenty-four women parish pastors, and I think that is good."

"Relatively," I admitted. "Do you hope to have your own parish even-tually, or do you prefer social work?"

"I'm not sure," she said. "I think I'd like to receive a call to a congregation, but you know if I marry it won't be permitted. No married woman may head a congregation."

"Would you like me to round up some female students to picket the bishop's office?" I asked and she laughed.

"Not just yet, but we girls may get around to that. There really is a good deal of irrational prejudice against us. For instance, what man would tamely accept the fact that no congregation would take him seriously if he's under fifty? And yet few women under forty-five or fifty are entrusted with a parish. On the other hand, we women have made a substantial amount of progress in West Germany since the war, so I ought not to complain, and I personally have a responsible and interesting job here. I must also admit that most of my younger male colleagues are very co-operative and they do take me seriously. They are quite ready to entrust me with any amount of responsibility provided I do the work."

I said, "They're not male chauvinist pigs, then?"

"Goodness, no! Not most of them. A few of the older and stuffier gentlemen look a bit askance, but as long as I do my work efficiently they don't complain. After all, they know I passed the same examinations they did, that I must be qualified. I think they also believe that a woman is especially suited to the kind of work I am doing."

Naturally I asked what that was. "Well, this whole department is involved in social work. We deal with foreign relief, development aid, scholarships for foreign students and apprentices, aid for unwed mothers, programs for drug addicts and alcoholics, work with the unemployed and ex-convicts and the elderly. We don't just preach to these people or send out missions. We have counselling services, we offer medical and psychological help, we find jobs and apartments and schools for people. For the elderly we arrange vacations and companions, eyeglasses or hearing aids, outings and hobbies. The works!"

"That's a tremendous program," I said.

"It's a whole gamut of programs," Ruth said. "Obviously, the Catholic Church has a similar program for its members. Sometimes we work together, especially on things like famine relief or development aid and we sometimes make use of each other's services. I have lunch now and then with my Catholic opposite number and we keep in fairly close touch."

I said that I had visited the Catholic offices and had toured a Catholic youth home. "They do a splendid job," Ruth said. "I sometimes envy my Catholic colleagues because they don't have the laity to contend with quite as much as we do! They can be more efficient than we."

"But they don't have women priests!" I reminded her.

"Not yet," she said. "Besides, I'm rather attached to our more decentralized tradition."

I asked just what her specific duties were. "The bulk of my work is with old people," she said. "As you know, Berlin's major social problem is the disproportionate number of older citizens we have to provide for. In West Germany the percentage of people over sixty-five is 12 per cent, in West Berlin it is 21 per cent—these are 1968 figures. That represents a considerable burden not only in pensions but also in providing apartments and in all kinds of service from medical through recreational."

"Of course," I said. "Not only do most of these elderly people not work, but obviously they require more social services than people of working age."

"They do indeed, and the Church rather than the state meets many of their needs. We feel that elderly people especially prefer to deal with Christians of their own background rather than with government officials, however dedicated or well qualified. We hope at least that we are warmer, more loving, more human. Certainly we try to be."

"Less bureaucratic," I suggested.

"Well, I think our atmosphere is less stringent and more relaxed, even though in any large organization which has to account for a substantial amount of money each month there are inevitable forms to fill out, regulations to comply with. There are more than I like. But after all it is not our money. We are only stewards. In spite of that we honestly try to achieve a warm and human atmosphere, and there's no question but that our workers are dedicated. State-collected tax or not, no one ever got rich by choosing a career with the Church, either as a pastor or as a layman."

"No, certainly not, but then civil servants don't get rich either, do they?" I asked.

"No, especially not in frugal Prussia! But some people are attracted to government service, I've observed, because they enjoy the status, the dignity of office, some because they like to exercise power. I hope and believe that we get fewer of these, although on the other hand we get some self-righteous ones. I do admit that not everyone who cries 'Lord! Lord!' is warm and loving. But we try, and by and large, we do fairly well."

I asked whether she only handled the problems of old people, and she said, "I do a zillion other things." She told me about just a few. "I know you're interested in the role of women in society. So am I, of course, and in my work I have a little something to do with women's problems. I'm involved in helping to counsel unwed mothers, in the supervision of our truly lovely country home for expectant mothers, married or not, where they spend a month or more before their child is born and up to eight weeks afterwards, and of our vacation home for mothers and babies where, again married or not, young women can enjoy a few weeks away from the city, away from their responsibilities. We have nurseries for the babies and arrange outings and entertainment for the mothers, or they can swim or lie in the sun, or just be lazy if that is what they need."

"It sounds lovely," I said.

"It is," she said. "And we don't preach, we just let them rest and enjoy themselves. Oh, we hold religious services, and we offer counselling and lectures or discussions on child care if the mothers want it, but we don't push, we don't act holier than thou. At least, we try not to."

"I'm sure you succeed," I said.

"Last month something happened which will interest you," she said. "We had a visit from a group of French Protestant women. We took them around to see our various offices and activities, and I arranged a luncheon and seminar for them so that they could meet with some of our professional women in Berlin. We had a fascinating discussion on comparative problems for women in our two countries."

"Which are better off?" I asked.

She smiled. "Ah, both our countries have problems, but in both we are coming along. Let's see, what else do I do? All kinds of odds and ends. You've no idea! I work in the 'Bread for the World' campaign, sending out speakers, speaking myself, arranging luncheons. I counsel with Germans who want to emigrate abroad. I work with the regular student pastor, that is, the pastor assigned as chaplain to the Berlin universities, to counsel foreign students, especially those from Africa and Asia. I work with a committee that helps Greek workers in Berlin. We work in cooperation with the Greek consulate to run a recreation center for them. I hold the religious services for our deaconesses, and every third Sunday I preach a sermon in one of our larger churches."

"Do you have any spare time?" I asked.

"Not much, but now and then I am invited as all other clergymen are to make a public speech at a luncheon or give the benediction on some official occasion, such as the opening of a new school or children's home, a graduation or festivity. Some days I find that I am simply rushing from one end of Berlin to the other. Others I am riveted to my desk trying to catch up on reports and paper work. This certainly isn't a nine-to-five job. I seldom finish up here before six and often have to take a briefcase full of work home."

"It is not an easy job, then." She smiled wryly. "Do you enjoy it? Would you recommend the clergy as a career to other women?"

"I enjoy every minute! And yes, I would certainly recommend the

career to young women. I think there are many facets of the work which
can better be handled by women than by men, and I think, since there
are always too few young men who want to attend seminaries, women
could be of immense help. As I said before, it is not a career for someone
who wants power or wants to get rich, but rather for a person who wants
to serve people, and I think that describes many women."

"I think so too," I said. I asked her to tell me about the training.

"That's not easy either," she said. "I started late. It didn't occur to
me as a young girl that a woman could be a pastor, and I didn't want to
be a religious nurse or a deaconess. I began to study chemistry. I took
several semesters of chemistry and worked as a lab assistant until I was
thirty before I decided to go back to the university to study theology."

"That was a very brave decision at thirty," I said.

"It was what I wanted and felt called to do," she said simply. "A degree
in theology requires a minimum of eight semesters, four years. I had to
pass exams in Hebrew, Greek and Latin and take courses in sociology,
anthropology and psychology as well as in Bible study, Church history
and theology. Nowadays a pastor must be a qualified counsellor and
social worker as well as a spiritual leader. All that takes time and work."

"Does one take a qualifying exam after the four years?" I asked.

"There is a general examination after four years. If one passes one
must work as an apprentice in the field for two years, and take a second
examination, and only then can he be ordained."

"That's exhaustive. Were there any other women students at the seminary while you were there?" I asked.

"A few," Ruth said. "Perhaps ten or so, but I don't know how many
qualified finally. I've kept in touch with three, but only one is now actually active in the ministry. It is still very hard for women."

We talked a little about Ruth's background and family. Both her
parents come from Saxony, but they had lived in Berlin since before she
was born.

"I was born and brought up here," she said. "I studied several semesters
in Paris and in Vienna and then returned to finish theology in Berlin.
I've worked in Austria and in West Germany, but I've spent most of my
life in Berlin."

She explained that her parents had lost their apartment during the war.
"Bombed out," she said, "like most Berliners. We'd owned a co-operative
apartment in the downtown area. For a good many years after that we
lived in makeshift housing, but late in the 1950s, perhaps 1958 or 1959,
we found an apartment in a new building in Schöneberg. It's very pleasant. The rooms aren't as large or the ceiling as high as in our old build-

ing, but they are sunny and comfortable, and we are close to a lovely park in a quiet neighborhood. We have been lucky."

I asked whether her parents still have friends and relatives in East Berlin and in the G.D.R.

"Oh yes, cousins and old friends. They write now and then, and we send an occasional package over. I know that economic conditions are much better over there these days, that the people no longer suffer any real need, but there are so many little luxuries and small useful things that they cannot buy! I send a package about once a month."

"Does your office have any contact with the East?" I asked.

"We are very much interested in developments over there, but as an organization we are not allowed to send over any packages. Only individuals may send packages to other individuals. It's surprising how after all these years of separation so many people here in the West still send off a monthly package to someone in the East. The Berliners are especially good about it. We never have to remind Berliners."

"Are Berliners more generous?" I asked, "or just more aware?"

"Well, they can't help being more aware, can they?" Ruth asked. "But I think they are also more mature socially, more cosmopolitan, less provincial than other Germans and probably also simply more generous."

"You like them," I said, and she smiled.

"Well, I am one. But yes, I love Berliners. I have always found them more spontaneous, more willing to sacrifice even for strangers than any other people I've known. The average citizen in Munich or Cologne has to be talked into contributing for the relief of earthquake victims in Peru or of starving babies in Nigeria, not the Berliner. He knows that the entire world concerns him."

"Do you find Berliners more likely to volunteer their time and work in fund-raising or in helping in hospitals and orphanages?" I asked.

"Oh, not like you Americans!" Ruth said. "One of the things I find most impressive about America is the willingness of upper- and middle-class women to donate not just their money but their time, their physical labor to charities and to their churches. That has not been the tradition here. The middle-class German woman is more apt to regard what you call volunteer work as undignified, not fit for a lady. She may give you a check or her old clothes but she is not going to roll up her sleeves and get to work. But we are trying to change that. We have a labor shortage in Berlin, as you know, and so we need volunteers for hospitals, day nurseries, old people's homes. It will take a bit of re-education, but we are working on it, and it's not surprising that we are having better results in Berlin than in the Federal Republic."

"Maybe Berliners are a little less stuffy as well as more generous," I suggested.

"I think so. I think they are quicker on the uptake too. They see the need and they respond. A couple of years back we had an amusing incident here in West Berlin. One day at noon all the air-raid sirens of the city began to scream. Something or someone had accidentally set them off. And what did the Berliners do? Scream in panic? Rush for air-raid shelters? Tear out of the city? Not a bit! They shrugged, laughed and made jokes."

"Sangfroid," I said and she smiled.

"We occasionally have technical failures even in West Berlin, but thank God we don't have failure of nerves. Good thing too, isn't it?" she asked.

I suddenly realized that I had stayed too long and that Pastor Ruth must have other duties. I thanked her and she walked with me to the elevator.

"I'll be looking forward to seeing your book," she said. "I hope that you will say something nice about Berliners, and I hope too that you'll do what you can to encourage more young women to enter the professions, all professions including mine."

"I will," I promised, and she smiled and waved as the elevator swallowed me.

21

The Evangelical Youth Center

"Are you and Carl old friends?" the young American pastor asked me.

"His aunt in Munich is a very old friend of mine. I used to live in her house in Bogenhausen. That's where I met Carl," I explained.

"I find it easy to make friends in Berlin," he said. "I've been here for a year now and I've already made some awfully good friends, people I shall want to keep in touch with when I go back to the States. Now this," he explained walking ahead of me into a large room, "is our meeting room."

Pastor Bill was conducting me through the Victorian town house which serves as a youth center for the Evangelical Church. Once the house had been luxurious. The rooms are spacious, the ceilings high, the floors parquet, but all luxury had been stripped away to make the house functional and to curb the cost of upkeep. The double drawing room we entered boasted no Oriental carpets, no brocade or velvet curtains. Folding chairs were stacked against the wall and at the end of the room stood a plain rectangular table.

"We use this for lectures or meetings," Bill said.

"And this used to be the dining room," he continued, leading me across the hall. "Almost a state dining room," he said. "Now we use it for coffee and snacks and for an occasional luncheon."

Several young men and boys were sitting in twos and fours at small tables scattered about the room. Some were drinking coffee from thick mugs, others drank Cokes in glasses of assorted sizes and colors. Some were playing checkers, others just talking quietly. One young boy was

286

sprawled in a comfortable chair in front of the window reading a paper-back.

"Hi, Pastor Bill," one of the young men called. "Don't forget you're supposed to drive us to the soccer game this afternoon."

Bill grinned, "No, I won't forget. Just you round up the fellows on time."

We walked through the dining room into a huge kitchen sparkling with chrome and tile and white porcelain. Three boys were washing and drying coffee mugs. A fourth was making sandwiches at the counter. We all said hello.

Bill pointed to the shelves and cabinets. "We've got an assortment of dishes and glasses, all gifts from volunteers. The boys do their own cooking when they want a snack or coffee, and they wash up afterwards. Of course when we give an official luncheon volunteer women come in to cook."

"Just who are your young men?" I asked.

"Well, the director and I are pastors for all the male Evangelical apprentices in West Berlin. That's a lot. I visit each vocational school in the city and talk with the boys of our confession."

"Do you give religious instruction?" I asked. "Or do you counsel?"

"Theoretically both," he said, "but actually I don't try to instruct them in formal religion. Mostly I just go into the classroom, perch on the desk and say 'Well, here I am. What do you want to talk about?' and they talk."

"Do they talk?" I asked and he nodded vigorously. "About religion or personal problems?"

"As a matter of fact, mostly about politics. These kids are amazingly well informed and they're interested in everything on earth, especially in anything about America. Of course they know I'm American, so mostly they ask questions about the States, clever questions."

Naturally I asked what kind of questions, and Bill answered, "All kinds. They want to know about the difference between our two political parties, about campaigns and elections, about urban problems, crime in the streets, drug addiction and of course about racial problems. They always come around to race."

"Do they ask to embarrass you or because they want to know?" I asked.

"Oh, most of them because they want to know. Trouble is I don't always know the answers. I went to a theological seminary; I'm not an economist or a political scientist."

"Are their questions that specific?" I asked.

He nodded. "Sometimes they are very specific or complex, and I have to admit that I just don't know."

"How do they respond to your not knowing?" I asked.

"Oh, they like it. I mean, I think it makes them believe me. I've never been a teacher before but I use the old teacher's trick. I ask them to look up the answers. I send them off to the U.S.I.S. library so often that I'll bet our friends down there could wring my neck!"

"I'll bet they're delighted! Do the boys actually go and look things up?" I asked, incredulous.

"Yes. They're terrific! They're not young scholars, of course, they're apprentices. They work in factories and shops part time and go to school only two days a week, so they're busy, but they are interested, and they want to know things, so they make time to find out. Mind you, they won't read anything too abstract or too complicated, but they will read good journalism and popular biographies. They're awfully interested in the Kennedys and in Martin Luther King."

"It sounds as though you have lively classes."

"We do," he said enthusiastically. "Of course, it isn't always politics. After a few sessions, when they come to know me, they often bring up personal questions as well. At first they ask about choosing a career, about getting along with the boss or with parents and then, when they see that I'm not going to be moralistic with them, they start to get more personal."

"You mean they ask you about sex?" I asked, and he blushed.

"Well, about love and marriage," he amended. "They ask rather young and naive questions like how a boy can know when he's in love, and when a young man is old enough to marry."

"Can you answer those questions?" I asked with mild malice.

"No! I've never been in love and I'm not married, but I can tell them what love isn't," he said.

"That is a great deal," I acknowledged. "In fact it's the most many of us ever learn."

He nodded. "It seems so, judging by most of the marriages one sees and hears about. Sometimes I get them to answer my questions, and I think they like that even better. I ask them about Germany, about Berlin, about their homes and families."

"Then you learn as much as they do?" I asked. As we talked we had been walking slowly through the house, looking into smaller rooms used for small meetings, for reading, for writing letters or playing quiet games.

Bill glanced at his watch. "I promised to take you to our club director at ten, so we have a few minutes. Would you like to sit here in the
sun and talk for a while?" He pointed to comfortable chintz-covered
armchairs next to a window facing the garden. The window was wide
open and the fragrance of summer flowers drifted in.

"Lovely," I said and thanked him.

"Funny," he said apologetically, "but Protestant clergyman here in
Germany are quite different from ours back home. A lot of ministers
I know at home take a dim view of smoking, and as for drinking even
wine and beer, that's downright sinful. Here?" he shrugged. "Well, I
don't mean ministers are drunkards or even that they're self-indulgent.
They're very abstemious and disciplined; in fact, maybe that's why they're
not afraid of cigarettes and a little alcohol; they know they won't go to
excess?"

"Yes, partly, but wine and beer are foods here. They are part of the
family pattern, a child growing up associates them with family meals
and with celebrations at Christmas and birthdays, not with saloons and
drunkenness. And surely, Bill, Lutheran ministers at home are not so
puritanical?"

"They are where I come from in the Middle West; at least the ones
I've known were. I went to seminary in New York so I've met your more
cosmopolitan East coast clergymen. I admit they're different, but I'm not
sure they're not just trying to be modern and 'with it,' while these Germans are just being themselves."

"You like the Europeans?" I asked.

"I've been here only a year, but I like them very much. I'm sure I'll
feel homesick when I go back after my second year," he said wistfully.

"You will," I assured him heartlessly. "I take it you like Berliners."

"Oh, they're terrific!" he said. "As I said, they're interested in everything, and they know so much about their city, about local politics and
government that they put me to shame. Gosh, I didn't know nearly as
much about New York when I was a student there. But I guess the situation in Berlin is special. They are sort of on the griddle, aren't they?
I suppose they have to be interested and to know. Anyway, even the
quietest, slowest of my pupils has a viewpoint and argues it articulately.
I'm impressed. And yes, I like them. They're so alive."

"Do you see many of the boys outside of school?" I asked. "Do they come
here to the center?"

"They're all invited," Bill said. "Friday evenings we hold open house
for boys from all the schools. We serve a buffet supper, and the boys
sit around and get acquainted. Uusually we don't have an organized

program on Fridays, just informal discussion, but we announce specialized activities, and those who are interested can sign up."

"You have subgroups, then, or committees?" I asked.

"Sort of clubs within the club. We have a discussion group, for instance, which invites guest speakers or shows films. We have a theater
group and of course we have sports groups, some who make up teams,
others who go and watch professionals. Once in a while a group arranges
a dance and they invite girls."

"I hope so!" I said, and he laughed.

"Twice a year we have a really elaborate dance, once in the spring, a
kind of spring festival, and of course at Christmas. Christmas is our
busiest time of the year, since after all we're a Christian club."

I asked whether many apprentices were genuinely active in the club
and he sighed, "Well, no, not nearly enough! Nothing like a majority
even come here, and of those who come, most are passive. Only a very
small minority actually take hold, accept responsibility and really run
things. But I suppose that's true everywhere. It was certainly so when I
was at college, and even at the seminary.

"And those boys who are active," he continued, "are really active.
When they're planning a party or an outing, they work all kinds of hours
to make the event successful, and they really are successful. So, I suppose as long as we have a willing and ambitious minority, we should be
happy."

Again he consulted his watch. "Almost time to see our leader," Bill
said. "I wish you could stay for lunch. Our Manchester visitors will be
back by then."

"Manchester, England?" I asked.

"We have about twenty young English apprentices here for a visit," he
said. "There are, of course, Christian youth groups in many countries,
which are affiliated. We often exchange visits, even with Catholic groups
in France and Spain or Italy, for instance. We've been exchanging visits
with the Manchester club for years now, since about 1960. In the summer they send a group to us, and every spring some of our boys go to
England."

"It sounds like a good idea," I said. "How do they travel?"

"We hire one of those big buses and cross the Channel by ferry.
When we get to Manchester the boys are farmed out to private families,
and the English Christian societies arrange tours to museums, factories,
soccer games and even to the theater. Here in Berlin the English youngsters stay with parents of our members or at the homes of adult volunteers. They eat either with these families or here at the club. Most of

the tickets for games and shows are free, so all in all they get a very cheap vacation. They'd have to, because as apprentices they aren't earning full-scale wages."

"It's a marvellous idea, and they really come to know Berliners too. It's much better than staying in a hotel or even in a youth hostel."

"We think so," he said. "Not only do they feel more at home staying with families rather like their own at home, that is, working-class families, where they don't have to feel shy or put on company manners, but they learn about German life, and our Berliners learn about English life. The English even learn a little of our language. Trade-school language courses aren't very advanced. Most of our boys don't know much English nor do their English counterparts know much German, but you'd be surprised and amused at how well they communicate. They all have pocket dictionaries or phrase books, Berlin hosts and English visitors alike, and they are constantly diving into a pocket for the book, thumbing through it for a phrase, and implementing all this with signs and gestures and a lot of laughter. They get along beautifully, and it's rather good for international friendship that both sides are equally bad at each other's language."

"No German technological superiority or English snobbishness?" I asked, and Bill just laughed.

"With these kids? Gosh no! They just have a ball."

We rose then to go to the director's office. As we passed through the hall Bill paused to show me the bulletin board.

"You can see here some of our activities for the next month or so," he said. "There are announcements and also lists where boys can sign up for trips or shows or games. We're having a jazz concert next Saturday, a film and discussion on Thursday and a dance in two weeks."

"Do they bring girls to the jazz concerts?" I asked.

"Some do," he said. "We don't encourage them to bring girls to discussion groups, not because we don't like females or disapprove of girl-friends, but because we think boys this age are more relaxed without girls around and will speak more freely. We think they need a place where they can relax among other boys and be themselves. Perhaps theoretically they ought to be able to do that with girls around, but in fact working-class boys that age usually do not, and we try to deal with them as they are, not as they ought to be."

"Probably sensible, and certainly Christian," I said.

"Look," he pointed. "Here are announcements of tours and camping trips. We hire buses or volunteers provide cars and groups go off to visit cities in West Germany or camp in the mountains or at the shore.

Our bus trips to Cologne or Munich cost only about a hundred marks. The boys bring their tents and food and cook along the way. Boys of sixteen or seventeen enjoy that, and it's a cheap way to see Germany."

"Do you often take them abroad?" I asked, and he nodded.

"We have a group going to the Soviet Union," he said. "And here is a list of volunteers to act as hosts for foreign visitors to Berlin."

"Do your youngsters pay dues?" I asked.

"No, there is no formal membership. Everyone is welcome to come as often as he likes, be as active as he likes. People just sign up for activities, and sometimes, as for bus tours, there is a charge to pay part of the cost. We get a lot of donations, soccer tickets for instance, and cheap theater tickets, and the general cost of running the club is subsidized by the Church Council through the Church tax."

As we walked toward the director's office, I asked the young minister how long he would stay in Berlin. "I'm supposed to stay another year. The World Council of Churches arranges these overseas tours of duty," he explained, "and I've been assigned here for two years. I wish it could be longer. I may just find some other slot in Berlin," he said, hopefully.

He had already told me that he was unmarried. I supposed him to be in his late twenties. "I have a furnished room here in Berlin," he said. "It's rather small, but it's within walking distance of the center, and I have a darling landlady. Well, she's a bit of a character. Her hair is a different color every week. I guess she likes surprises. One week it was bright red, the next a kind of muddy black, but mostly it's sort of mixed."

"Tortoiseshell?" I asked.

He nodded. "Yes, only she's not a cat. She's really very nice."

"So are cats," I said.

"Yes, of course," he said hastily. "My landlady is a gossipy, laughing, spontaneous soul. She tells me all sorts of scandals about old Berlin and even a few about contemporary Berlin. She seems to think I am a little boy and so she looks after me. She does my washing and mending, for which I'm grateful, and fusses and clucks when I have a sore throat or a cold, for which I am not. But she is kind, and she's a good cook."

"Do you eat there?" I asked.

"Two or three evenings a week," he said. "I often eat here when we have some activity. Like many Berliners, she lost her husband in the war and also was bombed out of her old apartment. She and her husband had a shop before the war, and that was bombed too, so they lost almost everything. She managed to salvage a couple of rugs and a few pieces of old furniture, and now she lives on her widow's pension and rents rooms. She has a tiny income, but she enjoys life. I suspect that in truth she's a very naughty, earthy old gal, but of course she is very respectable when Herr Pastor is around."

"You like her," I said.

"I enjoy Berlin," he said simply. "Well, here is the director's office. I will leave you. It's exactly ten!"

I laughed. "Pastor Bill, you not only enjoy Berlin, you've been assimilated!" I thanked him and wished him a good deal more happiness in Berlin.

"Wish that I find another job here, or get an extension on this one," he whispered, shook my hand and left.

I knocked, and almost immediately the heavy, panelled door opened and I stepped across the threshold into another century.

A tall, sober gentleman in dark grey welcomed me to an almost opulent room. The dark panelling and heavy dark furniture, the decorous velvet curtains retained the original atmosphere of the house. The room belonged to a century older than and a tradition different from those of the public rooms of the center. Like the difference between that young, light-hearted American and this deeply serious middle-aged German, I thought.

My German host bowed slightly and ushered me to a deep leather chair. "I've sent for coffee," he said in a quiet, deep voice. Almost immediately a spritely white-haired woman entered by another door, smiled; deposited a tray on the mahogany desk and left.

"I think perhaps I should pour," he suggested. "After all, this is a professional visit." I smiled agreement, much preferring to sit and watch and listen, grateful for the strong, Berlin coffee, served steaming hot in fragile, old Berlin cups.

"Biscuits," he said, "of a sort. Out of a box, I'd guess," but he offered the plate and I took one.

"Well, *gnädige* Frau, and what do you think of our center? Of our activities? Of your fellow American who runs everything so ably, with so much enthusiasm?"

"It works!" I said, sincerely impressed.

"It works," he repeated. "Oh, no, of course we don't accomplish miracles, and I'm not one of those sanguine people who believe that exchanging twenty young workers twice a year with the English will prevent wars. Rubbish! But it helps. We do what we can. In fact, if I may be permitted to say so, with God's help we keep trying to do more than we can." He took a sip of coffee.

"This week Manchester, next week Lyons. We're expecting a group of young French Catholics who are coming for the first time as a response to some work that a group of young Berliners did in Lyons. I don't know whether you know about 'Operation Reconciliation'?"

I said that I had heard about it and that I knew that the director was one of the founders.

"Well, a group of young men from Reconciliation spent two years in Lyons building a synagogue for a congregation of German Jews who had settled there as refugees during the nazi period. The local Catholic priest more or less adopted our youngsters, found them places to live, introduced them to his young people, and so on. Many young Germans made fast friends with the local French people, and so now they have invited some of their friends to visit us in Berlin."

"Operation Reconciliation is active all over Europe, isn't it? Do you receive return visits from all these places?" I asked.

"Indeed we do. Our people have worked in Israel, in the Soviet Union, and throughout Eastern Europe. We've had visits from Czechs and Greeks and Rumanians and we hope to welcome some Israelis soon."

"How do you manage the languages of all these East European visitors?" I asked, knowing he must speak French and English but wondering about Russian and Czech.

He laughed. "Sometimes we don't manage except with arms and feet. I can function in Greek and Hebrew because one learns those at the theological seminary. As you know much of the New Testament is in *koine,* not in the Greek of Homer or Sophocles, and many basic words are remarkably like modern Greek. But I am hopeless in Slavic languages. Still, we cope somehow." I was sure that he would always cope.

I could hardly ask bluntly whether he believed that projects like the building of synagogues and hospitals or day-care centers in countries which had been occupied by the Germans during the war could really build friendship and understanding except among the handful of local people who came into contact with the young German volunteers, but he seemed to sense my question.

"The idea behind Operation Reconciliation, you see, is not to make ourselves loved, not to buy friendship, or forgiveness. That would be presumptuous as well as foolish, wouldn't it? It would also be very poor theology, certainly for a Lutheran.

"No, our young people aren't buying honor with their voluntary work. They are building self-respect, building a personal sense of decency, of moral responsibility. They contribute their years and their effort, not to make themselves or their country loved but so that they can begin to love and accept themselves and their country, if that makes sense. They go as Christians, not just as Germans."

"But as German Christians," I said.

"Yes, that's true. They go to prove to themselves that they are both, and one hopes they will be able to live the rest of their lives accepting themselves as both. It's no panacea. Perhaps it's only a drop in the bucket."

"Perhaps it's a mustard seed?" I asked.

"We hope so, and hope too is our duty, nearly as important as love." I had finished my coffee. I knew he was busy. I rose and thanked him and he shook my hand.

"Come back to sit in on some of our meetings or suppers," he invited.

22

The City Mission

"I'm not preaching this Sunday, but I have to be at a service at one of our old people's homes. I said I'd read the lesson and have coffee with the old people afterwards," Carl explained.

"You've already been too kind," I protested. "I can take a taxi to the mission."

"You can do no such thing," he insisted. "I'll drop you off and pick you up at around eleven. I tell you what, we'll find a café in the neighborhood and, if you're finished much before eleven, you go there, order a cup of coffee and wait. I won't be late."

I thanked him meekly knowing that it does very little good to argue with Carl when he is determined on a good work. I agreed to be ready on Sunday by eight.

Of course he was punctual and so was I. I was waiting on the corner when the elderly blue Volkswagen puttered up, and Carl bounded out to open the door for me. "Another sunny day," he said exuberantly. "Lucky," he added, "because we're going to a gloomy part of the city."

"Is there a gloomy part of Berlin?" I asked, unbelieving.

"Oh, we have our slums too, you know," he said, driving on along the broad, cheerful street. "You'll see. Berlin even has a skid row, a refuge for alcoholics and derelicts, a den for ex-convicts and street girls."

"Berlin always seems so hygienic, so progressive!" I said, wondering.

"It is. And from what I've heard of other cities, whether New York or London or Hong Kong, Berlin's slums are relatively hygienic and our underworld very tame. Still, we do have them. Well, you'll see," he predicted and drove on through the mid-city streets, then across town alongside somber railroad tracks, driving block by block away from the fashionable shops and lively sidewalk cafés, away from tall, modern apartment buildings.

296

"You see?" Carl asked. "It's gloomy already."

"Oh, not really gloomy!" I protested. "These are older houses. They seem a bit dark and drab, but the neighborhood seems perfectly respectable. Look how clean the streets are!"

"Well, the city cleans the streets," he said.

"The city cleans the streets in the Bronx and in Brooklyn too, but you should see them."

We drove on a few blocks farther into the district, and then Carl turned right into a side street and parked the Volkswagen about halfway down the block. "We're early," he said, "so let's have a look around."

We climbed out of the car and began to stroll down the almost deserted street. "Sunday morning," he said, "nothing much open." A row of shops with flats above lined one side of the street. We paused to look in turn at a stationery shop, a laundry with a price list in the window, a bakery displaying yesterday's loaves and a few dispirited cookies, a fruit and vegetable shop, its crates and bins covered. The whole street seemed wrapped in Sabbath stillness; even the pub on the corner was closed and silent.

"You see," Carl said, "it's drab and grey."

"Well, everything's closed because it's Sunday," I said reasonably. "The shops look clean." The windows were narrow, the stone of the buildings was darkened by age but the neighborhood seemed perfectly respectable.

"Those two old women trotting along to fetch their Sunday papers seem almost prim," I insisted.

"So they are," Carl admitted, "but they're poor. They may be widows living on pensions, perhaps from the East. Probably they have no relations here and so they live alone in a small room somewhere in this neighborhood."

"That's sad, Carl," I said, "but it isn't a slum! Not a real slum."

"Well, some day you'll have to take me to see a real slum. This is the best we can do in Berlin." He walked back with me to near where he'd parked the car. "There, across the street in that building that looks like a private house," he pointed, "that's your mission church. If you finish much earlier than eleven, walk around the corner and you'll see a dim little café. It's not elegant, but it's clean and as you said respectable. I'll find you." He climbed back into Bluetooth and drove off.

I looked at my watch. Of course it was still early. In Berlin I am almost always early, but I decided that I could be early for church. I walked across the street and up the shallow steps to the door of the mission. I had not yet knocked when the door opened wide and the

Fig. 17. Street children in an East Berlin working-class neighborhood (photo by Landesbildstelle, West Berlin)

mission pastor himself stood in the door smiling at me. I introduced
myself and he shook my hand, bowing.

The pastor was a distinguished-looking man. Not more than middle
height, he had a shock of white hair, brilliant blue eyes and a robust
laugh. Dynamic, I thought as he greeted me and led me inside.

"Did you know that a court pastor of the Hohenzollerns founded the
City Mission?" he asked. "Now I am the back-court pastor!"

"Are there still back courts in the old sense?" I asked. In old Berlin,
before the First World War, the poorer sections of the city were known
for their back courts. Even in such neighborhoods the relatively affluent
commanded the rooms or flats facing the streets. Though the houses
were old and inconvenient, the front rooms caught the sun and were
cheerful. The cheapest rooms and flats were those which faced the
back courtyard. These were dark and dismal.

Painters, cartoonists, playwrights and song-writers made the denizens
of Berlin's back courtyards famous, the unemployed and unemployables,
the petty thieves and prostitutes, the elderly and abandoned.

"I thought the back courts had all disappeared," I said.

"Most of them have," the pastor said. "All those that remain are scheduled to be demolished. One by one, these dismal neighborhoods are dis-
appearing, but there are a few left, and of course into these the social
rejects crowd. These are the people we serve."

I shook my head. "Berlin looks so spic and span; Berliners seem so
tidy, so well dressed. It's hard to believe there are slums and a skid row."

"We keep our slums discreetly hidden," he said, "and I suppose we
have a relatively small antisocial element for a big city, but both exist."
He led me through the meeting room in which his congregation holds
its services. It was a plain, rectangular room. Wooden folding chairs
stood in rows. At the front of the room a small square table served as
the altar; on it was a square wooden cross. To the left was a small,
electric organ. On the right a row of windows let the morning sunlight
flood the room.

We walked down the center aisle, across in front of the altar, through
a door at the left. We found ourselves in a square, utilitarian room
obviously used as a sacristy, an office and a small meeting room. Just
beyond it a second door stood open, revealing the stove and cabinets
of a kitchen.

"It's early yet—let's chat for a while," he suggested and so we sat at
a long conference table and he began to tell me about his mission
church. "Mostly old women," he said. "The really poor in our city usually are old women. Anyone who has worked regularly during his life-

Fig. 18. Elderly women in a working-class neighborhood, West Berlin (photo by
Landesbildstelle, West Berlin)

time receives a fairly decent pension. A retired man or women who was just a simple laborer receives enough to live modestly, but the widow of a laborer—well, they say it's not enough to live on but too much to die on."

"I suppose it just covers food and shelter," I said.

He nodded. "Very simple food and often rather mean shelter. These widow's pensions were never meant to support an old woman entirely. It was supposed that she would have some savings and very probably sons and daughters or at least nephews and nieces, grandchildren, someone to help her. But today so many of our women are all alone in the world."

"Refugees?" I asked. "Or have their relatives been killed or emigrated?"

"Many of each," he said. "There are so many tragic old women in West Berlin with not a soul in the world; many others have relatives abroad or in the East but no one here. In this district our women are lonely and isolated old people. Some of them have no other recreation, no other source of friendship than the mission. You should see the dismal rooms and flats they live in. No central heating, no hot water, and often the only toilet in the building is a little privy in the courtyard. When Grandma wants to use it, she has to totter down four or five flights of stairs and out into the cold courtyard, even in the snow and rain. Those are my parishioners."

"It doesn't sound like Berlin," I said.

"It's not the Kurfürstendamm or the chic suburbs."

"Do you have only elderly women in your congregation?" I asked.

"Mostly," he said, "but we also have men who are alcoholics or misfits, young women who are married to drug addicts or alcoholics, prostitutes, and some very sad youngsters."

"Don't the young people leave the neighborhood?" I asked.

"The ones who are successful in school, in learning a trade, leave when they are old enough, but there are the younger ones who live with mothers who are sluts and fathers who are drunks or petty crooks. There are orphans living with an old grandma or *tante*. Some youngsters just don't make it in school and never are going to make it. They stay on in this neighborhood."

"Do they come to church?" I asked.

"Mostly not," he said. "I have to go after them, and often I can't do much for or with them, not until they're in real trouble."

"Sad," I said.

"Berlin is a depressing place for the kind of youngster who doesn't do well in school, who isn't especially gifted, who doesn't have many interests. The boy who has a challenging job, the bright young man or woman who has intellectual or artistic interests, these can be happy in Berlin. Berlin is an exciting place for the arts and sciences, for business and technology, but for the kind of boy who has only a routine, monotonous, unskilled job, what is there for him to do? In Hanover a bored boy can hop on his motorbike and tear out of the city to a lake or to the shore, to another city, but where can the West Berliner go? Only as far as the Wall, or the G.D.R. boundary. It's as though he were on a carousel: he can go around and around but he is always surrounded."

"Don't some of them leave the city?" I asked.

"Some do. They get jobs in West Germany or try to emigrate. Some don't have the energy, the enterprise, for that, and they feel trapped. And then they trap themselves into a life of vice or crime; they take to alcohol or drugs or gambling. Some end in jail, some on the streets, many here. Some commit suicide. Here in Berlin we have the world's highest suicide rate, and I suppose my parish holds something like the record for the record city."

"Don't you sometimes feel hopeless?" I asked.

"I sometimes feel that I don't do enough," he said. "I have one advantage, though, and that is my white hair. Even these rough and sometimes desperate kids can relate to a grandfather. The image of father either doesn't mean anything to them at all, or it's entirely negative. Try to tell one of these street kids that he should love and trust God and pray to Him as 'our Father' and he will look at you as though you were a lunatic. He might say, 'Father?' scornfully and then, 'Have you seen my father?' and show you a drunken brute or lazy lout. But a grandfather is something they understand. Grandfathers are very rare since the war, but there are a few around, and they are usually trusted and loved, and so generally they are willing to trust me.

"Sometimes I get discouraged," he went on. "About a week ago a down-at-the-heels man turned up here toward evening. He was an alcoholic like so many. He began to tell me his problems, and he rambled, and I'm afraid I was a little impatient. I was worried about one of my elderly parishioners who was alone and sick in her little cold-water flat and I'd promised to bring her some supper. I'm afraid I cut the man short and told him to come back the next day.

"He was apologetic, but I thought I had reassured him. He promised to come back in the morning and left his name and address. The next day he didn't turn up. I was awfully busy. We had a couple of emergencies that day, and in the evening I had to rush to an old man who was dying.

I spent most of the night with him, and so the next day I was overtired and again very busy. I'm afraid I forgot about the depressed alcoholic.

"On the fourth day it suddenly occurred to me that he had not come back. I asked my assistant whether he'd heard anything, and he hadn't. I hunted through my desk and finally found the slip of paper with the name and address and walked around there. It was only a couple of blocks away. I spoke to the landlady, and she said she hadn't seen him in two days, so I trudged up the dark stairs to his third-floor back room. I was the first to find him. He was lying across his unmade bed with his throat slit."

"Awful!" I said.

"It wasn't the first suicide I'd found, *gnädige* Frau, but this one I felt was my fault. I'd forgotten about him."

I wanted to say something but there was nothing to say. The pastor looked up at the round, stainless-steel electric clock and said that it was almost time for the service.

"I'll show you in and then leave you, but don't forget to stay for coffee with us afterwards."

I thanked him and we went back into the meeting hall. I took a chair in a back row near the open windows and waited while the room gradually filled. The pastor had been right. Most of the people who filed in and quietly took seats were elderly women, but all of them looked tidy and respectable. Their clothes were dowdy and certainly not new, but they were clean and well pressed and many of the old women had spruced up venerable suits with a bit of lace or a fresh flower. They looked well groomed and almost festive in their Sunday best.

A trim young woman wearing a navy blue suit with a frilly white blouse walked to the front and sat at the electric organ. The congregation became silent as she began to play an old-fashioned hymn. Everyone seemed to know the words of all the hymns and of the service by heart. The pastor did not follow the traditional Lutheran liturgy. The service was very simple, consisting of several well-loved hymns, an opening and closing prayer, a short Bible-reading and a very short sermon. After the benediction and a moment of silent prayer the young organist played a rousing recessional. The pastor walked to the rear door without ceremony, and as the congregation left he shook hands and chatted a little with each person. I stood and listened, noting that he gave each lonely old person or discouraged young one a personal message.

The last to leave was a fragile, grey-haired woman. He walked with her to the door and waved an almost tender good-bye, then he turned and escorted me to the sacristy. Mrs. W., the organist and wife of the assistant pastor, already had the water boiling. She came out of the kitchen to shake my hand and promised me coffee instantly.

Her husband, young Pastor W., also greeted me and asked how I'd enjoyed the service.

"Please excuse these rather rough mugs," Frau W. said. "They belong to our youth group and they're pretty much of a hodgepodge."

The pastor explained why he had adopted an informal, unconventional order of service. "I find our Lutheran liturgy very beautiful and very appropriate for large churches, for normal congregations, but this is an informal church and a special congregation. What our people need most is warmth and affection, a personal touch. The liturgy is lovely, but it is impersonal; in it the pastor is an authority figure, a priest. Here I have to be their friend, be close to them, not above them, so we've worked out this program, and they seem to like it."

"They sing lustily," I said.

"They do indeed," the organist commented, "and usually even on key, old though most of them are. That's because we are careful to choose songs they know. I'd love to experiment with something new or exciting, but not here. This is not the place for it."

"No, not here," her husband said. "This isn't the place for us to express our wants. These people need too much from us."

"We want our whole service to be warm-hearted and free," the pastor said.

"You know," the young assistant interposed, "the members of our congregation aren't just spectators at the service, they're all missionaries. They're a remarkably active and very generous congregation, poor though they are. Every person who was here today has assumed the responsibility of visiting and talking to at least ten other people in his neighborhood during the week, even strangers."

"Do they invite them to church," I asked, "or give them tracts?"

"Both," Pastor W. said. "Sometimes they just talk and try to cheer them up and see whether they can help them in any way."

"Our members also raise money for famine victims," his wife said. "Poor as our people are, they collected almost a thousand marks to aid starving children in a recent overseas disaster."

"That's amazing," I said.

"They need to be unselfish, *gnädige* Frau," the pastor said. "It gives their lives meaning. Most of them have no one to love them, and so they need to love."

"It's very wise of you to put them to work," I said.

"We work too," he said vigorously.

"We are very busy. This is no five-days-a-week job," the young pastor said. "We have other missions besides this one; a mission for the blind, one for prisoners and a midnight mission especially for prostitutes."

"*Ja, ja,*" the older man said nodding. "I have to preach to the ladies of the evening. Frau W. forbids her husband to do it, and my white hair protects me." We laughed.

"Of course, I've read that in Paris the street girls go to service at the Madeleine, but I'm surprised they go to church in Berlin."

"It is not just a cliché of fiction that many prostitutes are deeply religious. Many are. We have regular members of our midnight congregation. We don't try to reform them or make them feel guilty. They already feel guilty or they wouldn't be there. We give them what they need, and that is a sense of friendliness, a sense that someone cares about them as people. We try to make them feel self-respect if only because God loves them."

"Does it help, do you think?" I asked.

"Oh, *ja,* I think so. They are not saints, my magdalens, but at least I think the ones who come to service regularly are a little less unhappy."

"And our pastor works very hard begging," Frau W. said.

"Indeed, I do!" he said. "I am a famous beggar. I put on my clerical collar and go to all kinds of places to beg. Sometimes I embarrass people, but often I embarrass them into giving money. I walk right into bars and nightclubs, banks and boards of directors' meetings and I talk about Jesus."

"And they give?" I asked.

"Sometimes I guess they give just to get rid of me, but sometimes the most unlikely and worldly people really get interested in our work. Last week I walked into the Europa Club, which is a very fashionable and sophisticated club at the Europa Center. There was a rather noisy party going on and one gentleman turned to ask what the pastor had brought along to the party. I answered 'news about God,' and I think I shocked the poor man. He certainly thought such a blunt answer in questionable taste!"

"Did he walk away?" I asked.

"No indeed! He gobbled a bit like a turkey cock, but then he asked whether I was sure I knew so much about God. I answered that of course God knew more about me and him than we could know about Him and he blushed, but he did ask me to talk about the mission, and before I left I'd collected quite a few checks. Sizable ones too."

"Good!" I said. "You're brave."

"One must be brave," he said simply. "One must not be afraid to appear gauche or foolish. One must be willing to be a fool for Christ. I go everywhere, into bowling alleys and pubs, into chic parties and stuffy meetings. I talk with people of all classes, all ages. I tell the respectable people of Berlin not just about God, and many of them don't know Him, but also about the Berlin they don't know, the Berlin of the back streets and back courtyards, the Berlin many of them would prefer to forget. It's amazing how these seemingly shallow, selfish, worldly people can be touched, in both senses of the word." We laughed.

"They give, and it's not only Berliners who do. I beg all over West Germany. We are the free corps of the Church. We are supported only by free-will gifts, not by the Church tax. Every penny we spend, we raise. There is one congregation in the Siegerland in West Germany which has adopted us as their special project. I travel there at least once a year to report on our activities and give a series of lectures on Berlin, and I always come back with thousands of marks."

"That's wonderful," I said.

"It's good for them. The Church tax is too impersonal. Christians should make a personal, individual sacrifice once in a while, not for an abstraction called 'the Church' but for real, individual people.

"I beg from everyone, even from cabinet officials and from our Mayor.

"I travel a lot," he said. "An itinerant beggar! Of course, V.I.P.s also travel a lot, so I frequently run into some prominent man at the airport waiting for a flight. I make it a point never to sit next to a political or business leader, but just a few minutes before we are about to land, I approach him and begin a conversation. That way he is not afraid that I'll preach to him for the whole flight." We all giggled.

"No, these days it doesn't pay to bore people. No one has time for long sermons. I've made rather a specialty of very short sermons. I give a series of what we call 'Minute Meditations' late afternoons at the Kaiser Wilhelm Memorial Church. Each meditation lasts exactly four minutes. I never run over. It is gratifying how many young people come, both young workers and students."

We all finished our coffee and politely refused Frau W.'s offer of more. The pastor continued, "It's not any good being long-winded and stuffy these days. Jesus used a direct approach, and that's what we churchmen must do too. As long as there are poor and desperate and lonely people in Berlin we will raise money to help them, but we have to do more than that. We have to make our prosperous, sometimes smug, successful Berliners remember and think about their less fortunate brothers and sisters."

"These people in our district need friendliness and concern and love," Frau W. said. "Government can supply their pension and provide medical care and even new housing, but only individual human beings and God can give them warmth and love."

I thanked them all and strolled thoughtfully down the somber street to wait for Carl at the little café.

23

Renate

Renate was one of the people I met in East Berlin quite by accident. I very often go over to East Berlin on my own without having any specific appointments or goals and just take photographs, wander along the main streets and back alleys, browse in shops, make notes on prices and goods and talk, if possible, to East Berliners.

One day I had crossed over after an early lunch and had gone window-shopping along the Karl Marx Allee, conscientiously comparing prices and goods with those of the previous year. I spent some time prowling among the crowded shelves of a bookshop, coveting some of the cheap editions of art books but dismissing them as too heavy to carry around.

It was a glorious June day, but after two hours of wandering I was beginning to long for a shaded sidewalk café and something to drink. Somehow the official restaurants named for East European cities, Moscow, Prague, and Budapest, set along the Karl Marx Allee like so many sturdy fortresses of public nutrition, did not appeal. I longed for something gay and light, suitable to a brilliant spring afternoon, and thought wistfully of the many colorful cafés along the Kurfürstendamm.

Surely there must be one here! I told myself, and remembering a hazy vision of outdoor tables and gay umbrellas somewhere near the Hotel Berolina, I turned and walked in that direction. My memory had been accurate. Within minutes I arrived at a sidewalk café resplendent with doll-sized white metal tables and chairs, all empty. I wondered why. It was exactly the German coffee hour, and the weather was perfect. I shrugged and sat down at one of the small tables. After a minute or two a white-uniformed waitress leaned out of the door to tell me that it was the wrong time for outdoor service, presumably because the sun was shining or it was Tuesday. I sighed. Indoor coffee did not appeal to me but sitting did, and I was as thirsty as I was curious about all aspects of life in East Berlin.

Fig. 19. Sidewalk café in downtown East Berlin (photo by Landesbildstelle, West Berlin)

Inside it was warm and stuffy, as I had feared, but there were a few tables next to the windows on the shaded side. I chose one and was just draping the too heavy jacket I had been carrying over the back of the chair when a second uniformed young woman hurried over to me and whispered in a polite but worried tone, "It is forbidden to hang coats on the chairs!" She pointed to a coat rack.

Having complied with Order Number 372, I sat down gratefully and ordered a pot of coffee. It appeared with gratifying efficiency and was hot and drinkable. I began to glance over the notes I had made. When I looked up, I noticed a young mother with two attractive little girls sitting at the table next to mine. The children seemed from another century, with their long blond braids, their home-made, hand-embroidered pastel cotton dresses, one green, one pink. The mother smiled at me, and before I had finished my coffee she leaned toward me and spoke.

"I couldn't help noticing that you are taking notes, and I wondered whether I dare ask if you are a journalist."

When I told her that I was working on a book about Berlin and that I came from the United States, she said, "Oh, may we come to your table and talk to you? My girls have never met an American."

She introduced them as Gertrude, who was nine, and Ilse, seven. The girls stood, curtsied and smiled politely but looked awestricken.

Of course, I invited them to join me, and Renate was soon telling me about her work. I had hoped to meet an elementary schoolteacher, preferably informally, so I was delighted when she said she taught second grade. She turned out to be extremely well-informed, enthusiastic, and voluble, in short a Godsend.

She was a small-boned woman with a rounded, motherly face framed by a cap of shining blond hair. I guessed her to be about thirty-five, cheerful, and patient, my idea of the ideal teacher for the second grade. She said that she had always wanted to be a teacher but that she had married before she had finished training. Her husband was an engineer, and they lived in a semidetached house in one of the suburbs in which Berlin abounds.

"After Ilse was born, seven years ago, I decided that I would go back and take up my training where I had left off. There was still an acute shortage of teachers in the G.D.R., especially elementary schoolteachers, and so the government began a crash program to help people, especially married women, qualify quickly. I applied and was immediately accepted."

"Seven years ago?" I asked. "How long did you have to train?"

"Well, since I already had some credits I did it in two years. The program gave us the basic essentials, and then we could continue our training Saturday mornings or evenings and summers. I had to go Saturdays for only one year, but I still like to return for a summer or evening course now and then to keep up to date."

"Did you begin teaching right away? What would that be, five years ago?" I asked.

She nodded. "Immediately, and I was lucky to find a job in our neighborhood school so that I can walk to work. Later Trudy began at the same school and I could take her every morning. Now Ilse is there in the second grade, and Trudy goes to a school just a few blocks away."

"When you started teaching, Ilse was only a baby. How did you manage?"

"Ilse was two and Trudy four, so they were too young to leave with just anybody, neighbors or baby-sitters, and there weren't yet enough nursery schools, but, luckily, my mother lives near us and she doesn't work, so she looked after the girls until they both reached school age. Now she takes them evenings or Saturdays if I have a class or a teachers' meeting."

"You *are* lucky," I said, "but you still must find that you have a lot to do looking after a family and teaching full time too."

"A tremendous lot, but by now the girls are big enough to help a little. We do our shopping on the way home from school, and weekends they help with the cleaning and laundry. Trudy is quite a good needlewoman. She mends all our clothes!"

The girls dimpled.

"This weekend," she continued, "we had a real spring cleaning. The girls worked so hard that I thought they deserved a treat, so today after school we came here for ice cream."

"We had ice cream with fruit and lots of whipped cream," Trudy explained.

Renate smiled. "We don't have ice cream after school every day," she said, apparently fearing I would think her an indulgent mother, "but the girls are such a help."

"You are lucky they are both girls," I said.

"Yes, and lucky in my profession. This way I leave school about when they do, and we walk home together. They don't have to wait around until I finish office hours. Naturally, I have lesson plans to prepare and papers to grade in the evening, but they have homework, and they also do the dishes after supper while I get to work."

"They don't mind that their mother is always busy?" I asked.

"Oh, no. They both want to be teachers, don't you?" Both girls nodded.

"Of course, at that age many girls do, but mine see how much I love teaching, and they also like school. They know how lucky they are because I tell them that schools weren't that pleasant when I was a child."

"Did you go to school in Berlin?" I asked.

"No," she said. "My father was one of those country doctors who treat the whole countryside and whose bills are never paid. We lived in a ramshackle old house in a village not far outside Berlin, and my two brothers and I went to the village school."

"The old-fashioned, one-room kind?" I asked.

"Exactly. All four primary grades in a single room in an old, musty, dingy, drafty building, and only one harassed teacher trying to keep her first-graders drawing bunnies, the fourth-graders from cheating on their arithmetic problems, and the third-graders writing a composition while she whispered a story to the second-graders. Poor teacher!"

"But I'd bet she loved it as much as you do," I ventured.

Renate looked surprised; she reflected for a moment and smiled.

"You're right! She was certainly harassed, but poor Fräulein Winters did love it, and we learned something too. She was a splendid teacher now that I think back on it, but there's no question that today's children are better off in their bright, cheerful schools with lots of sunlight and flowers and modern equipment."

I was less certain than she, but I was impressed with her dedication.

"We have just about done away with village schools in the G.D.R.," she said. "Some children still attend the first two grades in their village; others begin right away in the district school, which serves several villages. Naturally, these district schools are larger, more modern and better-equipped, and there is a teacher for each class. With a larger pool of pupils, the school can have special teachers for music or athletics, and that makes the program more varied. They can have a library, a gym, workrooms, and labs."

"But the children are away from home all day," I said.

"Yes, but they have a good hot lunch at school and buses take them back and forth. Besides, these days, even in the country, many mothers work, so they are grateful to have their children looked after for most of the day."

"The G.D.R. has done a lot of reorganization of the school system, hasn't it?" I asked.

Renate nodded. "Yes, we put a lot of emphasis on schools here. I think it would be fair to say that the main aim of the socialist educational program has been to eliminate the traditional division of children into academic and nonacademic schools. We have gradually transformed our school system step by step, so that by now all children attend a basic school. We call it the *Allgemeinbildende polytechnische Oberschule:* comprehensive polytechnic high school. Why we should call it a high school when there is no lower school except kindergarten, I don't know, but we do."

She grinned in her relaxed, friendly way.

"How long do all the pupils stay together in this polytechnic school?" I asked.

"Most of them through the tenth grade," she said. "Some enter special trade schools in the ninth grade, but most stay through the tenth. Eventually we hope to extend the polytechnic school to twelve years. We already have a few twelve-year schools."

"How do pupils qualify to enter the university?" I asked. "Do you still have the *Abitur?*"

"Oh, yes," she said. "Naturally, within the polytechnic schools the child has a choice of curricula during the higher grades. Those who show a decided academic bent go on to the eleventh and twelfth grades and then take their *Abitur* and enter the university. Others attend a combined technical and academic school for three years, then take their *Abiturs,* and enter a university."

"And the rest?" I asked.

"They begin work as apprentices immediately, and some attend a trade school in combination with their apprenticeships. Some of them later apply for admission to universities or attend evening schools, of course. Many of our best university students are former factory workers, housewives or skilled artisans."

"How do you sort out the children?" I asked. "How do you help them decide which path they will follow?"

"We are very conscientious about that," Renate said. "Of course, I teach only the second grade so I have nothing to do with that, but I have several friends who teach in the eighth and ninth grades, and they tell me about it. As soon as a child enters the eighth grade, his teacher and the parents' council for his class begin to review his entire record."

"Parents' council?" I asked.

"Well," she explained, "every school has a general parents' council elected by all the parents for the whole school to supervise the general running of the school. It has committees in charge of the library, the cafeteria and so on. The council appoints a subcommittee in charge of each class."

"I see," I said. "And does this subcommittee work regularly with the class teacher?"

"Yes. At least once during each marking period the teacher reports on each pupil to the committee. Pupils who seem to be having special problems may be called in to meet with the council committee and the teacher, or his parents may be invited to the meeting."

"This happens every year in every class?" I asked.

"Yes, but in the eighth and ninth grades the work intensifies. Each pupil takes a series of achievement and aptitude tests, his whole record is reviewed and perhaps his earlier teachers are called in to give their evaluations. Meanwhile the youngsters are given every opportunity to learn about the various professions open to them. Whole classes or groups of classes visit factories, mines, farms and laboratories; they meet with trade unionists, skilled workers, managers; they look at films, read brochures, talk with counselors. The Pioneers also help."

"The party youth organization?" I asked. "What do they do?"

"They hold what they call olympiads every year, contests in art, music, science, mathematics and, of course, sports. We encourage every older pupil to enter at least one of the competitions, and sometimes we discover latent talent. There are children who are simply not challenged by day-to-day classwork or who are frightened by exams, but they throw themselves into a contest and really show what they can do, and they may be exactly the youngsters who are going to be successful research scientists or writers or musicians. So, in trying to decide a child's academic future, we take into consideration more than his school grades and test scores."

"That's good," I said. "Who has the final word, though?"

"We listen to the child's wishes and consult his parents, but the decision lies with the parents' council."

"Suppose you still make a mistake?" I asked.

"We do, of course, from time to time. In that case, the child can transfer to another program or he can attend evening school," Renate explained. "One way we guard against the consequences of mistakes is through the polytechnic program itself, of course."

"Doesn't that mean that all your secondary pupils, even those who are going on to the university, learn some kind of skill?" I asked, having read about it.

Renate nodded. "It's a good idea, I think. Every young person who is planning to go into a profession must also choose a trade, a skill, take courses, become an apprentice and qualify as a skilled worker in his field. When we first began the program, we thought it didn't matter what skill a pupil chose, but now we try to direct the youngster into an area which reflects his interests and fits in with his professional goals. That is, if he wants to be a medical doctor or dentist, we suggest that he become a lab technician or dispenser, something on that order."

"That way, if the young person discovers he wasn't cut out to be a doctor, if he doesn't make it, he has something to fall back on which reflects his interests. Yes, I can see that that is rational," I agreed.

"There is more to it. If he becomes a doctor, he will have a greater understanding of the work of the people under him and will be better able to get on with them. Naturally, the original aim of the program was to preserve a classless society, to keep young professional people and intellectuals from developing into a separate class, a remote elite. Under the polytechnic program, academic students work right along with trade-school pupils as apprentices. They may share a workbench or microscope; they eat in the same canteen, travel on the same bus, meet each other's families. We hope these experiences will establish a kind of solidarity which will last."

"Does it?" I asked. "Or are the youngsters separated by their different goals and interests?"

"I don't know. It's too early to see how it will work out. I just know the theory, but at least we are giving them a chance to know each other."

"Even if it succeeds, do you think it will be worth the cost in our highly specialized, technological society, where the young academic person has more and more to learn in his own field? Doesn't this program deflect time and energy from his intellectual development, delay his qualification?"

She nodded. "The curriculum suffers, of course. There are only so many hours in a school day, so many weeks in a term. We must make room somewhere. We have lengthened the term, but there is still sharp competition among the disciplines for the hours in each day's schedule, and you can guess which subjects go by the board."

I nodded, guessing easily. "The humanities."

"Yes, but there are compensations. So far we are finding that the young people get better grades in their academic subjects now that they are also learning a trade, perhaps because they are more stimulated or they begin to feel more like adults and become more serious, more responsible. The quality of their academic work doesn't suffer, but, of course, you are right. The emphasis on secondary education is narrowing. We have begun to include courses in cybernetics, in computer programming, in the regular secondary curriculum. Obviously, we must offer more math, more of the sciences, and pupils must specialize more narrowly sooner. It is necessary. Society needs engineers, technicians and scientists, but I agree with you that the humanities suffer."

"Don't forget you were known as a nation of philosophers and poets," I said.

"Among other things," she said and smiled. "I know, and I mourn our traditional humane education, and I agree that early specialization is dehumanizing and it saddens me. The modern world makes these demands and humanness, warmth, beauty have become luxuries. I regret the loss," she said. "I have loved the humanities too, but I quite honestly see no other way."

"First things first," I said, "but in the final analysis, we arrive at the question of which things are first."

"Exactly," she said and smiled a very warm, rather sad smile. "Oh, goodness!" she said. "It must be late! I must take my lambs home and start making supper. I have papers to grade too. When I get started talking, I am a terrible chatterbox!"

"Both of us," I said.

She gathered up her packages and helped the girls put on their light jackets.

"I hope we can meet again. Do you think that would be possible?" She asked it diffidently because it so often is impossible. "I thought you might like to visit one of our Pioneer day camps on the outskirts of the city."

"I'd love it," I said.

We arranged to meet the following day after Renate and the girls had finished school. We walked together toward the Alexander-Platz, where I planned to catch the subway. As we approached the square she pointed to a tall, up-ended oblong building.

"That belongs to us!" she said proudly. "It is the House of Teachers, a kind of club for members of the teaching profession, built with money raised by the F.D.J. and the Pioneers. Would you like to look inside?"

I had a dinner appointment with Elisabeth in West Berlin, but I said that I had time for a quick look and I would certainly be interested.

We wandered into the glass-walled reception hall. Several women and a few men were sitting in the lounge, relaxing, reading newspapers or periodicals or chatting with friends. Renate showed me a bulletin board near the elevator.

"You see," she explained, "here is the list of activities for this week: films, lectures, a string quartet on Friday, an exhibit of children's posters in the library."

The library featured an assortment of professional periodicals and journals as well as general literature. There was a recreation room, rooms for conferences and meetings, a lecture hall.

"It's an attractive building," I said, and she nodded agreement.

"It's a pleasant place to stop in when I'm shopping in the area, and sometimes I arrange to meet friends here who teach at other schools. I also come for a concert or lecture now and then and bring my husband. Teachers are important here in the G.D.R.!"

Outside again we strolled toward the subway entrance. I thanked Renate for her time and said good-bye to Trudy and Ilse. They curtsied and she shook my hand. We agreed to meet exactly there the following afternoon.

"Don't worry if you're delayed at the crossing. We'll wait. If it should rain, we'll wait inside the House of Teachers."

Luckily the next day was also brilliantly sunny and comfortably warm. There had been no delay at the checkpoint, and so I arrived punctually at three to find Renate, Trudy, and Ilse hurrying toward me. The girls, each dressed in green-and-white-checked pinafores, braids bobbing as they ran, greeted me gaily.

Renate was shocked when I suggested that we take a taxi out to the Pioneer camp.

"It's far!" she said. "It will be expensive!"

I assured her that it was a special occasion. "It will be an outing for the children," I said, "and besides, I can deduct it from my income tax."

Apparently Renate did not understand about income tax or deductions for professional expenses, but she accepted the treat for the girls, and we climbed into an aged taxi just delivering travellers to the Hotel Berolina. Taxis are still rare in East Berlin, so we were extremely fortunate.

Renate was right. It was very far to the camp. We drove the full length of the Karl Marx Allee, out past the zoo, and on into suburbs almost like rural villages where the streets were lined with tall, ancient trees. The taxi turned into a side road and drew up before the broad gates of the Ernst Thälmann Pioneer Park.

I thanked the driver and paid him.

"You might have trouble getting back," he said. "I could call back for you at five or five-thirty if you like."

Renate again insisted that we could return by tram, but I said that by then, the girls would be getting tired and hungry. "You have to get home to make supper!" I told the driver we would be delighted, and we agreed to meet at the gate at five-thirty.

Trudy and Ilse had already wandered ahead into the park. We caught up with them at a miniature kiosk where they were examining postcards. A girl of about thirteen, dressed in the blue uniform of the F.D.J., stood behind the counter.

"Mama, look!" Ilse cried, holding up one of the cards. "A little train. Isn't it darling?"

"We are going to ride on the little train," Renate assured her, taking out her change purse to pay for cards for each of the girls and one for me. "You see over there?" She pointed to a tiny cottage built like a village railway station. Both girls nodded excitedly. "That's the train station." They both shouted happily and rushed ahead.

"Nothing inhibited about your girls," I said.

She grinned. "They are very quiet in school, but I am happier if they let loose after school. Children need to run and shout and laugh once in a while, and today they are excited."

"Of course," I said. "It's fun to see them enjoy themselves. I am excited about the little train too. Where does it run?"

"All around the park in a kind of circle. This is a very large park, you see. It covers a whole forest and includes one good-sized lake and some ponds. There are bicycle paths and footpaths, but the train helps the children get from one part of the park to another, from one activity to another a little faster. Besides, they love it. The children run the railroad themselves. You'll see."

At the doll-house station we bought tickets from a serious girl with brown plaits, surrendered them to a younger girl as we passed through a turnstile and waited next to narrow tracks for the miniature train. Renate and I had to stoop to get into the train. It was designed for children. It was run by the children. A boy in his late teens was the engineer, a second boy of about fourteen served as conductor and still another boy, perhaps twelve, acted as guard at the crossing. Trudy and Ilse were enchanted.

"Mama," Trudy asked, "can Ilse and I help run the train some time?"

"Of course," Renate answered. "You belong to the Pioneers. If you sign up at the camp next summer and put your name down for train duty, you will have your turn. At least you will probably be old enough, Trudy. Ilse will have to wait a while."

She explained to me that the older Pioneers take turns working on the railroad, serving as guards, ticket salesmen and collectors, conductors and even engineers.

"But, of course, only the oldest children actually run the trains, and they have to take a course."

"I hope so!" I said, and we laughed as our train sped along through the evergreen forest. At the first stop two or three children wearing knapsacks got on board. The train chugged past a lake where we could see dozens of youngsters swimming, diving, splashing, tossing balls or lying in the sun. Several passengers carrying colorful beach bags got out at the lake station.

The train plunged back into the forest. We made several stops, passed a soccer field, a skating rink, an amphitheater, the arts and sciences center and several camping sites.

"We'll get off at the furthest point," Renate suggested. "Then we can begin to walk back. That way we can see most of the camp projects and activities. If we get tired, we can always get back on the train."

I agreed, and we got off at a wooded station, deep in the interior of the huge park.

"There is a road back and there are trails through the wood," Renate said.

The girls looked up at us appealingly.

"A trail, by all means," I said.

The girls grinned and scampered ahead. Renate and I tramped along behind them inhaling the clean, crisp, pine-scented air.

"It's almost chilly here under the trees," I said.

We passed two boys in their late teens on bicycles and later a troop of smaller children trotting behind two adult leaders. We came to a clearing and discovered a group of boys playing soccer. Later we passed an archery range and then four youngsters playing badminton and still further a campfire surrounded by fifteen or twenty young people engaged in a spirited discussion.

We had walked about twenty minutes when we arrived at a picnic area which seemed to be some sort of headquarters. A cluster of rustic buildings surrounded several wooden tables and benches. In a clearing to the right, a covey of small girls in green tunics were leaping and bending under the direction of a spindly young woman in tights. On the left, in a large half-tent, some very young children were weaving baskets and raffia mats, sewing colorful aprons and stuffing rag dolls. At the central picnic table, four or five athletic-looking adults in shorts and shirts seemed about to sit down to coffee.

A balding middle-aged man with blond hair and glasses, who was the director, came over and welcomed us. Renate introduced me and explained why I was there, and he immediately invited us to join them.

"An American!" he said. "Well, it's not often we have American visitors. Do come and have coffee with us!"

He introduced his colleagues, and they all welcomed me heartily.

"America!" a sinewy blond said. "Really from the United States? I mean, not Canada or South America?"

She could hardly believe my assurances.

"You don't look like an American," she said, "but I've never really seen an American close up. Normally we see only the buses filled with tourists and now and then some of your young G.I.s who wander over."

"And movies," an older woman interjected. "We get foolish ideas about America from your movies."

She was the oldest of the group, and it was she who began to pour coffee from an immense pitcher into the waiting mugs. She offered steaming mugs to Renate and me.

"The girls can trot over to that tent," she suggested, pointing to the left. "They'll find fruit juice and cookies."

"May we?" Trudy asked her mother, and Renate nodded. She and I sat at the table and sipped our hot coffee.

"Are you planning to go back to the States?" the athletic blond asked. "Aren't you a little worried? From what one reads in the papers and sees in newsreels, I should be afraid to go there!"

I told her that even my West German friends feared for my life and safety.

"It's not nearly so bad when you are there," I assured her. "The newspapers and films make it seem much worse. We do have crime and racial disorders and student unrest, and, of course, I am conscious of it all, but in the midst of it, one doesn't really notice and certainly one isn't afraid."

"In a way it must also be exciting," a young man suggested almost wistfully.

His comrades laughed. "Helmut thinks he's a Bolshevik!" one of them jibed. "A revolutionary *manqué!* Actually he's as gentle as a lamb and would faint if he saw a bomb."

The camp director and his staff were all friendly, hearty and uncomplicatedly extrovert, but I found them also highly indoctrinated, almost frighteningly dedicated, almost fanatic. The director was inclined to didactic sermons on the inherent evils in the decay of late capitalism, on the economic foundation of racial problems, on alienation and moral decadence. I found it difficult to turn the torrent of ideology, to ward off the anxious and well-meant sympathy of the counselors, to persuade them to tell me about their camp.

"Do tell me about some of your activities!" I implored, glancing at my watch and remembering the taxi-driver scheduled to call for us at five-thirty.

"Goodness, yes!" the older woman said. "This poor woman has come all this way to see our camp, and here all of you do nothing but talk to her about America."

Her colleagues laughed and agreed and began to compete in offering me information.

"Chiefly we're a day camp for city children," the director said. He explained that some children come to the camp every weekday all summer; others sign up for a number of weeks or for weekends. "We are also open for after-school and weekend activities in spring and fall."

"The children usually come in groups from their schools," the lamb-like Helmut said. "Those who have signed up meet in front of their schools early every morning. The teachers on duty that day check them off and shepherd them onto buses which bring them here."

"Do the teachers come too?" I asked, "and do teachers have to participate in the camp work or is it voluntary?"

"Oh, voluntary," the strenuous blond assured me. "They sign up for it, and they needn't work every day. Some just check the kids in in the mornings and again in the afternoons, so they are free all day. Others come along to the camp and help here, and, of course, they are paid as counselors."

"Do the children from a particular class or school stay together after they reach the camp?" I asked.

"Oh, no," Helmut said. "They disperse. We don't want the children to be regimented here. We encourage each child to choose the activities which especially interest him. If a youngster prefers to go off on his own or with one or two friends, he can just tramp through the woods or take his bicycle; he can photograph birds or collect leaves or go swimming or play tennis or badminton with a friend. He just has to report back for the evening roll call in time to catch the bus back to his school."

"If he prefers group activities, he can sign up for classes in crafts, sports, or academic work or he can join a swimming team or play soccer. We have a good many group activities and competitions." the older woman said.

"You know," the director offered, "although, of course, we do not compel any of the youngsters to go in for any activity which doesn't interest them, we do encourage every pupil to choose a balanced program to get the most out of his summer. We advise every young Pioneer to work for a badge in one of each of our types of activities, sports, arts and crafts, and academic. Their awards and achievements here at camp are entered on their school records, and it all helps when they apply for the university or for jobs later."

Helmut explained that he is the chief swimming coach. "There are coaches for each sport," he said. "We divide the children into small groups roughly according to age, and we assign a goal to each group, let's say, speed, form, endurance and so on. We grade each child and each group every week on progress toward the goals, and at the end of the summer or the end of a course, we award a plain badge to each child who has achieved the goals. We give silver and gold badges to those who excel, and we have a little ceremony at the end of the summer to present the awards."

We had finished our coffee, and the counselors seemed eager to get back to their charges. We shook hands all around, and the director led Renate and me off to inspect some of the classrooms. We entered one of the log cabins and found that a class had apparently been studying the geography of Latin America. A large colored map of Central and South America featured an enlarged Cuba circled in red. The bulletin board displayed children's drawing of their concepts of life in Cuba. Pictures of llamas and of Inca ruins hung on the walls.

"Here are some exercise books," the director said, handing me two or three notebooks from a pile on the desk. I glanced at the carefully transcribed questions and the neat, precise answers: the major exports of Ecuador all in the exact same order, data about the climate, about topography, about natural resources, all apparently learned by rote.

"Of course, they memorize," the director said puzzled. "How else could we measure their achievement objectively?"

He explained that the normal procedure in a class session was to ask one child to read a passage from the text aloud. A second child then is asked to explain what the first child has read. A third child continues the reading. At the end of the lesson, one child summarizes what has been learned, and all the children write the summary in their notebooks. The following day the teacher gives a quiz on the previous day's lesson.

"If a child fails the quiz," he said, "he must repeat the same quiz the next day and go on repeating it until he passes. That way," he said proudly, "all the children eventually pass and win their badges."

We looked at several rooms and stopped by to observe the small children at their arts and crafts. We passed the weary dancers resting in the shade and watched the energetic blond instructing six or seven girls in archery.

"You mustn't think," the director pleaded, "that our youngsters only do work on their holidays. Most of our program is pure fun. It is recreation, and, as I said, no child is compelled to take a course or enter a competition, but, on the other hand, we do feel that, even during the summer vacation, a socialist child should be reminded of the importance of achievement and growth."

Fig. 20. Entrance to the *U-Bahn* at the Alexanderplatz in East Berlin, Teachers' *Haus* in background (photo by Landesbildstelle, West Berlin)

Trudy and Ilse came running to us laughing happily.

"The teacher gave us this!" Ilse said, showing her mother a green and red raffia basket. "I helped to make it!"

It was more than time to leave. We shook hands with the director and with the older woman, who had rejoined us, and thanked them for their hospitality. It was too late to walk back, so we found the nearest railway station and waited for the next train. As they collapsed into the tiny seats on the train, Ilse and Trudy laughed and chattered happily, telling us of the children they had met, a story they had heard.

"They had a wonderful time," Renate said, as we stood in front of the subway stairs at the Alexanderplatz.

"They're exhausted!" I said.

"And dirty," she said smiling, "and they are never dirty! But they loved it."

She thanked me for taking them, and I thanked her for her time and help.

"I know that you cannot like everything about our program, about our teaching methods," Renate said. "Probably you disapprove of our emphasis on norms and achievement, but I hope you like us."

I assured her that I did, and we agreed that it was a very lovely park. Renate and I sincerely liked each other and had enjoyed our meetings, but we knew that we should probably not meet again. They waved as I turned and headed down the subway steps.

24

Elisabeth

Bertha, the stocky Bavarian maid at my hotel, smiled and nodded. *"Ja,* Frau Doctor, just down the path next to the meadow." She pointed, and the already tightly stretched lacing across her dirndl's bodice looked as though it would burst. "Please be sure to close the meadow gate," she reminded me, "so that the cows don't stray. After that it's just a short walk through the woods and you will be almost on the doorstep."

I thanked her and set off briskly across the courtyard and through the meadow. The placid Alpine cows, sleek and tan, regarded me with mild interest. I called a polite good morning to the haughty bell cow, which she acknowledged with a gracious nod. It's hot! I thought with a rush of surprise because it is so rarely warm in the Bavarian Alps even in high summer. I was grateful when I left the open meadow, dutifully closing the gate behind me, and headed for the shade of the pine wood. The cool fragrance of the forest was delightful, and so it seemed only a few minutes until I arrived at the far edge. Bertha was right, I came out of the forest, walked along the only road I saw, and just around the first bend I found the sanatorium, a sprawling, white stucco oblong, built in the modern Bavarian style with broad, overhanging timbered balconies.

I pushed the bell, but when no one answered I tried the door, found it unlocked and went inside. "Hello?" I called softly but received no answer. I walked further into the lobby, a dark cubbyhole with a shiny tiled floor, whitewashed walls hung with Oriental tapestries and brasses. Straight ahead through an open door I could see an office but it was empty. I called again and still no one appeared. I saw sunlight through a door to my left, so I walked across what appeared to be the dining room, an open room furnished in Bavarian peasant style, the tables already set for luncheon, colorful with bright red, blue and yellow cloths

325

and napkins. Beyond the dining room was an open door leading to the garden.

The garden was lovely, a blend of formality and casualness. The immaculate lawn was dotted with brightly colored deck chairs on which amazingly healthy-looking patients sunned themselves. Tall trees, conifers and stately beeches, stood at strategic points to provide shade, while silver birches, flowering shrubs and flower beds created splashes of color. A swimming pool dominated the center of the garden.

I looked around, half-aware of the opulence and elegance, half-searching for my friend. I walked slowly around the garden, exchanging polite nods with patients, none of whom was Elisabeth. A slim woman with crisp white hair had just looked up from her deck chair to ask whether she could help me when I saw a familiar, tall figure in a blue terry robe hurrying down the path. I thanked the stranger, and I turned to meet Elisabeth.

Elisabeth beamed, shook my hand and then gave me a friendly peck on the cheek. I studied her face for evidence of sickness and was reassured that she looked well.

"No, well," she said, "I have half a dozen ailments, as you know, but none of them is any worse than usual. I came here only to cure end-of-the-semester exhaustion. It's a wonderful place for a good rest."

"It's gorgeous!" I said.

"It is nice, and the people are so delightful, the doctors, the nurses, the other patients." She explained that she had regular massages and treatment for her chronic illnesses. "I'm on a diet, of course. I'm supposed to lose twenty pounds."

"Have you lost weight?" I asked, knowing she had been there for a week. She grimaced.

"*Ach,* I'm a grave disappointment to the doctor. I've lost only two pounds, and sometimes I gain them back. I think he weighs me three times a day."

Elisabeth is Rubensian, middle-aged, the mother of four grown sons. She is always overworked and overcommitted and her illnesses are not minor; nevertheless she always looks radiant and vital. Her short dark hair, fluffy from the heat of the Sauna, fell in soft waves around her face, which was slightly flushed. She looked younger than her age, good-natured and motherly.

"Come," she said, "let's go and sit on that blue bench over there under the big beech. There is a patch of shade for you and sun for me, and I shall call Frau Ingrid and ask her to bring us something cool to drink."

"Tell me about the boys," I said after we were settled.

"Boys!" she said. "I still call them boys, but they are young men. The twins are about finished with their law degrees, you know, and Peter is working on his habilitation."

Elisabeth's huband was killed in an accident when the twins were twelve; Peter and Heinz Dieter were in their teens. She has a doctorate in sociology and had always taught a few courses, so she found it relatively easy to begin teaching full time. By now she is a well-known and respected member of Berlin's academic community, and she has made a secure, comfortable life for her sons.

She and the boys had to move to a smaller house after her husband died. They found a semidetached house in a middle-class, suburban neighborhood just at the edge of the Grunewald. The neighborhood is unpretentious, respectable and convenient. Each house has its long, narrow garden; the streets are shaded and quiet; and yet two blocks away buses and subways rush to mid-town within a half hour.

The house is long and narrow, just one room wide, but three stories high. The ground floor contains only a small, modern kitchen and a combined dining and sitting room, which opens onto a terrace leading to the garden. On the next floor are a small bath, a cubbyhole bedroom and Elisabeth's sitting-room study. The boys' rooms are on the top floor.

"It has never really been big enough for a woman and four boys," she said, "but in the early days housing was scarce and so was money, and later I realized that the boys would soon grow up and go off on their own."

Most of the furniture is postwar and utilitarian, but a few pieces of old furniture, odds and ends of Dresden porcelain, a single Persian carpet, seem to have been salvaged. The family lives unpretentiously, but their lives have a style, a distinctive pattern. The high tea on Sunday afternoons when two or more of the boys are at home illustrates this style. The food is simple, even Spartan, but Elisabeth and her daily helper arrange the cheese, the bread and butter, the cold cuts and salad with flair. The teapot is never empty and continues its rounds as long as the conversation bubbles. Politics, music, religion, the state of the theater are discussed with enthusiasm, courtesy and no little wit. Everyone participates. Everyone's comments are considered, pondered, replied to, sometimes sharply, sometimes facetiously, but always with an underlying affection and respect. There probably is a degree of competition among the sons; certainly there is an occasional argument, but I have never sensed an undercurrent of tension or of hostility, and obviously there is no generation gap.

This is not to say that there have never been problems but that problems when they arise are faced frankly. For example, there was the shock when Heinz Dieter decided not to complete his *Abitur*. That was several years back, when he was nineteen. One day he came home from school and explained to his mother that he had made up his mind not to take his final examinations, not to go on to a university. Elisabeth was startled and worried. Both she and her husband came from families in which academic education had been taken for granted. She had never doubted that all four sons would attend a university.

"What do you want to do, Heinz Dieter?" she asked.

"I'm not sure," he said, obviously sure that he did not want to be an intellectual. "Join the merchant marine, I think" he finally admitted. Elisabeth told me that she could understand that an atmosphere which was too intellectual, in which two brothers were academically gifted and both parents had doctorates, might discourage the ambitions of an only slightly above-average child. She had often told me that she thought it was a cruel mistake to force children into academic molds, into the higher professions, just to live up to class status or parental ambitions. The time had come when she had to practice her preaching.

She did. She accepted her oldest son's decision with understanding and with humor, assuring him that he must make his own decision but that she would always be glad to help. He hugged her and went up to pack a bag. He enlisted, served a year or two at sea and then applied for admission to the merchant marine academy in Hamburg. First he had to make up missing credits toward his *Abitur,* but they accepted him. He is now first mate on a merchant vessel and already has master's papers and is only waiting for an opening to be captain of his own ship. A few years ago he married a sensible girl who is as understanding and easygoing as his mother, and he seems to be content and successful in his nonacademic career. His mother is delighted that it has worked out well.

"*Ach,* we have always had sea captains in the family," she said. "My family comes from an old Hansa town, you know, and my husband's family produced a few naval officers."

The three others have been unswerving in their progress toward degrees. One of the twins, Fritz, ran into a little trouble when he was about fourteen. He had never done as well in school as his twin, who was usually first in their class, but he had never failed. Suddenly one spring he failed several subjects and his mother was distressed to learn that he would have to repeat a year at school.

"Best thing that ever happened to him," she told me. She explained that although the twins look very much alike, so much alike that I still have trouble telling them apart, they are not identical. "They are very different in temperament, in character and ability. Fritz has the stronger personality. It was always Fritz who had the lead in the school play, who organized dances and led debates. George, on the other hand is quieter but it far more gifted intellectually.

"Fritz could never win in academic competition with George, and so as long as they were in the same class he never tried. He just coasted, and finally he failed. Once they were separated and Fritz found himself with all new classmates who thought of him just as Fritz, not as George's inferior twin, he began to feel like a new and separate person, and he discovered that he could really do very well in school. He never won any prizes but he managed to get satisfactory grades. He had no trouble completing his *Abitur*."

That summer she told me that both twins were studying law, George in Munich, where he was preparing for his final examinations, Fritz at the Free University, where he had about another year to go.

"They're nothing alike," she said. "Both are studying law, but they have very different goals. Fritz, my happy extrovert, wants to enter private practice and then go into active politics. George will take the civil service exams and enter one of the ministries or become a judge."

Peter, the middle son, was the only one to choose the academic profession. *"Na, ja,"* Elisabeth said gratefully, "they have all turned out well, and that is a small miracle."

They have turned out extremely well, and considering the events of their childhood it seems to me a major miracle. Both Elisabeth and her husband were active in the antinazi resistance. Her husband was a relative of Count Moltke, one of the founders of the Kreisau Kreis, the secret antinazi group which included both conservatives and socialists and met at Moltke's Silesian estate, Kreisau, to draft a postnazi constitution. Both Elisabeth and her huband became intimately associated with the planning of the group, she as a sociologist, he as an economist.

Even the most discreet and theoretical antinazi activities involved danger in a Germany dominated by terror. Uncertainty, tension and fear must have permeated the household while the older boys were babies. The twins were born in a situation of stark terror. In January 1944, Count Moltke was arrested. The government brought no immediate charge against him, but during the months he was in prison, subject to interrogation, no member of the conspiracy could breathe quietly.

Meanwhile, more active elements of the opposition were planning the attempt to assassinate Hitler. Only those closest to the center of the plot knew the precise target date, but Elisabeth and her husband knew that a climax was approaching, that the situation might explode at about the time when their third child was due.

"You'll have to get out of Berlin," Eduard told her. "In any case, it isn't safe here with these around-the-clock raids. I'd feel that I had a freer hand and I'd certainly have a freer mind if I knew that you and the boys were safe in the country." She objected, of course, because she did not want to leave Eduard and her friends just before the crisis, but she knew that his advice was sound, that he would worry more if she stayed.

"By asking around among our friends, we heard of a remote farm in the East, not too close to the front but far enough from Berlin, and my husband arranged for me and the two boys to go out there. I left in June, hating to leave, worrying every minute I was away," she once told me.

"Did the twins arrive in July?" I asked.

"I didn't know they would be twins," she said. "I expected only one baby, and it was due just around the twentieth of July."

"Oh!" I said and she nodded grimly.

"You can imagine what those weeks were like just before the twentieth. When I could get to a telephone and reach my husband, which was seldom because very often communications were broken by the bombings, we couldn't say anything. We had to be so careful. Of course we all used a kind of code," she added.

"Like 'how is Uncle Helo's cold' or something?" I improvised.

"Something like that, but it wasn't like really knowing, not like being there and sharing all the news. Of course I worried. For me it was far worse than being there."

"Of course," I said, "but men always imagine they're being chivalrous when they rush us off to safety."

"Well," she suggested, "perhaps we just imagine we are cosseting them when we let them. Anyway, it was pretty dreadful before the twentieth, but it was sheer torment afterwards. As soon as a brief bulletin came over the radio that something had happened, I kept my ear glued to it, and wouldn't you know? Just then my labor started."

"Oh, no!"

"I didn't say anything to the farm wife right away. I was afraid she would ship me off to a hospital, and who knows what I might have said if they gave me a whiff of anesthetic. I couldn't risk it, so I waited until it was too late to go, then I asked her to hide me somewhere."

"Was she sympathetic?" I asked.

"Well, yes and no," Elisabeth said. "She was a woman, and if she was a little rough and uneducated, she was basically decent. She was also a mother, so of course she sympathized with me and with the babies, but she was a devoted nazi, one of those simple German women who trusted their Führer."

"Oh, God, she would be, wouldn't she?"

Elisabeth nodded. "Well, she was that kind of person. I had waited through the news blackout before telling her that the baby was imminent. Just as she was preparing a makeshift bed for me in the barn, I heard the bulletin that Major Remer had crushed the revolt, arrested the major conspirators and the S.S. Colonel Skorzeny had been appointed to investigate the plot."

"You didn't know who had been arrested?" I asked.

"No," she said. "I didn't know where my husband was or what had happened to him, nor did I know what had happened to any of our friends. I was frantic, but by then the labor had begun in earnest, so I had to hurry out to the barn. The farm wife grumbled all the time she was helping to deliver the baby that all 'aristos' and intellectuals were a dirty bunch of traitors and she ought to turn me in."

"Brrr!" I said. "The baby, or rather babies were born in the barn with just the peasant woman as a midwife?" I asked.

"And pretty rough and unsanitary she was, our good Frau H., but the delivery was a quick one, thank God, and she soon had me and the baby, one baby please note, wrapped in blankets and she went off to fetch some warm soup and tea. Luckily, she left the radio. I was as weak as a drowned cat, but I grabbed it and tried to get some news. There was none, just more diatribes and threats of vengeance which made me feel sick."

"I suppose you felt sick anyway," I said. "But what about the twin? Was he born later?"

She shook her head and smiled. "No, we found him!" She laughed merrily at my expression. "Yes, true! When Frau H. came back with my soup, a good, rich farm soup which had been simmering on the stove, she began to clean up the rags and towels she had used in the delivery. She picked up one towel into which she'd scooped what she thought was placenta and it kicked."

"What?" I squealed.

Elisabeth paused and contemplated. "Goodness," she said, "I hope there won't be too many *bons bourgeois* who read your book."

"Never fear," I said, "they won't get any farther than the barn. Maybe we could supply free seasickness pills?"

"It is disgusting, isn't it?" she said. "But life wasn't tidy and sanitary in those weeks."

"No," I said, thinking of the interrogations and executions. "But you said it kicked?"

"Yes. What Frau H. had thrown carelessly away was actually a second baby."

"Obviously he was all right."

"He was perfect. We just washed him off, and he was none the worse, and as you know he's turned out quite well."

"He's a lamb," I said, "but what an experience, and what an environment for babies and toddlers!"

"Shocking, horrible weeks. I had to stay in the barn after that, and I never knew whether Frau H. was going to call in the police. She kept mumbling and threatening, saying all kinds of awful things about people like me. Well, you can imagine. She loved her Führer, and it was people like me who had tried to murder him, to destroy Germany as she saw it. I'm sure she believed that my husband and I were involved. Over and over she said 'You're probably a traitor too,' but she never did call the police. I suppose she felt sorry for the babies."

"How long did you stay there? And how long was it before you heard from your husband?"

"Weeks," she said. "Hellish weeks. You can guess what I was imagining all those weeks, that he was being tortured, that he had been shot or hanged. Then suddenly one day there was a message from him. He was alive and free."

"Wasn't he arrested?" I asked.

She nodded. "Oh, yes, he was rounded up with everyone else even distantly connected with the plotters, but the conspiracy had friends inside the Gestapo, and somehow through a fluke he was released."

"Did you return to Berlin?"

"Oh, as soon as I knew he was safe I went back in spite of the bombings and the danger of the investigations which were still going on. I had to see him, talk to him, find out everything that had happened."

I said that I could understand that. "Besides," I said, "East Germany was getting close to the front so your farm was none too safe."

"No, and I could never really trust Frau H. I was more relaxed in Berlin in spite of the danger, and danger there was because we had hardly got settled when our house was bombed and was almost totally demolished."

"Oh, no!" I said. "But you were all safe."

"All six of us, and that was a blessing. So many of our friends were not. No, we even managed to crawl back into the rubble and pull out some pieces of furniture, some jewelry. We found a temporary apartment and lived there until the end of the war."

"You were in Berlin when the war ended, then?" I asked.

"All of us. My husband worked for the Berlin city civil service as a transportation expert, so his work continued even though the war ended. As a matter of fact, he was treated well by the Russians at first, despite his class origin, because he was an accredited victim of National Socialism. There weren't all that many who had survived."

"No," I said. "So he kept his job?"

"He was promoted. There were so many vacancies caused by denazification and by officials' leaving for West Germany. We suffered from shortages the same as everyone else, but we were comparatively well off. We always knew that the Russians could never really trust anyone of my husband's background and views. He'd never made a secret of his anticommunism, but at first they needed him, and so we knew that for a while we were safe. But only for a while."

"I remember that just as soon as the city revived a little, the Russians began arresting class enemies and what they called nondemocratic elements," I said.

"They did indeed," Elisabeth said. "By the fall of 1945 waves of arrest were commonplace. Naturally, we began to get nervous."

"Again," I said.

"Yes, we were beginning to think tension was normal. We were almost philosophical about it. Every day the government posted a list of civil servants who were to be dismissed on political grounds. This was the signal that some were to be arrested; others simply disappeared, presumably to labor camps in the Soviet Union."

"You watched the lists?"

"More than that. The Russians were very like the nazis in that they followed a predictable routine. They worked according to a pattern, so it was often possible to outguess them. If a man was scheduled to be arrested the police would be waiting for him when he arrived at his office in the morning or when he returned after lunch. Almost never did they walk into someone's office during working hours."

"Strange," I said.

"It was their way," she said, "and so we worked out our own procedure. Every morning we went together to the neighborhood of his office. Then I walked ahead as far as his office building. I scanned the street in both directions, looked at all the entrances, back and side, looked through the corridors and inside his office. If the coast was clear, I walked back outside, gave a discreet signal and went home. Then Eduard knew he could go safely to his desk. We repeated the procedure after lunch."

"Strenuous," I said, "but didn't they sometimes arrest people at home?"

"Sometimes," she admitted. "We didn't sleep at home. We farmed the boys out for these weeks with friends, and each night we slept at the home of different friends, never at the same house two nights in a row."

"When things were that bad, why didn't your husband just leave his job and go over to the West or to West Germany?" I asked.

She said that her husband thought his work was necessary and that he should stay on as long as possible. "Naturally, we both knew that eventually he would have to escape."

She did not explain, but I assumed that her husband believed that it was important to keep as many noncommunists in the city government as long as possible, if only to help individuals as a nonnazi Gestapo official had once helped him. Inevitably, however, the day arrived when he had to flee.

"The Russians weren't a hundred per cent predictable, of course," Elisabeth said. "One day my husband had asked me to meet him for lunch at the Adlon. I think he just felt like celebrating. If you remember the Adlon in those years, there wasn't much left of the hotel except a shell, but the old restaurant was still standing. Somehow they had swept it up and refurbished it, and somehow the kitchen did wonders with whatever bits and pieces of food were available. Lunch or dinner at the Adlon was still elegant, and the food was delicious if meager, the service impeccable. I always found it rather shocking, all that formality in the midst of ruins. Anyway, my husband wanted to have lunch there, and so I turned up.

"When I arrived I found that he hadn't yet appeared. I asked for a table, waited a while and then decided to order my lunch. An elderly waiter had just brought my soup, I had sipped the first spoonful, when in rushed my husband. He threw some marks onto the table took my elbow and said, 'Leave the soup! Come!' The waiter understood at once and pointed to a side door. We ducked through the kitchen and out across a courtyard. We heard a commotion, a clattering of boots and shouts behind us, but we didn't stop to look. We just made a run for the Brandenburg Gate, which, as you know, was very close." She laughed. "I was slimmer and younger in those days or we'd never have made it.

"We dashed across into the Western sector, turned sharply into a side street as soon as we could and mingled with the crowd. We darted into the first shop we came to and browsed, because of course in those days the Russians could come freely into the West, but they didn't find us."

"But as you say, even West Berlin wasn't really safe in those years. Many people simply disappeared from the streets of West Berlin. What did you do?" I asked.

"We stayed," she said. "We knew it was only comparatively safe, but we both wanted to stay. The transportation office in West Berlin was glad to find a place for my husband, and we even found a house large enough to live in with four children. We rounded up the boys, moved in and began to enjoy life. We had to be careful for we were never entirely secure, but we had a few happy years.

"As you know, Eduard was killed in an accident in 1956. Of course the boys missed their father, and naturally we had a bad time for a while, but I managed to switch to a full-time teaching job. We moved to a smaller house and we got by. We always had to be frugal. Clothes and food and books for four boys do not come cheaply. We never used butter when margarine would do, and my boys never had more pocket money than they knew what to do with. They worked Saturdays and summers as soon as they were old enough. They were proud when they could buy their own clothes and perhaps have enough left over to buy me a present."

It seemed tame and almost unreal to be sitting in a calm and peaceful garden talking with this relaxed, glowing woman knowing what I knew about her past, and yet most of the men and women who help to run the colleges, the churches and the industries of Berlin have some kind of drama, very often tragedy in their past. That too is part of Berlin, part of Berliners.

"Now, Anne, what do you want to know about my college?" Her question forced me back to the present.

"It's a college to prepare kindergarten teachers, isn't it?" I asked.

"The official name is a social pedagogical institute. Doesn't that sound very German? We train young people to be kindergarten teachers and youth leaders."

"What do youth leaders do?" I asked.

"They run youth centers, recreation centers, summer camps, things of that sort. Our school is the largest of its kind in Germany, so we take many students from the Federal Republic as well as from West Berlin, and many of our graduates go off to work in West Germany or even abroad."

"What age are your students?" I asked, carefully making notes.

"We are not a university level college. Applicants don't need an *Abitur* to enter; most of our applicants have completed the 'middle diploma' at fifteen or sixteen and then subsequently worked in the field for a year or two. That is, they leave high school at fifteen or sixteen, take jobs as helpers in nurseries or camps to gain practical experience and then enter our college when they are about seventeen."

"Do you require an entrance exam?" I asked. "Must they have had very high grades in high school?"

"No. We place more weight on good letters of recommendation. We are most concerned with the kind of people they are, whether they really like and get along with children. We want girls and these days also young men of good character and wholesome personality, and we demand only reasonably good grades."

"I can understand that. How long is the course?" I asked.

"We have two levels. The lower-level curriculum takes two and a half years, and then the graduate qualifies to teach in a kindergarten."

"In other words, she, or possibly he, can start to teach at about twenty? That's a bit younger than in the States."

She nodded. "Some of our students choose to return to complete the second phase of study. We like them to work in the field for three or four years before they come back, and then the advanced curriculum lasts for another two years. When they complete this phase they are qualified to become directors of youth centers or of children's homes."

"Could you tell me something about the program?"

"It's not easy," she said. "Our students at both levels work very hard, but then I suppose all teachers and professors think that. But ours really have a strenuous program. In the first place, they attend school for a full eight-hour day, five days a week."

"Wow!" I said, thinking of our fifteen hours a week program.

"They spend about thirty-five hours a week in the classroom, the rest in chorus, dancing and play production. Our curriculum includes normal subjects like German, psychology and my course in politics, and also professional courses in teaching arts and crafts, dancing and music and physical education for children. The students have to master all these skills and then learn how to teach them to small children."

"Do you have children there for them to practice on?" I asked.

"Oh, yes. We have a day nursery, a kindergarten, a center for handicapped children and an after-school center for older children, so our students have plenty of opportunity for observations and for practice."

"Sounds ideal."

"Well, I think we have pretty good facilities and our youngsters get a good training. Each student has one child each semester to observe. She sits in his classes, observes his behavior and performance, takes notes on his reactions to the teacher and to other children and later discusses her notes with her advisor. At the end of the semester she submits a paper."

"I suppose you have student-teaching?" I said.

"We have a pretty thorough system. Each primary level student must serve a practicum of eight weeks in each of three semesters. She chooses a different institution to work in for each practicum. The upper-level students do their practicum in government youth offices and in youth centers: six weeks with the government and then six to ten weeks in a center. Upper-level courses include the study of welfare and youth laws, advancd sociology and psychology."

"It sounds formidable," I said. "How do you select students for the upper level?"

"We are a little more selective at the upper level," she said. "Our admissions committee evaluates each applicant in terms of her—or his— total experience, not just the academic record. Very often the committee will reject an applicant who has too little practical experience or who seems immature, but will recommend that she reapply after an additional year or two in the field."

"Do you ever take older students, married women, for instance, who did not enter right after high school?"

"At the moment we have a special campaign to encourage more mature students to enter our program," she said. "There are many women who did not have the grades to qualify for admission when they were seventeen, but they have proved through many years' experience that they could be excellent teachers. We now accept applicants who lack academic qualification but who can substitute at least seven years of practical experience in the field or in related fields."

"How do these older applicants work out?" I asked.

"Some of them turn out very well, although some, as you can imagine, find that they have problems with their academic work. They are, as you would expect, generally conscientious and reliable, but many lack the perceptive ability of younger girls."

"They are slower to get the point?" I asked.

"No, I mean they just don't see. In their observations of children, for example, they often simply fail to notice nuances of behavior and attitude that would be apparent to the younger girls. They seem less sensitive to the individual child. I don't know why. This is just something I have observed. Perhaps they are too used to children,, perhaps they have accumulated too many preconceived notions about the way children in general behave to notice the way a specific child in particular is behaving. But, despite this, by and large, they do well."

"Do you get many male applicants?"

"We encourage young men to enroll. As you know, the kindergarten and day-care centers traditionally have been matriarchies. We almost didn't dare hope to attract young men to jobs as kindergarten teachers, but we wanted to recruit them as youth leaders, camp directors. However, as I've said, in order to qualify for the youth-work posts, they must first take the kindergarten training, and, do you know, many young men discover that they enjoy it and just settle down to teach small children? Several men that I know are now working in kindergartens or day-care centers, and they love it."

"Do most of your students pass," I asked, "or do you have many failures and dropouts?"

"We have relatively few failures at the higher level. At the primary level, perhaps a third drop out or are asked to drop, usually before they take their examinations. The few we lose at the upper level usually leave voluntarily during the first semester."

"Goodness," I said, "I have a lot of notes. Could you just tell me a little about your faculty, and then I think I'll quit. You said at the beginning that your college doesn't have university rank, and yet I know that you used to lecture at a university. What about your colleagues? Would they be qualified to teach at universities?"

"We have two sorts of faculty. We have those who teach straight academic subjects like politics, psychology and German, and these generally are qualified to teach at a university. I think we all have doctorates, at least, and could have habilitated had we taken that path. However, obviously the teachers of crafts and creative dancing are not academic people, though they are very highly qualified specialists."

"Those of you who are in the academic areas do not, I take it, have to publish or perish?" I asked.

"No, thank God. We are under no compulsion or pressure to do original research or to publish, but some of us do manage to turn out a paper now and then. But we work much longer hours each week than do university professors and we have more direct contact with students. I think our work is a good deal more tiring."

I agreed that it probably was, knowing how seriously Elisabeth takes her work, how much personal concern she shows for her students.

I asked whether the institute endorsed any particular educational doctrine and she said no. "We believe in diversity. Our teachers represent most of the major schools of thought in education and psychology. We like to encourage an atmosphere of freedom, to present various points of view and let each student choose for himself the philosophy of teaching that suits him best.

"Of course, there are limits," she added. "I was thinking of the non-authoritarian kindergartens. Do you know them?"

"I know them in Berlin," I said. "Don't they call them *Kinderladen?* Children-shops?"

"Yes, because they usually rent some inexpensive store for their kindergartens. Have you visited any?"

"No," I admitted, "but I'd like to."

"I'll take you to one or two when we're back in Berlin. I know some of the youngsters who run them. They're mostly left-wing students and young intellectuals, some of them the children of close friends of mine, kids who are part of the Extra-Parliamentary Opposition."

"I understand that they're sort of do-it-yourself nursery schools, run by the parents," I said.

"Exactly. The object is to provide cheap day-care centers for mothers who want to attend school or who need to work by sharing the child-watching duties. By the way, I think in principle that idea is excellent," she said, interrupting herself.

"So do I," I agreed, "and I think it's awfully good that the fathers help out for an hour or two when they can."

"Splendid," Elizabeth said. "But they also intend their nurseries to be what they call antiauthoritarian, and there I think they go off on some pretty silly tangents. Don't misunderstand me—I believe, if anyone does, in an antiauthoritarian, or at least a nonauthoritarian society, and I agree that self-government and freedom must start in the nursery, but their way of trying to achieve those goals is simply to let the children and babies do anything they want. The results, I can tell you, are not only pretty messy, they are downright brutal."

"Messy I can see," I said.

She smiled. "Messy, indeed! The whole core of the program of these schools is that there is no program. The toddlers can do anything they like and need not do anything they don't like, such as be toilet trained."

"Ah," I said, "many of our young intellectual mothers feel the same way. Bits and pieces of Freud, you know."

"Unsanitary bits and pieces, if you will excuse my saying so," Elisabeth commented saltily. "Ugh—you should smell those rooms. I think they feel they would be violating their instincts if they cleaned up after the babies."

I laughed. "I suppose they have their hands full."

"Well, of course they do," she said, exasperated, "because they don't

Fig. 21. A street concert in downtown West Berlin (photo by Landesbildstelle, West Berlin)

teach the children anything. You can imagine how some of my old Kreisau friends feel about having their grandchildren brought up in such surroundings. The whole point of the program is that it is, as they say, un-structured. Children may do whatever it enters their heads to do even if it is to bang Heinzi in the face with a toy train or push Hilda into the sandbox. You should hear the screams and yells and the weeping. It is bedlam. You see, they believe that any training, even the gentlest, most rational, teaches the child to conform to authority and thereby represses his healthy instincts, makes him inhibited and neurotic and robs him of his ability to make his own decisions."

"Well, one sees the logic. Obviously they've been steeping themselves in Freud's *Civilization and Its Discontents*," I observed.

"More likely Marcuse's interpretation. Marcuse is a sort of prophet or apostle with them. These youngsters believe passionately that They, some nameless Establishment, have cleverly instituted repressions and taboos specifically to render the general population neurotic, denatured and docile. They genuinely believe that there is a subtle, gigantic, age-old plot, a conspiracy to preserve the authoritarian society and stifle individual liberty, and they are determined to thwart the conspirators and explode the plot."

"You say the children cry a lot," I said. "Are they very unhappy?"

"Miserable, if you ask me," Elisabeth answered. "Don't misunderstand me, I have a great affection for some of the young parents and sympathy for their desire to make their children free. Some of these young mothers and fathers I've known since they were infants, and no one desires freedom more than I, I am sure. I just believe that total anarchy does not lead to freedom but to tyranny, even in a nursery. The kindergarten which has no direction, no leadership, turns into a jungle, almost a torture chamber in which the toughest, most hostile children terrorize and dominate the smaller, less aggressive ones."

"I can see that," I said. "Don't the mothers try to stop one child from bullying another? What if one actually gets hurt?"

"In practice the mother of a child who is hit or knocked down may very well cuff the offender, but in theory she is not supposed to. The theory is that you just pick up the assaulted baby, dust him off, kiss him and tell him to get on with it."

"I suppose," I mused, "they actually believe that all toddlers are created equal?"

"However egalitarian they are, and for goodness' sake, I'm an egalitarian of a sort, they can see that all children are not the same size or physical strength. And just watching them for a few days, whatever your theory might be, you can see that they're not all equally aggressive or active. Some are just passive and timid."

"Of course," I said. "And I think that all children, whatever their temperament or prowess, need a sense of direction. It gives them a feeling of security. Little children can't cope with the world alone. They need to be taught, they need emotional support, don't they?"

"Well, we think so at my school," she said. "We believe that small children need nest warmth, the kind of security they get from knowing that someone is there and will care for them, will see that everything is all right."

"I certainly agree in principle," I said.

"Children need and like discipline. An occasional slap on the backside is a good deal kinder than bangs on the head, or than allowing the child to bang others on the head. These young radicals, however much affection I have for them, annoy me with their simplistic views of freedom and socialism. I think I am a socialist of sorts, but that doesn't stop me from using my common sense and my eyes. I believe in freedom, but I think that children learn to be free by learning to be responsible, that you can't have optimal freedom without a reasonable degree of order, in a nursery, in a classroom or anywhere else."

"Well, you know I agree with that, my dear," I said.

"Would you like to get up and wander in the shade?" she asked. "It's warm in the sun, but under those big trees it should be cool and pleasant."

We got up and began to stroll. "How do you assure that your teachers will administer discipline mixed with affection?" I asked. "How do you prevent reasonable order from turning into dictatorship?"

"Not easy," she admitted. "In the first place you have to be selective about teachers. At my college we begin by being as careful as we can in choosing students, and we weed out any that do not show their affection, their patience with small children. When I observe our girls during their work experience I find most of them excellent in doling out discipline. Most of them are offhand and detached about it, with just occasionally a 'No, Hans' or 'No, Lili, that is not how we do that. See,' and then showing them. Once in a while a light slap on the wrist to underline the 'No,' but no fuss, no drama. Small children need firmness along with affection and patience and that is what we try to inculcate. Come visit our school and talk with our young student teachers. It's better for you to go and see our girls in action than just to listen to me talk about them. Real children are more important than any amount of theory."

"I'd love to when we are both back in Berlin," I said. I glanced at my watch. "Do you know it's almost time for your massage?"

"Time for your lunch too, I suppose," she said. I walked with her back to the sanatorium, and we agreed to meet late the next afternoon. As I strolled back through the cool woods I thought over what she had told me and wondered how typical of older-generation progressives Elisabeth's views were. Very, I'd guess, I told myself.

The following day she felt strong enough for a more ambitious walk through the Bavarian countryside. As we walked I asked her about her many visits abroad.

"I don't really like travelling," she said. "With all my various ailments, buses, trains and planes are wearing, but I like seeing other countries, other societies, and meeting the people," Elisabeth said. She told me that she had visited the Soviet Union, the United States and Israel as well as many European countries.

"I was awfully impressed with some of the modern English schools," she said. "I went over with a group of teachers to tour their schools, and then some English teachers returned our visit. Good idea, I think."

In answer to my question she answered, "What impressed me most about the English children was their love of debate, of discussion, and their delightful manners in discussion. Alas, one of our German national shortcomings is our bad debating manners. If a German discovers that your viewpoint differs from his he is likely to take it as a personal affront, but I found that English children from primary school through the university seemed to accept differences of opinion as normal and desirable. They enjoyed debate. If we Germans could learn to do that, I'd feel more optimistic about our democracy."

I asked about her reaction to Israel, and she said that she liked Israeli society very much. She told me about one experience.

"In one kibbutz I visited there were three physical therapists, all three highly qualified, but the kibbutz needed only one. What did they do? Send two away? Assign two to other work? No, they shared."

"How?" I asked.

"Each of the three took on a third of the work and then each spent two-thirds of her working hours in some other, less interesting work, in the kitchen, for instance, or on the farm. I thought that was impressive, and it wasn't exceptional. I met a tractor driver at another kibbutz who told me he had been a doctor in Berlin. There are dozens of cases on every large farm. People are willing to sacrifice their interests for the community, and they think nothing of pride, of status. I can't imagine many Europeans of the traditional academic class doing that—they are too conscious of their dignity."

"Can you eat a peach on your diet?" I asked extracting two from my tote bag.

"I can if you brought napkins," she said. "They slurp." I produced a stack of paper napkins and a fruit-knife. We found comfortable rocks in the shade of a cluster of trees overlooking a pasture and sat down to enjoy the peaches.

"You know I'm not really a Berliner," she said. "My family comes from one of the old Hansa port cities. We were always mixed up in local government and politics, so I suppose interest in politics comes naturally to me. I don't mean that I'm active in a political party, I'm not. I have never been a member of any party, and now I refuse to join, not like the former nazis who are afraid of making a second mistake, but because I feel that a teacher of politics should be nonpartisan."

"I'm not, you know," I said slurping just a little.

She nodded. "No, of course I know that you are active in a party in the States, and that is a viewpoint I can respect, but for me, I prefer to keep my independence. I don't even vote consistently for one party. If I describe myself as something of a socialist, I mean in theory, not that I am a follower of the S.P.D. I quite often vote for an individual C.D.U. candidate or reject the S.P.D. stand on specific issues."

"But you are active in politics in the sense that you try to influence decisions, aren't you?" I asked.

"You mean I serve on committees and attend meetings, things of that sort? Yes, of course I do. I have many friends who are active in all three parties, and of course I discuss issues with them. I've often been on citizens' committees to study various problems. I think I do most of that kind of work through the Church."

"Evangelical?" I asked, although I already knew. "Are you an active member of a congregation?"

"Well," she said, tidily burying her peach stone and stuffing the used napkins into her bag, "I wouldn't say we are a very churchy family. We belong to our local congregation, and of course I pay the Church tax. You know that my husband and I were part of the Christian antinazi group, and so of course we identify with the Church, with religion. To be honest though I almost never go to church!"

"It's hard for a professional woman who also runs a household," I submitted.

"It is. I am tired on Sundays and I always have so much reading to do, people to telephone, papers to grade. However, I do serve on boards and committees and speak at panel discussions. Our local pastor is a good friend of the family. He understands and puts up with our habits."

"The boys?" I asked.

"Oh, they're all believers, I think. Anyway, they seem to be, but they never seem to have time to go to church either, although the twins have participated in some of the youth activities and we all go to church concerts now and then. I suppose we're a pretty unorthodox family. Still, though, I keep in touch with the Evangelical leaders in Berlin, and I help out where I can."

Elisabeth and I met each day while I was in the village. She was kept busy as sanatorium patients are with a series of treatments and consultations, and she was cautioned to rest quietly for several hours a day, but her program usually allowed a few hours for a walk, a drive to a nearby lake or to a colorful, medieval town across the Austrian border or for tea in the sanatorium garden. She introduced me to her doctor, to several nurses and to a few fellow patients, and I was delighted to find that most of them were Berliners.

"You meet Berliners everywhere," an elderly male patient told me. "Go into the jungle in Burma or Brazil and what do you find? A Berliner sipping Löwenbräu out of a can, listening to Bach on his transistor tape-recorder!"

"I certainly have met Berliners everywhere," I admitted. "Not in Burma, because I've never been there, but in Amazonian jungles, in Hong Kong and Teheran, and certainly in Bavaria."

"All over Bavaria," he nodded. "Most of us live in Munich."

One evening just before I left the valley, Elisabeth invited me to come over after the evening meal. "We don't have anything one can call dinner," she explained, "and of course I can't drink wine, but I'll have some harmless glop, and you can drink wine."

I accepted, and we had a pleasant talk on the terrace overlooking the garden and swimming pool. I knew that she should be in bed by ten, and so at nine-thirty I rose to leave. "I'll walk with you," she insisted. "You can't trot through that dark woods alone at this hour!"

"In bucolic Bavaria?" I said. "I'm not afraid of cows."

"There might be bulls," she warned, walking with me.

"Halfway!" I insisted firmly, but we soon became so engrossed in talk that we had crossed the woods and were almost across the meadow before I realized that we had gone more than halfway.

"Oh, well," Elisabeth shrugged, "I've come this far. I'll go on with you. Berlin?" she continued. "As I said, I'm not a Berliner by birth or background, but by now I've become one. My family and I have gone through so much with the Berliners, the nazi terror, the trials and executions, the bombings, the rape of the city, the blockade and all the years of tension. The Wall."

"Don't you get worn out with it?" I asked.

She nodded. "Obviously I am worn out physically, often emotionally, and from time to time I have to get away. And yet I don't think that I could move away. One can't, you know. One can't simply desert, run away from problems and from friends who have to face the problems. We've become part of the city. It's important that one stay."

We had reached the door of my inn. The country sky was black, the stars dazzling.

"We've come too far," I said. "Come, I'll walk you back to the meadow." We laughed like schoolgirls, our laughter cutting through the darkness, disturbing the placid cows, who eyed us disdainfully. The stately bell cow shook her head, clanging her deep-voiced bell.

"*Na,* Berlin," Elisabeth said. "Doesn't it seem far away? It is so silent here, so remote. One feels timeless, as though history and politics and reality did not exist." I nodded. "It's hard to leave all this and go back," she said, "and yet, to be honest, I can hardly wait."

The year before I joined Elisabeth in her Bavarian village, I spent a good deal of time with her and her family in Berlin. That summer I stayed at a comfortable small pension not far from the Kurfürstendamm. Several times a week Elisabeth would join me for lunch or pop into my pension for late-afternoon coffee to talk over my latest interviews and discoveries or to tell me about her many projects and activities or to report on the doings of her sons.

Toward the end of my Berlin visit that summer Elisabeth's middle son, Peter, arrived for part of his vacation. Naturally I thought that, with her son there on only a brief visit, I would see Elisabeth less often. Instead I quite often saw both Elisabeth and Peter. He took us to drink wine in a student pub; he took us for evening strolls along the Kurfürstendamm; he escorted us to the latest films, to a concert and to the theater. Coming from a society in which division according to age groups is almost a ritual, I was amazed and impressed. Peter apparently enjoyed the company of his mother and his mother's friend.

Peter is no mama's boy, and he is not a conformist. He was in his late twenties that summer and had just completed the draft of his doctoral dissertation in political science.

"Two or three weeks in Berlin," he said, "and I'll go back to Göttingen and polish the thing off. All it needs is cutting here, rounding out there, and, of course editing. It shouldn't take more than a few weeks," he assured us. Of course it took the year, but he got the degree and was immediately invited to teach at one of the newly opened West German universities.

Peter is neither tall nor short, about average height for a German man. He is slim and wiry, has clear-cut, regular features, hazel eyes and brown hair. He wore his hair longer than was the fashion for businessmen, but it was clean and neatly combed. His clothes were more casual than is conventional for city wear, but they were not bizarre. He is intense, energetic and serious, perhaps the most complex of Elisabeth's four sons, but like the others he has a lively sense of humor, an effervescent enjoyment of living. Like his mother and brothers he is given to spontaneous, joyous laughter, which often puzzles more sober citizens.

"He's our family revolutionary," Elisabeth warned me before we met for the first time. "Not, you know, that he is really a revolutionary. I'd say his politics are slightly to the left of mine, considerably to the left of my conventional twins. But, no, he is not really a new leftist. He's far too much of an individual to fit into any pattern. He has more sympathy with the Extra-Parliamentary Opposition than the other boys do, more respect for its leaders."

"But he's not a member of any of the radical groups?" I asked.

"Oh, no. Sympathize he might, but I think he would feel rather silly actually joining a group. No, he is interested theoretically. His mind is basically theoretical, while the twins are straightforward and practical. I suppose it's no coincidence that the twins both chose to study law while Peter chose political science."

One evening I had arranged to meet Elisabeth and Peter at a small café in a back street near my pension. They were waiting when I arrived. Peter rose, pulled out a chair for me and signalled the waitress to bring me wine.

"Would you like to see a cabaret tonight?" he asked. I said I'd like to.

"It's not a real cabaret," his mother warned me. "It's a student show."

"I wouldn't say it's not real, Mother."

"Not professional," she amended. "The script was written by two students; there are student actors, stagehands, electricians. They've hired an old barn of a theater and done the sets themselves. It won't be elegant."

"Or professional," Peter admitted, "but I thought you might find it fun. It will probably be very left-wing and rudely anti-American, but I suppose you won't mind."

I said I'd promise not to mind, and so when we had finished our wine we made our way down the street to the barnlike, improvised theater. The production was of an off-Broadway version of the traditional Berlin political cabaret. The room was long, narrow and dingy. The walls were decorated with vivid, psychedelic posters. At the front near the stage were a few small tables for patrons willing to pay an extra mark or two. The remaining space was filled with rows of plain wooden chairs.

"We have the cheap seats," Peter explained as a young girl in black tights and a turtle-neck jersey blouse showed us to plain seats in a back row.

"Probably not worth paying the extra marks for," Elisabeth remarked.

"No, I couldn't get better seats. They were sold out. Let's splurge and have a drink," he suggested and waved several times to attract the attention of a young man with long blond hair and horn-rimmed glasses who was serving as a waiter.

"Only fruit juice for me," his mother reminded him.

He ordered one wine, one beer and one fruit juice, which arrived just as the lights dimmed. We all found the skits witty and well-acted. Politically the writing was far from subtle or original. There were the usual accusations against the C.I.A., against police brutality to students, against monopoly capitalism. There was criticism of trade unionists who care only for a higher living standard, a piece of the action, of Bonn politicians for being cryptonazis, and of American society as racist. The major villain of the production was Axel Springer, who was portrayed as an evil genius manipulating public opinion and policy through his monstrous publishing monopoly. The evening ended with a dirge decrying war, a paean to pacifism.

Capsulized it sounds dreary, but the lyrics were clever, the music original and lively, the production fast-paced and sophisticated. "I enjoyed it," I said sincerely as we filed out. Elisabeth and Peter agreed.

Later when we had arrived at an exotic-looking restaurant on one of the streets parallel to the Kurfürstendamm and ordered Turkish coffee, Peter frowned and uttered judgment. "The production was O.K."

"Not amateurish at all," his mother conceded.

"The music wasn't bad."

"I thought it excellent," I said.

"But, my God, the politics! I mean, I know what they were trying to do. They were trying to get their viewpoint over to a general audience, so they thought that they had to be simplistic, paint everything in black and white, but I don't agree with them. I think that kind of thing backfires."

"I'm not sure it always backfires," I said, thinking of some successful propaganda of the past, "but I agree that this was mistaken. They weren't playing to a broad, general audience but to a very narrow, specific one. I don't think there were a handful of *bons bourgeois* in the house tonight, do you?"

"All students and young intellectuals," Elisabeth said. "I think I was the oldest person there."

Over our second cup of the sweet, thick coffee, Peter said that he thought perhaps the problem was that the authors really thought in simplistic terms. "Not that simple, you know, but overly simple. I know a lot of these new-left intellectuals, and I find that when we talk for a long time they always tend to fall back on clichés and moralistic dogma.

"I agree with most of the leftists on the description of the problems. I agree that most Bonn politicians are a mess, but I think they are inefficient, unimaginative or corrupt, not that they are nazis. Honestly. I know what nazis are and I dare say my mother knows who they are, the ones that are left, and nazism in Bonn is not our problem."

"There are some old nazis in Bonn, Peter," his mother pointed out.

"Oh, sure there are, and there are some trimmers, but I'd bet our radical friends never mention that. I believe that there are men in business who only care about profit, and men in trade unions who only want higher wages, but I don't buy the conspiracy bag. Frankly, the idea of the chairman of the board of General Motors sitting down with the Joint Chiefs of Staff and pondering where they can launch the next war is childish."

I said I agreed. "Then you're not a Marxist or neo-Marxist?" I asked.

Peter shook his head. "I'm not really anything," he said, almost regretfully. "I mean, I don't think that economics alone determines policy or history, although I'd be a fool not to admit that it plays a part, probably a major part. No, I think there's a lot to be said for psychological motives: fear, ambition, pride, insecurity and sometimes just plain stupidity."

"Sometimes," I suggested, "policy results from private ambitions, from private rivalry between generals, between cabinet ministers. It's interesting to speculate what role sheer chance plays in determining policy and history."

"Like which general happens to be commander in Berlin when the blockade begins, or who happens to be president in the U.S. when the Wall goes up, and what other crises are occurring at the time?" he asked.

"Exactly. Whether there's unemployment or inflation, whether there's an election the next year or not for three years. All of these factors play a role."

"It seems so," Peter said, "and so it's childish to oversimplify. I think the U.S. involvement in Vietnam is not so much a conspiracy as it is the result of your leadership's having got stuck there. They have got frozen into one way of thinking, one way of looking at world politics, at war.

Now they can't break out even though they may want to or need to. Actually, it's tragic rather than evil."

"What about the Soviet leadership? Aren't they frozen too?" his mother asked.

"God, yes! Those poor guys are even worse off because they're stuck with a dogma and a rigid party machinery. Well, look at Czechoslovakia. Instead of welcoming the Czech attempt to liberalize socialism, taking it as an example, as a way out, they were almost compelled to throw in their tanks and crush the reform. Yes, that's tragic too."

"Do you endorse the Yugoslav or Swedish forms of socialism?" I asked.

"Not really," he said judiciously. "I believe in fairness, in social justice, in humanity, not terrorism or repression, but I also dislike any form of centralized authority, and all the types of socialism I know lead to bureaucratic centralism. I guess it's our Kreisau background, but I have always believed in decentralization, in a federal form of organization, in maximum local and private control. How you are supposed to preserve that or rather achieve it, and still have social fairness, I don't know. I think Israel comes closest to my ideal, but perhaps they only achieve it because they are under a constant state of siege, in constant crisis."

Elisabeth nodded. "That's certainly a factor, and Israel is still a young nation. Its founding generation is still more or less in charge."

"I guess we're all cynical." Peter said.

"No," I said, "not really cynical. It doesn't help to solve a problem to pounce on an easy answer that doesn't hold water. That's not a solution, it's a soporific."

"True," he said. "I suppose the underlying problem is just the state of technology, or urbanization. Maybe we are all nostalgic for the old rural, organic community, left- and right-wingers alike. Maybe with complex technology, highly sophisticated, interrelated industry it doesn't matter what kind of government you nominally have; maybe it must inevitably be bureaucratic, inefficient and a little corrupt? God, I'm not an anarchist or a Luddite, but I can't help sympathizing with their frustrations and despair. I'm not the kind of person to throw rocks, much less bombs, but sometimes the sheer helplessness makes me wish I were."

I said, "Then you don't have any theoretical solutions?" He shook his head gloomily. "What do you teach your students?"

He grinned, "The same as you, I suppose. I teach them the questions and prod them into thinking about them, but I don't provide answers."

"You explode their easy answers?"

"Sure, that's my job. I try to make them think logically, think on the basis of facts, and think things through, and I try to encourage them in spite of everything to keep alive, to keep human, to be people, feeling, loving, individual people, you know. What else can one teach?"

"That's a great deal," I admitted, and his mother agreed.

"How is Peter?" I asked Elisabeth when I telephoned her from Munich the following year.

"*Ach,* Peter!" she said and sighed. "Our leftist, not quite revolutionary Peter is about to be married."

"Doesn't he approve of marriage?" I asked, knowing that some young intellectuals do not.

"Well, he doesn't approve of the idea that two people who love each other have to be married, and frankly I agree with him about that."

"Yes, so do I if they're not really sure they want to stay together and if there are no children involved."

"Well, in this case there's no baby on the way; there are just the girl's parents, who are very strict, very conventional Catholics, and there is the school the girl works for. She's a teacher in a private Catholic school, and they simply refused to keep her if she lived in sin."

"Oh, dear, that's a complication," I said.

"Much as they didn't want to marry until they were better established professionally and financially, at least until Peter had finished his habilitation and they knew where they were, they now have to marry or separate. Of course there was a tearful scene. The girl said she would leave him, and of course he rushed off to get the license and book the church."

"Naturally," I said smiling.

"The wedding, if you please, will be held in full baroque splendor." She told me the name of a famous and very beautiful Catholic church. "The bride will wear white and a veil, and there will be bridesmaids, a reception and all the trimmings. So much for intellectual revolutionaries and nonconformism."

"Elisabeth, dear, you said he was theoretical."

"Aren't they always?" she asked. "Well, almost, and thank God, when the chips are down they are just almost ordinary and really rather nice youngsters, even if this one is my son."

25

Pastor Carl, II

"Do you think the sun will hold out?" I asked Carl. "I've been almost too lucky this summer."

"There are a few clouds," Carl said, "but I think you can count on enough sun to get good pictures for another hour or so. After that if it rains we'll go and drink tea and pretend we're in England."

"Or beer and pretend we're in Bavaria!" I countered, and he grinned. "First, though, I want to get some pictures of the Wall and if possible, people near the Wall."

"Well, we'll try," he said. "We're almost at Checkpoint Charlie, but you don't want anything as trite as that. Charlie is a cliché, literally."

"No, I won't snap him, but I'd like a good lonely segment where I can get a long shot of towers and barbed wire, perhaps a few guards with dogs and guns."

"If we're lucky maybe we'll see a refugee just leaping to avoid a land mine."

A few minutes later I asked, "Don't I recognize this neighborhood? Aren't we somewhere near the City Mission?"

Carl nodded. "Very near, but instead of turning west up ahead, we'll drive east to the Wall. That big street runs straight into the Wall. There's a lookout tower that we can climb, and you might get some photos from there."

I have never grown used to the Sleeping Beauty quality of streets and neighborhoods intercepted by the Wall. Where the Wall cuts across it is as though life had been frozen. Up to the Wall, traffic moves, shops thrive, pedestrians stroll and shop, children run and play, and then abruptly all movement stops.

On Saturday mornings there's very little traffic close to the Wall. Carl pulled his blue Volkswagen up to the curb not more than twenty or thirty feet from where the street bluntly ended.

"No rain yet," he said, scanning the sky, "but unfortunately no local color at the moment either. Oh, well, you must make do with watch-towers and militant guards." He led me to a flight of improvised wooden steps and we clambered up.

"There," he said, "you have a whole vista of the Wall. Luckily it curves just ahead right after that watchtower. It makes a good shot, doesn't it?"

"It does indeed," I said, carefully measuring the light and adjusting my camera. "Look!" I pointed. "Here come two guards with a feral-look-ing Alsatian. Let's see whether I can get them at a good angle." I focussed the camera and waited until they came closer.

"They know you're photographing them. I suppose they're used to it," Carl said. "Weird feeling, isn't it? There are those two fellows armed to the teeth just a few yards away. We could toss a stone and hit either one. I don't know much about up-to-date military hardware. My infantry days were a long time ago, and as I've told you I did most of my fighting in the orderly room, but that looks like a very sophisticated rifle the comrade on the left is carrying. Mean-looking weapon."

I took several shots and then noticed the guard inside the watchtower in the middle distance. "Look, Carl," I said, "he's watching us through field glasses."

"Should I wave?" he asked.

"Better not," I suggested, snapping the guard in the tower, "he might think you're tossing over a grenade."

"Grim sight, isn't it? It's as though there were a prison camp stretching off as far as you can see in either direction. Wall, barbed wire, tank traps, death strip. You see they've torn down all the houses anywhere near the Wall to make this wide-open strip, which they mine and patrol. In the old days there were often apartments right up against the Wall. At first they just blocked up the windows facing west and put barbed wire on the roofs, but despite that too many people crossed over that way. Now the Wall is more efficient and it looks more permanent."

"You're right, it looks exactly like the more penal kind of prison. Do you think if we drove further along we might find some people?"

"We'll try," he said, and so in five minutes we had parked a little further north, again in a dead-end street. We visited several points along the Wall and I took a series of photographs, all painfully similar. Carl remembered a large Lutheran church perched on a hill quite close to the Wall. He thought that from the hill we might get a more distant view. We parked next to the church and strolled across the grounds.

"You see," he pointed out, "right on the edge of the church grounds is the Wall, and look! What a shot that is! Lucky the sun is still with us."

"A playground!"

He nodded. "Many of our churches run day-care centers for the children of working mothers. The church hires nurses. You see, there's a young woman in uniform sitting under the trees watching the children."

"But look at the children. What are they, two, three, four years old?—two on swings, three climbing the slide, and those darling little ones playing in the sandbox. What a picture! Exactly at the foot of the Wall." I hurried closer and began adjusting the camera.

"Can you get a shot which shows the projection of the Wall?"

"I'll try," I said and did. "There," I said closing my camera, "that's enough of the Wall! Let's go somewhere more cheerful."

Carl grinned. "No matter how far you get away from this rotten thing you don't ever quite forget it in Berlin."

"No," I said, "of course you don't, but could we try?"

He took my elbow and led me back to the car. "I tell you what, we can drive out to the Wannsee and have lunch at a lakeside restaurant. If the weather holds we can sit outside in the sun and pretend we're at a lake in Bavaria in the Alps."

We did. A half-hour later we were strolling beside the Wannsee, breathing in pine-scented air, watching sailboats in the distance and a brace of rowers closer to the shore.

"Saturday, and still sunny," Carl said. "The restaurant will be crowded. It's a good thing we came early. Should we order an apéritif?"

"Moselle and Herva," I said. We found a table that was both sheltered and sunny and that commanded a delightful view of the lake. Carl ordered the drinks from an elderly waiter who remembered me from the summer I had spent at the Trott Haus, not far away. We exchanged surprised greetings and he shuffled away.

"We didn't quite get away from the Wall," Carl said. "Look, over there, across the lake. I don't think you can see where the barbed wire begins, but it's out there marking the boundary of the Zone—oops—the G.D.R. You can't see it from here but around that bend where the lake widens you can look across and see the shores of Potsdam."

"Potsdam," I said and I thought of my visit there with my communist guide.

The waiter returned bringing our drinks and I remembered something he had once told me. "Weren't you in the Ninth Infantry?" I asked as he set down the glasses skillfully.

"*Jawohl, gnädige* Frau," he answered. "I lost that finger at Smolensk," he showed us. "Lucky it was on my left hand!"

I told him that the Herr Pastor had served with the Ninth, and the two veterans plunged into an exuberant exchange of reminiscences. They shook hands vigorously, and our waiter promised us the best of everything for lunch.

Carl smiled wistfully. "What do you think of Operation Reconciliation?" he asked.

"I'm not sure. The volunteers don't believe that their program is a cure-all, a magic formula to transmute hatred into love."

"No, I suppose not. I still can't like it. There are too many Germans, outside the Church but especially in it, who seem to get almost sensual pleasure from wallowing in guilt. I can't help it, it sickens me."

"Isn't it natural for them to feel guilty, especially Christians who acknowledge a sense of personal responsibility to God and to society, to history?"

"A sense of responsibility is one thing," Carl said, slowly sipping his Moselle. "I'm responsible, I hope. Guilt when you are not individually guilty is something else. It's arrogant, it's spiritual pride, or else it's very sick."

"There must be thousands of people still alive who have a legitimate sense of personal guilt," I suggested.

"Of course there are, but certainly not these kids who go trotting off to East Europe and Israel. What are these youngsters guilty of? They weren't even born in 1945, or at most they were babes-in-arms. If they have guilt feelings it's because they're indulging in adolescent fantasies of being a good deal more powerful and important than they are or are ever likely to be, or else they are pulling that old kid trick of blaming everything on their parents, poor slobs."

I couldn't help laughing. "You're right about that, probably," I said. "The parents of the most militantly self-castigating kids probably spent the war selling drygoods over a counter."

Carl's bearlike roar rang out over the Wannsee. "There speaks the daughter of a hundred generals!"

"Daughter-in-law," I said modestly. "But seriously, how many of their parents had any real responsibility?"

"Precisely," Carl said, still laughing. "Probably most of their papas did just about what I did in the war, wielded typewriters or pencils."

"*Na, ja,*" I added, "or perhaps took some potshots at Russians or even Americans, who were damned well shooting back!"

"So you agree with me?" Carl said.

"Obviously," I said, "I agree that most of the kids who go off kibbutzing have no personal guilt to expiate, even if they reckon unto the third and fourth generations, but they may sincerely feel that they share in a general, national guilt, mayn't they?"

"Precisely my point, Sister Anne, they may not! Responsibility, yes, guilt, no. Two reasons, psychological and theological. Guilt can only be personal, not general. To imagine that you are guilty for actions which occurred before you were born or over which you exercised no influence, let alone controlled, is just plain sick. Theologically, if you really are guilty and are truly sorry, if you confess your guilt and ask forgiveness, then you are forgiven; that's the end of it. Not to accept forgiveness is not a sign of higher virtue but of spiritual pride."

"But what about legal, historical responsibility? Isn't it a virtue to want to make good, to compensate?"

"I have nothing against building projects in themselves," Carl admitted. "As a Christian, I think good works are always a good thing. If these works were offered in a spirit of compassion or of love for one's neighbor, I'd stand and applaud. In fact I do applaud our Peace Corps efforts, our West German technical aid to developing countries, our aid to war-devastated areas. I work as hard as the next fellow on all these efforts, but moral masochism is something else, and frankly, it's never a very lovable trait."

"I think I see your distinction," I said.

"It's still early for lunch," Carl said. "Let's dissipate with another Moselle and Herva," and before I could answer he signalled the waiter.

"No wallowing in guilt for you!" I said, and he laughed.

"No indeed! There's something cheap and vulgar about crawling in an agony of guilt, of wailing *mea culpa* when you know perfectly well you have no guilt. It's a cheap way of feeling virtuous, and that's always disgusting, and it's a snide kick at the people who had decisions to make and made them in situations you can't even conceive of."

"O.K.," I said. "There's something in that."

He grinned. "You're being civilized and tolerant and allowing me my hang-up?" he asked.

"No," I said, "emotionally at least I think I agree with you. Breast-beaters always make me want to run for the nearest air-sick bag or bat them on the head, or at least go away and leave them some rag of dignity, but I'd not yet elevated an emotional reaction to a philosophical principle, much less a theological one."

"Am I doing that? Well, maybe, but I think it's a little too easy to be ashamed of one's country and a good deal harder as well as more worthwhile to accept the burden of the past, accept oneself as German and go on from there to make one's country decent."

"Certainly I agree with that," I said.

Our waiter brought the drinks, and he and Carl exchanged a few comments about Russian winters. "Well, now," the waiter quipped, "if I knew where you preached, Herr Pastor, I might darken the doors of a church once in a while!"

After the waiter left, I said, "Carl, I've seen that with a lot of men our age and older, Americans and Englishmen as well as Germans."

"Seen what?"

"You seem more alive when you talk with a fellow veteran about the war, especially about life at the front, than at any other time."

"I never thought about it," he said, "but I think you're right. I feel more alive. Is it just because it reminds me of when I was young?"

I shook my head, puzzled, and he went on. "No, I think it's because we all were more alive then. Perhaps it's the danger, the atmosphere of high adventure; perhaps it's just being away from women."

We laughed. "Escaping Nanny?" I asked and he nodded.

"I mean it. You have no idea how much fun it is for men to get away from women for a while, however much we love them. You don't have to be chivalrous or watch your language."

"Fine thing. You'd rather be shot at by a couple of million Russians than have to wash your ears." He laughed hopelessly. "But I do understand what you said about excitement, about adventure. I always feel more alive when I'm riding a fast horse or driving a powerful car, or, for that matter, when I'm in love. Do you suppose it's just adrenalin?"

"How unspiritual and deflating!" He picked up the menus the waiter had left and tentatively handed me one. "Should we order lunch?"

We agreed that there was no hurry, but we both studied the menu.

"I suppose I've become an anachronism in Germany and in the Church," Carl said, looking up. "I was never a nazi. I don't think that I was a nationalist, but now in this age of self-hatred, of antinationalism I seem as much out of step as I did back in the day of nazi emotionalism. Well, I guess both extremes are emotionalism. If you ask me, both are pathological, and they make me feel crawly."

I smiled and said, "Me, too, a little. Yes, you're a funny German. You don't hate Germany, and you're a Lutheran who doesn't hate Luther, but isn't it intriguing that I've never met a Berliner who hates Berlin, whatever his political hue or psychological hang-ups?"

"That's true, isn't it? It's intellectually fashionable to hate your country, but it's quite acceptable to love your city. Do you think that's because a city is no threat to anyone?" he questioned.

I said, "I think you're right that power and success and prestige are anathema and underdogs are in, but in a sense Berlin is a threat, and it's certainly a symbol of some very unfashionable adjectives: sturdy, independent, tenacious, hard-working, even, Heaven forefend, noble! Berlin is no antihero. It's very close to a classical tragedy."

"It certainly has a fatal flaw: it's in the wrong place."

"Perhaps that's why it is acceptable, because it is obviously tragic?"

"No good," Carl said, "Germany is tragic." He brooded for a minute and then smiled. "Let's have lunch. That's another of those profound problems that we shall have to settle later. Anyway, Pharisee or not, I'm grateful that I am not a self-hater. It must be rather uncomfortable to be the kind of person who despises what he is and who also thinks that most of his own countrymen aren't worthy of him!"

We had a delicious lunch and then decided to walk along the lake. "It does look a little like Bavaria, doesn't it?" I asked.

"A little, except that the sky here isn't quite so intensely blue and there are no mountains," Carl said.

"And the air here is Berlin air."

"Well, it is," he said defensively. "How many years ago is it that we went skiing in that village in the Alps?"

"Oh," I said, suddenly remembering the year I had lived with his Aunt Ursula in Munich, "forever ago!" I found that the memory of those cold, mountain days came flooding back to me.

I had met Carl only once before that, but his aunt had looked distressed when she opened his letter that morning at breakfast.

"Oh, my!" she said. "Carl is coming this afternoon and I have an appointment in the country. I can't get out of it. Could you entertain him? I'll be back late in the evening."

I had no commitments, and so I gladly agreed. Uschi pressed a botttle of sherry into my hand as she left, dripping scarves and mittens and shawls. "I think he likes sherry!" she said, and pecked me on the cheek.

Carl arrived at about four, looking like a bear in a tan *Loden* coat and a Muscovite fur hat. He was covered with a light dusting of powdery snow, which he shook off exactly like some large furry animal. We drank sherry and afterwards he insisted on carrying me off to Schwabing, Munich's Latin Quarter, for a Bohemian dinner of goulash and red wine.

Over dinner, almost in the middle of a sentence about Berlin politics, he interrupted himself to say, "You're looking pale. Are you working too hard?" Naturally I denied it, but he swept on: "You need a few days in the cold country air. Why don't you drive me to my bucolic Alpine village tomorrow? If you can, stay a few days and get in some skiing. I'm sure the peasant family I stay with will be able to put you up, and it would be great fun for me."

"You come here to get away from everyone, and I know you have some reading to do and an article to write. What you want in the mountains is solitude, not gossiping females!" I said, privately wondering how I could possibly leave my work, stale though I knew myself to be.

"Nonsense," he was saying. "I have three weeks. Lots of time to settle down to read and to write, but a few days of good gossip would be relaxing for me, and stimulating. You know we always shoot sparks off each other! Besides, think how much nicer it would be for me to be driven to the Alps than to take a cold, stuffy, crowded train! You can do a good work."

"Well," I said, quickly assessing what I had to wear and how much money I had until the end of the month.

"That's settled," Carl said. *"Tante* Uschi will be hurt if we leave too early. Perhaps we could take off after lunch? It's less than two hours to my valley."

By the time we left the next day it was snowing lightly, and before we had driven more than a few miles we were in the midst of a full-scale snowstorm. The roads were excellent, and my car was sturdy and built for Bavarian winters, but even so the drive took more than two hours. We were both chilled and a little weary when we slipped between two Alpine ridges and down into a silent valley. In the hollow, scattered like tea leaves at the bottom of a cup, lay the clustered houses of a typical Bavarian mountain village.

"If you painted the scene it would be *Kitsch,* wouldn't it," Carl said, "but with the fresh snow falling doesn't the reality take your breath away?" He showed me where to turn off to reach the small farm. Fortunately the house was only a short drive from the road, and the snow was not yet too deep to be passable.

"Good thing you didn't plan to go back tonight," Carl observed as we tumbled out of the car and stamped our feet. "It looks as though the storm is getting worse."

"I hope your hostess has a bed for me," I said, dragging out an overnight case while Carl struggled with suitcases and skiis. Before we could carry in the luggage both Herr and Frau T. rushed out, shook hands forcefully and stripped us of most of our burdens.

"Ja, ja, Frau Doctor!" the angular but energetic farm woman assured me. "It's no trouble at all. You can sleep in the room I've prepared for the Herr Pastor. I have made up a good warm fire in the stove up there and the bed is freshly made. You will be comfortable, and the Herr Pastor can sleep tonight in the sitting room."

I was about to protest, but she silenced me with a warm smile, "No, no, he will be quite cozy there. There's a big couch I bought especially for winter visitors. I'll make it up next to the stove. Tomorrow night he can move into one of the bedrooms, but you see I'll have to heat it during the day. He'd freeze there tonight!"

I let myself be persuaded, and a little while later Carl and I were seated in the almost too warm sitting room in front of a colorful tile stove drinking mulled wine. The snow tapered off by evening. By the time we walked briskly into the village to have dinner at the inn just a few powdery flakes swirled around us. It was exactly cold enough to give us an appetite for the hardy country food. We devoured fried potatoes and enormous schnitzels and consumed half-liter carafes of Kalterer See, the light, red Tyrolean wine of the Alps. We lingered over the wine, exchanging gossip and testing opinions, enjoying the pungent odors of burning coke, savory food and old wood mingling with those of drying *Loden* and leather.

The next morning I was down early, but I found Carl dressed and waiting, his improvised bed already made. He rose and put down a New Testament as I came into the room.

"Breakfast is on its way," he said. "Frau T. has already been into the village to fetch fresh rolls."

"She must have been up at dawn!" I said, looking at the tidied room.

"She was," he said. "Well, I guess cows wake early even in winter, and her husband had to see to them."

Frau T. bustled in, burdened with a tray piled with crockery and breakfast. "Ah, good morning, Frau Doctor!" she said. "If there's anything special you'd like for breakfast, just tell me!" I assured her that rolls and coffee were my usual fare.

"Ah, well, the Herr Pastor will want an egg and a bit of cheese, I know," she said, carefully setting out plates and cups and then pouring the coffee. "The egg will be ready, I'll just fetch it," she said and disappeared. Carl and I sat down and began to enjoy the excellent coffee, the crisp, still warm rolls.

"*Ach,* those women!" Frau T. said as she returned with the egg. "When I went into the baker's this morning for the breakfast rolls there were already several waiting. I no sooner got inside the door than I realized that they'd been gossiping. The big news all over the village is that the Herr Pastor has returned but that this year he has brought his cook with him!"

"His cook?" I said, and Carl and I both roared. Frau T. chuckled and went back to her kitchen.

"She thinks it's a joke, you know," Carl said, half-seriously, "but I'd bet anything she believes exactly what the others believe."

"That I'm a cook?" I asked, still laughing.

"My dear girl, in Bavaria a Herr Pastor's cook is not necessarily his cook."

"Don't they know you're a Protestant minister, not a Catholic priest?" I asked.

"I guess they know, but here in this isolated village they probably don't really know any Protestant ministers. To them a Herr Pastor is a priest, and if he turns up with a woman unless she's obviously his mama then she must be his cook. 'Cook' meaning the woman who lives with him, regardless of culinary activities."

I giggled. "Do you mind?" I asked.

"No, I guess not, not if you don't mind the slight to your social status, but I think I mind for them. What an attitude!"

I nodded. "Women to them are just appendages. I do rather resent the idea that I exist only as something you brought along with you, like a pair of skis or extra baggage. After all, it's my car, and who drove through the snow?"

"I apologize," he said, grinning, "but you're right. To them a woman is just an appendage, Adam's rib, and the only purpose of a woman is biological: sex, reproduction,"

I interrupted, "And cooking!"

"The idea that a woman is a person, that a man and woman could be friends, is beyond their imagination. They're not Puritans. They don't reject sex. Their whole attitude toward life is earthy, and they almost cynically take it for granted that their priests will not keep their cooks in the kitchen, the rule of celibacy notwithstanding.

"To me that seems hypocritical and yet I know they are a deeply religious people."

"I've lived down here a while," I said. "I guess I've grown used to Bavarians, but of course they're very different from North Germans, especially from Berliners."

"They sure are," Carl said. "I can't help liking Bavarians, especially the people in these remote villages, but I also can't help disliking some of their values and attitudes. I don't claim that my Berlin parishioners are all pillars of morality, but by and large they're honest, not hypocrites. Some of my younger people live together before they're married, but they don't make a charade of it."

Later that day, while we paused in the shade of a large fir to catch our breath between cross-country runs, Carl pushed a strand of hair back off his forehead, leaned against the tree and blinked at me. "You know, I've been thinking of this question of Bavarians and Berliners, of their basically different attitude toward sex, toward the body."

"So have I," I admitted.

"No wonder. I was remembering as we came down that last slope that not so long ago in the Rhineland a Catholic bishop protested against allowing Catholic girls in public schools to take gym with Protestant girls."

"Protestant girls?" I asked.

He nodded. "Well, in public schools, Catholics and Protestant kids take some classes separately. Not just religion, which is natural. Religion is always taught by visiting clergymen of each faith in separate sessions of Catholics or Protestants."

"I know," I said. "In some Bavarian schools there are two entrances, not for boys and girls, but for Catholics and Protestants."

"Exactly," he said. "Well, in some places they teach two kinds of history as well, but this bishop wants two kinds of gym."

"Why?" I asked, already guessing.

"He said that the attitude of Protestant girls toward the human body is different from that of Catholic girls. What he meant is that Protestants take their showers naked and probably prance around the locker room half-dressed."

"But girls?" I asked, "little girls?"

"They pound this modesty business into them very early. In many convent boarding schools even quite small girls aren't ever allowed to be naked or to look at their own bodies. They have baths and showers in a kind of shift."

"That's rather awful," I said.

"It's all part of the same sense of values as imagining that the only possible relationship between any man and any woman is sexual. I think it's worse than just unhealthy. It's a perversion of God's gifts. God made our bodies and he made them beautiful, made them for us to enjoy fully."

"Well, of course I think so," I said, "but then I've been brought up to value and take care of my body. I always danced and swam and played tennis. As a child I was always in and out of tennis dresses, danc-ing tunics, bathing suits, always in and out of showers. I think I spent every summer half-dressed or wrapped in a towel!"

"Well, yes, but you were brought up a Protestant. That generally is the north European attitude. Nakedness in itself, like sexuality in itself, is not sinful. It's the misuse that is sin. It is prostituting the body and

sex, using either as a commodity, as a weapon, using other people as
objects, that is sinful." Carl had said.

"You're day-dreaming," Carl said, recalling me to the present and to
Berlin.

"I was," I admitted. "I was thinking of that skiing trip and of the
conversations we had about Bavarians and sex."

He grinned. "Oho! You were insulted because they thought you were
a cook."

"I was insulted because they thought I was an object!" I said. "No, I
wasn't thinking about that part of the conversation so much as about
your own views on matters corporal. I was wondering what you think of
contemporary views, about situation ethics and communal marriage and
women's lib."

"I knew you would," he said with a sigh. "It's too complex for a sunny
Saturday afternoon on the Wannsee. Why don't you and I collaborate on
a treatise on the subject? Perhaps three short volumes?"

"Before or after we do the book on Yorck von Wartenburg?" I asked.
"And I don't want a treatise, just top-of-the-head reactions."

"O.K.," he said. "I'm agin it. I feel almost like my colleague at the
diocese. I used to think I was a liberal, even a radical, but these young
radicals have pushed me farther and farther to the right, until by now I
feel like Father Time or Colonel Blimp.

"Oh, of course, I agree with the young people's objection to hypocrisy
and to legalism. Jesus set some pretty clear-cut precedents condemning
hypocrites and placing the spirit over the letter of the law. But by trying
to separate the sexual act from the total human personality, by trying
to treat sex as though it were an activity which occurs in a vacuum, divorced from social, human responsibility, they are making the same mistake as the Puritans we both decry. Sexuality is part of the whole person,
one aspect of the whole personality. So is maleness and femaleness. You
bear your double-X chromosomes in every cell of your body, so how can
you escape them by wearing trousers? Not that I object to trousers, mind
you, as long as they are utilitarian and not escapism."

"I agree with you about sex as part of the whole person. So did
Freud, by the way. A person can't divide himself into segments without being sick. There's no such thing as 'just sex': the whole person,
including mind, spirit, social background, past, future, is always part
of everything a person does," I said.

"Exactly," Carl agreed. "The same persons who talk about liberating
women also talk as though a man could live with a woman without in-

volving her whole life, her entire personality. I'm not making the legal-istic distinction between a ring on the finger and no ring, but between responsibility and irresponsibility."

"Of course," I said, " and so far I agree, but regarding women's lib, you surely don't think that my double-X chromosomes condemn me to wearing hats in church and peeling potatoes?"

"Well, you know I don't think women are negligible. Lord! My mother isn't. I have a number of female colleagues, and I am all for encourag-ing women to enter the ministry, to study at universities, to enter all the higher professions. I think we need more women in politics and gov-ernment, more women judges and lawyers, but I think we need them because they are different from men, not because they are the same. I think women are in many ways superior to men."

Naturally I agreed, but I did not say so. Instead I asked, "How?"

"*Ach,* you know all the tests as well as I do. They are more patient, less physically violent, less selfish. Between us, I think that they are generally more grown up than we men, so why should they want to be like imitation men? They should be women lawyers, women judges and women professors and be proud of their femininity."

"By feminine you don't mean delicate or chi-chi, I take it?" I said.

"I didn't say bourgeois," he said, "bourgeois though I am. No, I mean essentially, instinctually female. I think it is an exalted, rather trium-phant thing to be. As I said, I don't mind if women wear trousers because they're more practical or warmer or just the fashion, as long as they look attractive while they're wearing trousers, as long as they don't ape the manner and the behavior of their inferiors."

"But we all do it! It's the age of revolution."

He shook his head. "In some ways it's the age of depravity. In some ways the pendulum seems to be swinging to both extremes at once." I giggled and he pretended to glare.

"Seriously," he said, but he smiled, "I doubt that there's ever been as much vocal objection to the exploitation of women, of sex, or more blatant, cold-blooded exploitation."

"The media?" I asked, "the mass press and films and advertising?"

"All of those, but also big business. Not long ago a friend of mine flew to New York as a consultant for a German industrial firm. He visited the president of one of America's major manufacturers and after they'd had a brief preliminary business talk the American suggested confidentially that since the German had never been in New York be-fore and might not have friends he might want to make use of his sec-retary. My friend thought this was unusually kind, but he said he probably wouldn't need a secretary during his short stay. The president smiled and became still more confidential. He explained that he meant his visitor could make use of her as a woman, that she was paid an exceptionally high salary and accepted extra duties as a condition of employment."

"Oh!" I said. "What did your friend do?"

"Well, obviously he couldn't do what he would have liked. Instead he thanked the corporation president correctly if not cordially and got out, but he was disgusted and furious. Not only was he furious at the invasion of his privacy, at the thick-skinned insult to himself, but he was indignant for the girl, who was obviously regarded as a hack mare to be rented out by the day or hour."

"I don't blame him, and I agree with you about exploitation," I said. "I also agree that this kind of depersonalization is the opposite side of the coin of puritanism. Both sicknesses come from the same infection."

He nodded. "Genuine morality, I believe, dervies from the affirmation of life, from respect for all of God's gifts, the body, the senses, freedom and personality and from regarding other human beings as precious in God's sight, as our brothers and sisters."

"Well," I said, glancing at my watch and at the sky. "I hope some day you will write a treatise, and some day perhaps we will get around to writing our book on Yorck. But right now it's getting cloudy, had you noticed? If we don't want to get drenched I think we ought to get back to the car."

"Gosh," he said, "it is," and we began our walk back to the restaurant.

"I think my landlady would make tea for us," I suggested.

"Good," he said, taking me by the elbow; "then if it rains we can pretend we're in England or, if you prefer, in Bavaria."

"Do you really want to pretend you're out of Berlin?"

"Na, ja," he said, "sometimes one has to pretend. Sometimes one has to get out. But I have no intention of leaving. I guess I really have become a Colonel Blimp in spite of myself. But this sandbox, this Prussia with its gallant, tragic people, its multilated, endangered capital, its fabulous Berliners, is where I belong; it is something I am part of, and it is part of me. I'm never quite whole, never quite myself anwhere else."

"I know," I said. "Could it have started to rain already?"

26

Eric, II

On my most recent visit to East Berlin I found Eric and his sector of the city both changed and the same. The *S-Bahn* cars were cleaner and there were more West Germans and foreigners travelling in the middle of the week than there used to be. There were still no West Berliners. The passengers seemed more relaxed, less self-conscious, as though travel to and from East Berlin had become more commonplace, but we still rattled over the bridge past the grim guards and barbed wire, and my stomach stubbornly contracted as we rolled across the border as it has done for a quarter of a century. At the Friedrichstrasse crossing the border guards and customs officials were more informal and a little friendlier than in years past, but they still examined packages and luggage, and Western currency is still controlled, Western publications still forbidden.

Once through the bureaucratic barrier I walked out of the station and around the corner to another entrance to take the subway. I found the subways changed. Here too the walls were bright with clean, pastel tile, and just as in West Berlin the underground stations boasted shops offering flowers, books, fashions and even antiques. I browsed in one shop, amazed to discover religious books, Dürer's praying hands and a crucifix priced at fifty-five marks. Just for tourists? I wondered, hurrying aboard my train.

Outside in the street I also noticed a difference. There were more people wandering or walking briskly, and they were far better dressed than a few years ago. Many young girls wore their skirts at the length fashionable that season rather than at a length two years out of style. A few young men wore sideburns but timidly and with restraint. There were very few beards in a year when Madison Avenue and Wall Street boasted bearded executives.

Fig. 22. Fashion photographer and model on Unter den Linden, East Berlin; VOPOs in background (photo by Landesbildstelle, West Berlin)

I stopped to look at an Intershop, which sells luxuries in exchange for foreign currency, and found the cameras, books and porcelain attractive. The young saleswoman was equally luxurious and attractive, smartly dressed and discreetly made up.

She is wearing eye make-up! I thought, astounded, and I admired her well-cut hair and equally well-cut dress. As I came out of the shop a young man in a boxy sports jacket stopped me and asked diffidently whether I could exchange some money for him. He was willing to pay me the black-market price in East marks for any foreign currency. It seems that some commodities can only be found in an Intershop, but East Germans cannot buy them without foreign currency. I wondered how many foreign and West German visitors dabble in this illegal but profitable activity. "Lots," Eric told me later, "because it thrives."

I passed two girls of about fifteen. One was dumpy, bulging in all the wrong places with puppy fat. Her ill-fitting, drab skirt hung unevenly, and she clumped along on stubby legs. Her companion, equally plainly dressed and heartily licking ice cream on a stick, had the face and figure of a Dresden shepherdess. I wished that I had my camera in focus or that I dared ask them to pose.

Clusters of construction workers, looking and acting for all the world exactly like New York hard-hats, laughed and joked and flirted robustly with me and immediately volunteered to pose. A string of schoolchildren wearing knapsacks or carrying books, chewing candy or gum or gnawing on apples, looking just a little plainer than their West German counterparts and perhaps a little quieter, were also willing to pose. Friendly people, I thought, and very kind, somehow nicer than West Germans, even than West Berliners, and I wondered whether it is only because they have been less spoiled, at least until now.

Even the placards, omnipresent witness of a socialist society, had changed. There seemed to be fewer of them, and they were not only less obtrusive, but they were more cheerful. The Berlin bear, long portrayed in West Berlin as a playful, dancing cub, now had grown almost equally light-hearted in East Berlin.

I walked through the construction area at the Alexanderplatz, cautiously stepping over stacked pipes, skirting bricks and tools, smiling at hard-hats or grinning at their comments, taking occasional snapshots. The new Alex was an impressive project, German in style not Russian. The television tower, fourth highest in the world, was also impressive. The area ultimately will include apartments, office buildings, shops and a tall international hotel, all centered around a broad open plaza. The entire area stretching from the Alexanderplatz railway station, past the

Fig. 23. Elderly man feeding pigeons in the Alexanderplatz, East Berlin (photo by author)

new hotel and the House of Teachers as far as the old city hall, will be transformed into a modern, elegant, and very lovely downtown center.

When I arrived at the Hotel Berolina I glanced at my watch and found that I was a little early for my appointment with Eric. I walked into the lobby and found it crowded with foreign visitors. Several young men dashed past me chattering in rapid French. I wondered whether they were students. There were a number of young girls and a sprinkling of older women, all rather dowdy, with lumpy figures, ill-fitting clothes, ill-cut hair—probably, I thought, from some corner of Eastern Europe. They looked decidedly less prosperous and less modern than East Berliners.

A sleek Mercedes sight-seeing bus pulled up in front and disgorged a surge of prosperous-looking West German tourists. Some of them had dumpy figures and lacked a sense of style and yet even the plainest among them bore the indefinable but unmistakable stamp of affluence. Looking over the people wandering through the large hotel lobby I found it reasonably easy to sort out the pecking order: West German, East German, Soviet, and last, Eastern European. The general standard of East German dress and appearance had greatly improved, but a West German was still clearly discernible: well-cut hair, better-quality shoes and handbags, better-tailored clothes, with small touches like jewelry, gloves, make-up and scent.

Clearly Eric was not waiting inside the lobby, and I went back outside to see whether he had arrived and was waiting there. It was a pleasant day, and so, even though he was not yet there, I decided to wait for a while in the fresh air. Two boys of about ten came up to me, stared, and one of them grinned.

"You're waiting for someone?" he said, and I said I was.

"Are you from West Germany?" he asked, and his young companion eyed me suspiciously.

"No," I said. "I live in the United States."

"America?" he said, wondering, and his friend's glare became still more hostile. "You mean you just came here? When? How? Did you fly? On a jet?"

"A big jet to Frankfort," I said, "a smaller jet prop into West Berlin." I said that I had arrived just three days ago.

"All planes from America should crash!" the hostile friend said.

"Don't pay attention to him," the friendly boy suggested. "His father's an official."

I grinned. "What's yours?"

"A doctor. You have to be something to live around here," he ex-

plained, gesturing at the apartments lining and surrounding the Karl
Marx Allee. "An official or an intellectual or a manager. Otto thinks he
has to hate all West Germans and especially Americans. Are you from
the C.I.A.?"

I laughed and asked whether he expected me to tell him if I were. "I'm
a teacher," I said.

"Oh, an intellectual." He nodded wisely. "I'd like to visit America
and fly in a big jet. If I'm a doctor like my father, maybe I can."

"I hope so," I said.

"You're wearing a cross!" his young friend accused. I nodded. "That
means that you're a Christian? Do you go to church?"

"Sometimes," I said, "when I am not travelling or too lazy."

"An intellectual?" he said, incredulous.

Just then Eric walked up, looked at the two boys and asked, "Are you
flirting with two young men or are you trying to recruit them for the
C.I.A.?"

"You too?" I said, laughing.

We strolled back into the Berolina. "Let's have a coffee at the new
coffee bar," Eric suggested. We found stools at the central counter and
persuaded a harried young man in a white coat to serve us small cups of
strong, fragrant coffee, real, not *ersatz*.

"Your coffee has improved!" I said, sipping.

"Yes," said Eric. "We have more exports so we can afford to use a
little of our foreign currency for a few luxuries."

He offered me a West German cigarette and lit it successfully with the
first strike of the match.

"Your matches are better too," I said.

"Everything's better."

"Strange, isn't it, that small things like matches should lag behind for
so long."

The coffee was excellent, probably the direct result of the growing
East German trade with Latin America.

"Our whole consumer industry has improved," Eric explained. "Until
about 1964 we were forced to reinvest most of our profits in capital expansion. The whole thrust of our productivity went into producing goods
for export or into capital goods, machines, factories."

"I realize that," I said. "You lost proportionally far more through dismantling than West Germany did, and you had no Marshall Plan."

"Quite true," Eric said, "and yet by 1965 we had reached the rank of
sixth or seventh in the world in terms of gross national product. Between
1950 and 1961 our productivity in basic industries almost tripled; in

metal industries it quadrupled; and yet our living standard couldn't rise proportionally because most of that production was in capital goods."

"You were losing people too," I said.

"Three and a half million by 1961," he said. "Of course, some were elderly people who emigrated legally, but many were young doctors or engineers or skilled workers. It's quite true that since the Wall has curbed the illegal flow of talent and skills our productivity has risen."

"I take it that your seven-year plan was successful?" I asked.

"Overwhelmingly," he said proudly. "We expected to increase overall productivity by eighty-eight per cent between 1959 and 1965, and we exceeded that. I brought some statistics for you. They're in the car."

"And this has gradually permitted an increase in consumer goods?"

Eric nodded. "During the past five or six years we have slowly been able to increase consumer-goods production. We've gradually reallocated profit until now only twenty-five per cent needs to be reinvested. That means seventy-five per cent of all productivity is available for distribution."

I said, "You also have more trade with nonsocialist states, don't you? I suppose that means you can import more of their luxury items."

"Most of our trade is still with the other socialist countries—seventy-five per cent in 1969, but that means twenty-five per cent with capitalist countries."

"Therefore coffee," I said, emptying my cup and extinguishing my cigarette. "What shall we do this afternoon?"

"Anything you like," Eric said. "I haven't made any plans. I have tickets for the ballet for Tuesday if you can come over, and I thought we could have dinner this evening at the *Rathaus* because you like that, but I didn't plan anything today. Would you like to see Potsdam again?"

I picked up my bag, and we walked slowly to the door. I shook my head. "I don't think so," I said. Once had been enough. Three or four years back Eric had arranged a drive to Potsdam as a special treat for me, and we had visited the famous palace, but I had found the shabbiness, the decay, the neglect depressing. Tourists came from all over Middle and Eastern Europe, even from the Far East, to pay their admission fee to see the palace of Frederick the Great, but the palace seemed run down and dispirited. Old Fritz had deserted it, taking the *lares* and *penates* with him. I had no desire to return to the empty shell. If he were alive, you would not be here, I had thought then, glaring gloomily at my pedantic, doctrinaire escort.

"Well," he mused, "what about a collective farm? Or the zoo? Or the races? There are trotting races this afternoon just outside the city."

"Biological, aren't you?" I said. "Are you catering to what you consider my political philosophy?"

Eric laughed. He laughed more frequently and more easily these days, even about ideology.

"My dear Doctor Anne, I have never accused you of being a National Socialist! After all, you are a follower of Stauffenberg, so we consider you a National Bolshevik."

"Heavens!" I said, "what's that? It sounds catching."

"Unfortunately, it is not. A National Bolshevik is, well, let's see, how do I explain?"

"A revolutionary conservative?" I ventured.

"A progressive conservative or a progressive with strong national feeling."

"All right," I said. "I plead guilty, but I'm not sure poor Claus Stauffenberg would agree. I'm not sure I can accept the tribute of being one of his followers except in the academic sense, and that takes no great moral courage."

"Well, where shall we go?" Eric asked.

Over the years Eric had escorted me all over East Berlin and its outskirts. One day we had taken an all-day cruise on one of the ships that plow through the rivers, lakes and canals that surround Berlin. Another day we had driven out to visit a collective farm and been amused by arriving right in the middle of a furious argument among the farmers about the coming election of a supervisor. One farmer had been both a little drunk, even though it was not yet noon, and extremely irate. He kept insisting belligerently that he would be damned if he would vote for "that fellow" and was apparently trying to convince his colleagues, by violence if necessary, not to vote for him.

We had visited the zoo, a large hospital, a prison, a student home, an old people's home, a factory, a co-operative garage and dozens of private East Berliners. We had been to the opera, the ballet, to films and to the Distel, East Berlin's political cabaret. We had eaten at lakeside restaurants, in neighborhood pubs, in school or factory canteens and in elegant international restaurants.

"Let's just drive," I suggested, "and perhaps have coffee at one of the lakes, and you tell me about yourself. I have interviewed so many people in East Berlin but never you."

Eric blushed. "You don't want me for your book," he protested. "No, you want interesting people like professors and factory workers and youth-group members and retired dancers. Not me."

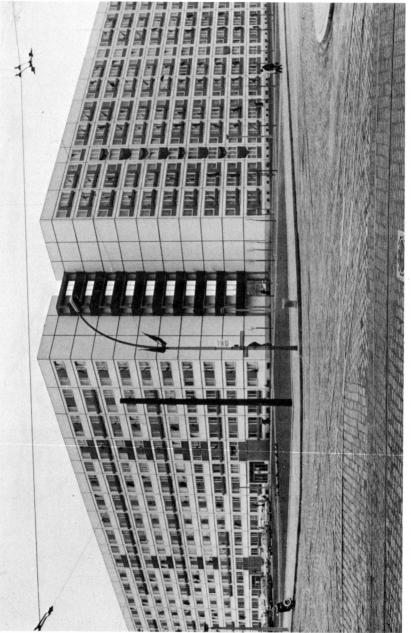

Fig. 24. Apartment building in East Berlin, 1970 (photo by Landesbildstelle, West Berlin)

But, of course, I realized that I knew him far better than any other East Berliner.

"You are not really a Berliner, are you?" I asked, and he admitted that he was not.

"You see, you can't use me!" he insisted. "I was born in a small village in Saxony. Actually it's only by chance that I'm not a West German."

When I asked "How?" he explained that his father had been mustered out of the army in the West, and in those early days it would have been possible for him to have stayed there and arranged for his family to join him. For some reason he decided against it and returned to the Soviet Zone. I did not ask Eric whether he was glad or sorry, but I had the impression that he looked just a little wistful.

"Your father was in the infantry, wasn't he?" I asked.

Eric nodded. "He fought from 1941 straight through Stalingrad on the Eastern Front, but he was one of the lucky ones. He was wounded just before the airports fell and was evacuated from Stalingrad. It wasn't a bad wound, but, by the time he was fit for service again, his old unit had been wiped out or captured, so he was reassigned to the West."

"Since you were able to go to the university, I take it that your father was never a nazi," I said.

Eric grinned. "He was never a Party member, but if you ask me, he's still a nazi. Of course, he doesn't admit it except when some of his old army comrades get together and they drink too much beer. Then they start singing their old songs and get sentimental."

"That embarrasses you?" I asked.

He nodded. "It used to. I've got used to it, and things are more relaxed here than they used to be."

By then we had arrived at the rural outskirts of the city and were driving under great, shady trees.

"Did you study politics at the university?" I asked.

"Economics," he answered, and he explained that he had achieved about the level of an American master's degree. "I wasn't a brilliant student," he admitted, "not cut out for an academic career, but I was good enough to pass the civil service exams."

I realized that I knew almost nothing about his personal life, and so I began to ask questions. He told me that he had been married for about two years.

"We have a new baby," he said. "A girl. I'll show you her pictures when we stop for coffee."

Janita was six months old.

"We live in the suburbs now," he said. "After the baby arrived, we qualified for a larger apartment, so we started hunting and were lucky enough to find a whole house. It is old-fashioned and small. Just two tiny bedrooms, a little box of a parlor, an old gas stove, and hot water from one of those little electric boilers over the sink, but we have a garden overgrown with lilacs and roses. We even have a couple of small apple trees. It is very pleasant and better for the baby than a city apartment."

"Do you garden?" I asked.

"No, but my wife is learning. She's a city girl and never had more than a window box, but she got a couple of gardening books from the library. She spends a lot of time outdoors while the baby is sleeping in her carriage, so she potters."

"Do you have any pets?" I asked, remembering that he had always seemed nervous whenever we had encountered a dog, especially a watchdog.

"No," he said. "I don't like dogs."

"Cats?" I asked.

"I've never paid much attention to cats. Actually I can't understand the fuss some people make over animals. It seems a waste of time to me and a little silly."

I nodded realizing that Eric very likely considers anything but work and ambition silly. There is nothing playful or light-hearted about the sober, industrious Eric. I wondered whether he would think it silly to play with his daughter. Certainly I could not imagine him crawling on the floor with her or bringing her absurd presents. When I am not irritated by Eric I often feel a little sorry for him.

He turned off the main road and drove along a narrow, country road which threaded between tall pines and firs. The scent of evergreen forests grown on sandy soil reminded me of Pastor Carl. Just over there, I thought, a few miles if we could drive directly; but the only way I could get back to that West Berlin forest would be to return to the center of the city, cross at an official crossing, then travel back to the outskirts on the Western side. And Eric cannot get there at all, I thought. Absurd!

"There's our lake," Eric said, pointing to the left. It was one of the smaller lakes surrounded by a sandy shore, evergreens growing almost down to the waterline. There were two small sailboats scudding across the far end of the lake. At our end a small cabin announced that it served beer and coffee. Eric parked the car and came around to help me out.

"Can I leave my notebook here?" I asked, sure that I could.

"Of course. In East Berlin no one would steal anything. This isn't New York. Have you got your revolver? Your tape recorder? You'd better take those with you."

"Of course," I said. "Revolver in my purse, and see this?" I held up a garden-variety ball point pen. "The latest thing in tape recorders."

"Aha!" he said. "The C.I.A. is ahead of us again. I suppose that cross you wear is really the microphone."

"You guessed. What a rotten agent I am!"

We both laughed as we trudged through the sand toward a wooden table under a tree. I reflected that Eric had come a long way to be able to joke and laugh about the C.I.A., even to laugh spontaneously about anything. I wondered whether he had mellowed or simply had grown accustomed to me.

"Remind me to give you the newspapers I brought for you. I thought you'd like to see what our press has been saying about the four power talks," Eric said.

"Thank you, I would."

"I brought some from each of the parties so that you'd have a cross-section."

I knew about East German cross-sections. It is true that East Germany has a variety of political parties, more than West Germany. It is also true that each party has its own newspaper, but it is just as true that on any given day the news and editorials in any minority party newspaper will be almost verbatim the same as those in *Neues Deutschland,* the official communist organ.

Eric ordered coffee and for himself cake, having by then learned that I never eat it. My mind continued to pursue the question of the minority parties.

"Do the parties other than the S.E.D. manage to recruit young people? What kind of young men and women, for instance, join the C.D.U. and become active in it?" I asked.

"They get some," Eric answered sceptically, as if wondering how it was possible. "Some young people from conventional, middle-class families with a religious background want to keep their identity. They want to be active in politics, but they can't bring themselves to join the S.E.D., or perhaps they don't want to offend their parents, so they join the C.D.U."

"But is there any point in it?" I asked as he lit my cigarette.

"Some," he said. "Of course no seriously ambitious young person would join the C.D.U. or L.D.P. [Liberal Democratic Party] or the peasants' party because obviously the real power, real policy-making lies with the S.E.D., but young men with modest ambitions can work their way into the hierarchy of the C.D.U., let's say, and make a comfortable career."

"But never attain power. Isn't that frustrating and a little humiliating?"

"Yes, I think so, but they may feel that they can have at least some influence without going all the way and joining the majority. I guess it salves their consciences."

However, I knew that many clergymen, Protestant and especially Catholic, disapprove of the C.D.U. and prefer their church members not to be active in it. "Real Catholics," a priest had told me in confidence, "either do not vote at all or if they feel they must vote, vote C.D.U. as a symbol of opposition to communism, but they do not join the C.D.U. and are certainly not active in it because they know it is a puppet party, that the so-called coalition government is pure fiction."

"Of course, any really sensible young person," Eric was saying, "joins the S.E.D. not just because it offers more opportunities, although obviously it does, but also because he wants to help in the building of socialism. It's a challenging project and it's exciting to be part of it. It's rather futile and ineffectual, I think, to insist on remaining in the impotent opposition." He grinned, "But then I'm a socialist and always have been. I guess you find me a bit of a fanatic."

I denied this. "What about other young people who refuse altogether to join either the S.E.D. or any of the minor parties? Do you have many who just drop out, as we say in the West?"

"Some," he admitted. "You must have seen a few young men with sloppy clothes and beards, adolescents who ape the hippy style of the West. There is a minority which listens to West Berlin radio, watches their television, copies the latest slang and fashions. Libertines," he said contemptuously.

"Libertines?" I said puzzled.

"Hedonists!" he said. "Self-centered, antisocial types, but there are only a few, and they are unimportant. Most of our young people are enthusiastic or else ambitious."

Our coffee arrived, not as good as that in the Berolina but drinkable. We talked a little about my book, and Eric asked whether I had encountered any interesting West Berliners since we had last met. I told him that I had interviewed Axel Springer, and he was impressed.

"Springer!" he said. "One of our worst enemies. What an arrogant man. Do you know he built his publishing house right over a public street? That mammoth building of his is two blocks long, you know, so he just built right over the street. Imagine. He couldn't get away with that in a socialist city. When we unify Berlin, he'll have to pull that monstrosity of his down."

I smiled. I wondered whether Eric really believed that Axel Springer would be waiting in Berlin if the East ever took over the whole city.

After we finished our coffee we strolled along the shore of the lake,

then drove slowly back into the city to have an early dinner at the Red
Rathaus's famous rathskeller. We talked of politics, of women's liberation,
of prison reform, the profit motive and prostitution. Eric's conversational
style has grown more relaxed. And yet his comments on social, political,
and moral questions are still predictable, still doctrinaire, still straight
down the fairway of the current party line.

He dropped me in front of the Friedrichstrasse station at about nine.
Dinner had been delicious, and we had drunk our traditional bottle of
the excellent Hungarian Stierblut. There had been fresh berries for
dessert, French cognac and genuine coffee, a most unproletarian meal. I
thanked him for a pleasant day, and we agreed to meet at six on Tuesday
to have a drink at the Berolina before going to the ballet.

"Sleeping Beauty," he said, "and there's a great ballerina from the
Soviet Union. You will like it."

I said I was sure that I would, and I walked toward the entrance of
the station. A young nun was standing near the door holding an offering
box. She held it out to me and smiled shyly. As I fished in my purse for
my remaining Eastern coins, she explained:

"We get quite a few contributions from Westerners going back. They
have to get rid of their East marks and some of them would rather give
the money to us than to the Red Cross inside."

"No one bothers you, Sister?" I asked, and she shook her head.

"Our order is much smaller than it used to be, and we have trouble
raising money, but we manage. We even recruit some novices from time
to time. God bless you," she said, as I dropped my truant coins into the
box.

I wished her goodnight and hurried on into the waiting hall, almost
empty at that hour. Even then, though, there were a few of the perennial
elderly travellers, mostly old women, saying tearful farewells to middle-
aged daughters or young granddaughters, sometimes to a son, and then
trudging on through the barrier, carrying battered suitcases much too
heavy for them. However often I pass by, trying not to see, not to intrude
into the private family tragedy, I never become fully immune. I hate the
Friedrichstrasse *Bahnhof.*

There was no delay at the crossing, and I found a West-bound train
waiting. Within a quarter of an hour I was sitting next to a window,
watching the empty streets and political placards of East Berlin give way
to the watchtowers, barbed wire and Wall of the border. Then we hurtled
across the Spree into the lights and bustle and vitality of the West. That
still has not changed.

When Eric talks about the economic growth of East Germany he often grins and boasts that the G.D.R. has world status. It certainly has status within the Soviet orbit; it has certainly achieved economic and technological growth. Its material achievements in the past decade have amounted to a second German economic miracle. With gradually growing affluence the atmosphere has eased, producing a sprinkling of chic girls wearing eye make-up and boys sporting beards, a shower of neatly dressed, well-fed, decently housed citizens. However, there are still early-morning lines in front of bakeries because, while there is now always enough bread, freshly baked breakfast rolls are still scarce, and at the butcher's the housewife must often take what is available rather than the meat she would prefer. Luxuries are still rare and expensive. There is still the sad trickle of emigration of the elderly. The guards at the Wall still shoot with real bullets at East Germans, who still, despite the growing affluence, try to escape.

I have never learned to like Eric, but over the years I have learned to tolerate him and even to admire the very real virtues he possesses. I can never honestly say that I enjoyed a day spent in his company, but I am grateful for his tireless energy in trying to help me. I enjoy visiting East Berlin, and I genuinely like many East Berliners. Still, as I stepped off the train, glided down the old escalator, marched briskly out into the light and clamor of West Berlin and headed again for the protective bustle of the Kurfürstendamm I breathed the usual sigh of gratitude, not for the opulent shops or the atmosphere of fashion and success but for the sense of purpose and vitality. "First things first," I thought and settled down at a busy sidewalk café to sip my late-evening coffee and glance at two newspapers with two different viewpoints, delighted that one was inexcusably vulgar.

27

Kurt

Ever since my first visit to Germany in 1947 I have wanted to meet a genuine nazi. Over the years I have met any number of Germans who had been perfunctory nazis, who had joined the party *pro forma* for professional or economic advantage or for safety. I have also met people who at one time had been convinced nazis but who later became disillusioned either because of nazi brutality or simply because Hitler had lost the war. I did not want to meet opportunists or former nazis. I longed to encounter a real, live present-day nazi, one who still believed that the National Socialist ideology was basically right, that the world would be a better place today if nazi Germany had won the war and who would say so.

For two decades I never met such a person. Then I met Kurt. One day I was having lunch with a retired military man in Munich, a very dear, old friend. I complained to him that I never seemed to meet a genuine nazi. He laughed, pulled his little red book and a pen out of a breast pocket and scribbled a name and telephone number on the back of a card.

"You are going to Berlin next week. Give this man a call," he suggested.

Doubtfully I accepted the card, and sceptically I dialed the number when I arrived in Berlin. A man's voice, deep and gruff, answered, and I explained who I was, that I was working on a book, and that I would like to meet him. He immediately agreed to have coffee with me the following morning and said that he would call for me at my pension at eleven.

The next morning I worked for a while after breakfast organizing some notes, arranging appointments. Sigrid had said that she would stop by to drop off some information about the S.D.S. some time between ten and eleven. Once or twice I glanced at my travel clock and thought that the morning seemed very long, but I was busy and soon forgot about it. When the clock read quarter to ten, I stopped to shower and do my face. When I had finished it was only ten, too early, I thought, to begin to dress. I slipped into a negligee and returned to my notes, vaguely wondering how soon Sigrid would arrive.

A few minutes later I heard a knock on my door. Assuming it was Sigrid, I called out, "Come in," and quickly finished the sentence I was typing. The door opened, and I looked up. I blinked and looked again. Instead of Sigrid I found myself staring at a very substantial and startled man. Absent-mindedly unaware of the inadequacy of my coverage, I stood up, apparently a mistake. I began to say something like, "Oh, I thought you were Sigrid," and suddenly found myself enfolded in a bear hug. The brief exchange of views which followed placed a considerable strain on my *savoir faire* and, in all fairness, on his. I am not sure that my diplomacy would have extended to convincing my precipitate and misled visitor both to retreat into the hall and to wait while I dressed except for Sigrid's entrance on cue as *dea ex machina*. Her spontaneous burst of laughter turned the tide and she led him like a docile lamb out into the hall to wait. I hurried into a dress, straightened my hair, grabbed a hand-bag, and rushed out to find them chatting away like old friends. The three of us left the pension together, Sigrid bound for the university, Kurt and I for our coffee. We waved good-bye to Sigrid as she boarded her bus, and Kurt burst out laughing.

"I am sorry," he said, "but you have no idea how you looked in that Eve costume."

"I'm sorry," I said, "for the misapprehension."

"No matter," he said. "I'll dine out on it for weeks."

"With names changed to protect the innocent?" I added.

"Oh, of course," he protested. "I shall just say Eve. Now, Eve," he said seriously, "where shall we have our coffee? Not one of the larger cafés, I think. Someplace where we can talk." He seized my elbow in a firm grip and piloted me swiftly down the Kurfürstendamm.

"Pity," he mused, "you are too young to have been in Germany before the war. Do you know you are a lot like that Mitford girl? What was her name? Not Nancy, and not the leftist one. Unity! You remind me very much of her as she was then. Of course, I was only a kid, but I was a literary kid, a kind of hanger-on at Munich studio parties."

"Was she a great success?" I asked.

"Terrific," he said, "The Führer insisted that she was the perfect Germanic girl. You Anglo-Saxons often are, you know, and besides, Hitler had a weakness for the English."

"Weakness, perhaps, but he misunderstood them totally," I said.

He nodded. "He did, didn't he? With tragic consequences. If he hadn't pushed them too far, had not underestimated their pride and tenacity and their basic realism, we might be living in a very different world today."

We had arrived at a quiet café, and he guided me to a table deep in its recesses, remote from the crowded street. An elderly waiter wearing a shapeless white coat shuffled over to us, and Kurt ordered pots of coffee.

"Anything with it?" he asked.

I thanked him and said no.

He shook his head in mock seriousness. "Americans! You eat like birds. It's a wonder to me you stay alive."

He ordered fruit *Torte* for himself, "with whipped cream and lots of it!" I kept to myself my concern for the collective German digestive system, to say nothing of its waistline. Kurt was not fat but he was a large man of bearlike proportions.

"Well," he said with a relaxed but appraising grin, "what do you think of having morning coffee with a genuine, dyed-in-the-wool National Socialist?"

"I don't know yet," I told him.

"Do you really believe that I'm the first one you ever met? I may be the first to admit it."

"I've often wondered about some of the people I've met socially or in interviews," I admitted, "but I'm very sure that no one I know well is anything like a National Socialist."

"I'm not talking about card-carrying members, *gnädige* Frau. I'm not one myself although I once was. I'm talking about viewpoint, ideology," he explained.

"So am I," I said, "and I know the viewpoint, the ideology of all my friends."

"We live in a rather small world, you and I. After all, we were introduced by a mutual friend. We have many mutual acquaintances. I have a fairly good idea who your friends are, very pious and proper and clean-handed people."

"Well," I said, "they are, aren't they?"

"Are they?" he asked, raising a bushy eyebrow. "If you'll forgive my frankness, I'd call them moral snobs. They look down their long, delicate noses at people they consider nazis, and they very carefully avoid coming too close to them, but don't they actually want the same things we do? They are just not willing to pay the moral price. They want other people to get their hands dirty."

"If you mean that they're patriotic, of course they are, but national feeling doesn't make them nazi, does it? Or is that part of your definition?" I asked.

"No," he said, "I'll grant you that even Willy Brandt and his crowd have some national feeling. It's a question of degree, I'd say."

"Yes," I agreed, "I'll accept that, but it's also a question of means. Most sane people want their country to be prosperous and safe and also, if possible, to be honored and respected. It's a question of what means one can or ought to use to achieve that."

"A question of the moral price," he said. "My point is that your dainty conservative friends are quite willing to have us pay the moral price. They want the results. They remind me of a society woman who wants to have lovers but who also wants to protect her reputation."

He blinked in sudden embarrassment. "I don't mean you, of course."

"No, no," I said. "You obviously think I have no reputation." He laughed and said, "I've said I was sorry, Eve."

"You know," he continued, "it was the conservative Bismarck who was fond of saying that if you want to make an omelette, you have to break eggs. Well, your friends, my dear Eve, would like nothing better than to have the omelette elegantly served to them, preferably with champagne, but they want us to break the eggs."

"Terrible indictment!" I said.

"But you don't believe me?" he asked.

"No, not really. I am willing to believe that there are some people who call themselves conservatives who are exactly like that, but honestly no, not the people I know well."

"Ah, well," he said philosophically, "you are loyal. Conservatives are."

After a pause he added, "What do you want to know about me except that I sing the Horst Wessel *Lied* every morning before breakfast?"

"Three times?" I asked.

"At least. Five times on Sundays."

"Instead of church?" I asked, and he grinned.

"Well, in the first place, you're obviously not a Berliner. How did you get here?"

"No," he said. "I am obviously a Bavarian and probably just as obviously the son of a peasant. My father owned a good-sized, prosperous farm at the foothills of the Alps. I was the second son, and my father sent me to the university in Munich so that I could earn my living."

"Does your older brother run the farm now?" I asked.

"He was killed at Alamein, but he left a son. My nephew studied agriculture at the university, and he runs the place like a laboratory, every-

thing all mechanized and modern. It pays, and I suppose he has to keep up
with the times, but I am not at home with technological farming. I like
the old ways.

"However, I don't have to earn my living by farming, and young Sepp
does."

"How did you happen to become a writer?"

"I always wrote, even as a boy. I went to a good Catholic private school
run by Dominican brothers. By the time I had my *Abitur,* I was fed up
with religion and with too much discipline, but I had learned to write a
decent German. The monks had knocked most of the Bavarian dialect
out of my style. God, I hated them, but I admit that they were good
teachers."

"Did you intend to be a writer when you entered the university?" I
asked.

"Not really. I knew that I could write, but I wasn't sure I could earn a
living by writing. My father wanted me to be a lawyer or a teacher, but I
couldn't decide. I just took courses. I found that I wasn't really a scholar.
I was far more interested in the theater and in politics than in studying."

"Many students are," I said.

"In those days Munich was an exciting city to be young in. I gave up
the idea of a university degree after two or three years of cutting lectures
and got a job on a local newspaper. Evenings I started writing my first
novel. That was about 1937 or 1938."

"Did the first novel sell?" I asked.

He shook his head. "I guess it was pretty awful stuff.

"Then the war came along and kept me pretty busy for a while. I was
a reservist and was called up early in 1940. I spent most of the war writing, not fighting. I was assigned to the Army Information Office, and
they put me to work writing scripts for army documentary films. I got to
all the fronts, though, and even got shot at a couple of times. I was
wounded once when we were filming in northern Italy. Must have been a
mistake."

By then he had consumed his cake, and we had both finished our coffee.

"It's still early, and we have got only up to 1944. Would you like some
wine?" he asked.

"Isn't it too early?"

"Not for a very light, dry wine." He signalled to our waiter, who
seemed to be dozing, standing propped against the wall.

"This lady would like a half liter of a dry, pleasant Moselle," he
ordered.

"Where were you when the war ended?" I asked.

"In Bavaria. Of course, as a party comrade I was interned, but since I was pretty small fry, they let me out after a few months. Naturally, I had to be denazified like everyone else, but since I hadn't been a party official or any kind of V.I.P., the worst that happened to me was that I was forbidden to write for any branch of the communications media or, of course, run for office or work for the government."

"What kind of work could you do? Did you go back to the farm?" I asked.

"Yes, I went home for a few weeks to get back on my feet. I was pretty thin after the internment camp, hard though that may be to believe now."

I smiled and asked whether after that he was able to find any work in Munich.

"Odd jobs," he said. "Everything from sweeping out a pub or delivering prescriptions for a pharmacy to doing translations of English mysteries. Gradually I started doing a little free-lance writing under a pen name, nothing political, of course, and I began working on my second novel."

"A nonpolitical novel?" I asked.

"A straightforward war story. After all, I had seen a lot during the war and met a lot of soldiers. The book sold pretty well, and I slowly began to be known under the pseudonym. By then the legal restrictions on former Nazi Party members, especially unimportant ones like me, were easing bit by bit. For example, I found I could travel. I went to Ireland and wrote some articles and then to Italy, and I slowly worked up a modest reputation as a free-lance foreign correspondent."

"When was that?" I asked, "about 1950?"

He nodded. "Something like that, perhaps 1951. Ever since 1945 I'd wanted to write a novel about Berlin. I'd been back here a few times, but my old apartment had been bombed out, and there just weren't any flats to be found. In 1951 an old friend of mine wrote me that he was emigrating to New Zealand and said I could have his flat right in downtown Berlin off the Kudamm, so I flew up and grabbed it. I was in Berlin during the most exciting part of the reconstruction, during the seventeenth of June uprising in the East. I think I learned to love postwar Berlin even more than I'd enjoyed the rather hectic gaiety of the nazi Reich's capital."

"I know," I said, "as you would a sick child. I understand that the Berlin novel was a success. It was famous."

"It did well, and I was beginning to be solvent. I thought I could afford to begin writing a few political articles, and incidentally, also get married."

"Did you marry a Berliner?" I asked.

"No, I married a Bavarian girl, but I brought her here to live and by now she's as much a Berliner as I am. We spend holidays in Bavaria and sometimes she travels with me to Ireland or Italy or Greece, but she is always happy to come back to Berlin. Good thing, too, now that we have three school-aged children, and she can't get away as easily."

"Has your political writing interfered with your literary success?" I asked.

"Not really," he said. "These days I do a lot of films for television, mostly travel and feature films, once in a while a mystery or short play. I guess you know that our TV channels are left-leaning. The government bent over so far backwards to keep the information media out of nazi hands that they turned them over to left-wing radicals, who seem to enjoy nothing more than running down everything German."

He stopped because the waiter was approaching with our wine, waited while he set down the small pitcher and glasses, half-filled the glasses, half-bowed, and shuffled away.

Kurt raised his glass, "To you, Eve."

I laughed and took a sip of the wine.

"Well," Kurt went on, "one-sided as the TV bosses are, they like my films, and the public seems to like them, and, so long as I stick to non-political stuff, they go on using them, even though by now they know full well who and what I am. My books sell. Apparently the public doesn't care whether a travel book or adventure story was written by a nazi."

"Are you a nazi?" I asked. "Are you really?"

"I describe myself as a National Socialist."

"But you don't belong to any neonazi organization, do you?"

"Any so-called neonazi organization, you mean, like the N.P.D.? No. Romantic restorationists depress me. I'm not a misty-eyed espouser of lost causes. I'm not one of those old party comrades who sit around in musty beer halls or meet in dingy cellars to wear their old arm bands and sing nostalgic marching songs, moaning about the good old days. They are just pathetic. History doesn't go back. It never restores. Frankly I don't think there's the slightest chance of a return to anything like the old National Socialism in Germany."

"Then what do you mean? Just that you reject both communism and the major Bonn parties?" I asked.

"Not exactly," he said. "But obviously the old Ulbricht crowd in East Germany is nothing but a bunch of boring bureaucrats, insipid pseudo-socialists, unimaginative grey mice parading as heroes of the revolution. They are about as revolutionary as my Aunt Bertha and about as exciting."

"Do you find dullness the unforgivable sin?" I asked.

"Don't you?" he returned. "Our revolution, whatever else you want to say about it, was fun. It was tumultuous, adventurous and exciting. It was glorious to be alive and to be part of what was happening in Germany in the 1930s. Oh, I don't mean the Jewish business or the war, so don't raise your pretty eyebrows at me. I mean the whole intoxicating drama of resurgence, the reassertion of German honor and influence. That was exciting!"

"And the West Germans?" I asked.

"*Ach,* Bonn!" he said and added a Bavarianism.

"Who are the leaders of the S.P.D. and C.D.U.?" he asked. "With a few notable exceptions, and I admit there are some, most of them are third-rate party hacks chosen more for what they are not than for what they are or stand for, and, at that, some of them are third-rate former nazis without even that justification for their elevation. Look at the way they deal with the very real crisis of our drift toward anarchy. The Bonners and the West Berliners, too, are scared silly of using the power they have."

He poured wine into our glasses and continued, "I'm willing to grant that a libertarian political democracy is a pleasant thing. I wish it could succeed! But once again, it is showing that it does not succeed. Bonn is going the way of Weimar. Democracy just cannot deal effectively with enemies of democracy who refuse to be bound by rules of procedure and of fair play; it can't cope with revolution."

"Do you think the weakness is inherent in political democracy, or is this particular weakness the result of special circumstances?" I asked.

"Well, I personally think that it is both a general weakness and a specific Bonn one. The Bonn politicians are especially impotent because they are afraid not only of their own shadows, but they're afraid of ours."

"The nazis?"

"They are terrified to take any sort of resolute action because someone, anyone, especially anyone abroad, might whisper 'nazi!' They have painted themselves into a corner where they are damned if they do resist the anarchists and destroyed if they don't."

"Do you really think that West Germany has arrived at a revolutionary situation?" I asked.

"I do, Doctor Eve. Not that I think for a moment that those infant amateurs of the new left have a hope in Hades of winning if they precipitate a revolution! If and when a real crisis comes, the final outcome will not be to their liking. The overwhelming majority of ordinary Germans, both middle-class and trade unionists, the rank-and-file citizens who cleaned up the rubble and rebuilt the cities and the industry, who sweated their way back to prosperity and to some kind of international acceptance, the people who pay the taxes that support the universities and pay the stipends to students, these people are about fed up and will not tolerate being dictated to by a small minority."

"But small minorities have brought about and controlled revolutions in the past. The Bolshevists and the National Socialists were once small minorities," I submitted.

"Of course. According to Lenin, a small, highly disciplined cadre is the best tool for engineering a revolution, and I agree with him, but these kids aren't disciplined. They're a bunch of self-indulgent adolescents who couldn't subvert, much less reorganize, a Sunday school! How could they hope to run a sophisticated, technological urban society for as long as a week? They can't even run their own communes."

He laughed and lifted the wine pitcher and found it almost empty. We shared final half-glasses, and he suggested another half-liter. I said, "Heavens, no!" and refused more coffee as well.

"Perhaps we could take a walk?" I suggested.

"All right," he said. "What about the zoo?"

"The Berlin zoo is one of my favorite places," I confessed as he took me by the elbow and led me out into the Kurfürstendamm. "I've taken some fairly good photographs there."

"I go there," he said, "when I feel stale after writing too many hours or when a plot just won't jell. Sometimes I wander about after lunch or between appointments, looking at the people as much as the animals. You know the Berliners love their zoo."

"Both zoos," I said. "I've visited the one in East Berlin, and that, too, is overflowing on Sundays."

He nodded. "All Berliners. You know, of course, that the bombing of the zoo infuriated the Berliners more than anything else about the air war? They accepted the bombing of factories or even of cities because they could see that the morale and the nerves of workers were part of Germany's military strength. It was awful, but war is war, and after all, we Germans bombed London. But when the Allies bombed the zoo and the Berliners could hear the cries of injured and dying elephants and tigers and rhinos, they were simply furious!"

"I can understand that," I said. "Animals are so helpless and so obviously unmilitary, but I'd be inclined to guess that the zoo was bombed by mistake. You know how that kind of thing happened. The pilot was chased away from his target by heavy flak, and the bombardier had to drop his bombs somewhere. I remember hearing flyers joke about the tons of bombs they dropped in the Grunewald. No one shot back from the Grunewald."

He nodded. "Of course. I've heard that, and it's probably true. I'm sure no one intended to bomb the animals, but at the time one is less reasonable."

We had arrived at the zoo entrance. Kurt bought tickets and pushed the turnstile for me to ease through. By then it was about noon and handfuls of workers and office girls had joined the mothers and grandmothers with small children strolling through the zoo.

"So many old ladies!" Kurt said.

"Everywhere in Berlin," I said. "It's a city of old ladies."

"Well, at least they have the zoo and lots of parks and lakes and sidewalk cafés, the old dears. It's depressing, though, a little like an old people's home."

We walked along the path, threading our way among the numerous prams, skirting gaggles of toddlers.

"Shall we have a look at the predators?" Kurt suggested, and I agreed promptly. Absently, he guided me toward the distant sound of militant roars.

"I'm not sure I made it very clear what I meant by saying I am still a National Socialist."

"Well," I said, reflecting, "at least you made it clear what you are not, that you reject both the East German brand of socialism and the Bonn compromise. Is that it?"

"That's certainly part of it. Mind you, I'm not a spoilsport who enjoys standing on the sidelines and saying, 'I told you so.' I am not petty enough to underestimate or deprecate the accomplishments of the Bonn government. Certainly I never approved of Konrad Adenauer's subservience to the Catholic hierarchy nor could I forget his separatist past, but I'd be a fool to deny his greatness, and I don't. Erhard may have been weak as a parliamentarian, but he was responsible for what really was an economic miracle, and I give him all credit. There are individuals in both Bonn parties who have brains and courage and even patriotism. I'm not bitter and I'm not a fanatic. I just can't help believing the historical evidence which shows that liberal democracy brings about its own destruction."

"But you just admitted that Erhard's economic liberalism sparked the economic miracle, and you know what a mess economic controls had caused, both the fascist and the occupation controls, and you can see the effect of centralized planning over there beyond the Wall," I submitted.

"I'm not an economist, and I'm probably willing to grant you the efficacy of at least a degree of economic liberalism, but political libertarianism is all too likely to lead to permissiveness and then to anarchy. Plato said it, not Hitler, and, woman, it's doing it in front of your eyes!"

"If you'll forgive my mentioning a pendulum," I began, and he laughed.

"All right, I'm not doctrinaire," he assured me.

"In history there have often been periods of license succeeded by periods of downright prudery not necessarily enforced by a totalitarian government.

"Before the pill and before the modern technological revolution, which has entirely changed the role of women and of the family, there used to be a natural, built-in regulator to restore restraint. There no longer is, and look what is happening to West German society! Well, for example, I've written a couple of plays which have had a modest success, but to get a play produced these days it has to be about nude homosexual drug addicts!"

I laughed and sympathized, having also written plays about fully clothed heterosexuals with pleasant manners.

"All right," I said, "as a fellow disgruntled playwright, I grant you the excessive permissiveness and tastelessness of our era, but surely a totalitarian dictatorship is a cure worse than the disease?"

"You misunderstand me, *Gnädigste*," he explained. "I am not talking about my preferences but about, forgive the pompousness, historical necessity. It is not a question of what I want or would like but of what will happen."

"You sound suspiciously like our brothers and sisters over there."

"As Goebbels once said, two and two are four even if the Devil also says so. But I firmly believe that the Bonn government—any liberal democracy in fact—is totally unable to cope with the anarchy of the new leftist revolutionaries, with the moral decay which springs from excessive permissiveness or with the complex problems of modern, urban technological society which require planning and regulation. The leftists, old and new, have no answer. The German communists are a bunch of tired old party functionaries spouting a tired old nineteenth-century ideology. The new leftists are a crowd of infants howling for total license. The real revolutionaries in this country are the hard working, rather unimaginative, increasingly disgruntled average citizens, who are tired of all this nonsense, tired of paying taxes out of their hard-earned income to support it and tired of being told to be ashamed of being German. They are the stuff, I think, of which real revolutions are made."

"I see," I said. "You're not saying that you favor this middle-class revolution, just that it is likely?"

"Exactly. It might turn out to be pretty awful. I do not think it will be a restoration. When and if it happens, it won't revive the old slogans, the old banners, and certainly won't restore the old learers, but basically, it will be a revolution against both the old and the new left, against permissiveness and decadence."

"Who will be the leaders?" I asked.

"I don't know. Perhaps trade unionists, perhaps businessmen, but someone or some group will grasp the historical moment, crystallize the discontent and resentment and offer a program of regeneration. The new group will not call itself national socialist, of course, but you and I will recognize both its social and political base and its basic program."

"I have heard Americans predict much the same thing," I admitted.

We had long since slowed down and were standing under a cluster of trees some hundred feet from a row of cages. The roars were titanic. We strolled closer and saw that two powerful male lions in neighboring cages were hurling reciprocal insults at one another. Both males reared on their hind legs and thumped their forelegs against the wall separating them, roaring their outrage and challenge. In one cage a sedate lioness stretched and yawned, contemptuous of her mate's crude fury. In the other a temperamental young female growled and bristled and stalked back and forth, urging her male on to combat. Kurt and I looked at the caged lions, looked at each other, and laughed.

"Aren't they silly?" I said. "They both know they can't break down that wall."

"I don't think they really want to, they are just enjoying the drama of combat. Instinct, my dear. Both males are having a terrific lot of fun, and so are those lionesses, even the bored-looking one. You can't outlaw instinct, Eve, and you can't sweep it under the rug forever. It's far too much fun."

"Incorrigible!" I said, and then I took his elbow. "Come away, Comrade Kurt. I've got to go and take pictures of another wall."

"You're never far away from it in Berlin. Depressing place, and yet, one goes on living here, I guess because it's also exciting. Like the lions we're in a cage tossing epithets back and forth across the Wall, but our cage is Berlin, and, Bavarian though I am, I love it."

"You plan to stay?" I asked as we walked briskly toward the zoo gate, but even before he answered, I knew what he would say.

28

The Canon

On one of my visits to East Berlin, perhaps five or six years ago, I told Eric that I wanted to see some churches and, if possible, meet some clergymen. He looked puzzled and mildly offended, so I asked whether it was impossible to visit churches and religious leaders.

"No! No, of course not," he protested. "It is perfectly possible. There is no reason why you should not visit churches. It is just that I cannot understand why you should want to."

"It's not forbidden?" I asked diffidently.

"No, certainly not. Nothing is forbidden. We are very liberalized here." This, of course, was in the days before the Soviet incursion into Czechoslovakia, during the years when Eastern countries were beginning to decentralize their economies and to boast of de-Stalinization. Even Ulbricht's German Democratic Republic, last stronghold of Stalinism, spoke smugly of liberalization.

"You can visit a bishop; if you like, two bishops," Eric said magnificently. "But why should you want to? Religion is unimportant in the G.D.R."

"If it is unimportant, then that is important," I said, but he continued to look puzzled.

"Only old women and children go to church here," he said flatly.

"If that is true, that is historically very important, and I should like to see it for myself."

He shrugged. "Well, of course, I shall take you, but I don't see why religion or churches interest you. The Church has no perspective."

Now I was puzzled. "No perspective?" I said. "Surely whatever one thinks of religion, perspective is exactly what one would expect of Christian leaders. Surely they must view history from the perspective of two

393

thousand years' experience, to say nothing of viewing it *sub speciae aeternitatis.*"

Eric blinked in utter incomprehension. He shook his head as though to clear it. "The Church has no perspective, no how do you say *Aussichten* in English? No future."

"Oh," I said, enlightened: "Prospects." And I remembered that German and English are languages divided by a common classical heritage, that especially in East Germany words are apt to take on secondary, ideological meanings. I soon discovered that the word "perspective" is a favorite term in the jargon of party functionaries predicting progress.

Resigned, Eric climbed into his small car. "All right," he said, "churches. What kind? Protestant or Catholic?"

"Well," I said, "I want to see both, but since it's Saturday, we'd better look for Catholic churches."

"Does it make a difference?" he asked. "No churches will be open on Saturday."

"Catholic ones will," I said confidently.

He shook his head, "Not here," he said.

"Catholic churches all over the world are open every day," I said, "and especially on Saturday. They have confession."

He shook his head stubbornly. "Not here," he assured me, but he drove on, smiling tolerantly as though he were humoring a small child who insisted on hunting for tigers in the garden.

We drove away from downtown Berlin to a more residential neighborhood, and we soon saw a steeple in the offing. We pulled up in front of a large, red-brick church. I jumped out of the car, ran up the church steps and read the name on the announcement board. It was a Protestant church, and it was closed.

Eric smiled politely when I told him, and he drove on to the next neighborhood. The next church, slightly smaller, was also Protestant and closed. So was the third. By then Eric was smiling discreetly as though to say, "Tigers, indeed!" The fourth, however, was Catholic and was open.

"Do you want to come in with me?" I asked, but he just shook his head. I climbed the steps and crossed the porch. The church was a cumbersome nineteenth-century building decorated with the usual nineteenth-century, sentimental paintings. The windows were high, the interior gloomy. I made my way to a center pew, sat quietly and glanced around. Eric had been right in predicting that I would find only women and children in the church, but there were women of all ages: adolescent girls, young working women, mothers with small children, and middle-aged women as well as grandmothers. A few of the younger girls studied their prayer books, fingered their rosaries, or just closed their eyes and prayed or meditated and then rose and left. Most of the women seemed to be preparing for confession. One after another rose and went to stand in line behind one or the other of the confessionals. The church was far from crowded. There were perhaps a dozen to fifteen women at any one time; those who left were replaced by newcomers, a steady trickle if not a stream.

I studied some of the faces as tactfully and unobtrusively as I could and found worried mothers, hopeful or frightened young girls, young wives radiant or discontented, older women wistful or resigned, all serious, intent, and seemingly devout, strikingly similar to the praying women one sees in West Berlin or West Germany or anywhere in Western Europe.

After about twenty minutes I rose and walked out quietly. Eric smiled patiently and asked whether I had now seen enough. I said that I wanted to see several more to get an overall picture, and he sighed and dutifully drove on. Most of the churches we found were Protestant and were closed, but we discovered a few Catholic churches, all of which were open, and in each the pattern repeated itself. Now and then I observed a man, sometimes even a young one, but I counted many women of all ages, and they seemed very sincere.

At mid-morning we pulled up in front of a slim, grey stone church.

"I think this is a Protestant church, so I don't know whether there's much use in your going to see whether it's open," Eric said.

However just then a car drove up and parked in front of us, discharging several passengers who walked up the steps and entered the church. Moments later a second car arrived, and four festively dressed people stepped out.

"Do you suppose it's a wedding?" I asked, not wanting to intrude if it was.

"Possibly," Eric said, "but there's no harm in asking."

I decided that I could risk asking an usher. Just as I reached the top step the center door opened, and a short man dressed in dignified black and wearing a black homburg looked out, bowed slightly, and asked whether I had come for the service.

"Service?" I asked rather stupidly.

He said, "Sabbath service," and then seeing that I did not understand he explained that a Jewish congregation was holding its service in the church.

"We are a very small congregation," he said, stepping out onto the steps. "Not many of us are left. Of course, we lost our synagogue—first the nazis took it, then the English bombed it, but the Protestants in this parish have been very kind to us. They let us use their church Saturdays for our service and evenings now and then for meetings and socials. They helped us during the nazi time too. The old pastor, dead now, and some of his friends sheltered some of us all through the war. Otherwise many of us would not have survived. Some of us, of course, were abroad during the worst years and came back."

"But you don't want to hear that old story," he said. "Would you like to come in? We're orthodox, but I can show you the women's section. You are very welcome."

I would have liked to stay, but I hesitated to ask Eric to wait through an entire service, so regretfully I refused.

"Come back," he suggested, "any Saturday. You will be very welcome. There aren't many Jews left in East Berlin, and the government is not fond of us. They don't like the Protestants to help us, but they go on doing it. We are no longer important here, but perhaps we are still interesting. Do come back."

He smiled a kind and deprecatory smile, bowed again, and I thanked him and left.

"Oh, Jews," Eric said. "Of course, the Jews who count are in the Party and don't belong to the Synagogue any more, and most Berlin Jews who survived are in West Berlin because they are capitalists."

He put the car in gear and asked, "Where next?"

I said that I would like to talk with a priest but that I could not interrupt one who was hearing confessions. Eric thought for a moment and then looked inspired.

"The headquarters!" he said, by which I assumed he meant the bishop's palace, and he accelerated vigorously and drove off.

"It's been rebuilt," he said indifferently, pointing to St. Hedwig's Cathedral as we drew up in front of the classical building. I had first seen the shell of St. Hedwig's in 1947. Then it had been boarded up to protect visitors from being injured by collapsing walls or floors. It had been impressively restored.

"Have you been inside since it has been rebuilt?" I asked Eric. He said no. "Wouldn't you like to come in and see how they've done it?" I suggested.

"I've never in my life been inside a Catholic church," he said, "and I don't intend ever to go into one!"

I was astounded by his vehemence. I remembered that he had once

Fig. 25. St. Hedwig's Cathedral, Roman Catholic, in East Berlin (photo by author)

told me that he had visited Italy, and so I asked him whether he had never inspected the Italian cathedrals.

"No, never," he assured me.

"You were in Florence?" I asked and he nodded. "Venice? Rome?"

"Yes," he said, "all over Italy and, of course, I visited the museums, but why should I go into churches?"

"You didn't go into St. Peter's?" I asked, and he admitted that he had walked around St. Peter's square and toured the Vatican museum.

"I just don't like churches," he said contentedly. "Don't hurry, I'll wait for you."

I decided not to hurry. It was a bright, sunny day, and when I stepped across the threshold into this dim vestibule I blinked. I walked on into the body of the church, stood, looked around and sighed with delight. The restoration had achieved a delicate balance between modern austerity and traditional opulence. The atmosphere was almost submarine, a little, I thought, like a stage set by Wieland Wagner, stark simplicity, deftly touched by grace and fantasy.

There is no nave in St. Hedwig's Cathedral. The main body of the church is a large hexagon topped by a high, classical dome. I glanced up at the cupola. A skylight at the apex held a hexagonal cross. St. George and St. Andrew? I wondered. Ribs of medium grey outlined the contours of the dome. The high windows were of stained glass in modern, geometric design, an interplay of yellow, grey and off-white squares.

The central altar, framed on three sides by the circle of benches for the congregation, was of stark, dark grey marble and bore a single square-shaped cross. There were no statues, no paintings. Behind the altar was a mural proclaiming the names of martyred apostles, Peter, Andrew, James *et al.* In front of the altar a circular staircase led down to the crypt.

I slipped onto a bench made of dark wood and wrought iron. The lighting in the church was muted and almost liquid, but the blend of greys was fresh and vital. Glass globes strung like large grey pearls hung from the ceiling in a double circle to provide artificial light. A double column of twelve pairs of marble pillars framed the center of the church.

Here too I noticed a steady stream of penitents and petitioners, chiefly women and young girls, but here in downtown Berlin there were also men praying and even a few going to confession, workmen on their coffee break or office clerks taking an early lunch hour. Here too were some obvious West Germans visiting and sightseeing. As I sat and observed, a bustling priest shepherded a group of tourists down the stairs into the crypt.

After a few minutes I got up and walked quietly back to the vestibule. I found a sign explaining that the church had been restored with funds contributed by individuals and by the Church hierarchy in West Germany. I read, looked at photographs of the interior of the church before the restoration and fished in my handbag for a coin for the contribution box.

An elderly priest in a shabby cassock approached me diffidently and asked whether I was a visitor from West Germany. When I said that I was an American, he offered to guide me around the church, but, remembering the patiently waiting Eric, I declined.

"I shall come back next Sunday, though," I promised, "to hear Mass," and he told me the times.

"Come for the ten-thirty Mass—it has the loveliest music," he suggested.

I agreed to try to be there for it. Then I asked him whether it would be possible for me to interview one of the priests at the diocesan office. I hesitated because by then it was almost noon, but the priest promptly reassured me that surely someone would be available to speak with me.

"I knew it is not possible to arrange appointments in East Berlin," he said kindly.

He led me out of the cathedral and around to the back street, where we entered the remnant of a partly destroyed building. We both nodded absently to a woman receptionist, and I followed the father up an uncarpeted flight of stairs and into a small sitting room.

"If you will wait here," he said, "I shall arrange something for you."

I thanked him and he disappeared. I had barely time to settle myself on a rather hard couch and glance around at the small, sparsely furnished room when a young, dark-haired priest appeared at the door and told me that Canon R. would see me.

"I'm afraid he can give you only ten minutes," he said. "We are very short-handed here, and Canon R. is especially overburdened."

I assured him that I understood and followed him down the long corridor. He held open a door for me, and I entered a small reception room. A weary-looking elderly woman, almost obscured behind a wooden desk piled high with files, told us to go right in. We went through the door beyond her desk and found ourselves in another small, spartanly furnished office. There was one very plain, slightly battered wooden desk, three straight-backed wooden chairs and some bookcases. Papers and books were piled everywhere.

A distinguished-looking elderly priest rose from behind the desk to greet me. He seemed worn and truly overburdened. I was determined not to take too much of his time. He was probably well over sixty, with the spare, sharply defined features of a seventeenth- or eighteenth-century bishop of impeccably aristocratic lineage. His bow was courtly, his smile charming and kind, the hand with which he gestured me to a chair was elegant and graceful.

"It must seem very rude to begin a conversation with a lovely lady by warning her that I can spare only a few minutes," he said, but I assured him that I understood.

"I shall try to keep my questions both modest and brief," I said.

"Surely," he said, glancing discreetly at my hemline, "a contradiction?" I laughed and knew at once that we should have an amusing and sparkling interview.

"Could you tell me," I asked, "how it is that the bishopric of Berlin is only that, a bishopric, and yet the bishop is an archbishop? Why isn't Berlin an archdiocese?"

"Berlin is only a diocese. The territory included a lot more than just Brandenburg. It is a very large and important diocese; nevertheless it is, as you say, only a bishopric. The bishop, however, carries the rank of archbishop and cardinal in his person, not as the result of the rank of his diocese. He is archbishop, but he rules only a bishopric."

"Oh," I said, enlightened, "and this is the bishop's chancery?"

The canon nodded. "Yes. The cathedral and chancery are here in East Berlin as they always were, but the cardinal himself resides in West Berlin. Since the Wall was built he has a secondary seat in West Berlin, but he is one of the few people who is allowed to travel back and forth to visit his office in East Berlin. He comes regularly about three days a month.

"And the rest of the month?" I inquired.

"We have a suffragan bishop here who actually administers the Eastern part of the diocese. The diocese of Berlin is virtually split. It is administered *de facto* as two separate sees."

We talked a little about the status of the Catholic Church in the East.

"Church attendance," he said, "is very poor. Perhaps only one to two per cent of those who are officially Catholics attend regularly, and many have dropped out, that is, officially declared that they are no longer Church members. Of course, there is great pressure on them, especially on the young people."

I told him that I had seen surprisingly many young women and even some young men praying and going to confession.

"Oh, yes, many do stop by furtively, briefly, for a quick prayer or even for confession, but most of them do not come to Mass," he explained.

I asked about vocations.

"No, of course, we don't have enough seminarians, but the wonder is that we have any, and we do have a steady trickle. Some of them are excellent, too, and some of our lay people are very devoted, very dedicated. Perhaps in times of oppression, the weak hangers-on are weeded out and those who remain are genuine, productive Christians?"

He assured me that certain individual congregations across the G.D.R. were very active, filled with lively, religiously conscious Christians.

"Of course, such congregations, indeed such individuals are rare these days here, but perhaps they were always rare everywhere."

Our conversation drifted from religion and diocesan administration to the wider and more mundane spheres of politics. We found ourselves in swift and automatic agreement on most questions of basic values, and we discovered that we both liked to laugh and to turn phrases. Our chatter and laughter leaped and cantered. When I looked at my watch, the proposed ten minutes had soared to a full hour. I gasped guiltily.

"Father R.!" I said, "you said ten minutes! Do you know it's almost one o'clock?" I pushed back my chair as though to rise and he held out a hand.

"Please don't go yet unless you have to," he said. "I'll send for coffee and biscuits. Lunch can wait. That is, unless you have an appointment?"

I thought briefly about Eric waiting in the car. He had assured me that there was no need to hurry, but surely there were limits to his patient tolerance of my eccentric whim to investigate churches and interview the clergy. I hesitated, picturing him smoking, perhaps fuming. Then I glanced at the canon's exquisitely chiselled head, the delicate wisp of gleaming silver hair, the elegance of the hands crossed on the desk, the glint of wit and of discreet wistfulness in the cool blue eyes and I settled back in my chair. I told him about Eric, and he laughed and with un-Christian callousness advised, "Let him wait! He is young and a functionary. He probably has no soul, but, if he has, waiting will be good for it."

He walked to the door, opened it, and asked his secretary to find some coffee and biscuits for us. We settled back to our conversation about West German, West European and world politics, about trends in education and civilization, about love and morals and art and the theater and even about feminine fashions. The coffee arrived and was better than most I had tasted in the East. We sipped and nibbled plain sugar biscuits and talked on. Finally my conscience intervened.

"I have really kept you too long," I protested and rose to my feet reluctantly but resolutely. He walked with me to the door and took my hand.

He held it lightly by the fingertips. "Don't apologize, *Gnädigste*," he said. "You have no idea what a pleasure it was for me to be able to talk freely to someone from the outside, just to say what I feel and mean without having to pussyfoot. It has been a joy."

I thanked him and he bowed over my hand. "You also can have no idea how delightful it has been for me after all these years to spend an hour or so with an elegant woman. There are beautiful women everywhere, but elegance is the product of civilization, of affluence and leisure. Here we have all the necessities but few of the amenities, few of the graces, and I am not at all sure that grace and elegance are not necessities. They are products of the spirit and they nourish the spirit. Our G.N.P. is rising, but surely man does not live by productivity alone."

I nodded and agreed, thinking back on my shopping excursions, on my observations of East Berlin women.

He brushed my hand lightly with his lips in a courtly hand-kiss and raised an eyebrow. "Worth? Or Guerlain?" he inquired nostalgically.

"It has been a very long time," he said. "My mother wore Worth's scent and had her clothes made in Paris, but that, of course, was in another world. Thank you for coming. It is comforting to be reminded that such things still exist, at least for a little while longer."

I thanked him and ran down the stairs and across the courtyard to Eric's car. Eric was pacing up and down in front of the cathedral but as always, his control was perfect. If he was annoyed, he said nothing. He smiled wryly and asked whether I was starved.

"You must be bored to death," he said, "after spending two hours with that bunch of superstitious reactionaries." I smiled and let him take me to lunch.

29

Eleanor

More than once, probably because it is usually summer when I am in Berlin, I have visited Eleanor on or near the twentieth of July. One year I called her on the nineteenth and she asked me to come to tea on the twentieth. "I'll have to be at one of those dreadful ceremonies in the afternoon, so I may be a little late getting back, but you just make yourself comfortable and I'll be along," she explained.

Eleanor lived in a small house tucked away in a quiet street near the Botanical Gardens in West Berlin, a neighborhood in which all the streets are named for flowers. That year I had a car, and so I was grateful that hers was a neighborhood in which I could always find a parking place. I drove almost to her door, left the Volkswagen, walked up and rang. Almost instantly Marthe, Eleanor's housekeeper answered.

"*Ach,* lovely roses!" she said after we had exchanged greetings. "Yellow! The Frau Gräfin will enjoy them. I'll put them on her desk." She went off to put them into water, leaving me to find my way to the sitting room. French windows opened onto an informal garden, redolent with the fragrance of high summer flowers. I stood staring out absently at the garden, undecided whether to go outside to wait or to stay in the cooler room.

Marthe bustled in carrying the roses in a crystal vase. "Would you like me to bring your tea now, Frau Doctor? She should have been back half an hour ago, but you know what these official do's are like. They never end when they should, and then just when she wants to get away, some bore buttonholes her. They wear her out, these receptions."

I said that I would wait for tea, and just then we heard the outside door open and close. Marthe set down the roses and hurried out, and a minute later Eleanor swooped into the room calling, "Anne!" I jumped up and kissed the proffered cheek.

403

"Oof, warm," she said. She was a little flushed and her hair was wind-blown, but she looked lovely, not a bit older than when I'd seen her the year before.

"Was it horrid?" I asked.

"Awful," she said, tossing a large square handbag onto the floor. "Shall we have tea right away or would you like a schnapps first? Schnapps, I think, I need one!" She turned to extract two slim glasses and a decanter from an eighteenth-century cabinet. "You'll like this," she said, handing me a cordial glass. "It's pear." She dropped into a wide wicker chair, raised her glass and sipped.

"These twentieth of July affairs get worse every year. I don't know why I keep going. Each year fewer of the real resistance people turn up and each year there are more and more speeches by ambitious, pushy politicians trying to parade as resisters. This time there were all kinds of Bonners, people one never heard of, and of course they all elbow themselves forward, hoping to be seen, hoping to be photographed for the press or TV. Whenever they come around with the cameras I try to hide, hoping no one will recognize me."

"Bad company," I said and she nodded.

"These hypocritical Bonn people all rush to be photographed with any of the opposition people they can snare on the twentieth of July, but any other day of the year they wouldn't have time to give any of us an interview and certainly not a job."

"Why do you go, my dear?" I asked, thinking she looked tired and wishing she could have stayed at home.

She smiled and shrugged. "Well, of course, some old friends turn up. One sees friends one doesn't see again perhaps for a year. Your friend, by the way, was there this year. Usually he can't be bothered." She re-filled our glasses. "Ah, well, I suppose we are a bunch of cranks and anachronisms, but nevertheless all this hoopla and show business makes me just a little sick."

We settled down to a comfortable chat about who actually had been at the ceremony and what I had been doing in Berlin. Marthe brought in the tea tray. "Sand *Torte* and fruit tarts," she said, setting down the tray. "Made them myself, Frau Doctor, especially, because I know you watch your calories."

"There you are," Eleanor said grinning, "if you eat only two pieces of each you will hardly gain any weight." I laughed but I knew I could not refuse Marthe's baking. Eleanor poured and handed me a delicate cup.

I stirred my tea, enjoying the pleasant, relaxed feeling of being back in one of my favorite corners of Berlin, savoring Eleanor's very personal atmosphere. I have known Eleanor for years, for so long that I have forgotten when or how I met her. She is one of the relatively few genuine survivors of the nucleus of the German antinazi opposition. She has been helpful to me through the years in my search for background and understanding of the aims and work of the Kreisau Kreis.

She and her husband were both active in that famous and ill-fated circle, which was founded by two Prussian counts, Helmut James von Moltke and Peter Yorck von Wartenburg, both descendants of illustrious military families. The circle was named for Moltke's Silesian estate Kreisau, where the plenary meetings took place.

"This was not just an association of counts," she once told me. "It was no group of anachronistic gentlemen or reactionary cranks. The aim of the group was to lay down concrete plans for postwar, postnazi society and specifically to draft a democratic constitution which, while providing for maximum, or perhaps I should say optimal, liberty, would avoid some of the weaknesses of the Weimar constitution."

"Big assignment," I said.

"Tremendous," she agreed. "To make this draft anything but a purely academic exercise, we had to include all elements of the political and social spectrum in the planning."

"Elisabeth and her husband," I suggested.

Eleanor nodded. "Yes, they are a good example of the kind of people we had with us. He was an aristocrat but he certainly was no dyed-in-the-wool conservative. They were both intellectuals, scholars in their fields, probably what I would call Christian socialists."

"Slightly left of center, I'd say," I submitted.

"Well by now, of course, their views are quite moderate and middle-of-the-road, but they were definitely left for those days. Then we had some old Socialist Party men and trade-union leaders, many of whom had served in prison or concentration camps and been released because the nazis considered them powerless."

"You had a good many Church people," I prompted.

"The Church was very important in our planning. Both Moltke and Yorck were convinced Christians, as were most of us. The majority of us conservatives had been brought up as Protestant Christians, Lutherans, but as young people our religion was routine, conventional, formal, just part of our family background. Some of our people became converted to a more personal, more serious view of religion while they were students. They read the theologians and religious poetry, and they joined groups of Christian students. Some became serious Christians later as they went about their daily lives, practicing their professions as part of nazi society."

"I can understand that sensitive, conscientious people might look to the Church, to Christianity, as a standard in a situation that seemed inhuman, immoral," I said.

"Inhuman, immoral and something more," she said reflectively. "The nazi view of life lacked a spiritual dimension. These men sought that dimension. They gradually found that their Christianity had become real, alive, personal. Of course this led them to reconsider the Weimar period, the causes of the rise of nazi nihilism and the triumph of Hitler."

"I can see," I said, "that the clever scepticism, the worldly cynicism of the Weimar intellectuals and of Weimar art can be seen as a cause."

"Do you remember the Weimar marriages? Complacent husbands, broad-minded wives, each going their own way. Society was a world of intrigues, flirtation, sensuality. Divorce, which was almost unheard of in good families before the war, became commonplace in sophisticated circles, homosexuality was flaunted. Weimar Berlin was brilliant, of course —it was artistic, lively, almost hectically productive, but it was corrupt, decadent and basically nihilistic. Yes, I am convinced that the loss of values, loss of moral certainties and loss of spirit of the postwar era prepared the ground for nazi brutality."

"You agree with Voltaire, then, that it is safe enough for philosophers to be deists or agnostics but not for cooks and butlers," I said.

"Especially when there are so many cooks and butlers," she said.

"And if you elect one of them chancellor," I added.

"Exactly. It was the combination of the growing mass-democracy, which so easily turns into demogogy and mass hysteria, and the undermining of faith in absolute values that made the Hitler phenomenon almost inevitable. In any case, the Kreisau people thought so, and they intended to try to establish the new postnazi Germany on a sound Christian foundation."

"Even your socialist members, I understand," I said.

"Oh, yes. Our socialists and trade unionists had suffered personally from nazi nihilism, and many of them had lived in K.Z.s or in prisons in close contact with fellow prisoners who were Christians, often priests and ministers. Many became close personal friends of clergymen or of landowners, aristocrats, all class enemies, and they learned to admire them as well as like them."

"I've read some of the letters and diaries of Christians in nazi camps and prisons. I can understand why an atheist or sceptic would admire, even envy them," I said.

"Some envied them enough to become converted, others just admired them, thought they had something valuable for society. No, I don't mean they were opportunists, pragmatists. I mean they honestly, sincerely admired the spiritual strength, the depth of conviction of the Christians."

"I know," I said. "I've met some of the socialist survivors. Frau Leber, for instance, and Frau Suhr."

"Splendid women!" she said. "Did you know Jeanette Wolff? The old socialists turned out some pretty tough warriors. Some of them were our staunchest supporters. I think that has been one of the greatest accomplishments of the Kreisau work. In addition to providing some proof for history that not all Germans were nazis or acquiesced in nazi crimes, to the simple statement that 'we are here, we are German, we are part of the German tradition and we oppose nazism root and branch,' we also laid the foundation for co-operation and friendship between conservatives and socialists, between the Church and the old left. Class warfare couldn't survive the K.Z.s and certainly not the executions."

"Class didn't survive," I said, "did it? Only money."

"Only Bonn; *Na, ja,* you're right, but the disappearance of strictly class-based political parties is a great blessing. Class identification with all its emotionalism, its hatred, made it almost impossible for otherwise moderate politicians to co-operate in the national interest or to prevent the rise of the nazis."

I agreed, of course. "You conservatives also accepted a good measure of socialism in your postwar plans, didn't you?"

"Yes, but not as a pragmatic *quid pro quo.* We genuinely believed that it was not only necessary, but also that it was moral, just. We believed that postnazi Germany must be founded on a system of social justice and also that it must be a frankly, officially Christian society. We wanted to lay a foundation for co-operation between the Church—both churches—and the government."

"You mean include religious instruction in schools, continue the Church tax, that sort of thing," I said.

"That and more. We hoped that the government itself, the heads of the major parties, leading men in trade unions and in the professions would identify with the Church, with Christian principles, be active as laymen and so give moral leadership to society."

"Ambitious ideal," I said.

"Yes," she acknowledged, "but in some sense it has worked out. Adenauer and the leaders of the C.D.U. did identify themselves with the Church. So did many trade unionists. In Berlin Willy Brandt was a strong supporter of religion, as you know."

"That's quite true, my dear, and yet?"

She nodded thoughtfully, "And yet, we now have a materialistic, amoral society. I agree, but we tried. One must try."

"Oh, I agree with that," I said. "Then what your constitution was going to try to do, as I understand it, was to incorporate principles of Christian morality, of democratic socialism and of individual liberty?"

Eleanor agreed. "Even the most conservative members were realistic. They saw that by the time the war ended the world would have changed too much technically, economically and psychologically to make a return to pre-Hitler social and political institutions practical. Moltke and Yorck and many other aristocratic members had been reared in the principles of monarchy, but they realized that a return to the 1914 constitution, to the old form of Hohenzollern monarchy, was just not possible."

"Some of them did hope for a restoration, though, didn't they?"

"Yes, there were individuals in the group who thought a liberal, democratic monarchy under one of the younger Hohenzollerns, perhaps Louis Ferdinand, would be feasible, but the Kreis as a whole was never formally committed to the idea. The general concern of the group was to preserve the nucleus, the heart of Western culture, to protect the rights and dignity of individuals while at the same time providing for social progress."

"Not easy," I said.

"Certainly not. We held many meetings, many discussions, and appointed many subcommittees to try to work out possible formulas."

"I know. Elisabeth said that she and her husband worked on papers on economics and on social problems to present to discussion groups."

"We had all kinds of experts, economics, sociological, judicial. Count Moltke's chief aim was to establish a decentralized society, returning as many decisions as possible to the local or county or provincial level. This way not only did he hope to conteract the growth of bureaucratic centralism but he also hoped to inculcate a sense of direct, individual involvement of the citizen in public matters. He wanted to restore the sense of community which has been so badly undermined by the growth of modern industry, by the trend toward urbanization."

"That sounds almost new leftist," I said.

"Much of the new left ideology has roots in our talks or at least in the ideological sources of our views, but I'm afraid that our methods and concrete goals were very different," she said.

"The Kreisau group actually drafted a constitution, didn't it?"

"Yes. You see, we believed that it was going to be important to have our plans ready, at least to have clarified our thinking in order to avoid a psychological vacuum when the nazis collapsed. We were afraid that, unless the democratic leadership was ready with a well-thought-out plan, power would pass by default to neofascists or communists."

"You started to make postwar plans very early," I said.

"Moltke and Yorck began preliminary meetings back in 1942. Then they began to gather the various members of the groups, men of all backgrounds and persuasions."

"Wasn't it awfully dangerous for a large number of known antinazis to meet in those years?" I asked, knowing that it was.

"Of course, and so they met in twos and threes, often here in this little house, usually somewhere here in Berlin. It was a long, tedious process, sifting individual views, trying to arrive at generally acceptable principles and platforms, but finally they decided on a plenary meeting at Kreisau. Once they had worked out all the preliminaries they hoped to be able to draft a constitution in a single meeting, so they took the chance of calling everyone together."

"Didn't the Gestapo get suspicious?" I asked.

"Well, of course they were aware that both Moltke and Yorck were unfriendly and that they had an assortment of rather odd friends. Yes, they knew something was going on, but they had no concrete evidence. Later when Count Moltke was finally arrested on general principle as an antinazi, they weren't able to convict him. They held him in prison from January 1944 until after the assassination attempt in July, and probably would have released him if the failure of the attempt hadn't turned up Kreisau documents."

"Moltke himself wasn't involved in the assassination plot, then? I mean, not in the earlier plots before he was arrested?"

"No. Of course he sympathized with the plotters. Some of them were his own Kreisau people, but he personally refused to be involved. I believe that he was doubtful about the moral and political wisdom of founding the new Germany on an assassination, no matter whose, and by 1944 he thought it was too late to do any practical good. By then, he thought there was no way out of total German defeat."

"But still, he was arrested. Didn't they bring up that old charge of being an anglophile?"

"Well, as you know, he'd studied law in England, and of course he had a lot of friends there, but even the Gestapo with their famous methods couldn't find enough evidence to bring him to trial."

"But Yorck was directly involved in the plot wasn't he? He was close to the plot leaders," I said.

"Yes. Until Moltke was imprisoned, he accepted his friend's viewpoint, but after January 1944 he moved closer to the planners, and when the attempt actually occurred on July twentieth, he was at the War Department Headquarters in the Bendlerstrasse. He was arrested there with Ludwig Beck and Stauffenberg and the other key men when the plot failed and was tried under Judge Roland Freisler with the major conspirators."

"Those must have been dreadful days," I said. "When did you know that your husband had been arrested?"

"Oh, right away. Like the other women involved and many of the men, I just had to sit at home and wait for news of whether the plot had succeeded or failed. Like everyone else, I suppose, I sat next to the radio, but for hours it was out of commission, and there was no news at all. I don't know how many pots of tea I drank during those hours. Finally I heard the official news that the plot had failed, that Beck and Stauffenberg were dead, the other leaders arrested. Then I knew."

"Were you allowed to see your husband?"

She shook her head. "No. None of us were. I think that was the worst part, knowing they'd be tortured, not being able to see them."

"Almost a whole month until the trial," I said, imagining.

"And even then, we weren't allowed to attend the trial. That was on 8 August."

I remembered the films I had seen of the trial, a film made at Hitler's orders to intimidate future potential conspirators and to shame and degrade the haughty aristocrats and military leaders who had dared to attempt to kill him. I had not been able to sit through the unspeakable film, and my husband or brother or son had not been on trial. The appearance of the defendants testified to eighteen days and nights of debasing abuse. Their front teeth had been filed to points so that when they spoke they hissed. Belts had been confiscated and they had all grown so emaciated that when they stood to testify they had to hold up their trousers in order not to lose them. Hitler wanted them to look desperate and ridiculous. Their restraint in the face of the vicious Judge Freisler's abuse; their inherent dignity and their quiet conviction triumphed over his intent.

"No, we weren't allowed inside, and I suppose I am just as glad now, but I waited outside the courthouse all during the trial," Eleanor said. "It only lasted one day, of course. Freisler made short work of justice. I made friends with one of the guards. As a nazi he was convinced that the conspirators were a bunch of traitors, but he was human. He agreed to keep in touch with a friend inside to let me know what was going on.

Every half-hour or so he'd go inside the door to borrow a match or get a drink of water and bring me back news. I knew when my husband was called to testify; I knew when sentence had been passed.

"The guard told me that the minute the sentence was delivered, all the defendants were hustled into vans and were taken to Plötzensee Prison, where they would be executed. I thanked him and rushed home. I wanted to write a letter to my husband, hoping he would get it before they killed him.

"I wrote the letter and then I took the subway and a bus to Plötzensee. It's a horrid place, like a fortress. The police officer at the desk told me that I would not be allowed to see my husband, but that I could leave my letter. He promised to see that he got it. I handed it to him, and then I suddenly thought that perhaps the men had already been executed. I asked the desk officer and he said, 'No, of course not! We don't execute prisoners the same night that they're sentenced. Do you think we are inhuman?' But of course, that wasn't true. He was already dead. They had executed them as soon as they arrived from court."

I remembered how they had died, strangulated by piano wire, suspended from steel meat hooks.

"And you," I asked, "when did they arrest you?"

"A few days later. Hundreds of wives, relatives and friends of the conspirators were rounded up. Anyone who had even been connected with the plotters, even casual acquaintances, were questioned. It was a terrible time. I was one of the lucky ones," she said.

"You survived," I said. "How?"

"I'm not sure, really. Well, obviously I'd had nothing to do with the actual assassination attempt. Those were the first ones tried and executed. After that, well there were just so many of us that they couldn't try us all at once. They did us in batches. The trials went on, one after the other, for months. It wasn't until January 1945 that Moltke was finally tried."

"I suppose they kept him that long hoping to discover more about the resistance," I ventured.

She nodded. "I think so, but obviously they learned very little. As he said himself, he was finally convicted and executed not for any specific antinazi action or for any plotting, but simply because he was a Christian."

"I remember," I said. "Freisler said 'We want the whole man!' meaning 'We, the nazis.' A Christian can't accept that, and so is automatically a traitor."

"Exactly. We prisoners in Tegel were allowed to receive visits from

Pastor Harald Poelchau, the Lutheran chaplain at Tegel, and he was one of our group. It was through his visits that I knew what was going on, who was on trial and who had been executed. He told me about Moltke's trial.

"During January and February Poelchau grew very pessimistic. He warned me that my turn for trial was growing nearer and that very likely I would never leave the prison alive. I tried to get used to that idea, but by March he came with the news that perhaps history would intervene. The Red Army was getting closer and closer to Berlin. We might just survive after all.

"Well, as you know, in April they arrived. The Red Army liberated Tegel and released all of us survivors. They treated us like heroes. That helped, you know, those early days of the Soviet occupation. They gave me a little paper to show in case any Russian tried to molest me, but I think that by then my scarecrow appearance was safety enough. My little certificate helped with getting food and fuel too. Those first weeks and months after the war ended, after I was released, I was still dazed."

"You didn't stay numb very long, though," I said.

"I couldn't. I found myself not only a widow and dreadfully alone because so many old friends had died or been killed, but also very poor. Our estates in the East had vanished, and so had our income. I had studied law before I married, but I'd never finished my degree or taken bar exams. Now I studied my assets. Our little house was undamaged. Unlike most of our friends, I still had all the china, crystal, rugs and furniture we'd had here in Berlin. Of course the things in the East were gone, but I still had much more than most of my friends."

"You were entitled to a pension as a victim of fascism, weren't you?"

"I was, and as the widow of a victim. It wasn't much, but then my rent here was low, and I can live on next to nothing when I have to. I did for a few years. I went back to law school. I found that I enjoyed it. It occupied my mind, and I found that I was a far better student than I'd been before I married; things came much more easily to me. I finished requirements and passed my exams in record time, and then I applied for appointment as a judge. It was simple to gain appointment in those days, since so many judges had disappeared, fled or been disqualified, and I was a genuine, bona fide antinazi. They welcomed me with open arms."

"Of course," I said.

"Interesting to begin a whole new life at forty," she said, "but I found those years very productive, perhaps because so much of the past had been swept away."

Much of the past had been swept away, but as we sat sipping the last of

Fig. 26. Execution chamber in the prison at Plötzensee, West Berlin (photo by Ullstein Bilderstein, West Berlin)

the aromatic pear liqueur on a twentieth of July a quarter century after the assassination attempt, the past was still with us.

"Now," Eleanor said, relaxing in her wicker chair, "we can have some good gossip later, but I know you wanted to ask me some questions about my work for your book. What would you like to know?"

She assured me that she was neither too warm nor too tired to answer questions. "On the contrary, it will do me good to get those Bonners off my mind. Oh, I don't mean that some of them aren't very decent, and I know you know me well enough to realize that I believe that with all its faults Bonn is a thousand times to be preferred over the G.D.R. I don't have to tell you that. But sometimes they are depressing, precisely because one expects so much more from them. But let's forget them. What do you want to know? And if you are going to take notes, my dear, please don't forget to eat your *Torte* too, or poor Marthe will be offended."

"I'll try," I promised, hastily taking a bite. "Could you tell me the exact title of your court and whether it is an appellate court?"

"It is the Berlin State Court for Juvenile Cases, and we are the court of second instance, that is, on the first appellate level. I am the director or chief judge. There are three professional judges and three lay judges."

"What are the lay judges?" I asked.

"Usually from some related profession," she explained. "One might be an educator, one a physician, one a sociologist, something like that. Sometimes we have a clergyman or a trained youth director."

"Just what young people and what kinds of cases come before you?"

"According to Berlin law a child is a person under the age of fourteen. Between fourteen and eighteen, if he commits a crime, he is called a youthful offender; from eighteen to twenty-one he is a young adult. Our court deals with appeals in cases involving felonies committed by youthful offenders. We also hear cases involving offenses committed against children or young people."

I asked whether her court had a good deal of discretion in choice of punishment and she said yes. "We try to be very careful when we are called upon to pass sentence on a first offender. It is a serious thing to send a young person to prison for the first time, knowing that in so many cases he will be beginning a lifetime of crime, imprisonment, release and more crime, more imprisonment. So many of those who are once sentenced become hardened, professional, incorrigible criminals."

"Can you mitigate the sentence?"

"We look into each case thoroughly, and if the circumstances warrant it, we can substitute therapy, vocational training, counselling or assignment to a foster home for imprisonment. So often, young people have been led astray by bad company or poor supervision. Don't misunderstand me, I'm not advocating softness. If the crime committed was brutal, if the young offender is sadistic, destructive, then leniency does not pay. A judge must be realistic. Where it is clear that the young person involved is not basically a criminal, at least not yet, then the judge must be humane and enlightened, but he must suit his decision to the actual individual. Lately, I am afraid we have had an increase of brutality, of sadism, of cases in which leniency would be a grave mistake."

"Youthful sadism?" I asked.

"Yes. I suppose it is only natural considering the tension, the boxed-in feeling one gets in Berlin since the Wall. Perhaps what is really surprising is that the overall crime rate has not risen since the Wall. One might have expected that it would. What has increased is the severity, the brutality of crime. It has been a qualitative change."

"Change in psychology?"

"Or *Zeitgeist*," she said. "You probably remember that, right after the war, Berlin was an amazingly safe city from the point of view of crimes against persons. The number of thefts rose. People were hungry; all commodities were scarce and no matter how hard one worked one couldn't obtain them; and therefore if you left a coat, a bicycle or a chocolate bar unguarded you could expect to have it stolen; but you could walk through a public park or down a deserted street at any time of night without fearing a brutal attack either by a sadistic robber or by a rapist."

"No young men," I said. "I mean, there just weren't any young males and very few middle-aged ones—wouldn't that account for it?"

She nodded. "It was a factor, but even before the war Berlin was not known for crimes against persons. There were robberies but rarely with violence, and sadism was what it should be, a rare aberration. Now it is too frequent. Oh, we always had an occasional drunken brawl or family fights which could erupt into violence but almost never cold-blooded, pre-meditated violence."

"You have now?"

"There has been a series of vicious, senseless crimes. You know, assault on elderly women, mass rape by a gang of teen-aged boys of a single fourteen- or fifteen-year-old girl, brutal attacks on old people to rob them of a pittance, that sort of thing. I know that is commonplace in New York and you have no Wall, but here it seems that violence has increased since the Wall and I can't help believing there is some connection. Perhaps not, perhaps it's the result of modern, urban living, but I think uncertainty about the future, prolonged tension and being shut in have something to do with it."

I asked whether Eleanor agreed with some of my other acquaintances that West Berlin was growing provincial.

"I'm afraid so," she said. "We are a *cul de sac,* cut off from our natural hinterland. Normally cities grow as young people from farms and small towns pour into the city looking for opportunities or education or just excitement. You know the saying that the best Berliners come from Breslau? Well, in the past many Silesians, Pomeranians and Saxons migrated to Berlin each year, but now that these provinces are cut off we lose all the talent and energy of young settlers.

"I'm afraid it's true that today the center of gravity in industry, business and even in the arts is in West Germany, not in West Berlin, and therefore we keep losing talented, ambitious young people. Those who stay and settle for second best are in danger of becoming isolated and therefore narrow-minded and provincial."

"Someone told me the other day that the fact that big jets can't fly into Berlin has made Berlin a second-rate city, and I think there's something in that. The major international flights are from New York, London, Paris and Tokyo to Frankfort. Anyone wanting to come to Berlin from another world capital usually has to change planes," I said.

"True," she said. "I hadn't thought of that. I think the atmosphere of tension in Berlin, the consciousness of always living under pressure is very bad for young people growing up, bad for their nerves and for their perspective. They begin to believe that Berlin and the Berlin question are the center of the world. I think as many young people as possible ought to leave the city for a semester or two in West Germany, or better still abroad."

"Massive exchanges? Even of trade-school kids?"

"If possible, yes. I think Berlin youngsters should be encouraged to travel, to spend at least a summer now and then in England or France or Sweden, just to get out."

"But you want them to come back?"

"Oh, of course. And I think most of them will always want to come back, but they'll come back a little more relaxed, a little more realistic. I always want to come back," she said. "I love to travel, but I never feel quite at home anywhere west of Berlin. My parents were West Germans, but I was born here in Berlin. When I married, my husband and I went to live in Silesia, and I loved it there. Silesia is so open, the people are so free, so generous, so spontaneous. I confess that I am often homesick for Silesia and for Silesians, but Berlin and Berliners are my first love."

"I knew you'd say that," I said. "Do you like the Brandenburgers?"

"I like them, admire them, love them. They are a tough, inventive,

humorous people; they had to be to win a living out of the barren sandbox of the empire and still find life worth living. And the Berliner is
lively, generous, amazingly courageous. I've been through a good deal
with them.

"Did you know," she went on, "that Berliners read more newspapers,
magazines and books on current affairs than other Germans? And Germans generally read a lot. The Berliner is intellectually curious; he wants
to know, and he is open-minded, world-minded."

"You like living here?" I asked.

"Oh, I love it. It's genuinely delightful, despite the tension. The
streets are uncrowded, the residential neighborhoods are quiet and tree-
lined, the communications excellent. I can always find a parking space,
buy a theater ticket, get a good table in a restaurant. It's not overcrowded, rushed and hectic like so many modern cities. I tried to drive in
Paris during rush-hour last spring and it was awful."

"But the politics," I began.

"Good for one's sense of values," she answered. "It is frustrating never
to be able to drive off to the country; it is annoying always to encounter
the Wall; it is strenuous to live constantly under tension; but all that is
good not only for the character but also for the personality. It forces one
to live within one's self, to live with oneself. One must concentrate on
one's family, home and friends, on hobbies and work. In other words, one
must develop inner resources."

"That I had not thought of," I said, "although I've noticed a depth in
Berliners, perhaps a maturity, that I miss in West Germans."

"In my case, I concentrate on my house, which I love, and my garden.
I find that knowing I can't escape when I feel restless or bored forces me
back on myself, forces me not to be bored, compels me to concentrate on
essentials and forget frills. When a person learns to be happy and relaxed
here in Berlin in spite of the Wall, in spite of the threats and uncertainty,
then I think he has grown up."

"He has become a Berliner," I said and she smiled.

"I would be a hypocrite to pretend that I like living in a divided city,
that I enjoy the constant pressure of international tension. I wish the
situation were different, of course. Every year when I drive across the
Zone into West Germany and know that I am out, that I can breathe
freely for a few weeks, I could shout with joy. But then after a few weeks
of rest I find I am just as excited, just as happy to cross back."

"And the future?" I asked.

"Oh, my dear, in January and February of 1945 I made up my mind
that I had no future, and since then I have stopped worrying about it.

One lives each day, one loves one's friends, one works and fights, of course, but worry is useful to no one. I love Berlin; I shall stay. I don't know whether there is a future, but we Berliners have already been through so much, what really can happen to us? Come, have another schnapps and then we must see whether our good Marthe has some supper for us. I am hungry after that ghastly Bonn charade."

She refilled our miniature glasses and we sipped slowly. "Twentieth of July," she said. "You were here last year on the twentieth, weren't you?"

30

Plötzensee

On one of those rare days that only the illusive, irritable summers of England and Germany seem to produce, a glorious day of dry, crisp air, golden sunshine, pure white clouds and brilliant color everywhere, a day beautiful enough to be painful, Carl drove me to Plötzensee Prison. We drove silently through downtown Charlottenburg, then out through grim industrial districts, past the giant Siemens electrical works, past long rows of workers' housing, past miles of railroad-marshalling yards and finally reached the prison. It was ugly and menacing, as one would expect, a complex of fortresslike buildings surrounded by a high, massive brick wall.

Carl drove in through the main gate and parked his Volkswagen in a stone-paved courtyard. A guard pointed to a separate building about the size of a large garage, to our left. It was a square brick block, one-story high, with narrow, barred windows. The door stood open. No one was in sight, so we walked inside. There was nothing to see except the dull red of the bare brick walls, the inside view of the narrow barred windows and on the walls, perhaps seven feet high and five or six feet apart, a row of heavy steel meat hooks.

On the evening of 20 August 1944, the same evening on which they had been found guilty and condemned to death for the unsuccessful attempt to assassinate Adolf Hitler, the major conspirators of the twentieth of July plot were executed in this room. Within minutes after sentence was passed, they were rushed to Plötzensee in Gestapo vans, marched to this execution chamber, garrotted with piano wire and suspended from the meat hooks. The whole process of execution was filmed by Gestapo photographers for the historical record and for the edification of possible future conspirators.

Carl and I stared at the now empty meat hooks. The memory of a conversation with General Frank Howley, United States Commandant in

419

Fig. 27. The meathooks from which the leaders of the anti-Hitler plot were hanged in August, 1944; Plötzensee, West Berlin (photo by Ullstein Bilderstein, West Berlin)

Fig. 28. Maria Regina Martyrum, Roman Catholic Church, West Berlin (photo by Landesbildstelle, West Berlin)

1945, flashed through my mind. He had once explained to me in excruciating detail the painfulness of death by wire strangulation. Carl glanced at me and led me out into the courtyard. We barely took in a memorial plaque listing the names of the martyrs. My mind noted mechanically that a wreath laid by some civic group was wilting.

Carl and I blinked as we emerged from the dimness of the execution chamber. Overhead a flock of birds chirped. In the courtyard we found a wooden bench shaded by a tall tree and Carl led me to it. We sat without speaking, listening to silence and to the bird chorus.

Just then a Mercedes bus pulled into the courtyard through the main gate, and a procession of boys in their late teens streamed out. They were neatly, conventionally dressed in navy blue or grey suits, prim ties, and smartly polished shoes, obviously upper-middle-class boys from a private Gymnasium somewhere in West Germany. The bus bore a Rhineland license plate. Two male teachers, one young and wispy, the other middle-aged and substantial, emerged and led their troop into the square block-shaped building behind us. Carl and I turned to watch and listen.

The youngsters, cheerful, attractive boys, probably well brought up, trotted behind their tutors in twos and threes, hurriedly, uninterested, indifferent. One whistled as he strolled beneath the steel hooks, two or three others must have made some joke and laughed raucously. Casual, still uninterested and indifferent, they trooped back out of the execution chamber, across the courtyard, and onto their bus, trailed by the dutiful teachers.

Carl and I waited, silent, exchanged a glance as the powerful bus roared out of the prison yard through the main gate. He stood and extended a hand to help me up. "Shall we go visit the nearby Catholic church, Mary Queen of Martyrs?" I nodded.

Ten minutes later as we climbed the shallow steps of the modern Catholic church dedicated to the memory of the executed plot leaders and of all Christian antinazi victims, Carl shook his head. "Affluence," he muttered, "and a shallow, spiritless materialism, and, over there," he nodded roughly in the direction of the Wall to the east, always in Berlin not far to the East, "a narrow, spiritless dogmatism and bureaucracy." He smiled a little wryly. "Come, let's join our Catholic brothers and sisters and pray for those kids and for us."

The church was austere and silent, the walls grey, unrelieved by side altars or paintings. The nave was almost empty. We found seats, sat quietly and pondered Plötzensee, the resistance leaders who died there and their descendants both affluent and dogmatic. A modern and stylized Mary presided over the church, promising solace to martyrs, comfort to the conscience-stricken. *Maria Regina Martyrum, ora pro nobis.*

31

Ted

"Why a big Mick like me should give a damn one way or the other about a bunch of Krauts, I don't know!" Ted exclaimed and we both grinned. As I looked up to smile at him I grabbed my hat just in time to keep a gust of wind from blowing it off. It was a raw, blustery day. The wind pursued us down Fifth Avenue like a whole squadron of furies.

"Why do I come back to this miserable city?" Ted asked, guiding me around the corner out of the wind. "It's not sentiment," he insisted, "just habit, I guess."

"It looks grey and grim today because of the weather," I offered half-heartedly.

"New York is grim!" he said emphatically, "and I am grateful every day of my life that I don't live here. I have grown rather fond of my particular bunch of Krauts, you know."

"I'd noticed," I nodded, still clutching my futile hat. "You used to accuse me of being soppy about them, if you remember."

"Oh, you!" he said with a deprecatory gesture. "You like everybody."

"Even the Irish," I admitted coyly. "The coatroom for gentlemen is over there," I said and disappeared to check my things and to cope with wind-whipped hair. It was fun seeing Ted again. We had never been close friends, but we had known each other since I first arrived in Berlin in 1947 straight out of Columbia Graduate School. In those days Ted was a tall, slim, sandy-haired reporter, not long out of the army, not much longer out of Fordham. He is still a reporter and a free-lance writer, still tall, but now he is portly and the sandy hair is streaked with grey. He had changed subtly. He looks like a Berliner! I thought, snapping my handbag closed and rushing out to meet him at the elevator.

He was glancing around the lobby, and when I appeared he pressed the bell. "Lovely building," he said appreciatively.

"Wait until you see all those women and no men in the dining room!"
I warned.

"I like women," he assured me as we stepped into the old-fashioned
brass-embossed elevator. "I'd have to, to stay in Berlin this long. There
are still many too many women, especially old women."

"Just like my club," I said. We found a table close to a window overlooking the city. While I ordered drinks from the waitress, Ted looked
out at the offices and terrace gardens of Rockefeller Center and across at
the façade of St. Patrick's.

He shook his head. "Strange to be in New York. It's not home any
more: it's changed and so have I."

"We Berliners," I began and he laughed.

"Whenever I hear an American say that I think of Frank Howley."

"You were on his staff, weren't you?" I asked trying to remember.

"P.R. Officer," he said, "a very junior one. Howley was a great guy to
work for."

"The Berliners liked him. He was the kind of soldier they understand, direct, straightforward and no nonsense," I said.

Ted nodded. "He liked and admired them after he came to know them.
Like most of us, he entered Berlin feeling like a conqueror, intending to
give nazis and war criminals short shrift, but he was shocked with what
he found."

"He told me. He found a city in ruins and instead of war criminals
only women and children and old men."

"Do you remember how it smelled? Did it still smell when you got
there?" he asked.

"No," I replied. "Perhaps I didn't wander on foot through the parts of
the city that had been worst hit. I remember the stench in Nuremberg,
though, when I flew down to sit in on one of the trials."

"It was sickening when we got to Berlin in 1945," he said. "It wasn't
just the obvious smell of unburied bodies rotting underneath rubble, but
also broken gas mains, shattered sewer pipes, uncollected, unburned garbage. It was the general smell of destruction and devastation.

"I was a pencil soldier who fought the war behind a desk, but I'd
travelled through war zones. I'd seen dead and wounded men, bombed
towns, streams of refugees, even battlefields right after the action, but
none of that prepared me for Berlin. I thought I was a tough son of a
New York City cop, but that first sight of Berlin was too much for me.
It was like being kicked right in the midriff. It certainly knocked out of
me any idea of swaggering like a big hero."

"You're not the ax-grinding type, Ted."

"I'm not a good hater," he admitted. "In fact, I've never hated anybody except the English and now and then a senior editor, but I suppose I had as many preconceived notions as most Americans about nazis and Prussians and all the rest."

"You were expecting maybe the Master Race?" I asked. "A whole town bursting with glorious Siegfrieds and bouncing Brünnhildes?"

"Something like that, I guess, and what did I find? Scarecrows. Old men, cripples, ragged kids and, oh God, the women! Do you remember the *Trümmer Frauen?*" he asked. "Were they still sorting the rubble when you arrived?"

I told him I remembered. "All in black," I said, picturing the women loading the railway cars, then pushing or pulling the cars along rails improvised on city streets.

"Berlin was a hideous mess," Ted said. "Do you know that one of the first things Howley did was order seven plane-loads of drugs for the Berliners? I think he was more shocked at the rape of the city by Mongol troops than by the physical destruction. Young girls, old women, anyone female! Thousands and thousands were raped, and of course afterwards in our sector we had to take care of them. The Berlin hospitals had no drugs and few supplies of any kind. Some hospitals didn't even have running water or electricity. The water system was polluted, dysentery was epidemic, and venereal disease was rampant. How could you hate?" he asked.

"Well, Howley soon got the city functioning again."

"We and the Berliners," he said. "Those of us who worked with the Berliners to get the city cleaned up, the gas and electricity working, the buses and subways running, soon learned to respect and to like them. There weren't nearly enough of them, but they worked like tigers to get Berlin ticking again."

I nodded. "Did you speak German in those days? It seems to me that when I first met you you only knew bits and pieces."

"I never did learn it formally," he said. "Even now my kids speak better German than I do, but I gradually picked up a good deal. In the early years we conquerors expected Germans to be able to speak English."

"I don't think I remember," I confessed, "whether you stayed on in Berlin after you left the service or came home and went back."

"I was sent home at the end of 1946," Ted said, "but by then I already had decided that I wanted to go back. Before I joined the army in 1941 I'd worked as a cub reporter on a New York paper. I had only a B.A. and two or three years' experience, so I couldn't expect a very glorious job, but my paper took me on again and agreed to let me go back to Berlin.

In addition I made a free-lance arrangement with a couple of other papers and magazines. I had to live on a shoestring, but I got back to Berlin. Eventually I got a better job with a wire service, and still later with one of the TV networks, so I've made a pretty good career out of our Berlin."

"When did your wife join you? Does she like Berlin?" I asked.

"Fran loves it! She gave up our New York apartment and her job and moved to Berlin during the summer of 1949. She arrived just after the currency reform went into effect, so she missed the experience of the Black Market. By the time we had found an apartment and started house-keeping the German economy was just beginning to revive, but even so it was an adventure living on the economy those days. We were both young and adventurous, though, and we loved every minute."

"Did your children go to school in Berlin or did you send them home?" I asked.

"We had two kids when Fran moved to Berlin. Three more were born in Berlin. All five went through school in Berlin, the first three in the American dependents' schools, the youngest two to German private schools. My middle boy is studying engineering in Munich, the youngest is in the army and was lucky enough to be stationed in Frankfort, I guess because he knows the language."

"Close to home," I suggested.

"Sure. He flies in weekends when he's off duty. My youngest girl is al-most ready for college. She's still with us in Berlin, and she's having a hard time deciding what to do with herself. She doesn't want to leave Europe, and yet we don't quite like the idea of her attending the Free University." He shrugged. "Well, there's time yet."

"You don't regret it?" I asked. "Transplanting your family?"

"Oh no, anything but. There are problems for the children, sure, but we've all had a fascinating life. The kids have travelled all over Europe, including East Europe; they've visited North Africa and Israel. They all speak at least one other language besides German and English, and I think, on the whole, they've turned into more interesting people than if they'd grown up in Brooklyn or the Bronx."

Having consumed two rare and juicy steaks, Ted and I decided to have cognac and cigarettes in the lounge.

"Now, if my more German than the Germans' sons were lighting your cigarette for you, they would stand up. They'd probably click their heels," Ted said, lighting my cigarette by comfortably leaning over from his armchair.

"We Berliners expect that," I said primly.

"Funny, isn't it, how a people, a city can get under your skin. I've been tense and worried all spring, not about myself or my kids, but about Berlin."

"The negotiations?" I asked. "Don't you approve of Willy Brandt's *Ost Politik?*"

"Brandt!" Ted exploded. "Do you know I remember when I liked him!" The Tyrolean waitress brought our drinks and spoke to me in a dialect which Ted did not even recognize as German until she said *"Bitte!"*

"Hals und Beinbruch!" I said using the sanguinary Luftwaffe toast for those about to fly. Ted grinned and raised his glass.

"Tomorrow, Berlin!" he said, almost not believing in the two different worlds.

"You are seriously worried?" I asked.

"Damned seriously. I admit that not everyone is. Some of my close friends in both parties are reasonably optimistic, largely on the grounds that the Soviets are going to be worried about China for some decades to come and because the development towards European unity is encouraging. We might yet rescue the baby from the vanishing bath water."

"But you are not sure?"

He shrugged. "I guess you'll think I'm just an unreconstructed Cold Warrior, and maybe I am. Maybe I've lived through too much, seen too much that I can't forget. What puzzles me is how Willy Brandt can forget."

"Has he forgotten, Ted? I have an old friend in Bonn in the F.D.P. who is basically as realistic about the Soviets as you, more conservative than you, and he insists that nothing real has been sacrificed in the Moscow Treaty or the Four Power Accord."

"Is an atmosphere real, Anne? Is morale real?" he asked intently.

"Of course. In my world they rank among the very few realities."

"You and I are old blockade comrades. We remember Berlin when. I remember the S.P.D. when. My God, how can anyone forget such socialist giants as Ernst Reuther and Kurt Schumacher?"

"Or Jeanette Wolff and Annedore Leber," I added.

Ted nodded. "Terrific people, almost literally. They had integrity and guts and saw things clearly, but then maybe issues were more clear-cut in those days." He shrugged dispiritedly.

"I remember something that Annedore Leber told me when I first met her," I reminisced. "You knew she was running the S.P.D. newspaper, *Telegraf,* right after the war? Just before the blockade, during the weeks and months that the Russians were putting pressure on Berlin socialists and trade unionists to persuade the S.P.D. to merge with the communists and to allow the communists to take over the unions, the Soviet authorities naturally tried to muzzle the socialist press. Frau Leber told me that she was called to Soviet military headquarters at the Karlshorst and politely invited to co-operate. With equal politeness she refused to commit herself. A few days later the Soviet Military Authority called her back and were more forceful; finally they threatened her. I asked her whether she had hoped that the Western powers would support and protect her, but she said no, not at that time, it was too early. She realized clearly that if she said no she would be standing alone, that there would be no protection, that she might very well end in a concentration camp or simply disappear, as so many others had."

"But she said no," Ted repeated. "She went on publishing the *Telegraf* as an anticommunist, socialist paper."

"Yes," I said. "Do you know why? She and her husband were antinazis. They were involved in the resistance. Her husband, Julius Leber, was imprisoned by the nazis and later died in a concentration camp."

Ted nodded. "I remember."

"Well, you might think that people who had experienced so much horror, people who knew exactly the price of resistance to total power would be afraid to say no, that they would be the first to give in to pressure. Frau Leber said with her it was exactly the opposite. After she came home from the Karlshorst she found that she was shaken, and she was afraid. This was no naive Joan from a village who had never suffered the flames. Annedore Leber had been well seared, and she had no desire for fire, but she said that she remembered the early days of the nazis and reflected that if enough people had only said 'No!' then, the world might be very different today. She said that she felt that she and her friends had said 'Yes' too often, that they had retreated in the face of terror too often, and that quite simply she could not do it again; physically and spiritually she could not."

"And so she said no," Ted finished. "Apparently she got away with it. I mean, she wasn't arrested and she went on publishing the *Telegraf* long after the split in 1948."

"She went underground for a few days. That is, she developed a diplomatic flu or something of the sort and just stayed away from her office and refused to answer the telephone; fortunately just then the government split. The noncommunists bolted from the East Berlin *Rathaus* and moved to the West. After that, she was relatively safe in the Western sectors."

"Brave woman," Ted said. "There were a lot of brave women and men in Berlin in those early years, and not just in the West."

"You mean the seventeenth of June?" I asked. "I missed that."

"I was there," he said. "I was in East Berlin. I actually saw young East Berliners throw stones at Soviet tanks."

"Do you suppose those workers thought they could win? Did you think so?"

He shrugged. "It's so long ago—1953. Another world. I don't know what they—we—hoped, but we hoped for something. Now?"

"You're really that pessimistic, Ted?" I asked.

"I can't help remembering how different the S.P.D. used to be, how different Willy Brandt was. I also keep remembering the times my photographer and I rushed out to where something was happening on the Wall."

"Refugees?" I suggested.

"A refugee or someone trying and not making it. As you know, it still happens. Almost every week there's at least one incident. Some make it, some half-make it, some don't. I still can't get used to the sight of some poor devil being dragged back, sometimes bleeding from rifle wounds, sometimes shattered by a land mine."

"You didn't see that young woman who stepped on a mine just around Christmas, did you? The one with two young children?" I asked.

"Lost both legs? No, thank God. Last year Fran and I were spending Christmas in the Alps. But I've seen enough, too much." Ted grimaced and reached into his pocket for cigarettes.

"Do we or don't we?" I asked as the waitress appeared and asked about more drinks. "Tempted?"

"I'm not worried about my liver," Ted explained, "it's my waistline, or what's left of it!"

"There," I said, "however much you worry about Berlin, it hasn't turned you into a wraith. Waitress, two more, please."

Ted laughed. "Well, I may be a crank, but no one has ever yet accused me of being ascetic. I may get grey hairs in Berlin, but there's no shortage of calories, as you know."

"Too well. All right, let's agree that Ulbricht and now his successors haven't changed their spots and that guards at the Wall still shoot to kill, some of them, but might there not be some point in *détente* in spite of that as long as the West doesn't bargain away anything substantial, anything dangerous?"

"Oh, I don't object to negotiations. It's the rhetoric of this *détente* episode that worries me. Not only me, you know. Some very prominent politicians and political analysts are worried. You know Axel Springer, don't you?" Ted asked.

"I've met him," I said. "His organization sends me a lot of material."

"I heard a speech he made in Stuttgart this spring, and I found it very convincing, very scary.* Springer believes that the Soviet Union hasn't altered its ultimate goals an iota since 1945, that they want now what they have always wanted: the consolidation of their military gains in the Second World War, the sovietization of all Germany and hegemony in Europe, and he seems to conclude that the new agreements are a giant step toward achievement of all three goals."

"I've read that speech." I said. "Certainly the Moscow Treaty seems to achieve the first goal: the virtual legitimization of World War Two conquests. The others?"

"There's little question but that the Russians have increased their military, especially their naval, strength in Europe. They are obviously not relying on any *détente*. They already have a four-to-one submarine superiority over N.A.T.O. in Europe and they've made the Baltic a Soviet lake."

"Yes," I said. "I read that they demanded that all non-Baltic states be prohibited from sending warships into the Baltic. That would have excluded most N.A.T.O. ships, and the Scandinavians and West Germans were worried, but N.A.T.O. refused to comply."

"N.A.T.O. refused, but the Russians are still building up their Baltic fleet, the largest of their four fleets. The Red Army is also developing new and powerful armored units, and this year the Soivet Air Force participated with the East Germans in strategic maneuvers in the G.D.R. That doesn't add up to disarmament or to a softening of policy," Ted asserted.

"If you want peace?" I questioned.

"Prepare for war? Of course, but what kind of peace do they want? Peace on their terms. Springer pointed out that the East German Party chief Erich Honecker was very frank and very blunt. He attributed Bonn's desire to seek *détente* simply to the military superiority of the Eastern bloc, but he said 'in our image of the enemy nothing has changed.' Note that, 'enemy.' He doesn't pull punches."

"Honecker speaks for the East Germans, and they have always been prickly. Perhaps they are disgruntled because they see how greatly the U.S.S.R. values West German technology and economic strength. Perhaps they feel they've been sold out for a mess of Bonn's capitalistic pottage?"

"Possibly," Ted admitted. "And yet those two top Czech General Staff officers who defected this spring [1972] indicate that the Kremlin's plans by no means exclude the use of war to attain political objectives. The

* His speech before the German Atlantic Society in Stuttgart on 7 March 1972.

Czech officers were very specific. Since 1965 the Russians seem to have adopted the theory that limited and local war involves less risk. Should hostility break out, they would see that the attack was carried out by only one bloc state. They would use the public fear of nuclear war to keep the war from spreading, to try to confine the hostilities to Europe. The Czechs said the estimate was that the Russians, or their ally, presumably the East Germans, could reach the Rhine within ten days. Meanwhile the Soviet Government would apply every kind of pressure to end the war by political means, on its own terms of course, before universal war could break out."

He shook his head seriously. "That doesn't sound like peace and brotherhood to me. Meanwhile it is obvious that the Russians are exploiting every weapon to soften up the West for eventual attack, to build up psychological readiness to accept a political solution, in other words, surrender."

"You take a dim view," I said. Ted nodded. "Surely Brandt is no weakling, and certainly he is not a communist sympathizer as some of his extreme critics say. He must have some aim in his *Ost Politik*."

"I don't see any except appeasement. I said before, I remember Brandt when. As mayor of West Berlin he was a staunch anticommunist. It was Willy Brandt who named the Ulbricht wall the 'wall of shame.' It was he who constantly criticized the C.D.U. for not caring enough about Berlin. Brandt is the political heir of Schumacher and Reuther. Now look at him."

"I know that some of his Berlin social democrats have bolted the party, or at least opposed the Moscow Treaty," I said.

"What's got into Brandt?" Ted asked. "He and Egon Bahr were never appeasers when they were in Berlin, but they began this whole idea of rapprochement with the Soviet Union during the Great Coalition when Brandt was Foreign Minister under Kurt Kiesinger. When? In 1967, I guess, when Brandt visited Rumania and talked off the record about the necessity for the Federal Republic to recognize the reality of the existence of the G.D.R.

"Of course, Kiesinger pulled him up short and repudiated the idea that West Germany was about to throw over the Hallstein Doctrine, and so Brandt had to keep quiet for a while."

"Until he took over in October 1969?" I suggested.

Ted nodded. "He began to talk about *détente* right away, and Bahr, who became his state secretary, went to Moscow in January, 1970, to begin the spadework. Brandt went to initial the treaty in August."

"You agree with Strauss [Franz Joseph Strauss, leader of the Bavarian

Christian Social Union], then, that the treaty is a sellout?" I asked. "It doesn't really say much, you know. It talks about peaceful resolution of disputes and the relaxation of tensions, but it doesn't actually recognize the Oder-Neisse Line *de jure*."

"No," Ted agreed, "but it accepts it *de facto* and it renounces the use of force. In fact, it describes present boundaries as 'inviolable' and that is pretty close to *de jure* recognition."

"But realistically, Ted, you don't suppose the Federal Republic, much less N.A.T.O., ever intended to use force to recover the Oder-Neisse territory, do you? And if they didn't, then what have they given up? Not the legal right to negotiate: they've specifically retained that, and certainly not the political right to apply pressure whenever and however they can."

"I meant what I said before about an atmosphere, about morale. By rushing to give up too much too soon, Brandt has created an atmosphere of insecurity. His negotiations have the smell of defeat. I agree with Strauss when he says that Brandt took the pauper's oath for West Germany in Moscow. He went too far. He may have thought he was just being realistic, but to the Russians that kind of acknowledgement of reality looks too much like moral collapse. They can see only one reason to give in, and that's not reasonableness, it's weakness. And where they see weakness, they do not accommodate, they bully. Lord, girl, you know that."

"You don't think there were Soviet counterconcessions?" I asked, and he responded vigorously.

"What? That West Berliners will be allowed to visit East Berlin and East Germany now and then? Does that compensate for the prohibition on the Bonn parliament's meeting in Berlin? That is an abdication of part of West Berlin's political freedom."

"But the treaty permits Bonn ministries to keep their offices in West Berlin. What are there? Something like twenty thousand federal civil servants working in West Berlin? They may continue, and Bonn parliamentary committees and political parties may meet in West Berlin. Originally East Germany opposed any Bonn presence in the city. Isn't that a concession?"

"Sprat to catch a whale," he said explosively. "What the Soviet Union got is the explicit acknowledgement that it, one of the four powers which have legal rights in Berlin, has the unilateral right to accept or deny West Berlin's rights. That's a whale of a concession."

"True," I said, "but then ever since the blockade hasn't the Soviet Union used force or the threat of force to influence, sometimes dictate, what West Berlin would or could not do? Isn't this just formalizing an existing situation?"

"I thought you were legal-minded," Ted asked, challengingly.

"I am. I'm just playing advocate of the angels for a change. I want to hear your arguments and not take your line of reasoning for granted."

"Sounds to me as though you'd gone all dove-ish," he said.

"Hawks, doves!" I said, grandly, "I'm an Athenian owl."

"O.K., owl, but just don't cuddle up to any Russian bears. We lose more owls that way." Ted took a sip slowly. "No, I think Brandt's excuse, to the extent that he has one, is that he believes his position is weak and that he has no choice but to negotiate."

"You agree with Axel Springer, then, that since the Wall some Berlin social democrats, including Bahr and Brandt, have become pessimistic. They think they cannot really count on the U.S. in a crisis?" I ventured.

"I suppose they think they can count on us in a major crisis, in a clear-cut case of the use of force," he said.

"You mean, if West Berlin were overrun by Soviet tanks, or if the East Germans actually invaded West Germany, we would act?"

"Under any foreseeable circumstances, of course we would. We'd have to. But in the last decade or so, they've concluded that they cannot count on us in small pin-prick crises. The Russians or East Germans bluster and threaten; they make ten demands and we negotiate and give in on one or two and think we have won concessions. If the S.P.D. leaders know that, if they can foresee the gradual erosion of West Berlin's rights and guarantees over another decade or two of similar negotiations, maybe they think it is better to trim their sails. I disagree with them, but I guess I can understand it." He looked miserable.

"A lot of Germans seem to agree with you," I said. "In March one of the polls reported that after three days of public, televised debate, fifty-three per cent of those polled had concluded that they opposed ratification of the treaty." (The poll was taken by *Die Welt,* 4 March 1972.)

"Your old acquaintance, Klaus Peter Schulz, broke with his party on the issue, saying that as long as VOPOs on the Wall shoot to maim or kill there is no *détente.* But of course Schulz is a Berlin socialist."

"He belongs to the party's right wing, too," I said. "Like you, he's an old Cold Warrior," I added, grinning.

"He knows the Russians." he said. "Damn it, all Berliners know the Russians by this time. I don't hate Russians. Most of us don't. I like Russians; I admire them; but I don't want Berlin to be swallowed up by them."

"None of us do, Ted, certainly not Willy Brandt. It's not a question of ends but of means, of what is the most realistic way to protect Berlin."

"How? By building up the G.D.R.? Do you realize how far the East Germans have progressed in the world arena since Brandt started his *Ost Politik?* Since 1970, Brandt has jettisoned the Hallstein Doctrine. Kiesinger used to break diplomatic relations with any state regardless of how important it might be to Bonn economically or politically, if it recognized the G.D.R. In 1970, when three developing African states recognized the G.D.R., the Brandt government didn't even lift an eyebrow. Did you know that Bangladesh was the thirtieth state to recognize the G.D.R.? They are almost a world power. Since the Moscow Treaty and the Four Power Berlin Agreement, Honecker is boasting that before long all three Western powers will recognize East Germany."

"Haven't the French already said they would?" I asked.

"Well, I don't know why they shouldn't, if the Bonn government more or less recognizes them. Yes, Foreign Minister Maurice Schumann announced that France would recognize the G.D.R. as soon as both German states became U.N. members, and I suppose that is reasonable. There is no question that there is a drift, a trend, but I can't like it or help worrying about it."

Ted glanced at his watch. "Gosh," he exclaimed, "have we been talking that long? I didn't mean to take your whole afternoon and depress you besides."

I reassured him about my spirits. "Tomorrow Berlin!" I added. "Are you glad in spite of everything?"

"Oh, sure. I'm always glad to get back to Berlin, but this time even more than usual. Not only because I am worried about Berlin but because I can't say that I like what is happening here either."

"Do you mean what is happening in America or in your family?" I asked.

"It's all part of the same," he said. "It's funny, but during the early years when my wife and I lived in Berlin, my relatives and hers used to think we had both become radicals of a sort because we actually approved of socialized medicine, city planning, public housing, that kind of thing. We knew some Russians and didn't think they had horns. We also thought that now and then the United States was mistaken or foolish, and we said so."

"And your relatives thought you'd become effete cosmopolitans?" I guessed.

"More or less. I remember, during the Kennedy administration and the first years of Johnson's administration, when we used to discuss Vietnam. Naturally they were all sharp-clawed hawks, like the good Irish-American patriots they are."

"And you?" I asked. "Had you acquired a more European perspective?"

"I must have," he said. "Well, it stands to reason. In Berlin I had one friend who was an English officer, who'd just got back from Malaysia. He had had direct experience with guerrilla warfare and he knew something about Southeast Asia. I had a French friend whose brother had been killed at Dienbienphu, and several of my German friends knew a good deal about the weaknesses of saturation bombing because they'd been involved in antiaircraft defense or in industry during the Second World War. They knew, none better, that massive bombing of cities just isn't what it's cracked up to be, even when the enemy is a highly industrialized, highly urban society."

"Did you believe them?" I asked.

"Not at first. I remember that you had told me that once a very long time ago, but I thought you were just tender-hearted, which of course a woman should be. But these were soldiers. They made me take a look at our own strategic bombing reports of World War II, and that started me reading some of the memoirs of air generals and strategists, and by God, they convinced me."

"But, I take it, you couldn't convince your relatives?"

"No. They thought I'd just got soft."

"They believed in technology, in bigger and better firepower. I have a friend who insists that that is our national religion, our creed."

He nodded. "Seems to be. I got nowhere. I even threw Dulles at them. You know—that in Vietnam we were fighting on the wrong terrain against the wrong enemy, but I guess they dismissed Dulles as a Methodist."

I laughed. "But now?" I asked.

"Now," he said with disgust, "my hawklike relatives are molting! Their feathers are frayed and not just at the edges. They fall over each other in their eagerness to make cooing noises. They make me sick, the lot of them."

"All of them?" I asked, unbelieving.

"Ah, no, not all, but so many! It seems to me like cheap opportunism, like running with the herd." He paused and took a deep breath. "No, it's worse than that. It's that smell of defeat, of defeatism that I spoke of before. I feel it all around me, I smell it in the air, and it frightens me.

"When I think back to the end of the war, when the victorious American troops entered Berlin," he stopped again and grinned wryly. "O.K., so I'm a jingoist. I don't want us to conquer the world. I don't want us to run the world. Maybe we tried to do too much, bit off more than we could expect to chew, but when I think about the change in the U.S. since 1945 I could explode. Sometimes, I guess, I do explode. Sometimes I just get drunk."

"Lucky you," I said.

He nodded. "Look what's happened to the U.S.," he exhorted. "In 1945 we had a monopoly on atomic weapons, and practically a monopoly on gold. In 1948 we forced the Russians to swallow their blockade, while the British kept Greece and Malaysia from being taken over. Containment worked, and for a few years some of us hoped for a rollback, at least in parts of Eastern Europe."

"Not after Hungary in 1956," I said.

"No, not after Hungary. And then the Wall, and then the freezing of the Czech spring, and now the German *détente*. It's all part of the same trend, I guess."

"Part of the same swing of the pendulum," I suggested. "Pendulums do swing."

"You mean they also swing back? Oh, I guess so, in time, but you and I only live now, and it's the rest of my lifetime and my children's lifetime that I'm concerned with. What's going to happen inside America and in Berlin to us as individuals, to the quality of our lives? That's what worries me." He crushed out his cigarette, half-smoked.

He went on, "A few years back my brother would have knocked his son's head off if he had come home from college with long hair or if he had caught him smoking pot. I used to be the one to urge him to be a little more tolerant, and he thought I'd grown decadent and over-sophisticated. Now? He just shrugs and says 'What can I do about it?' He seems afraid of his kids and basically unsure of his own ideas, his own standards. He used to be absolutely sure what was right, what was wrong, too sure. Now he has lost his moorings.

"Hell, even my sister the nun prances around with her skirts to her knees and a wisp of blue on her head you'd never know was supposed to be a veil. And my brother the priest plays golf every Thursday with his best friend the Presbyterian minister. Well, now," he said good-naturedly, "that part is all to the good, but the rest? I don't recognize my family."

"You've been away a long time," I suggested.

"I guess I see things from a more distant perspective. Perhaps I'm so far away from the trees that I can't help seeing the forest, the overall outline that my family here is too close to see."

"Natural," I said.

He nodded. "Of course, but I can't like it. I wish I could feel close to them, and I can't. I could shake them. I guess it's high time I went back to Berlin."

"Don't you sometimes want to shake the Berliners?" I asked and Ted grinned.

"Oh, sure, often, but they don't mind. I'm one of them now."

"We Berliners," I said as he took my arm and we strolled toward the elevators.

"I do sometimes want to shake our young Berliners, our students."

"Half of them aren't Berliners," I pointed out, "and really, Ted, the violent radicals are only a handful, a small minority."

"So much the worse for the majority," he said. "That's why I want to shake them. Why don't they stop the radicals? Why can't the moderates run their schools if they're such an overwhelming majority? Because they're either lazy or cowardly, that's why, and that's enough reason to want to shake them."

"I thought the universities were quieter this year," I said as we stepped inside the elevator.

"They are," he said, "but not really better. Oh, there have been some healthy signs. On the one hand there have been some laws reforming the course of study, and that's all to the good, and some moderates on the faculty have been organizing and talking about a rollback."

"I thought I read that the German Student Association had come out against the reform measures and that there had been some protests," I said.

"True. The student association had always favored proposals to shorten the course of study, but, when the federal government wanted to enact a law to try to do just that, they came out against it, calling it undemocratic. They complained that the plan to divide university curricula into short and long programs would divide the students into an elite and helots."

"That's silly. It's what they wanted, and no one in his right mind can argue that a research physicist needs only as many years' study as a veterinarian or a trial lawyer. That's absurd. Some courses just take longer."

"Don't argue with me; I agree with you, but the students have decided that any prescription about the length of study is an infringement on academic freedom."

"Well, it is, but that's a lesser evil under the circumstances. Student leaders have been protesting for years that the curriculum was too long. What is this rollback?"

"There's a group of professors called the Federation for Academic

Freedom which demands a return to a more balanced regime in the universities. They call themselves moderates; their enemies call them conservatives. At the Free University, fourteen professors resigned from the university senate because they said it was undemocratic, that it was controlled by a violent minority. Did you hear that one professor, a political scientist by the way, was threatened by his students last year? A bunch of young men threatened to toss him out of the window. Of course it wasn't a very high window, but still."

"Was it open?" I asked.

"I don't know, but a lot of professors all over Germany are fed up, and so are a good many politicians and taxpayers. In Bavaria the legislature passed a new university law in the fall of 1971, doing away with equal voting strength for students and re-establishing a clear majority of senior faculty on the governing committees and academic senate."

"Well," I said, "Bavaria is always conservative. What about the Spartacists? How strong are they?"

"Not very strong in numbers, but they scare me because they are openly, avowedly Kremlin-type Marxists, not juvenile adventurists. The Spartacus is officially the youth wing of the new West German Communist Party. You'd think they could never have got off the ground, wouldn't you? They have funds from the S.E.D. in East Berlin, of course, and they've made a working agreement with some of the left-wing socialist groups on campus. Berlin socialists are not so ready to co-operate, but in Bonn the General Student Organization chairman is a Spartacist, and the group is exerting power at many West German universities, power out of all proportion to the size of their membership."

"Popular front?" I asked. "How big is the German Communist Party? Pitifully small, isn't it?"

"It has only 33,000 card-carrying members and never polls more than two per cent in elections. If I remember correctly, it has about four hundred cells spread all over West Germany. No, it's neither large nor powerful, but don't forget it has direct support from the G.D.R. Neither Spartacus nor the New West German Communist Party is large but both exercise a good deal more influence than their numbers would indicate because they are highly organized, ruthless, and part of an international organization."

"So you want to shake them? The moderates? The lazy ones?"

Ted grinned. "I'd love to. I'm not really pessimistic, you know. Worried, yes. Concerned? Deeply, but somehow I have a residual faith in Berliners, in their common sense, their healthy minds."

"So you and Fran will stay in Berlin?" I asked.

By then we were being blown down Fifth Avenue; the wind was even colder and more cutting than before lunch. "I go east here," Ted said, glancing up at the street sign. "Did you ever picture what New York would be like with a Wall straight down Fifth Avenue?"

"Isn't there one?" I asked and he laughed.

"No, of course Fran and I will stay. We live there. It's our home. I suppose if worst came to worst, if the East ever really snapped up West Berlin Fran and I would get wind of it in time to get out." He shrugged. "I can't really imagine that."

"Thinking the unthinkable," I said.

"It is unthinkable for us. For now, for as long as life in West Berlin is livable, it's more livable for us there than anywhere else. We've been through too much with the Berliners. We've come a long way with them. We couldn't cut and run now. Besides, Berliners have come through so much, I can't help feeling they'll come through this, but meanwhile, like everyone else in Berlin, Fran and I just live from day to day."

"Everyone does, Ted, everywhere."

Ted nodded. "I know. I've seen that here in the States this time. Well, if we have to be insecure someplace it might as well be the place we belong." He took my hand and shook it ritually. "Thank you for lunch!"

"Thank you," I said, "and say hello to Berlin for me."

32

Anne

President Kennedy was neither the first nor the last American to declare *"Ich bin ein Berliner!"* Numberless Americans who have served, worked or lived in Berlin and many who were born there still keep a figurative suitcase in Berlin and return to visit whenever they can. Many remain nostalgic for the bouncy vitality of the Kurfürstendamm and still feel a sense of identity with the divided outpost city.

Adopted Berliners as well as the *waschecht* insist that Berlin *ist einmalig.* I have loved Berlin and Berliners almost since I first landed in the midst of the rubble and desolation in 1947. In spite of the wartime propaganda which I had imbibed along with my countrymen, in spite of the very real horror of the recent nazi past, the Berliners won me over almost without a struggle, as, indeed, they won over many Americans, from Generals Lucius Clay and Frank Howley on down.

Berliners inspire affection and admiration, or at least many of us old Berlin hands believe so. Throughout Germany the Berliner has the reputation of having a big mouth, of being saucy and irreverent, but he is also known for his humor, for his refreshing ability to laugh at himself and at his situation, however grim.

The Berliners I came to know I found warm-hearted, spontaneous and generous. During the postwar years of hunger and deprivation, when Berliners, along with other urban Germans, were subsisting on a daily diet of nine hundred calories, when peasants hoarded poultry and potatoes to barter them for fur coats and radios, the typical Berliner would cheerfully offer "the first slice of bread each day for the refugees."

The shock of my first drive from Templehof airfield across the desolation of downtown Berlin, past mile after mile of grey ruins to the United States Headquarters in Dahlem in the western suburbs has never quite worn off. Months later, vacationing in sleek, opulent Switzerland I

440

dreamed of the rubble, of the brutal incongruity of a window box with vivid red geraniums hanging from a bombed-out wreck of a building, only the corner apartment on the ground floor still habitable and obviously still inhabited, the rest an empty shell. I dreamed of the black-clad *Trümmer Frauen,* dusty black kerchiefs tied around their hair, shapeless, weary ghosts lifting brick after brick, tapping them to free them of rubble and tossing them, often with a laugh and a ribald joke, onto waiting coal cars. I dreamed of streets empty of men except for the too frequent cripples lurching on improvised crutches or the ubiquitous blind men wearing the warning arm band with three spots.

I remember my first winter vividly. It was bitterly cold. The ruthless wind sweeping from Siberia across the eastern plain whipped through the shattered city, chilling already cold houses, freezing underfed, raggedly clothed citizens. Morning after morning I watched shabby, bony children trudge through the high-piled frozen snow, many with feet wrapped in rags, to spend a dismal day in an underheated school, perhaps in a building still partly destroyed with missing windows, perhaps even missing walls. At noon they would eat watery soup, perhaps with a slice of unbuttered bread.

Day after day when I finished breakfast or lunch at the Truman Hall mess, slipping a roll or some slices of toast or a wedge of dry cake into my handbag for a typist or clerk, I was aware that United States policy prescribed that all leftover food must be destroyed rather than be distributed to the local population. Not even to children! I thought, wondering how children could conceivably be held responsible for the war or for nazi crimes. Having been reared on intensive infusions of the New Testament, I found living in Berlin in 1947 and 1948 a shattering experience.

Spring 1948 finally came and with it the freezing of the Cold War into the Soviet blockade. My colleagues whose duty it was to analyze political trends had long predicted some overt, hostile Soviet move, but even so when the blockade came we were shocked. It caught me in Rome enjoying my first leave since arriving in Europe. As a dutiful citizen I hurried to the United States Embassy. Our diplomats assured me that there seemed to be no immediate danger of war, but they advised me to return to Berlin immediately.

How? I wondered, since the friend with whom I had driven south was already on her way to Paris. That evening I boarded a crowded train to Frankfort, planning to fly from there. First, however, I decided to get a good night's rest. I checked in at the Frankfort hotel reserved for press and military government. As I crossed the lobby on my way to an early dinner someone called out "Anne!" and I turned and recognized two newspapermen from Berlin.

"Hi, Anne! Come have a drink," the man called Ted invited. "We're going to break the blockade. Want to join us?"

I blinked.

"Drive through," his friend Jack explained. "Come with us. It'll be a lot more fun than tamely flying back, and we might have a better chance of getting through with a woman along."

"Will the Russians let us through?" I asked dubiously, but of course I had already decided to join them. We had a good dinner, and then I disappeared to my bedroom, arranging to meet the two men early the next morning.

We set out on schedule and reached Helmstedt by ten. The British border guard tried to dissuade us from crossing into the Soviet Zone.

"What if you have a puncture or run out of petrol?" he asked, warning us that the British and American service stations along the *Autobahn* had been closed, that Allied jeeps no longer patrolled the stretch helping stranded motorists.

"Our car is in good condition," Ted insisted. "I had it thoroughly checked over in Frankfort, and we have a full tank of gas, a spare tire and a tool kit. We should make it."

"Do you have enough petrol to make it back in case they don't let you in?" our British comrade asked.

"Oh, probably," Ted said, but he later admitted that he deliberately avoided taking along a canister of extra gas to add weight to our argument that we could not return.

"You can still get out and fly in," Jack suggested to me, but I shook my head. I had got that far; obviously I was curious about our reception by the Russians. We all thanked the English soldier, waved and drove on.

"Well, here come our gallant Soviet Allies," Ted said as we drew up to the next barricade. "Let's see what they have to say." He smiled at the approaching Red Army soldier and handed out the car papers and our passports.

"Blockade," the Red Army man said in thickly accented English. "They won't let you into Berlin when you get there."

"We're willing to try," Ted said and the Russian shrugged.

"Well, we're not blockading the *Autobahn,* anyway not yet, but if you get stuck outside Berlin, don't blame me." He handed back our papers, having made a note of the car's license number, raised the barrier and waved us on.

"We're in the Sovzone," Ted shouted as the car raced along the *Auto-bahn*.

"In is the easy part," Jack said. "Can we get out?"

I remember few details of the drive except that in the Soviet Zone the road was still pockmarked from bombs and artillery fire. There were several shattered bridges requiring lengthy detours through dingy villages over narrow, bumpy roads. We met virtually no private cars and very few trucks, but from time to time we passed a Soviet Command car or a truck transporting Red Army troops. Occasionally we passed a single peasant or a group of farm workers plowing in adjoining fields, but otherwise the land adjacent to the *Autobahm* seemed deserted. It was a dull, desolate drive.

However, my press acquaintances were in a happy mood. They laughed and joked. We ate sandwiches and drank hot coffee, with judicious sips of whisky to keep out the cold as well as to keep up our spirits. Ted drove circumspectly, knowing that the Soviet M.P.s enforced their speed limits rigidly. Eventually, we entered the *Autobahn Ring*, which surrounds Greater Berlin, and finally we pulled up to the Soviet checkpoint at Dreilinden.

"Well, chums," Ted said, "this is it. Come on, baby, start hexing."

"Never mind hexing," Jack advised. "Look as innocent as a lamb."

"At school people called me Gretchen," I said, looking as innocent as possible.

A Red Army soldier, swiftly followed by a noncommissioned officer, marched up to us and leaned in at the open car-window. Ted casually handed out our papers. The soldier, who apparently spoke neither English nor German, tried to tell us by gestures that we could not go on and by a sweeping, circular arm motion that we had to turn around and drive back.

"I don't understand," Ted said calmly, and he gestured that we wanted to drive through. I got out of the car feeling that my influence might be greater alfresco. With as much innocence as I could muster, I spoke German to the hovering sergeant and discovered that although he could speak only fragments of German he understood the basics.

"Can't we go through?" I asked blandly as though I had never heard of a blockade.

"*Nein*, Frau," the sergeant said good-naturedly. "Blockade, blockade. Closed, closed." He too used gestures to indicate a road blocked off and again shook his head repeating, "*Nein, nein.*"

"Go back?" Ted said, pretending amazement and indignation. "We

Fig. 29. Cars waiting at the *Autobahn* checkpoint to cross from the G.D.R. into West Berlin, 1969 (photo by Landesbildstelle, West Berlin)

can't go back! We haven't enough gas and you've closed our service stations."

"*Ja,*" the sergeant said, "Go back, go back." He pointed southwest, "Helmstedt! English."

"No, no," Ted insisted, catching on to the style. "No gas, no gas. No petrol, no benzine. Get stuck." He gestured, his hands conjuring up a car stranded on the highway.

"Benzine?" my sergeant said shaking his head. "No benzine, *nein.*" Apparently he meant that he could not give or sell us any. "*Verboten.*" He looked puzzled and concerned and shook his head sadly over our mutual dilemma. "No Berlin, *nein.* Blockade," he explained tragically. "Orders, *verboten.* I can't help it. Orders."

"We can't go back," Jack interjected.

"No one allowed into Berlin. Blockade," the sergeant repeated in German.

"But we don't want to go into Berlin," I chirped innocently. "We live there." The sergeant looked puzzled as was only reasonable. "We live in Berlin," I continued. "We are just going home. I can understand that you have to keep new people out of Berlin, but we just want to get home. We are not taking anything into the city. Look. Look inside the car. We have nothing with us." I gestured widely, inviting the sergeant to inspect the car's interior. Ted and Jack, although not understanding a word of my German smiled blandly and nodded.

"You see," I said, and both the sergeant and the private peered into the car. "Nothing."

The sergeant nodded in agreement. "Nothing," he confirmed. "Well. . . ."

I knew I had won and that he was prepared to let us through.

"Here," I said, taking our passports from Ted and thrusting them under his nose. "You see, here are our addresses: Berlin-Dahlem and Berlin-Zehlendorf. We live in Berlin. Please can't we go home?"

He studied the alien passports ponderously.

I looked up at him soulfully and he blushed slightly and smiled in a fatherly way. He leafed through the three green passports. "Ha!" he announced with an air of discovery. "Passport! German word is passport, Russian word passport, English word is passport too! Ha! Ha!" He laughed heartily.

Ted and Jack had not understood the words, but they swiftly joined me in laughing. The sergeant laughed again and handed back the passports. "All right," he agreed. "As long as you live there, go ahead in." I thanked him and jumped back into the car. Ted started the engine before our sergeant could change his mind. No sooner had the bewildered soldier raised the barricade than Ted shoved his foot down on the accelerator and we shot through, all three waving happily and gratefully to the two Russians.

"God!" Jack sighed, not irreverently. "I never thought we'd make it."

"We're through," Ted almost shouted. "Of course, they wouldn't have done anything to us beyond keeping us for a night or two, but it wouldn't have been much fun, and think of the story we'll have to tell at the Press Club. People will be buying us free drinks for days."

When we arrived at the Allied checkpoint we were greeted with enthusiasm and disbelief. "Helmstedt told us you were on your way but we never thought you'd make it," a British soldier said. A British captain rushed up, congratulated us and offered us a drink.

"Come into the command post," he invited, "and stretch your legs and relax for a few minutes," and we accepted gratefully, but we stayed only long enough for a quick drink. We were eager to reach Berlin. Half an hour later at the West Berlin Press Club we were greeted like heroes arriving on Mount Olympus and again offered drinks. Our colleagues found it difficult to believe that a Red Army sergeant had been that friendly, but Ted and Jack and I have never forgotten him or our little blockade-breaking adventure.

Ever since that first year I have felt that I belonged in Berlin. Later I was transferred to Bavaria. I found Munich delightful, but still I seized upon every excuse to return to Berlin, flying in on one of the noisy, rattletrap, legendary C-47s. Each time I flew out and watched the red-tiled roofs of the city give way to the green of forests and lakes and then to neat rows of gold, green and brown marking the farms of the Soviet Zone I sighed and began to feel homesick.

During the years since 1948 I have returned to Berlin whenever I could. I saw Berlin pick itself up out of the rubble and grow into a bustling, productive, vital metropolis. I saw Berliners change from the scrawny scarecrows of 1947 to the well-dressed, briskly successful citizens of the 1960s and 1970s. I visited the city just after the seventeenth of June uprising in East Berlin in 1953 and just before the erection of the Wall in 1961.

On my many visits I have stayed at simple pensions, at amusing small hotels and at fashionable large ones; I have visited friends and lived at a student home. I have shopped for fruit and cognac and cookies at sleek supermarkets and at homely neighborhood shops. I have bought dresses and scarves and sweaters at fashionable boutiques and gadgets at cheap discount stores. I have browsed for antiques and books and

records, for cameras and sunglasses. I have gone to the theater and
to the opera, heard concerts and visited cabarets. I have strolled through
zoos in East and West Berlin, through parks and forests and along lakes
and canals. I have eaten and drunk my way up and down the Kurfürstendamm, sipped champagne in night clubs and Moselle in little wine restaurants, eaten goulash in student co-ops, *Würstchen* in working-class
pubs, and nibbled caviar in an austere restaurant favored by bishops and
Bonn dignitaries.

I have talked politics with taxi drivers, coatroom attendants and university professors, with radical and conservative students, with dear old
friends and with chance acquaintances. I have attended church at both
cathedrals and in mission chapels, sipped tea in the drawing rooms of
elderly ladies, coffee in the offices of innumerable officials, and beer in
factory canteens. I have interviewed pastors and prostitutes, countesses
and dressmakers, intellectuals, bureaucrats and hardhats, and over the
years I have stored up impressions, memories and even a few hard-won
generalizations. Perhaps it was inevitable that when I began searching
for a theme for a new book I chose Berlin. Perhaps it is more accurate
to say that Berlin chose me.

Some of my most valuable experiences occurred entirely by chance.
For example, one evening when I arrived in Berlin from southern Germany I had no hotel reservation, and it was growing late. As I drove
in from the western outskirts I happened to notice a sign announcing a
hotel. The building looked grim and shabby, in fact not very promising,
but I parked the car and went in. I decided to have dinner as a kind
of test, and despite the gloomy late-Victorian interior I found the service
friendly and cheerful, the food good. I decided to stay for the night.

By daylight the old hotel seemed a little less grim. Inside, the halls
were dingy with dark panelling and high, narrow windows, the stairs
were uneven and creaking. Outside the façade was grotesque, sporting
irregular turrets and balconies and an effusion of gingerbread. Nevertheless I decided to stay on. The couple who ran it were both respectable
and kind, the service continued excellent and I liked the food. My friend
Elisabeth laughed when she came to call for me and asked whether I
liked living in scurrilous lodgings.

"Scurrilous?" I asked. Later I hunted in my dictionary and discovered
that the word derives from the Latin *scurra,* meaning buffoon. Obviously
Elisabeth had meant the hotel was comic.

It was certainly a comic hotel, but I stayed there for more than a
month, not just because I enjoyed it but also because I discovered that
it was a staging area for the redistribution of refugees from the East and

living there gave me an excellent opportunity to talk with dozens of them informally. During the years just before the erection of the Wall, when refugees were pouring into West Berlin in a rising tide, new arrivals were housed and processed in a large emergency camp, but after they had been registered, questioned and given temporary papers they were sent to various small, inexpensive hotels throughout the city, where they stayed until they could find permanent housing or be flown out to West Germany. My small, scurrilous hotel was one of these temporary housing centers.

Morning after morning I chatted with one or more refugees, and I found that I had to revise my preconceived, oversimple views as to why they had fled. The youngest, not counting children brought over by parents, was a boy of eighteen whom I met the morning after he had swum across the Wannsee, arriving in West Berlin in just his swimming trunks, with no papers, no clothes, no possessions. At breakfast he was wearing black slacks and a black turtleneck sweater, both a little too tight. "Lucky they had anything long enough," he said and grined. He was about six feet four, slim but very muscular.

"I belonged to a work crew of seven boys," he told me buttering his breakfast roll generously and spooning on marmalade. "We were all eighteen or nineteen. We were laying new barbed wire under the water. All of us wanted to come over, but we knew that only one of us had a chance, so we drew lots. I won. Each evening before we quit we would all have a swim. While one of us took his turn to dive down and clip away some of the wire, the rest of us would laugh and splash and make a great noise. We did that every night so that the guards on the hill overlooking us got used to it."

"Clever," I said.

"Last night when the other fellows started their larks I took a deep breath, dove straight down and swam underneath the cut wire, coming up to the surface on the western side of the barricade."

"Couldn't the guards see you?" I asked.

"The wire gave a little shelter and I huddled against its shadow, keeping under water as much as possible. I could hear the fellows laughing and cutting up just a few feet away. Then they splashed out of the water, and I could hear them shouting and singing as they got dry and dressed themselves and walked away. I tried to lie as quietly as I could, but I got hungry. I guess I was scared too because those guys on the hill had rifles and machine guns. The water was cold, and as it grew darker it got colder. Summer or not, I nearly froze." He shivered, thinking of it.

"As soon as it was almost dark I began to swim for the western shore.

I swam underwater as much as I could, trying to avoid splashing. That's hard, especially when you know your life depends on it."

I nodded appreciatively. "Didn't they have searchlights?" I asked.

"Sure, but they turn those on only when it gets really dark. By then I had reached the shore. As a matter of fact they spotted me just as I was climbing up and they shot at me, but I flattened and was able to crawl behind some bushes. I lay there until it got darker and then crawled up inch by inch. A Western patrol found me within minutes after I got to safety, and I guess because I was wet and cold and maybe because of my age, they brought me right here. I have to go to get processed this morning after breakfast."

I asked the usual questions: whether he had relatives in the West, where he planned to settle. "No relatives," he said, "but an old school friend escaped last year and is living in Dortmund. He has a good job there and a flat, so I'll go to him first until I can find a job and a place of my own. Once I'm settled, I may try to go to nightschool. I'd like to be an engineer."

"Couldn't you have been an engineer in the East?" I asked.

"Oh, sure," he said. "I had a pretty good job for someone my age, and the money wasn't bad. My friends and I had a lot of fun. I didn't leave because my life was awful or anything. We get along, but somehow all my friends wanted to get out, I don't know quite why. Maybe we feel there's more opportunity here, more choice, or maybe it's just human nature to try to escape when you're locked in. All that barbed wire is a kind of challenge."

Another morning I spoke with a serious-looking man of about thirty-five who had got out with his wife and two children. He told me that he had been a plant manager in Chemnitz. "We're Silesians, but my parents fled as far as Chemnitz in the trek," he explained. "I had a fine job in the East. The work was interesting, and I had an excellent salary. I was able to travel for my firm. I visited Latin America, the Far East and the Middle East, but always, of course, without my family." He smiled, knowing that I understood that the government had feared that he would bolt if his family had been with him on any of his foreign trips.

"It may be years before we'll be able to live as well here as we did in Chemnitz. The firm gave us a comfortable, modern apartment, and I had a big car with a chauffeur at my disposal. No, I certainly didn't leave for material reasons although I admit that many people do."

"Did you have specific reasons?" I asked.

"It would be easy to tell you that I escaped because I wanted more freedom, and I suppose it's true, although I am not clear in my own

mind what one means by freedom. Not political freedom, I think, because I am not a very political person, but perhaps some of the small
freedoms that come with political freedom."

"Specifically?"

"Well, in my work I felt myself hampered by a web of bureaucratic
red tape, by regulations and restrictions, by people constantly snooping.
I felt as though a whole government apparatus was looking over my
shoulder, if that makes any sense. I wanted a chance to experiment, to
try out new ideas, to use my initiative. I also wanted the freedom to
choose my own friends, to be free in my leisure hours, not always have
to attend meetings and pep talks and join in collective amusements."

"Even in the West, businessmen have to play golf with clients, invite
the boss to dinner and go to endless business lunches and parties and
conferences," I pointed out.

"I suppose so, but surely there's a difference in degree. In the East
there seems to be nothing left over, no time at all for a private life, for
personal friends. Surely this is not true in the West." I admitted that he
was probably right.

"There was also the question of the children," he continued, and
I glanced over at his wife and children at a nearby table. His wife, a
pretty, fragile woman of about thirty, smiled and told the children
to say good morning. The girl was about twelve, pale with silvery blond
braids, the boy, a little darker, was about nine or ten.

"Next fall my daughter will be old enough to begin Confirmation Class.
We are Lutherans. I won't say we are fanatics or the world's most pious
Christians, but we have always been a religious family. It meant a decision. If I entered her in the Confirmation Class she would automatically
be disqualified from applying for the Free German Youth dedication
ceremony, and she would be barred from taking the *Abitur* or from
going on to the university. She's a bright girl and very musical. I think
she would like to be a teacher or perhaps a choir director. She might not
have the potential to be a student, but I should hate to see her barred,
and, on the other hand, one doesn't care to give in to blackmail."

"Where will you go?" I asked.

"I have a sister in Munich. There would be more opportunity for me
in the Rhineland, but I think my family would like living in Bavaria.
I may not find anywhere near as good a place in the West as I had
in Chemnitz, and I'm a little old to start over again. But then, after
the war many men older than I am had to pick up the pieces and make
a new life, didn't they? And most of them are doing well today." He

smiled and his chin jutted out confidently. "We may have a thin time for a year or two, but we are prepared for that, and in ten years?"

The trickle of refugees in and out of my little hotel continued throughout the weeks I lived there. Between May 1949 and the erection of the Wall on 13 August 1961, an estimated total of two million seven hundred thousand refugees fled from East Germany to the West, almost two million of these by way of West Berlin. In 1960 the total was just under two hundred thousand. By July 1961 the number had already reached more than a hundred thousand. The numbers increased daily, reaching about a thousand a day, when it was cut off by the building of the Wall on 13 August. It is estimated that approximately four million Germans from the East poured into the West between 1945 and 1961. That represents twenty per cent of the total East German population. Of the total number of refugees, about two hundred thousand chose to remain in West Berlin; the rest were flown out to settle in various parts of West Germany or to emigrate abroad. I talked with all three varieties.

Of the dozens I spoke with during those weeks, although most admitted that material considerations had played a role in their decision, very few seemed to have fled for material reasons only. A plastic surgeon and a general practitioner, for example, both said that they had felt hampered in their profession in the East. "I knew that there were exciting, revolutionary techniques and equipment being used in the West but I had no access to them," the surgeon explained.

"I realize that some doctors must stay on to serve the population in East Germany," the general practitioner said. "A sense of duty kept me there for years after I wanted to leave, but I finally decided I had to get out. For a dedicated doctor practice in the East is frustrating."

Technicians, engineers and corporation managers made similar complaints. None of them had ever experienced political freedom as adults, since most of them were under forty, but they sensed that they had lacked personal and professional freedom. Some sought religious, intellectual or artistic freedom. Some simply wanted to escape the greyness, the boredom of the Eastern bureaucracy. My fortuitous sojourn at the scurrilous little hotel had proved profitable. I had learned a good deal more than I had anticipated. In Berlin one is always learning about politics willy-nilly.

One day, perhaps it was in 1964 or 1965, I arrived early for a luncheon appointment at a fashionable hotel. I had spent the day strolling around East Berlin and had been delayed in crossing back, so I had rushed from the railway station and felt warm and grimy. Since my friend had not yet arrived I made my way to the checkroom to leave my raincoat and then to wash up and brush my hair before lunch.

"You look tired," the coatroom attendant said, sympathetically. She was a pale, neat woman with mouse-colored hair streaked with grey. She wore an old-fashioned black uniform with a black satin apron.

"I am a little tired," I admitted and told her that I had been tramping around East Berlin all morning.

"Ah, East Berlin," she said morosely, hanging my coat away carefully and handing me a stub. "I don't go there any more. I could, you know. I lived in Bremen after the war so I have a West German pass. I could go over to see my sister whenever I like, but you won't catch me there again."

"Did you have trouble?" I asked, sinking into a convenient chair to hear her story.

"Trouble!" she said. "They put me in jail. See, I used to go over about once a month regularly. I'd take my sister fruit and coffee and now and then maybe a nice bit of material for a dress, something pretty that she couldn't get over there, or maybe a toy for her grandchild. Sometimes we'd go tend our parents' grave. It's bad not being able to see Sis or visit the folks' graves."

"Why were you arrested?" I asked, thinking that I could not imagine a more innocuous, less political-looking person than this poor matron.

"Newspaper," she said cryptically. "Oh, I know it was illegal to carry Western newspapers into the East, but I did it accidentally. I had a paper stuffed down into the bottom of my shopping bag with food and some flowers on top. The guard made me unpack everything, found the paper —of course, it had to be a Springer paper, so that made him extra mad. He called his superior; they sent for the regular police and they marched me off to jail."

"Did they try you and actually sentence you?"

"Six months," she said tersely. "And I served all but a few days of the time. Worst thing was they wouldn't let me write my husband for the first six weeks, so the poor man didn't know what had become of me. Frantic he was, as you can imagine. He had his first heart attack in those weeks, and he died a year or so after I got back. I think it was the worry that killed him. He wasn't old, only sixty."

"I'm sorry," I said inadequately. "Was it terrible in the jail?"

"Awful. They put me in a big cell with about fifteen other women. One woman was at least eighty; two others were over seventy. Imagine jailing women that age, as though they could be dangerous criminals."

"Did they treat you badly?" I asked.

"No, nothing like that," she admitted, "and we got enough to eat. Nothing fancy, but it kept us alive. No, the bad part was the crowding, the lack of privacy and the dirt and smells. They hardly ever cleaned our cell and we didn't have a broom to do it ourselves. We were almost never allowed to have baths or even to wash properly, and we couldn't wash our clothes or hair. I had only the one dress. There wasn't a toilet, just one pail for the lot of us, and they emptied it only once a day. I don't pretend to be a great lady or that I'm used to luxury, but I've always been clean and respectable. It was feeling dirty and ashamed that was the worst."

"That must have been some time ago," I said, knowing that regulations had been gradually eased.

"In 1962," she said, "and I haven't been back since. Ah, well, my sister and I are no worse off now than the Berliners who can't travel back and forth to see their relatives."

"I've read that a third of all West Berliners have close relatives in East Berlin or East Germany," I said.

She nodded. "Some of them have husbands or wives or children over there. That's worse than just a sister, so I'm not complaining, but, still, I'd like to see her before either of us dies. I have a neighbor who has a West German pass and she goes over regularly to visit her mother. Sometimes she takes something for my sister. That helps, and we write."

My friend arrived, left her coat and bore me off to lunch, but I was depressed by the matron's story. I am often depressed in Berlin, despite the vitality of the atmosphere, the gallant humor and kindness of Berliners. It is depressing to watch small children playing in a nursery-school sandbox right under the watchtower of the Wall. It is extremely depressing to pass through the Friedrichstrasse station and unwillingly intrude on the final farewells of elderly emigrants to sons, daughters, brothers or sisters, knowing that the families may never see each other again. Christmas Eve in Berlin, when West Berliners march to the Wall with trees and flaming candles and place lighted trees all along the preriphery, when people who live or work along the border place candles in windows facing the East so that the whole Wall becomes a blaze of light, is more than depressing—it is tragic.

Berlin is a city of contrasts, of light and darkness. In one literal sense Berlin is a city of dramatic light and darkness. One of the sights which West Berliners show visitors from West Germany or abroad is the view from the top of the Radio Tower. The last time I stood on the observation platform overlooking the city it was a mild spring evening, but a

Fig. 30. The lights of downtown West Berlin: the Kaiser Wilhelm Memorial Church and the Europa Center, upper left (photo by Landesbildstelle, West Berlin)

strong wind swept ferociously around the tower, and my friends and I shivered, eager to get back inside.

Below us were the sprinkled lights of a fashionable suburb, ribbons of streetlamps and clusters of lights from private houses. The lights came closer together and became brighter off to the east, culminating in a crescendo of light along the Kurfürstendamm. Beyond that, the lights continued, thick at first, then sparser. Then came the pencil-line of dim lights that marked the Wall, highlighted here and there by harsh search-lights scouring the death-strip. Beyond that darkness. My friends and I stared, blinked and hurried back into the light and shelter of the top of the tower restaurant. Each year East Berlin adds a few more lights, but the contrast with the West remains.

But, obviously, Berlin is also a city of light and of gaiety; otherwise those of us who love it would be perverse masochists. Berlin wears its tragedy lightly and endures the tension with humor, kindliness and grace. Perhaps because I have grown used to the hostility endemic in New York, I am always startled and delighted by the amused tolerance, the helpful-ness of Berliners. A visitor who enters a restaurant alone will often be invited to join Berliners at their table, and not only only by lonely members of the opposite sex. Groups of young people, whole families and elderly couples have often asked me to join them or have begun to chat with me.

On buses and subway trains a question to a neighbor about one's destination can provoke a general conference among the passengers about the best way to arrive there, and it is not uncommon for one or more of the travellers to offer their escort. One day while driving in downtown Berlin searching for the Evangelical Academy I asked directions of two young men in a delivery van. They insisted that the way was too compli-cated to explain, so they drove ahead to show me where to go. I am sure that it was entirely out of their way. Another day when I was driving through a fashionable suburb I stopped a distinguished-looking elderly man to ask directions. He immediately offered to come with me to show me the way. When I thanked him but refused he smiled sadly and said, "Too bad!"

It is sheer fun to travel on a Berlin bus. The drivers and conductors are noted for their friendliness and their good-natured impertinence. Once on the run to Wannsee a driver called out to a fashionably dressed, obviously upper-class matron at a bus stop, "Well, Grandma, do you want to ride with us?" The woman, certainly not more than fifty, smiled happily and climbed on board.

One rainy day as I made my way to the door of the bus, skillfully shifting packages, briefcase, handbag and umbrella, the driver seized the tip of my umbrella and held it firmly. "You can get out, my lady, but the umbrella stays here!"

"What?" I said, startled.

With a perfectly serious face he explained, "It's raining and I left mine home!"

Waiters in even very fashionable restaurants are usually just as informal. Naturally, there are gourmet restaurants where the waiters preside over dining like a bishop and acolytes over a sacrament and, at the other extreme, restaurants where waiters are irritable, overworked and rude. However, my long-term experience has been that most Berlin waiters in most restaurants are relaxed, helpful and frequently amusing. Not long ago in one of West Berlin's most elegant restaurants, when I arrived rather early for lunch, I found three young waiters laughing and tossing plates to one another in a kind of gastronomic deck tennis. They grinned when they saw me and stood to mock attention.

In less formal restaurants at less busy times of day I have discovered that Berlin waiters often like to discuss politics with a friendly guest, and I have found them well-informed and deeply interested. Many have told me how grateful they are to the Americans for their past help and for their continued presence in Berlin, and it was not just because they believed that flattery would provoke a larger tip. More than one Berlin waiter has reproved me for extravagance when I offered what he considered a too generous tip.

This Berlin warm-heartedness and helpfulness is recognizable even in exile. One year I spent about nine dreary months in Bonn. One cold grey day when I was feeling especially dispirited I decided to cheer myself up by a shopping spree. I entered a small corner hat shop and began to amuse myself by trying on hats, most of them impossible. The saleswoman laughed and said she was afraid that she did not have any hats for me, but she ordered me to take off my coat. "The top button is loose," she said briskly. "You don't have to buy a hat, but sit there and get warm while I sew it on for you before you lose it."

"You're a Berliner," I said. She nodded.

"Neukölln, and homesick. Bonn!" she said indignantly. "Humph! Calls itself a city!"

One of my West Berlin friends had a special reason for appreciating Berliners. Ute values them because they respect privacy. Formerly the director of a Lutheran day nursery and now a teacher of speech therapy in one of West Berlin's excellent special schools for handicapped children,

Ute is a very quiet, sedate person. On sunny summer days she likes to get into her little car and drive out alone to one of the many lakes.

"I take my lunch and a book," she said. "I find a place on the sand to spread out my towel. After a swim I stretch out on my towel, enjoy my lunch, read my book, breathe in the clear air and look around at the other people, and no one ever disturbs me. Berliners are so orderly," she explained, "so disciplined. Even though the beach is crowded, even though there may be several large families near me on the beach, not even the children bother me. They run and play, of course, and they seem to be having fun, but they don't throw their balls at me or splash me with sand. It is as though each person or group had staked out a small territory and everyone else respects his boundaries.

"I suppose it has to be that way," she continued. "There are two million of us living in West Berlin and there are only a few places we can go weekends. Obviously every lake and park and forest is overrun, and yet I never have the feeling of being crowded, perhaps because the Berliner has larned this knack. Perhaps he has had to."

I agreed with Ute that in general Berliners are tolerant and considerate, but I smiled at the thought of going alone to a crowded beach, spreading out a towel, relaxing upon it in a bikini and expecting to be left alone. My experience with Berliners has been rather different, but then Ute looks exactly like a young woman who might direct a Lutheran day nursery. She is pretty, but in a style which leaves no doubt about her piety and propriety.

My experience has been that male Berliners are very gallant and flirtatious. Prussian correctness, Protestant piety, a Catholic conscience or simply middle-class inhibitions may bridle the expression of gallantry, and certainly I have never encountered a Berliner whose attentions were rude or embarrassing, but whether he be a courtly elderly gentleman or a brash young waiter, a distinguished churchman or a simple apprentice, a radical student or a retired general or naval captain, the Berlin man partakes of the European tradition of looking upon any woman as first of all a woman. I find it delightful.

Perhaps Berlin has grown less cosmopolitan than it once was. Some of my Berliners complain that Berlin is dull, since many artists, executives and scholars have left the city. Some have stayed; others have deliberately taken up residence there; but undoubtedly many cultural and intellectual and social leaders have moved away.

"After World War I," an old friend told me, "we said that little Austria without the Austro-Hungarian Empire was like a head without a body.

Fig. 31. The Kurfürstendamm by day, West Berlin (photo by Landesbildstelle, West Berlin)

These days poor Berlin is a body without a head. Its leaders have deserted it."

"Not at all," I protested, but he sighed. "We've become a middle-class city, philistine and provincial," he insisted.

It seems true that in recent years the smart shops along the Kurfürstendamm are just a little slower in adopting international trends, their styles just a shade less innovative and daring and a touch more conventional and bourgeois. Berlin matrons dress opulently, even fashionably, but perhaps with just a little less flair than before. Sigrid decries Berlin as *"Spiessig!"* but it is not, and Sigrid loves her adopted city despite her laments. However, it seems even to my partial eyes that Berlin grows just a little less cosmopolitan each year.

However, world city or not, Berlin remains a major cultural center. No person who loves music, art and the theater need be bored or lonely in Berlin. Both East and West Berlin support excellent opera companies, world-famous symphony orchestras and an abundance of legitimate theaters. West Berlin alone boasts sixteen museums, fifty private art galleries and an excellent art institute. Two hundred publishers make their headquarters in West Berlin; there are nine daily newspapers, two radio stations and a television channel. The universities of both parts of the city are of international rank and the various research centers are internationally renowned. For the artist, the scholar or the dilettante, Berlin remains an exciting and rewarding city. To me Berlin is a challenging city.

For a quarter of a century I have been involved with Berlin, with its history, its politics, its people. I have pored over surveys, statistics and monographs. I have wandered in every corner of the city. Most important, I have become acquainted with Berliners; I have tried to discover just who and what Berliners are. It would be pompous as well as invalid to base any hard and fast generalizations on such a rule-of-thumb cross-section, such an impressionistic appraisal, but perhaps a few threads are sufficiently distinguishable throughout the interviews to suggest a pattern.

Clearly one theme which recurs is the changing role of women, in the dramatic achievement of Berlin's women. To some extent the traditional German patriarchy which relegated women to the three *K's—Kinder, Kirche, Küche—*was less powerful in Berlin than in other German cities. Berlin has always been a progressive city. The Second World War's drain on man power, the exceptionally heavy casualties suffered by Berlin field units, and the Soviet postwar conscription of male labor, all accentuated the need for woman power in Berlin. During the war even the nazis were compelled to encourage women to enter more varied professions and to make training available to them. After the war Berlin was virtually a city of women.

The same women who had kept factories and offices running during the worst years of saturation bombing swept up the rubble after the war and began to get Berlin back on its feet. By and large it was women who carried the burden of the early phase of reconstruction, who, through years of back-breaking, hand-tearing, aging labor, years of grief and loneliness, picked up the tons of bricks, picked up the remnants of the shattered social structure, sorted out lost children, restored them to parents, unearthed school books and equipment, trained and recruited teachers, scrounged medicine, bandages and light bulbs for the hospitals and helped run the government. Women performed in every capacity, whether it involved heavy physical labor or serving as mayor of the city.

Today Berlin is still far more a city of women than is any other German city. The Berlin woman, whether she is seventy and exhausted by a lifetime of tension and crisis, fifty and old for her years, or an energetic, uninjured twenty, knows what her sex has contributed to the survival and restoration of her city. Although it is true that women still form a minority in the higher professions and that in active politics women still lag far behind, the percentage of women in more prestigious fields increases yearly. The number of girls who complete their *Abitur* and the percentage of women students in the fields of medicine, chemistry and engineering is rising steadily. Women have a long way to go to achieve equality in the policy-making, executive level of society, but Berlin women are a little farther along than their sisters elsewhere in Germany. My personal impression is that the Berlin woman is more fully consicous of her role as a woman and as a citizen.

Berlin is also a children's city. So many Berliners, even those not directly engaged in the education profession, Berliners of both East and West, Berliners of varying backgrounds and viewpoints, stressed the importance of schools, of the educational system. Communists, socialists, Christians and conservatives, all agree on the crucial importance of educating children in the formation of values and in developing the personalities as well as the intellect and skills of future generations. Revolutionary, reformer, bureaucrat and reactionary were one in their stress on the importance of education, from day-care centers and the kindergarten up through the university.

Who should educate whom and how are the issues that I found an almost perfect litmus test of ideology. No question that I raised during my discussions with Berliners more quickly brought basic beliefs into the

Fig. 32. Children on a West Berlin street (photo by Landesbildstelle, West Berlin)

open. I found all my Berliners, East and West, perfectly willing to propound their views on education.

One result of this all but universal concern with schools is that Berlin schools on both sides of the wall are efficient, the teachers and administrators seem highly dedicated, highly professional. The schools in general are modern and cheerful; the pupils seem relaxed, enthusiastic and successful. The schools, the educational system, and indeed Berlin itself are all child-centered, and I found this impressive.

I was also impressed by the extent to which the old Prussian tradition seems to have survived in Berlin, not only among nostalgic conservatives but also among socialists and even communists. The probity and correctness of civil servants, the universal respect for law, the frequent emphasis on frugality, diligence and simplicity, the repudiation of ostentation and luxury are all facets of the Prussian value-system.

Equally within the Prussian tradition is the respect for individuality, for freedom of inquiry, for the public welfare. The paternalism of the Hohenzollern electors and kings, their tradition of religious toleration, of intellectual freedom, their sponsorship of the arts and sciences, all contributed to the dynamism and progress of Brandenburg-Prussia and of its capital.

Both the traditionalist and the progressive strains of the Prussian heritage joined in opposition to National Socialism. By no means were all Berliners antinazi, and only a small minority actually shared the dangers of active participation in the antinazi resistance movement. The nazis, however, admitted that they regarded Berlin as hostile territory, and the active opposition included all levels of Berlin society, all shades of political opinion.

The tragic failure of the opposition resulted in deep personal tragedy for many individual Berliners. Its failure inevitably became an element of the overall tragedy of Berlin. The execution of thousands of men and women involved in the abortive July 1944 assassination plot robbed Germany and especially Berlin of moral leadership, and the loss has been sadly apparent. On the other hand, the record of the resistance, despite its failure, is part of the Prussian heritage, a moral capital on which Berliners can draw for a sense of pride and identity in spite of nazi crimes and wartime horrors. Moltke, Yorck and Claus von Stauffenberg are also a legitimate part of the past of every Berliner. Many of the widows and children of the martyred resisters are a living part of their inheritance.

The average Berliner is not a hero. He is probably not the conscious heir of his heritage, whether Prussian or otherwise. Consciously he is just himself, just a Berliner. He is probably not aware that there is anything special about him, that he is in any way unique, although he insists that his city is. Courageous, gallant, generous and possessed of a great sense of fun, of self-irony, the Berliner has until now accepted every challenge, every reality, however grim. He has squared his shoulders, gritted his teeth, cracked a joke and got on with the job of dealing with that reality. Bombing, destruction, death, defeat, desolation—the Berliner has embraced them all with high-hearted courage, with an impudent grin.

Since 1945 and certainly since 1947 the Berliner has resisted the division of his city, the loss of his identity. He dug in his toes and, powerless, defied a superpower, and, a little to his own amazement, he survived and his city survived, at least half did. It has been a very long struggle, with West Berlin isolated and vulnerable despite four-power agreements. Much of the excitement and glamor of the years of the blockade have worn thin. Tension and prolonged crisis have frayed nerves, stretched patience, hope and humor almost past the breaking point, but he still makes jokes about his situation, about himself. The wise Berliner is aware of the menace of history, but he is also aware of the stakes. There is a German saying that courage is when one fights in spite of—*trotzdem*. The Berliner is sceptical about the future, but he deals with today as it comes.

"The future?" one Berliner remarked, "who knows? But I shall stay. After all, it's my city. I'm a Berliner. I wouldn't really be alive anywhere else. Berlin is unique. I'll stay, *trotzdem*."

About the Author

Anne Armstrong received her M.A. and her Ph.D. from Columbia University. She is a member of the faculty in the Department of Political Science of the City University of New York. She has taught at Hunter College and Fairleigh Dickinson College and in 1947–48 she served as an intelligence analyst in Berlin and Munich. She is the author of *Unconditional Surrender: The Impact of the Casablanca Policy upon World War II*.

The text of this book was set in Baskerville Lino-type and printed by Offset on Hopper Offset supplied by Bulkley Dunton Linde Lathrop, Inc., New York, N.Y. Composed, printed and bound by Quinn & Boden Company, Inc., Rahway, N.J.